UNDER 30

2/18/05

Dearest Morgan and
Heather.

Well, you're "under
30" and I have a
play in here and was
given a few copies.

To two dear
friends, Love
Cat and
John

ALSO EDITED BY

Eric Lane and Nina Shengold

UNDER 30

PLAYS FOR A NEW GENERATION

EDITED BY *Eric Lane*
AND *Nina Shengold*

VINTAGE BOOKS

A DIVISION OF RANDOM HOUSE, INC. NEW YORK

A VINTAGE BOOKS ORIGINAL, AUGUST 2004

Copyright © 2004 by Eric Lane and Nina Shengold

Library of Congress Cataloging-in-Publication Data
Under 30 : plays for a new generation / edited by Eric Lane and Nina Shengold.
        p. cm.
    Includes index.
    ISBN 1-4000-7616-1 (trade paper)
    1. American drama—21st century.   2. Young adult drama, American.   3. Young adults—Drama.   4. Youth—Drama.
    I. Title: Under thirty.   II. Lane, Eric.   III. Shengold, Nina.
PS625.5.U54 2004
812'.540809283—dc22   2004043041

Book design by Mia Risberg

www.vintagebooks.com

Printed in the United States of America
10 9 8 7 6 5 4 3 2 1

CONTENTS

EXCERPTS

INTRODUCTION

The editors of this volume both acted in high school and college, and the median age of our roles was at least twice our own. It is one of our fondest goals to undermine sales of Streaks'n'Tips hairspray, talcum powder, and nursing shoe polish to undergrads whitening their hair to play Willy Loman and Mary Tyrone.

Not that there's anything wrong with assaying great roles. But what about all the great *new* roles that reflect the age and experience of the young actors who play them? What about all the great playwrights who write about this generation—passionate, volatile, coming of age in a world that keeps changing at Instant Messaging speed?

Here, then, is a collection of exciting, emotionally relevant scripts with leading roles for actors in their teens and twenties. As editors, we've searched for a diversity of voices, and are proud to present works by major American playwrights alongside emerging young writers. There are plays here of all lengths and styles: dramas and comedies, ensemble pieces and two-handers, with roles for actors of every experience level. Though some playwrights specify their characters' ethnic identities, many more have created opportunities for color-blind and non-traditional casting.

Annie Weisman's *Be Aggressive,* Allison Moore's one-act *CowTown,* and the collaborative play *War at Home* offer startling perspectives on the American high school experience. Weisman's fanatical Southern California cheerleaders push every limit, against a backdrop of freeway sprawl and rampaging mall culture. Moore paints a harsh Minnesota landscape, with a caste system of transplanted city kids, suburbanites, and untouchable farm kids. *War at Home,* created by Nicole Quinn and Nina Shengold from journal writings of forty students and community members immediately after September 11, 2001, offers an undiluted portrait of that day's effect on a high school one hundred miles north of Ground Zero.

This Is Our Youth, by two-time Academy Award nominee Kenneth Lonergan, and Jessica Goldberg's spare, lyrical *Refuge* examine young people struggling to live in a world in which parents are absent or treacherous, and siblings and friends make desperate efforts to fill the gap.

The offstage parents are equally clueless in Jenny Lyn Bader's *None of the Above,* a two-character romp that pits a private school princess against a scruffy SAT tutor, playing for much higher stakes than either imagined. And Douglas Carter Beane's comic tour de force *As Bees in Honey Drown* takes a "hot" young author through the celebrity spin cycle, abetted by a mysterious benefactress and an ensemble of four who play a smorgasbord of New York glitterati.

In David Ives's hilarious *Time Flies,* the characters are about as young as you can get: two mayflies determined to squeeze the most out of their twenty-four-hour life span. We've included a wide variety of short plays for two: Jeff Hoffman's graceful, quietly heartbreaking *Fishing;* Catherine Filloux's haunting *Photographs from S-21;* Carolyn Gage's surreal and powerful *Harriet Tubman Visits a Therapist;* Eric Lane's bittersweet gay romance *Sweet Hunk O' Trash;* and Craig Pospisil's surprisingly droll *On the Edge,* whose down-to-earth heroine isn't impressed with the melodramatic teen boy she finds hugging a window ledge.

Anyone looking for short comedies for larger ensembles will be delighted by Craig Fols's witty *Shari Says* and Tracey Scott Wilson's first-date zinger *Small World.* And Sam Shepard's *Icarus's Mother* (the only play in this book that's over thirty itself) is an acting bonanza, studded with adrenaline-powered monologues; its apocalyptic rogue plane takes on chilling new meanings for the post-9/11 generation.

We've also included excerpts from some of the many wonderful plays that we couldn't fit in their entirety: Frank Pugliese's gut-wrenching *Aven'U Boys*; Sunil Kuruvilla's whip-quick *Night Out* (from the Actors Theatre of Louisville's multiauthor collaboration *Snapshot*); Warren Leight's deft circle of couplings, *The Loop*; and Donald Margulies's *Misadventure* (from Louisville's *Back Story,* for which eighteen different playwrights wrote scenes for brother and sister characters created by Joan Ackermann). We urge actors who choose these selections to read the entire play—you'll find a wealth of information that will help you in your preparation and performance.

There is wonderful writing between these two covers, and this book will be a pleasure for anyone who enjoys reading plays as good literature, or wants to learn more about the generation born after the Vietnam War. First and foremost, however, we hope that this book will be a godsend to young actors in search of relatable roles for auditions and classwork as well as to college professors, drama club coaches, and young theater companies.

These plays were written to be performed. They're the genie in the bottle, waiting for young hands to bring them to vibrant, spectacular life. We hope you enjoy them.

NINA SHENGOLD AND ERIC LANE
December 2003

ACKNOWLEDGMENTS

So many people contributed to the creation of this book that we'd need the Dorothy Chandler Pavilion to fit them all. We'd like to thank all the literary managers, agents, and publishers who steered us toward hundreds of outstanding plays and helped us secure the rights for our final selections.

Particular thanks go to Michael Bigelow Dixon of the Guthrie Theater, John McCormack at the Zipper Theatre, Pamela Berlin of HB Playwrights Unit, Daniel Gallant of the Makor/Steinhardt Center, Michael Kenyon at the Public Theatre, Linda Kurland at Samuel French, Matt Love and Eleanore Speert at the Drama Book Shop, Maureen Nagy at Overlook Press, Sonia Pabley at Rosenstone/Wender, Tanya Palmer and Amy Wegener at Actors Theatre of Louisville, Doug Rand of Playscripts Inc., Tom Rowan of Ensemble Studio Theatre, Steve Supeck of Helen Merrill Ltd., Pier Carlo Talenti at the Mark Taper Forum, Gavin Witt at Center Stage Baltimore, everyone at New Dramatists, Jenny Lyn Bader, Sarah Bisman, Warren Leight, and the members of Actors & Writers.

As ever, we thank our own agents, Phyllis Wender and Susie Cohen, and Diana Secker Larson, our wonderful editor at Vintage Books, who made this a pleasure in every way. Our deep appreciation to the Corporation of Yaddo, Virginia Center for the Creative Arts, and St. James Cavalier Centre for Creativity in Malta, for their priceless gift of time and space to work on this collection. Grateful thanks to our fellow travelers Mark Chmiel, Steven Corsano, Shelley Wyant, Nicole Quinn, and Joe Reeder for reminding us how vital theater for young actors can be, and to Bob Barnett and Maya Shengold for making the journey a whole lot more fun.

Most of all, we'd like to thank the many playwrights who sent us their wonderful work, and we wish to honor the many collaborators—actors, directors, designers, crews, theaters, and audiences—who bring their words to life.

FULL-LENGTH PLAYS

AS BEES IN HONEY DROWN

Douglas Carter Beane

For Mom

As Bees in Honey Drown was developed at the Drama Department. As far as I can tell, all forty members did at least a reading of it and I can't thank them enough. It was also read at Portland Stage when Greg Leaming was at the helm with the following cast:

ALEXA	Kristin Nielson
EVAN	Bo Foxworth
PHOTOGRAPHER, et al.	Jeff Hayenga
RONALD, et al.	Kevin Geer
AMBER, et al.	Kim Daykin
WAITER, et al.	Lisa Benevides

and I can't thank them enough either. It was then workshopped at the late lamented Sundance Playwrights Festival when Jerry Patch was at the helm. (Is there a curse on this play for the artistic directors that choose it?) Anyway I thank them, but not enough.

The play's first production was by the Drama Department, where I am artistic director (hey, wait a minute). It opened June 19, 1997, at the Greenwich House. Directed by Mark Brokaw, sets by Alan Moyer, costumes by Jonathan Bixby, lights by Kenneth Posner, sound by David Van Tiegham. James FitzSimmons was the Stage Manager. The cast:

ALEXA	J. Smith Cameron
EVAN	Josh Hamilton
PHOTOGRAPHER, et al.	Mark Nelson
RONALD, et al.	T. Scott Cunningham
AMBER, et al.	Cynthia Nixon
WAITER, et al.	Sandra Daley

They all made me look good.

Four weeks later the play moved to the Lucille Lortel. Produced by Edgar Lansbury, Everett King, Randall L. Wreghitt, Chase Mishkin, Steven M. Levy, Leonard Soloway, by special arrangement with Lucille Lortel; and with Bo Foxworth going in for Evan, and Amy Ryan going in for Amber. New actors continue to go on and understudy, and I continue to look good. So they're doing their job.

I give my undying gratitude to Eric for inspiring the first act and Gene for inspiring the second.

Finally, this play wouldn't have happened if it weren't for Mark Brokaw, Mike Rosenberg, Mary Meagher, and Edgar Lansbury. And I know it.

CHARACTERS

This play is written to be performed with a cast of six. The actors play the following roles:

ALEXA VERE DE VERE
EVAN WYLER
PHOTOGRAPHER, SWEN, ROYALTON CLERK, KADEN
RONALD, SKUNK, MIKE
AMBER, BACKUP SINGER, SECRETARY, BETHANY, GINNY, A SECOND
   MUSE
WAITER, BACKUP SINGER, CARLA, NEWSSTAND WOMAN, DENISE,
   ILLYA, A MUSE

Part of the fun of the play is the four actors portraying all of glamorous New York. I wrote it that way and prefer that it be performed that way.

TIME

The present.

PLACE

New York City.

ACT 1

"Life"

Scene 1

(*A photographer's studio.*)

(*A seamless. A light shines on* WYLER, *a handsome young writer. He is in his late-twenties and he knows it. A flash of light as a* PHOTOGRAPHER *scampers around with a camera. A beautiful photographer's assistant,* AMBER, *stands next to a ladder sipping a glass of white wine.*)

PHOTOGRAPHER: Life. Life. A little more. I'm sorry, what is it you do again?

WYLER: I'm a writer.

PHOTOGRAPHER: That would explain it.

WYLER: What?

PHOTOGRAPHER: Why you're uncomfortable.

WYLER: That's the writer's job, isn't it? To be uncomfortable.

PHOTOGRAPHER: Amber, lose the shadow on his face.

AMBER: (*Adjusting a light.*) Amber wants to be dancing.

PHOTOGRAPHER: Quiet, Amber. So—what did you write?

WYLER: A novel. My first.

PHOTOGRAPHER: Amber, honey, more light.

AMBER: Amber wants to be dancing.

PHOTOGRAPHER: What's it about?

WYLER: Sorry?

PHOTOGRAPHER: Your novel, what's it about? Don't smile.

WYLER: It's this story of this guy who's in his twenties— (*He is suddenly plunged into darkness.*) Amber!!

AMBER: Amber says she's sorry. (*The light comes back on.*)

WYLER: —and this guy is like overwhelmed with this conflict of fantasy and reality—

PHOTOGRAPHER: Wyler, you any relation to—

WYLER: William Wyler, no. Nor Gretchen. My real last name is Wollenstein. And . . . well that's a little long for a book cover. And—you know there really are no, you know, Jewish themes in my writing so—

PHOTOGRAPHER: And you kept your first name which is Evan and— (*He points at his camera,* AMBER *looks in and focuses it for him.*)

WYLER: Actually my first name is Eric.

PHOTOGRAPHER: Oh.

WYLER: But I figured with the "w" and the "y" in the last name, a "v" in the first name would look so good and—

PHOTOGRAPHER: Well, you kept your initials. You won't have to change your sheets.

WYLER: I hadn't really thought of—

PHOTOGRAPHER: Great. Let's lose the shirt.

WYLER: Sorry?

PHOTOGRAPHER: The shirt. Let's lose the shirt.

WYLER: Is there something else you want me to—

PHOTOGRAPHER: You look like you have a nice build.

WYLER: Oh. I see. You're thinking in terms of a shirtless thing.

PHOTOGRAPHER: Right. Amber, lose his shirt.

WYLER: You know—I just don't know if—And I'm probably way, way out on a limb here, but I was thinking more in the genre of like a pullover V-neck and a button-down shirt and, you know, kind of leaning on a stack of Proust and—

PHOTOGRAPHER: Filterless cigarette, long dangling ash?

WYLER: I don't smoke, but right.

PHOTOGRAPHER: No.

WYLER: No?

PHOTOGRAPHER: This is so endearing. Look. I don't want to put you down. I'm sure you have a very nice, trenchant, tortured, art-damaged life. In your exposed brick grubby railroad flat on West repel me street. Filled with filth and far too much Henry Miller and dank air clinging with clove cigarette smoke and nostalgia for Bennington. But, I'm here to sell magazines, you're here to sell books. So, lose the shirt. (*A moment.* AMBER *is now at* WYLER'*s side. He thinks for a moment. The* PHOTOGRAPHER *goes over to set his camera in a different location.* WYLER *immediately removes his shirt.*)

WYLER: Selling books is selling books, right? (*He looks to* AMBER *for encouragement.*)

AMBER: Amber wants to be dancing. (WYLER *hands his shirt to* AMBER. *The lighting changes, a fan machine is now on. The feel is now sultry. The* PHOTOGRAPHER *returns to the seamless.*)

PHOTOGRAPHER: Now take your right hand and grab your left shoulder. (*As* WYLER *does so.*) This isn't so bad, is it?

WYLER: No.

PHOTOGRAPHER: No. Not at all. Now . . . fuck the camera. (*A flash, then darkness.*)

Scene 2

(*The Hotel Paramount.*)

(*Resplendent in a simple black suit,* ALEXA *toys with a strand of real pearls. A beautiful cape is draped over the back of her chair. A silver tea service and pastries are on the table.* WYLER *approaches the table.* ALEXA *is now effortlessly sliding a cigarette into an ivory cigarette holder. She looks up, gently shaking her Louise Brooks bob.*)

ALEXA: Evan Wyler!

WYLER: Alexa Vere de Vere?

ALEXA: Lamb. I hardly recognize you from your photograph without your *mammilia*. Have some *petit déjeuner*, though be warned the *déjeuner* here is very *petit*, sit sit. (WYLER *does so.*) I have the most shimmering new screenplay for you to write. I pray that you'll forgive me for not going through your agent but the moment I read your book and I found that you were listed in the phone book, I—

WYLER: No, no, that's OK.

ALEXA: I loved your book, did I say? I saw the seminude photo in a magazine and just lunged for a copy. It is fabulous and I NEVER use that word. You have got to do this movie!

WYLER: Thank you.

ALEXA: You are sans doubt my favorite new writer and, if Cheever is dead, you are my favorite living writer. The reason I called you is that I have been struggling—looking for *the* genius young writer to write this mouthwatering movie idea I have up my Gucci sleeve. David Bowie, no less, wants to play my father. He's a dear friend. David Bowie, not my father. Love this lobby, please. It's not so much a lobby as a lobby as told to Theodor Geisel. You see I want this film to be the story of my life, which is too entrancing, almost even for me, I mean here I am in the blush of my youth and I am working with Morris Kaden of Delta records, do you know Morris Kaden of Delta records, how did you come to be such an amazing writer? (*She takes a sip of tea.*)

WYLER: Which tea are you drinking, the orange pekoe or the Sodium Pentothal?

ALEXA: Repartee! You are *brilliant*. God. I love writers. They always have the last word, because they know so many. Gore Vidal says that. I say it too. What do we ever get of any bygone civilization but the poems left behind. I'm part Indian, I know things. Do you think David Bowie is dark enough to pull off an Indian? I mean a red-dot Indian not a woo-woo Indian. Try the boysenberry, it's a revelation.

WYLER: Have you ever thought of diagramming these sentences in your head before you speak them?

ALEXA: See, that's what I mean. Who else but a writer—they know so much about life, no one pulls the cashmere over the eyes of a writer. When I do my work in the music business I always say, "Let me have lunch with the lyricist," you know that I'm a record producer, but you know that. Mostly in England, do you love England?

WYLER: I've never been.

ALEXA: You would love. Everyone is gay. Truly. When you say the queen, you have to specify. How they procreate is beyo—How long did it take you to write this debut novel, it is a debut novel please say, "yes."

WYLER: Uh . . . yes? Nine years.

ALEXA: And it's ever so thin.

WYLER: Well, I'm not—writing doesn't come easy to me. I'm not particularly good at listening to people and figuring out what's going on in their minds. Or summing up with a grand sweeping statement. But—

ALEXA: But?

WYLER: But I do know when to use a semicolon.

ALEXA: What you say is music to my ears, and I work in the music business, so—You're not having any tea. Let's get down to cases. I am overt with joy about your book. There's a movie there, I just don't know that I'm in a position to make it right now.

WYLER: Right.

ALEXA: But I mean after our movie, who knows?

WYLER: Right.

ALEXA: What I'm doing right now is taking all my connections in record and film—I work in the recording industry, but you knew that—which are *legion*—and combining them to create a production company. I feel I've had enough success making money for other people to start making money for myself. You're a creative person, I'm sure you know the feeling.

WYLER: Yes, abso—yes.

ALEXA: My life has been nothing short of amazing. I mean I can't tell a total stranger three episodes and I must show you— (*She opens the contents of her purse onto the table.*) They are imploring that I make a movie of it. I was married off by my mother when I was fourteen—I had to lie about my age, which is to be encouraged, but not at fourteen—to the son of a significantly rich person. Then my husband died. I was penniless. Cannot find it—don't overlook the butter—and that's where I changed my life, with my philosophy. (*She stops to take a pastry from the plate.*)

WYLER: What's that?

ALEXA: A brioche.

WYLER: No, I mean your philosophy.

ALEXA: (*She is now a hub of activity between her cigarette in a holder, her purse contents, her tea, and her brioche.*) Well, I mean that's your job. As the writer. I only know that I'm living it. I need you to define it for me. Something to do with sketching out what you want to be and then coloring it in as it goes. Being what your dreams are, and . . . well, look at us now, I see your picture and just feel instinctively you know what I'm talking about. I read your book and now here we are at the Hotel Paramount over *petit déjeuner* and great lashings of butter and I'm offering you one thousand dollars a week to write the story of my life and—

WYLER: Really?

ALEXA: Oh, God. Haven't I told you? I have absolutely no mind for money whatsoever, that's what accountants are for— (*From within her Judith Leiber jeweled egg, she pushes aside pills and makeup and pulls out a wad of cash.*) And agents, though I don't believe in agents, do you?

WYLER: Mine is—

ALEXA: Let's not deal with them. They are such unbearable leeches. Why should she get a hundred of your thousand? I introduced myself. Here we are, one thousand dollars. (*She hands him a thousand dollars in twenties and a couple hundreds held together with a rubber band.*) I find that agents have no imagination. No taste for . . . possibilities.

WYLER: Actually, I agree.

ALEXA: Waiter! Let's keep this *entre nous.* I believe in cash, I think in this flighty world it's the only thing left with any impact. Now I don't see this taking more than a few months, the info-gathering part and then we'll work out a juicy amount for you to actually write it. Remember David Bowie wants to play my father. Maybe Iman could play my mother? If he could be darkened and she could be lightened. (*A* WAITER *glides by.*) Check please. I mean does this interest you in any way, shape, or form?

WYLER: Does this interest me? In any way, shape, or form? Well let's see. I've lived my life making sacrifices for the moment when I would see my first novel published. I've made sacrifices, lived sacrifices until this moment—I'm living in a place CNN would casually dismiss as third world. The people who are my age who don't do what I do have homes and cars and—I scrounge for subway fare. So I have my nine-years-in-the-making overnight success and you know? I'm thinking, oh this is where they pull back the velvet cord and I get to meet whomever I want to meet and do whatever I want to do and I'm still looking for fucking temp work to hustle together rent. Because no one ever tells you about that little breather period between critical success and financial success. Does this interest me in any way, shape, or form? Yes. I would say this interests me in every way, shape, and form.

ALEXA: Happiness!

WYLER: Just tell me what you need to know.

ALEXA: Only one thing. I ask it before any business relationship.

WYLER: What's that?

ALEXA: If you absolutely had to sleep with one of the Three Stooges, which one would it be?

WYLER: What? (*He starts to laugh.*)

ALEXA: No, really, lamb, the answer reveals your personality. I mean if you say Moe, I know you wish to be dominated— (WYLER *laughs harder.*) Which I, of course, am incapable of, and if you say Larry, well, I mean, God help you.

WYLER: I'm just trying to think of a situation where I would absolutely have to sleep with one of the Three Stooges.

ALEXA: Too funny. Now darling, what shall I do? My accountant, Martel Grushkov, wants a record of all these businessy lunches, but won't let me have credit cards because I just see homeless people and I want to buy them socks. I'll need a receipt of some sort—

WYLER: I could put this on my credit card and you can give me cash, if that could help.

ALEXA: Such a help. (WYLER *puts his credit card down, the* WAITER *takes it away.*) I hate my accountant, I should have known something was up when he said, "Shemp." So, pick a Stooge.

WYLER: Curly.

ALEXA: Oooh. Why on earth? Here's fifty dollars. (*She hands him two twenties and a ten.*)

WYLER: That's too much.

ALEXA: Please. So why Curly?

WYLER: Because he would make that high-pitched "whoo whoo whoo" noise at the climax. (*The* WAITER *comes with the check and card,* WYLER *signs it. She shovels things back into her purse.*)

ALEXA: The ONLY response. The Duke of Chichester, who would adore you, once told me, he's a brilliant international tax attorney, does all my claims, he told me Larry and when I said why he said so that he could hold on to the hair for dear life. (WYLER *laughs. She stands.*) This has been everything I hoped it would be and somehow just a little bit more. (WYLER *stands up and walks with her.*) We must start right away, I am feverish with enthusiasm. Now tomorrow is no good I've got—please let me hold your arm, there is no railing on this staircase and it unnerves me— (*She takes* WYLER*'s arm and places her head on his shoulder. They walk down the staircase.*) I gave you money for the check, right?

WYLER: Right.

ALEXA: Curly and high-pitched whoo whoo. Such genius. You were born for this life. Wyler. Are you Welsh?

WYLER: Uh. Yeah.

ALEXA: I could tell by your coloring. *A WELSHMAN.* I shall trust you anyway. Now. We shall begin. Tomorrow I must deal with rock stars and their egos. Not pretty, but Wednesday afternoon?

WYLER: Sure.

ALEXA: Just the afternoon, the night is fraught—your scent is tremendous.

WYLER: Ah—yeah—thanks—

ALEXA: But don't you adore the scent of soap on a man, you do love men don't you?

WYLER: Uh no. I don't love anyone. I sleep with men, but—

ALEXA: Oooooh. An emotional cripple, how enchanting! This way there can never be sexual tension between us, we can only be soul mates like Sally Bowles and Christopher Isherwood or Holly Golightly and whomever Truman Capote called himself. (*They are at the bottom of the staircase. They make their way to an elevator.*) Wednesday. Noon. Sixth floor of Saks. We've got to get you a suit before we lunch. Now if you will excuse me, I'm expecting a call from an investor in Milan who is, to put it mildly, endowed. (*She presses for an elevator, the door opens immediately to reveal a green-lit elevator.*) Oh look, we *are* in Oz. So there. (*She steps in.*) I don't trust this elevator. Well, hold on to something tight, close your eyes and sing Shalom Aleichem. My late husband always used to say that, he was Jewish, I have no idea what he meant. (*The door begins to close.*) Hooray. Lots of love. (*The door is closed.*)

WYLER: Excellent.

Scene 3

(*The men's changing room, Saks.*)

(RONALD, *a very effeminate salesclerk, enters with a suit.* WYLER *is undressing.*)

RONALD: She's a goddess.

WYLER: She's kind of—

RONALD: A bright, green goddess.

WYLER: I mean, man, to live like that. Not having to worry about money. Signing for everything. And the people she knows and—

RONALD: You working with her?

WYLER: Ah, yes.

RONALD: I hate you. She only works with the flawless. Everybody she's ever found has done the skyrocket thing. She's got a real eye for it. What do you do?

WYLER: I'm a writer. I'm going to write the story of her life. As a screenplay. (*He is down to his underwear and socks.*)

RONALD: Wait a minute. I didn't think I could hate you more, and now I realize, I CAN!!! Here, try these on. One hundred percent silk. Cry me a river. (*He hands* WYLER *a pair of socks.* WYLER *is changing his socks when the curtain is shucked aside and* ALEXA *strides in, shirt in hand.*)

ALEXA: Lamb, this shirt—

RONALD: Boundaries, boundaries!

ALEXA: Oh now, Ronald.

RONALD: Boys only in the changing room, no girls allowed. He-man woman haters club.

ALEXA: No fair, if I'm buying the suit I want to pick it out! I promise the millisecond a heterosexual male enters the room I shall scatter.

RONALD: Well—all right. But only because you're divine.

ALEXA: But gay men adore me, when in London I am FLANKED by the Pet Shop Boys! Lamb, the shirt, it's the ONLY solution for your frame. (*As* WYLER *puts on the shirt,* RONALD *and* ALEXA *play.*)

RONALD: Have you seen the suit?

ALEXA: Happiness.

RONALD: If you see only one suit this season, let this be it!

ALEXA: Women will see Evan in this suit and die. Gay men will see Evan in this suit, squeal and die. Straight men will see Evan in this suit, be confused and die. Lesbians will inherit the earth.

RONALD: And I have a tie, a masterpiece of a tie, a Guernica of a tie to go with it! (*He is gone. By now,* WYLER *has his shirt on.* ALEXA *hands him the slacks.*)

WYLER: Auntie Mame, long pants!

ALEXA: You behave or I'll tell Ronald you like him. Hurry lamb, I crave to see you in this suit.

WYLER: Alexa, I don't really—I'm not entirely comfortable—

ALEXA: The shirt?

WYLER: No. I just don't feel comfortable with you, after giving me a nice salary, just buying this suit for me. Please, let me pay for it.

ALEXA: Lamb, my dearest lamb. You will buy other suits. You will buy hundreds, nay, thousands of suits. You will buy suits in Italy, have them altered and shipped back to America. And they will sit in closets and you will never get to them and you will hand them down to assistants or housekeepers. This is the world that lies ahead for you. But this. This is your first suit. The suit you buy at the moment when you belong in a suit. It's a glorious moment. And you've let me share in it in some small way. And it is—and you are not allowed to laugh here, lamb—it is thrilling. Please. You are letting me share in the honor of the moment. The payment of the suit. It is my admission. (WYLER *puts the slacks on.* ALEXA *holds the jacket up for him in the subtle haberdasher manner. She has obviously done this before. He slides into it.*) There. There. You look . . . you are . . . sheer happiness.

WYLER: (ALEXA *leans forward and kisses him on the lips.*) What was that for?

ALEXA: For luck! An old superstition I've just invented.

RONALD: (*Sweeping in with a tie.*) Nicole Miller. I could kiss her on the lips with tongue.

ALEXA: Shoes! What has been going on in my *petite tête*? (*She is running out.*) Evan, what size shoe do you wear?

WYLER: Uh, twelve D. (RONALD *and* ALEXA *exchange a look.*)

RONALD and ALEXA: Hmmmmmm.

WYLER: Quit it. (ALEXA *is gone with a laugh.* RONALD *ties the tie on* WYLER.) Have you—has Miss Vere de Vere tried suits on a lot of other people?

RONALD: Here? A few. Also elsewhere around town. So I hear. And it's always the same. They come in and it's like you, I mean no offense, but who are you? Then a month later, they are the complete and total household name. And when they come back into the store they're big and famous and there's a fuss and . . . they always see me and. Smile. Like we've shared a special moment or something.

WYLER: I've never in my whole life, met anyone like her. I mean outside of a play or a book or a—

RONALD: She's a mixture of every woman I've ever loved in a movie.

WYLER: The way she is . . . so . . . amazing in every way. And yet just getting through a day seems a struggle for her. As strong and as powerful as she no doubt is, I want to protect her. Weird, huh?

RONALD: Here's a little secret. Between you, me, and the *New York Post*. If I were to fall in love with a woman, it would be her.

WYLER: God. Same here. Maybe we're closet heterosexuals.

RONALD: Impossible. Your suit hangs properly. Here. Look in the mirror. Get your bearings.

ALEXA: (*Before* WYLER *can,* ALEXA's *back! With an armload of shoes.*) Lamb, shoes in excelsia! I have cash for it all. Be a lamb and put this on your charge so my evil Shemp-loving accountant will have a record! Cologne! (*She's gone.* WYLER *looks into the mirror. He is mesmerized.*)

WYLER: Wow.

RONALD: Your first suit?

WYLER: Yes. (RONALD *smiles knowingly and leaves. As soon as he is gone,* ALEXA *reenters with a bundle of cash in her hands. Loose, an occasional hundred falling to the ground. She is also precariously balancing a tray of colognes and a suit bag.*)

ALEXA: I have the cash and cologne. And I've picked out a cunning little Lagerfeld traveling suit for myself. It complements your suit without matching it.

WYLER: (*Taking the cologne tray.*) Alexa, you're spilling money all over the—

ALEXA: What care I? Calvin Klein fragrances! (RONALD *reenters, picks up the fallen cash, hands it to* ALEXA, *then hands the check to* WYLER.) Have you ever noticed that his scents capture a man in any contemporary relationship? First he wants you. (*She hands a bottle to* WYLER *who is signing a check. She then hands a hundred to* RONALD.) Obsession. Thank you, Ronald. Then he promises to build a life with you. Eternity. (*She hands a second bottle to the now fumbling* WYLER.) Then he realizes what he's in for. And he is out of there. (*She hands him a third bottle.*)

ALEXA, RONALD, and WYLER: ESCAPE!! (*They laugh.* WYLER *is handed his receipt.* ALEXA *takes back the bottle of Escape and is about to spray it on his neck. She hands the money to* WYLER.)

ALEXA: Here's the cash, *mon chou.* Ronald, what's our time?

RONALD: One o'—

ALEXA: THAT CAN'T BE THE RIGHT TIME!!! (WYLER *turns just then, getting a face full of sprayed Escape.* ALEXA *takes the cash and shoves it into her pocket and gets up. She pulls the blinded* WYLER *along. Everything happens within a second.*) Lamb, we're late!

WYLER: Ow! (*They all laugh.*)

ALEXA: We're late for our meeting. (*She grabs* WYLER *by the arm and bolts. On the way out,* RONALD *hands them a large shopping bag.*)

RONALD: Here are Mr. Wyler's old clothes! (WYLER *and* ALEXA *are gone.*) Come back soon.

Scene 4

(WYLER'*s composition book/various.*)

(*First,* WYLER *holds a composition book. And a pencil.*)

WYLER: Notes on the life of Alexa Vere de Vere for eventual film script. Notes taken today. First in the limo. To the restaurant. (*He turns, he and* ALEXA *are in the backseat of the limo.*)

ALEXA: And truly, India. Well, when the Mountbattens—Mount-batten—Boring, but hardly worth blowing up—left they took my mother, white, and father, red dot, with them to London, which explains my rollicking Kathleen Turner of an accent and—Oh look. You're writing in a faux marble composition book with a number two pencil. In an age of Powerbooks. *SMASHING*. Ah, here we are! Now lamb, this is the place. Let the Regency have its power breakfast, this is the power lunch. Fortunes come and go over appetiz-ers. Once a Japanese businessman started choking on a Cae-sar salad. Stock to half the American film companies went through the floor. Everyone thought it was rage, but it was just a crouton. (*Back at the composition book.*)

WYLER: Later, in the limo after lunch. (*Back in the limo. They are joined by a model,* SWEN.)

ALEXA: I remember when I first moved to London I was a child, you may want to write this down, and I turned to Mother and I said, I don't care that Father has squandered our inher-itance on the tables with Princess Grace, I am not marrying that rich broker's son. But then I met Michael and let bygones be— (SWEN *turns the radio on loudly.*) Swen, must you toy with the buttons?

WYLER: I don't think he speaks English.

ALEXA: I know, but he is Nordic and he did a fashion layout that was nothing short of pornography and—

SWEN: Yah, yah. Photo shoot photo shoot.

WYLER: Where are we going?

ALEXA: The airport.

WYLER: The airport? I don't have—

ALEXA: Relax, lamb. We're not traveling anywhere, we're just picking up this *SIN*sational new band I'm signing, you'll adore. Swen? Rock and roll?

SWEN: Yah, yah! Rock and Rolla, Rock and Rolla!! (*Back at the composition book.*)

WYLER: After the airport, in the limo. (*The limo now is packed with a rock singer,* SKUNK, *his two* FEMALE BACKUP SINGERS, *and* SWEN. ALEXA *is talking to* WYLER *who is trying to get things down. The band is talking to* SWEN *about music. A tape of a percussion track rattles the windows. Salted nuts and champagne are being passed around.*)

ALEXA: My wedding was of course very simple, only five hundred, it was in so many tabloids and—it is far too noisy in here— (ALEXA *pushes the button that opens the moon roof. She stands up and is outside.* WYLER *stands up and joins her.*) There, that's better. Such the cacophony. The wedding was part Jewish, owing to the groom and part, well, I asked my refreshingly unspiritual father what religion we were and he thought perhaps Hindu, and I couldn't have cows milling about so it just had this sort of Eastern feel. And— (*A bottle of champagne is handed up to them.*)

SKUNK: (*A cockney.*) Here ya go, luv!

ALEXA: Bless you, Skunk. (*Back at the composition book.*)

WYLER: A restaurant whose popularity will last as long as any of the dairy items on its menu. (*Crammed around a table,* WYLER, ALEXA, SKUNK, SWEN, *and the two* BACKUP SINGERS.)

ALEXA: London was London then. The Clash, the Cure, the Smiths, the Pretenders, the Boy George, the parties, the pharmaceuticals, the beverages. I don't know what London is now. One day I awoke and it had become Luxembourg or something. How well I remember when my first release with Simon LeBon hit the airways. The critics were but peeling off cart—I stood there reading the reviews with my new discovery, Illya Mannon—well my mother could have written those reviews, not actually my mother, but my mother metaphorically. And I—dear ones, here I sit with my boys—I felt then no doubt how you two must feel. On the virtual circumference of fame. My Skunk. My Lamb. This meal has taken on a certain Disney on Ice quality. I feel I shan't recover.

BACKUP SINGER: Medallions of venison, anybody?

ALEXA: And here's Bambi! Now Skunk I have got the *only* state-of-the-art recording studio set up for Thursday and—

SKUNK: Did that money exchange do the trick—

ALEXA: Utterly, and the accountant has a big bulging envelope for you, unmitigated bonehead that I am I left it behind in his office, it is but winging its way to your hotel. (*She opens her purse amid all the food.*)

BACKUP SINGER: Oi! Luv!!

ALEXA: Let me give you something—

SWEN: Hey!

SKUNK: That's OK, that's OK. I'll get it later. We just got to make sure that there's a reverb at the— (ALEXA *accidentally knocks over a drink. Mass confusion.*)

BACKUP SINGER: Oi! Oi!!

ANOTHER BACKUP SINGER: Bugger!!

ALEXA: I'm sorry is there Scotch in—

WYLER: Alexa!

ALEXA: —the veni—I didn't get the reverb!

SKUNK: Gotta have the—

ALEXA: Too much information in my brain. My circuits are overloaded.

SKUNK: We gotta have a reverb!

ALEXA: I'm having a breakdown!! There's too much going on!

WYLER: Calm down, Alexa.

ALEXA: I smell burning toast, someone take my pulse!!

WYLER: Calm down, calm down. I'll take care of it.

ALEXA: I'm so—

WYLER: Just. Calm down.

ALEXA: How could I have forgotten that which is so basic? I mean reverb.

WYLER: I'll take care of it.

ALEXA: I am pouting with intent. Look at my face.

WYLER: (*Standing up.*) I'll take care of it. I'll call the studio, get a rewhatever for tomorrow—

SKUNK: Verb.

WYLER: Put it on my charge, we'll get Shemp to reimburse me. It is not the end of the world here. Relax.

ALEXA: You are an angel. A cherub. I'm not entirely sure what a seraph is but you are that also. Here's the phone number for the studio. (*She hands him a slip of paper.*)

WYLER: Got it.

ALEXA: Oh, lamb.

WYLER: Don't worry.

ALEXA: And on the back of that shard of paper is the number for Louis Vuitton. My new luggage set. Could you—

WYLER: Credit card, big envelope. You would be so lost without me.

ALEXA: Lifesaver.

SKUNK: (*Teasing.*) Careful of him, he's a Welshman!

WYLER: What?

SKUNK: Can't trust him, he's a Welshman. Name like Wyler, and that dark hair, you can't fool me.

WYLER: Oh. That. Yes. Welshman.

ALEXA: (*Placing a hand on* WYLER's *cheek.*) My little Welshman. Oh. If I were a boy . . . the mischief we could manufacture. (*Back at the composition book.*)

WYLER: The VIP lounge of an impossible-to-get-into-night-club. Pull back the velvet cord. (*The VIP lounge of a club. Music plays in the background.* ALEXA *and* WYLER *sit and sip cocktails.*)

ALEXA: And Michael, the Jewish husband of convenience turned to me and said, "We need time apart," and I said, "Separate beds?" and he said, "Separate cities," can you imagine my heartbreak? I was just— (*Enter a well-built woman,* CARLA, *wearing barely anything.*) Carla!

CARLA: Alexa, you used-up old tart!! What brings you back to New York?

ALEXA: Darling, I'm making the movie of my life, can you beat it? This is Evan Wyler, the writer, he's forming it for me, he wrote—

WYLER: It's great to meet—

CARLA: You wrote *Pig and Pepper.* Love that. Alexa you didn't snatch up the film rights to that did—

WYLER: No—

ALEXA: No, that's for someone far wiser than me.

CARLA: He should have his agent call me.

ALEXA: I'm acting as his agent now, his agent has but no imagination. We'll talk.

CARLA: You look resplendent. Drinks, Friday?

ALEXA: South of France, sorry. When I get back?

CARLA: Deal. (CARLA *and* ALEXA *kiss-kiss as* CARLA *exits.*)

ALEXA: Proving that it is possible to be underdressed for this affair.

WYLER: And that's how deals are made? No agents, no offices, no lawyers? Casually over cocktails.

ALEXA: My love, that's how a culture is maintained. Lawyers and such are for later. Initially it's not even cocktails. It's people passing and selling films on their way to the restroom. Over lunch a film executive mentions an idea at his studio, suddenly three other studios have similar ideas in development. A record producer plays a new song on the Hampton Jitney, by Monday five other labels are trying to capture that sound. All of us, the creative people, tearing about trying to feed a nation's insatiable appetite for entertainment. Making truckloads of money we never see so that we can discover something new and vivid to present to poor fun-starved modern civilization. The new becoming old almost before we find newer new. Humanity gasping for air under the weight of its own culture. All holding on for dear life as we create fresher and fresher possibilities. As bees in honey drown. This is it. This is what you've wanted your whole life, isn't it? To be a part of it?

WYLER: Yes. Of course. Who wouldn't?

ALEXA: And so you are. With this movie. Our movie. Where were we?

WYLER: "Separate beds, separate cities."

ALEXA: That may be our title. (*Back at the composition book.*)

WYLER: And finally, at four in the morning, on the Staten Island Ferry. Just because.

Scene 5

(*A Staten Island Ferry boat.*)

(ALEXA *stands at the railing.* WYLER *is by her side, holding the bag of his old clothing.*)

ALEXA: Tell me how much these new earrings are worth it!! God, look at that view! Try to include my new earrings in it.

WYLER: Actually I was wondering if there was a way that—

ALEXA: Lamb, I know what you're going to say. I've been so self-absorbed of late and I—

WYLER: No, that's not what I—

ALEXA: Well, I have and I apologize. I just feel we're coming up to the point where my philosophy begins and I don't want to break the rhythm. As soon as I get past my husband's sui-cide, which is haunting—

WYLER: It's not the—I'm just gathering all this information and if I knew what I was working toward, I might—

ALEXA: Oh, but a game plan. Of course. We'll talk a bit more and then you can write a quick treatment—the perfect word, as if films were somehow a cure!—just a twenty-page descrip-tion and then I'll go out and pitch it to the studios.

WYLER: But even as I'm writing, I—

ALEXA: We'll make a trip to Hollywood. Oh and look at your face light up. It truly is the finest word in the English lan-guage, far surpassing my other favorites—complimentary and royalties.

WYLER: But I mean—oh God, this is going to come out so awk-wardly. I shouldn't—I'm really bad at this and—

ALEXA: Lamb. Unknit that brow. And share.

WYLER: Alexa, this—everything I've been jotting down, about your past and your life it's all so—

ALEXA: What?

WYLER: Fictitious. I mean Mountbatten leaving India, that would put you at least over fifty and you're—plainly not and—

ALEXA: I was born in India. I left India at an early age. All right, an occasional factoid has been enhanced. But—honey lamb. I know how to interest people. Don't let me go through this venture with a virtual arm tied behind my back.

WYLER: And your name . . . is—

ALEXA: And how are Ma and Pa Wyler?

WYLER: That's not my—real name. That's—

ALEXA: You're not the person you were born. Who wonderful is? You're the person you were meant to be.

WYLER: What about the—

ALEXA: But enough of me. Even I grow tired. What of you?

WYLER: Me?

ALEXA: Yes, you. Mr. I-don't-love-but-I've-slept-with-men, what is your personal life?

WYLER: Huh? Oh. There's nothing to me.

ALEXA: Oh dear, you're not one of those I-am-a-camera types, I refuse to believe it.

WYLER: Sorry. No personal life. (*A pause as they look out at Manhattan.*)

ALEXA: Have you ever been in love?

WYLER: You start right at the top, don't you?

ALEXA: Yes?

WYLER: Yes.

ALEXA: Ahhhh.

WYLER: Yes. Of course. Once. Where would creativity be without unrequited love, right? (ALEXA *keeps looking off at the beautiful skyline.*)

ALEXA: (*Quietly.*) Right right.

WYLER: (*Into his drink.*) It's nothing, really.

ALEXA: Tell me, if you dare.

WYLER: Please. No big story. Honestly. Please.

ALEXA: Please?

WYLER: Nothing. No startling story never once before told. Just some guy. At school. Smart. And funny. And—what have you. From our, like, second time together he was there with the "I love you." Constantly. He would say it every time I did something correct or endearing. Just toss it out like a piece of liver to a finalist at the Westminster Dog Show. And. And I couldn't say it back. Felt it but. Coward. After a couple of months together when I finally realized that perhaps this was what they'd been writing all those songs about and I was ready to, I don't know, speak my emotions? He turned to me, on a bright winter morning and told me that though he cared deeply for me, he was no longer—wait—interested in pursuing the physical side of our relationship. (*They look at one another. They both know.*) Charming. And then he left and I threw myself into writing and—it's not the newest story you'll ever hear.

ALEXA: An acquaintance of mine, Bethany Vance, the alleged actress, at a party in London, I found out to be a masochist. No really. Whips, chains. Enjoyed to be tortured, as it were. I asked her what it was that inspired her to be treated poorly. She told me that the line between pain and pleasure was very thin indeed. I smiled to her ruefully and told her not to fret because the line between pain and love was virtually indistinguishable. (*Self-consciously, they both look at the skyline.*) But we're not like that, are we? We're not the ones people hurt. We are the creative people. We have art to protect us, even if our greatest creation gets to be ourselves. (*She takes* WYLER's *shopping bag and walks across the deck.*)

WYLER: Hey!

ALEXA: Come!

WYLER: Where are you goi—

ALEXA: We are saying good-bye.

WYLER: To whom?

ALEXA: To the old you. And all his woes.

WYLER: And who will replace him?

ALEXA: Lamb, I can't be expected to do everything. Say good-bye to the old you, Evan. First salute him. He has served you well. (WYLER *salutes the bag and laughs.*) And toast him that he may rest in peace. (WYLER *toasts the bag and takes a swig of his drink.*) Now say, "Good-bye."

WYLER: Good-bye, old me.

ALEXA: Good-bye, old you!! (*She hurls the shopping bag toward the mighty Hudson.* WYLER *watches it hit the water. He laughs. Softly,* ALEXA *slides her hand along the rail and places it atop* WYLER's. *He looks into her eyes.*)

WYLER: You're confection. Pure confection. (*They look at one another again. They slowly kiss.*)

ALEXA: Lamb?

WYLER: Baaaaaaa. (*They kiss again.*)

ALEXA: Lamb. We should not be doing this.

WYLER: Under no circumstance.

ALEXA: I mean Boswell never became involved with Johnson.

WYLER: I would have heard about it.

ALEXA: Well, I mean, I never saw a photograph.

WYLER: But then it was like seventeen twenty or something. (*They start to kiss again.* ALEXA *suddenly stops.*)

ALEXA: You took your wallet and keys out of those old pants, right? (*They laugh and kiss more fervently.*)

Scene 6

(*A bedroom at the Hotel Royalton.*)

(*The lights slowly come up on* WYLER, *in slacks and shirt from his suit, writing in his composition book.* ALEXA *enters in an oversized terry robe. She immediately plops on the bed and pulls her makeup and mirror out of a bag.*)

ALEXA: Now lamb—

WYLER: Baaaaa.

ALEXA: Please don't do that. I rather feel Shari Lewis's hand should be up your back. Don't look at me yet darling— haven't had a moment yet to dab on a foundation—How is our little film treatment—I think it's time we beat the path to Hollywoodland and shake those money trees.

WYLER: You think? Already?

ALEXA: This treatment will be—I'm wiring the Pulitzer committee, I swear to God, they are going to add a new category. Best American film treatment. (*They laugh.*) How is it coming along?

WYLER: Well . . . slowly.

ALEXA: Allow me to register my disappointment.

WYLER: I'm not particularly good at listening to people and figuring out what is going on in their minds. Or summing up
with a—

ALEXA and WYLER: Grand sweeping statement.

ALEXA: Yes. Semicolon. I recall. You're a very special sensitive
person. And you deserve the finer things in life. A match.
We are a match. Ying and yang or whatever. Hollywood?
Do we dare?

WYLER: Why not?

ALEXA: Oh, the possibilities. I've got us on the four o'clock.
American. Two side by side. We have a meeting tomorrow
at eleven a.m. Hark unto us, Brothers Warner!

WYLER: Great!

ALEXA: Oh, the places we shall go!!

WYLER: Excellent.

ALEXA: Two o'clock, Paramount. Five o'clock, Fox. A bidding
war by six, my humble estimation. Then, I'm off to the
south of France, you come back to little old New York. We
meet up again on Monday, and we decide where we shall go
to write it. Something decadent I think. New Orleans. Jazz
and louver doors and the spirit of Tennessee Williams to
bolster us on.

WYLER: Great.

ALEXA: Or an island. With no telephones.

WYLER: Hmmmmm.

ALEXA: Are you packed?

WYLER: For the island or New Orleans?

ALEXA: Los Angeles first, lamb.

WYLER: Right, right. (*They laugh.*)

ALEXA: So you go home and pack, I'll pack. I'll meet you at one at JFK at the Admiral's club lounge. Oh and could you pick up a carton of Dunhills for me, I shan't have time, and an L.A. paper or something so we know what's the latest and—

WYLER: Alexa— (*He begins to turn around to see her.*)

ALEXA: Don't look, don't look. I'm a sight, I'm sure. I haven't had time to dab on any makeup.

WYLER: We can't leave yet.

ALEXA: Why ever not?

WYLER: I haven't finished the treatment.

ALEXA: Oh that.

WYLER: I'm afraid there's something missing. In the story. It's a painful part. Maybe you don't want to deal with this first thing in the morni—

ALEXA: (*On the phone.*) Room service please. (*To* WYLER.) Why not? Fire away. This way the coffee and croissants will arrive just as I'm feeling my worst to cheer me. (*To room service.*) Coffee and croissants. (*She hangs up the phone and speaks to* WYLER.) There. Never venture down unless you have a ride back up. A skiing instructor once told me that, I've gone and found deeper meaning. Now, ask me anything, but don't look at me.

WYLER: Do you want to tell me about Michael? I mean, if you don't—

ALEXA: Dear God. Well. Michael. Mr. Michael Stabinsky. The name. He came to me at a time when I was—quite, quite low. I was what I imagine you would call a party girl. A London party girl. The type you see in the tabs still today clutching the arm of some ancient rock star with the byline "here with unidentified friend." The type whose love of fun and good times only belies a deep, plangent self-loathing and—Maybe after coffee would be—

WYLER: If you'd rather.

ALEXA: No. No, we've started. Let's finish. Just promise you won't look at me. Michael. Well. He was not handsome in a traditional sense. But he found something in me that was— special. Perhaps the way I find something special in others. Maybe. Too Freudian a side stop, I'll continue. And he became—smitten, obsessed with me. He was very much not of this century. Old world, if you will. I had seen him at countless, endless parties but never knew his—his father called upon my father. And set up an agreement for marriage. Surreal, no? The financial rewards for Father were . . . tangible. He and my mother forced me to marry him. I did not love him. Then. He was hardly attractive in a, as I say, traditional meaning of the word. But we married and—the comfort which that afforded was what I imagined. But what I didn't count on, what I didn't bank on was—the world he would show me. A way of life. A way of possibilities. The casual way with which he, because he was so bloody rich, could breeze through life and meetings and get things done. And he loved me so. So ceaselessly. And I came to love him. And after we were married a year and had taken those pointless religious and legal vows, we took new vows. Profound vows. Vows of true love. For eternity. He nurtured me, again as I do others now, he "found my genius" as he loved to say. He set me up in business. My connections in rock music from the party days were . . . extensive. I became a manager. He was so ungodly proud. But that life, any life in the entertainment field—phone calls, meetings, triumphs, disasters. Barely keeping afloat in the sticky sweet success. As bees in honey drown. Soon he became abandoned. All my good fortune. And he felt resentful of my success. He was sick of people asking at parties what it was that he . . . did. And one morning, in the middle of several overwhelming negotiations he called me, sobbing, to say that he . . . felt no longer a part of my life. And I, on a car phone whisking on to God only cares what now, Filofax on my lap. Cellular ringing at my side. Glibly snapped, "Then do something about it." (*She begins to cry.* WYLER *begins to turn.*) Please don't look at me. And when I returned late that night to my Chelsea flat. All was as it always had been. The candles blazing for dinner. The Mahler playing. And when I walked into the bathroom. Please don't look at me. He knew, you see that after a tense day at work I needed, nay REQUIRED, to unwind in a hot bath. "Why not give up this life, if you need to unwind from it?" he always said. Always. And . . . when I walked into that bathroom the SHOCK, the near electric shock. First of tile smeared with red red blood. Then in the bathtub. The tub, he knew that I would be heading for. His lifeless body. The wrists gashed with shaving razors. Blood and life escaping and—

WYLER: Oh God.

ALEXA: Don't look at me. An arm extended from the bathtub onto the floor and a steady stream of—Don't look at me. (WYLER *looks at her.*) Don't look at me. (*She turns away.*) Don't. Look. I am not what I appear to be. I am nothing. I am a worthless half-caste piece of shit from the London streets. Who has truly only ever been loved by one man. An ugly, unattractive, generous man who gave me my life and I destroyed him. Don't look at me. (WYLER *moves to the bed.*) Please don't. (*He gently takes her chin in his hand and moves it toward him.*) I'm nothing, don't look at me.

WYLER: I—

ALEXA: I am nothing.

WYLER: I—

ALEXA: I am not to be loved by anyone.

WYLER: I—I love you.

ALEXA: No one should love me.

WYLER: Evan Wyler loves you.

ALEXA: Don't look—

WYLER: I'm looking at you. And I still love you.

ALEXA: Don't. Ever leave me. Don't ever leave me. Ever.

WYLER: I love you.

ALEXA: And I . . . I love you. (*They kiss passionately.*) I love you, lamb. (*They begin to make love as the lights fade.*)

Scene 7

(*A newsstand.*)

(*A little shop. Covered with magazines all with smiling pretty people.* WYLER *walks in. A* WOMAN *attendant is there.* WYLER *looks at all the smiling pictures. He turns to the* WOMAN.)

WYLER: A carton of Dunhill cigarettes. And—do you have any Los Angeles papers or magazines that say what's going on there? I'm going to L.A. and I need to know what's—

WOMAN: Just a moment, I'll check. (*She goes.* WYLER *picks up a copy of a magazine and quickly riffles through to find his picture. He does and smiles. Just then* SKUNK *walks in.* WYLER *sees him first.*)

WYLER: Skunk, my picture's in this magazine, did you see?

SKUNK: (*He is furious.*) You!!

WYLER: Hey, what's—

SKUNK: You tosser, where the fuck is me money? (*He punches* WYLER.)

WYLER: What the—

SKUNK: You toerags owe me soddin' three thousand quid I put up. You and—

WYLER: What are you— (SKUNK *punches him again.* WYLER *is now bleeding.*) STOP!!

SKUNK: You and that bloody slag Vere de Vere. You soddin' having me on? You having me on?

WYLER: I didn't take any— (SKUNK *punches him again.*) I didn't take any of your bloody money, look. (SKUNK *threatens to punch him again.*) STOP!! Calm down. There's a mistake, an obvious mistake. I haven't taken anybody's money.

SKUNK: That cunt Alexa did and you bugger well work with her and—

WYLER: I don't work—I'm just writing with her and—

SKUNK: Flight from London, studio space, hotel all on me bloody tab and she never gave me nothing—

WYLER: I don't know anything about—

SKUNK: I can't even fucking get ahold of her or find her and—

WYLER: She has a meeting with you right now with Morris Kaden of—

SKUNK: Who the bollocks is that? (*The* WOMAN *enters.*)

WOMAN: Hey hey! Take this outside.

WYLER: I swear I don't—

SKUNK: Bullshit, you know.

WOMAN: I'm calling the cops!

SKUNK: You're a fucking grifter like her—

WOMAN: (*Into the phone.*) Yes, there's a fight going on here at—

WYLER: I don't know—I don't know!

SKUNK: Tosser! Who are you anyway?

WYLER: Wyler. Evan Wyler.

SKUNK: How do I know that? You're bugger well Alexa's assistant— (*He punches* WYLER *again.* WYLER'*s face is covered in blood. The* WOMAN *screams.*)

WYLER: I am me.

SKUNK: Who the fuck are you? (*A final punch from* SKUNK. *And a shove.* WYLER *lands on the newsstand. The hundreds of smiling faces cover his face.*)

Scene 8

(*A pay phone.*)

(MORRIS KADEN's *office.*)

(*The Royalton.*)

(WYLER *is now covered in blood. His face is cut. He holds a handkerchief up to his left eye. He is at a street pay phone. He dials information.*)

WYLER: It's a business. Delta records. (*A pause as he gets the number. He hangs up, puts a quarter in and dials.*) Yes. Morris Kaden please. (*A pause as the lights come up on the outer executive offices of Delta records, a stylish* SECRETARY *is on a headset, lazily flipping through a magazine.*) Morris Kaden please.

SECRETARY: And who may I say is calling?

WYLER: Just put me through to Morris Kaden.

SECRETARY: I'm sorry. Mr. Kaden doesn't speak to anyone unsolicited. And he does not return phone calls.

WYLER: Tell him this is about Alexa Vere de Vere, his employee.

SECRETARY: I'm sorry, that name again?

WYLER: Alexa Vere de Vere.

SECRETARY: I'm not familiar with that name at all.

WYLER: You probably haven't heard of her.

SECRETARY: Hon, trust me. I've heard of everyone.

WYLER: I'll hold.

SECRETARY: I'll hang up. (*She hangs up, the lights go out on her. A dial tone.*)

WYLER: Shit! (*He slams the phone against the receiver. Quickly dials another number.*) In Manhattan. Royalton Hotel. (*He gets the number. Puts in a quarter and quickly dials. The lights come up on the* CLERK *at the Royalton.*)

CLERK: Royalton.

WYLER: Alexa Vere de Vere. Suite 719.

CLERK: One moment. (*A moment.*) Ms. Vere de Vere has left for the south of France.

WYLER: Oh God.

CLERK: Is this Mr. Wyler?

WYLER: (*Hopefully.*) Yes, Evan Wyler. Has she left a note?

CLERK: Mr. Wyler. We have an outstanding bill here of three thousand dollars. Ms. Vere de Vere said you'd take care of it. (*The lights come up on a too trendy bar.* DENISE, *an up-and-coming actress, enters.* ALEXA *stands up.*) We've called on your credit cards and it appears you've reached your limit.

DENISE: Alexa Vere de Vere?

WYLER: Oh God.

CLERK: Mr. Wyler?

ALEXA: Cabbage!

CLERK: Is there another form of payment possible?

ALEXA: I saw the magazine photograph of you in that dingy little play and I knew then and there that you must star in the movie of *MY LIFE!*

WYLER: Oh my God. Hasn't she left a note? (*He slowly sinks to the ground and sobs.*)

CLERK: No. She's gone to Toulouse to think. She said you would take care of the bill.

ALEXA: We will away to Hollywood where we shall incite them to madness!

WYLER: (*Through sobs.*) It isn't true.

CLERK: Mr. Wyler? Mr. Wyler? Mr. Wyler, I can hear that you're still there, Mr. Wyler? Mr. Wyler?

WYLER: It isn't true. It isn't true, isn't true!

END OF ACT 1

ACT 2

"Art"

Scene 1

(*A glamorous dinery, to be sure.*)

(*Another trendy restaurant.* ALEXA *is talking with* DENISE.)

ALEXA: Art. Art. Art art art. *Je suis* knocked out by art. The homes of Hollywood are all about art, I cannot wait to show you. All modern and postmodern works have found themselves in Los Angeles County. San Andreas goes? The last six pages of Janson's, gone. Ross Bleckner is in every living room in Bel Air. And some of his paintings. Of course you ask any of these movie people why they have this art in their life and never ever in their work and oh the blank stares. In their minds it is all a sort of aesthetic penance. You shall see when we're there!

Scene 2

(MORRIS KADEN's *office/various.*)

(MORRIS KADEN *is going over some papers with his* SECRETARY. WYLER *stumbles in. The* SECRETARY *sees him first.*)

SECRETARY: Oh Christ, I'm calling security. (*She runs to a phone.*)

WYLER: What the fuck is going on?

KADEN: Who is this putz? Do I know this putz? Putz, who are you?

SECRETARY: (*At the phone now.*) We do not know this putz. I'm calling security.

WYLER: Something fucked up is going on with one of your producers.

SECRETARY: This putz is unknown to us.

KADEN: Which producer?

WYLER: Alexa Vere de Vere.

SECRETARY: She doesn't work here.

KADEN: She doesn't work here.

SECRETARY: We've never even heard of her.

KADEN: I've heard of her.

SECRETARY: You have?

KADEN: You—putz—what's his name?

SECRETARY: I don't know.

WYLER: Wyler. Evan Wyler.

KADEN: Wyler Evan Wyler, sit down. (*To his* SECRETARY.) Don't call security. Get this putz some damp paper towels and some Band-Aids. Hold all calls.

SECRETARY: (*As she exits.*) I don't know this putz, I don't know this producer, and I know everyone.

KADEN: (*Offers* WYLER *a glass of water.*) Here putz. Water. Drink. So. Alexa Vere de Vere, huh? God. Haven't heard that name for a while. How much did she take you for?

WYLER: Take? What do you—I don't get it.

KADEN: She took you. Which word eludes you? She, the subject. Took, the verb, vernacular for took advantage of. You. The direct object. (*The* SECRETARY *reenters. Hands the paper towels and bandages to* WYLER.)

WYLER: Oh no. Oh God.

KADEN: And from the looks this is very direct. Wyler Evan Wyler, God. Why don't you hand your credit card to my secretary so that she can see how much has been run up? (WYLER *does so.*)

WYLER: I think there's been a mistake. (*As the* SECRETARY *exits, he stands up.*)

KADEN: (*To his* SECRETARY.) Come in as soon as you know the amount. (*She is gone; he turns to* WYLER.) If you don't sit down now, I'm either going to laugh at you or cry for you. (WYLER *sits.*) OK. Alexa Vere de Vere. Let's start at the beginning. What magazine were you in?

WYLER: Magazine, how did you know—why?

KADEN: And was the unbearable adjective "hot" used at any time and not in reference to temperature?

WYLER: Hot writer.

KADEN: How literary. That is how you were found. Alexa, she— (*Lights come up on a stack of trendy magazines.* ALEXA *is riffling through a magazine.*) pores through those magazines as if, well, as if they really mean anything, until she finds someone who is in some editor's estimation— (ALEXA *rips out the page with* WYLER*'s picture in it.*) hot. (*The lights go out on* ALEXA.) She contacts them with some harebrained scheme about working together. Some album, or television show, or Broadway musical or whatever that particular artist would consider doing to get some quick vast cash. Take the money and run type of scenario. Some— (*He stops to think of a word. The lights come up on* ALEXA. *She is at the Hotel Paramount. We are back at their first meeting.*)

ALEXA: . . . this most mouthwatering—

KADEN and ALEXA: Movie idea—

ALEXA: I have up my Gucci sleeve.

KADEN: Whatever. Just enough to blow some sunshine up your ass. And the names get dropped.

ALEXA: David Bowie, Iman, Morris Kaden, the Duke of Chichester, etc. etc. etc.

KADEN: And the places.

ALEXA: London, India, Hollywood, south of France, an investor in Milan, Oz.

KADEN: And the disregard for money and prices and—basically the world everybody wants to live in. (*The* SECRETARY *reenters.*) Oh and the support team.

ALEXA: My lawyer, my international tax attorney, my Shemp-loving accountant. And agents, though I don't believe in agents, do you?

SECRETARY: Mr. Kaden.

KADEN: Yes?

SECRETARY: Just shy of fifteen grand.

WYLER: Oh my God.

KADEN: You got off easily.

SECRETARY: (*Handing the card back to* WYLER.) They said I should destroy the card in front of you with scissors. You look like you've already been through enough today. (*She exits.*)

KADEN: That's how she lives. Almost famous person to almost famous person. She knows you're champing at the bit to lose the almost and just be famous. See, first you're blinded by the appearance and the jewelry, then it's the cash. The cold green cash. The bait.

ALEXA: I read your book and now here I am at the Hotel Paramount over *petit déjeuner* and great lashings of butter and I'm offering you one thousand dollars a week to write the story of my life and—

WYLER: (*In a trance in* KADEN's *office.*) Really?

ALEXA: Oh God. Haven't I told you? I have absolutely no mind for money whatsoever.

KADEN: And she puts a thousand dollars in cash into your hand. With—wait, what does she say—

KADEN and ALEXA: I believe in cash, I think in this flighty world, it's the only thing left with any impact. (ALEXA *holds up the cash.*)

KADEN: A nice appearance. A little glamour, cash in your hand. Let the games begin. And they do. With the first bill, she sets a precedent.

ALEXA: Now darling, what shall I do? My accountant wants a record of all these businessy lunches, but won't let me have credit cards because I just see homeless people and I want to buy them socks.

KADEN: And she's so helpless.

ALEXA: I'll need a receipt of some kind.

KADEN: And you're helpful.

WYLER: I could put this on my credit card and you can give me cash.

KADEN: So helpful.

WYLER: If that could help. (*A* WAITER *breezes in and takes* WYLER's *credit card.*)

ALEXA: Such a help.

KADEN: And of course she pays you back immediately. The first time.

ALEXA: (*Showing two twenties and a ten.*) Here's fifty dollars.

KADEN: With too much.

WYLER: That's too much.

ALEXA: Please.

KADEN: But also another precedent is set. One of distraction during the transaction. (*The* WAITER *is back with a check for* WYLER.)

ALEXA: (*As he signs it.*) If you absolutely had to sleep with one of the Three Stooges, which one would it be? (*The* WAITER *takes the check.*)

KADEN: Those distractions are important.

ALEXA: (*Now standing next to* WYLER.) What care I? Calvin Klein fragrances. Have you noticed that his scents capture a man in any contemporary relationship?

KADEN: Because soon comes the first one where money doesn't exchange hands.

ALEXA: (*She hands money to* WYLER. WYLER *reaches for it.*) This can't be the right time! (*She sprays cologne in his face.*) Escape! (WYLER *sees that the money has not been handed to him as she runs off.*)

KADEN: And soon you never see cash again. It's all on your credit card. Can't call the police on her. You've been volunteering to pay. (*A light on* ALEXA *admiring a beautiful diamond bracelet.*)

ALEXA: And I've picked out this cunning little Lagerfeld traveling suit for myself. It complements your suit without matching it. And on the back of that shard of paper is the number for Louis Vuitton. My new luggage set. And tell me how much these earrings are worth it!! (WYLER *covers his ears.*) And I simply must pick up the oh so many things I phone ordered while you were writing. (*Lights down on* ALEXA.)

KADEN: You've helped pay for Alexa's five-star, world-class life. She gets the hot person to pay for her life and she is gone by the time the credit card bill arrives. On to the next hot person. She knows, her one bit of brilliance is that she knows. At that moment in time, when the artist first stands at the what— (*Lights up on* ALEXA *in the nightclub.*)

ALEXA: All of us creative people—

KADEN: Brink of success, they call it.

ALEXA: Tearing about trying—

KADEN: The artist wants to be—

ALEXA: —to feed a nation's insatiable appetite for entertainment.

KADEN: Through the looking glass.

ALEXA: Making truckloads of money we never see—

KADEN: Ready to abandon all morals and logic.

ALEXA: So that we can discover something new and vivid—

KADEN: Ready to be famous and, so it would follow, fulfilled.

ALEXA: —to present to poor fun-starved modern civilization.

KADEN: Ready to lose all problems.

ALEXA: The new becoming old almost before we find the newer new.

KADEN: Ready to lose the old life.

ALEXA: Humanity gasping for air under the weight of its own culture.

KADEN: You're ready to sign anything.

ALEXA: All holding on for dear life as we create fresher and fresher possibilities.

KADEN: Anything not to have to be you, anymore.

ALEXA: As bees in honey drown. (*She disappears.*)

WYLER: How many has she done this to?

KADEN: A lot. Hundreds maybe. A lot of new people all the time in magazines.

WYLER: Why don't they stop her?

KADEN: Well—it's a pretty elite club, the survivors of Alexa Vere de Vere. Nice company to be in. And who really wants to go public and brand themselves as a stooge? Or worse, someone who pursues fame? And well, maybe there's a bit of gratitude for the dear girl. Nothing like the first big screw. The screw that toughens the skin for all the future screw attempts. You know, Teacher says every time an artist is screwed, an angel gets his wings.

WYLER: Doesn't anyone ever get her back?

KADEN: Most people have lives. They move on.

WYLER: I'm not—I don't think I'm going to move on. I'm going to get her back. And I'll get my money back.

KADEN: Wyler Evan Wyler. She doesn't have it to give back. Move on. Why bother?

WYLER: Fifteen grand?!

KADEN: Consider it tuition.

WYLER: I'm different than—We slept together.

KADEN: Not unheard of with her. Just let go.

WYLER: You don't understand. I slept with her. And I'm gay.

KADEN: What do you want, frequent flyer miles? Forget about it.

WYLER: She said she loved me. I told her that I loved her. I'm not big on—I hadn't done that before. (*A look of great sadness passes* KADEN*'s face. He leans over and feels the material on the lapel of* WYLER*'s suit.*)

KADEN: Well . . . it is a great suit. If nothing else she made you buy yourself a nice suit. Her taste in suits—

WYLER: So—Oh God. So then—?

KADEN: Even I was a putz once. Why do you think I'm the expert? (WYLER *stands up to leave.*) Don't. Please. Just leave her be. (WYLER *is at the door.*) We all let her go on because in an odd way, she reminds us what we were foolish enough to think of giving up. To have her life. Her sad empty life. We all actually considered giving up ourselves.

WYLER: What do you know about her that's true?

KADEN: Oh. None of her. One hopes.

WYLER: You know where I might talk to someone who might know something about her?

KADEN: Geez. Uh. Offhand, not really. Maybe. You know who might know about her is the dancer, what's her name, Illya—

Scene 3

(*The telephone.*)

(WYLER*'s composition book.*)

(*Immediately following the last scene,* WYLER *has his composition book. He leafs through and finds a mention in his notes.*)

WYLER: Illya—

KADEN: Illya Mannon. (*We see* ALEXA. *She is as* WYLER *has written her on the page.*)

ALEXA: I stood there reading reviews with my new discovery, Illya Mannon. (ILLYA MANNON *appears. She is on the phone.*)

WYLER: (*Now on the phone with* ILLYA.) Illya Mannon?

ILLYA: Speaking.

ALEXA: I stood there—

KADEN: And there was that boy dancer in that video.

WYLER: I'd like to talk to you about Alexa Vere de Vere.

ALEXA: Quaking.

KADEN: Going to be big.

ILLYA: Oh Jesus. She still alive?

WYLER: What do you know about her that's true?

KADEN: And the sculpture performance person.

ILLYA: Who is this? You get taken by—

WYLER: Yeah.

ILLYA: Yeah well. Join the crowd.

KADEN: And that composer. With the animation.

WYLER: I want to find her. And I'm looking for—for want of a better word, the truth. Something to help try to find her.

ILLYA: What are you going to do once you find the truth?

WYLER: I haven't thought that far in advance.

ILLYA: Uhm. Well. You know I really don't know her. It was like one weekend and twenty-five grand. But you know who would know is—

KADEN: And the actress with the accents.

ALEXA: An acquaintance of mine— (WYLER *leafs through the composition book.*)

ILLYA, KADEN, and ALEXA: Bethany Vance—

ILLYA: She spent some real time with her—

ALEXA: The alleged actress.

ILLYA: She really got taken.

ALEXA: At a party in London.

WYLER: Bethany Vance? (BETHANY *appears. She is on the phone.*)

ALEXA: I found out to be—

BETHANY: Yes?

ALEXA: A masochist.

BETHANY: She said I was a masochist?

ALEXA: No really. Whips, chains.

BETHANY: You know that is just so typical, fucking typical. Fucker rips you off and then claims you into a circle of friends and then pins, like, intimate knowledge on you. But then, you know, I found out that like all her quote friends are people she's conned. All of them. The accountant, Martel Grushkov.

ILLYA: The investor from Milan.

KADEN: The Duke of Chichester.

ALEXA: Morris Kaden.

WYLER: Morris Kaden—

BETHANY: Morris Kaden, they're all alive and well and she's conned them. (WYLER *is now flipping through the pages of his book.*)

WYLER: The truth.

ALEXA: Illya Mannon, Bethany Vance, the Duke of Chichester.

ILLYA: That actor with the really great hair who can't act.

WYLER: I'd like the truth.

BETHANY: That singer with the six-note range.

WYLER: Just someone tell me the truth.

KADEN: That poet who can't rhyme.

WYLER: Overseas operator, London. I'm looking for a residence for the Duke of Chichester.

ALEXA: Martel Grushkov, my husband deserted me in the most far-fetched ways.

WYLER: Chichester, I guess.

ALEXA: The Pet Shop Boys.

BETHANY: And you know. What's his name? Him.

ILLYA: And Morris Kaden.

KADEN: Any putz.

BETHANY: The really famous one.

ILLYA: Did I mention Morris Kaden?

BETHANY: The celebrity.

ALEXA: The Clash, the Cure—My late husband always used to say that, he was Jewish.

WYLER: So you would agree that the names she drops are mostly people that she's conned?

ALEXA: The Boy George, Simon Le Bon, I am not marrying that rich broker's son, but then I met Michael.

WYLER: What about the husband who died?

ALEXA: Dear God.

WYLER: Michael.

ALEXA: Well, Michael.

BETHANY: Who's Michael?

ALEXA: Mr. Michael Stabinsky.

ILLYA: He's dead?

ALEXA: That name.

KADEN: Who's dead?

ILLYA: I thought he tried to kill her and she ran away.

BETHANY: I don't know a Michael.

ILLYA: Or he ran away.

BETHANY: Now a *MICHELLE*—

ILLYA: Somebody ran away. To Denmark.

KADEN: Is this the fiancé who died in the freak hovercraft accident?

WYLER: I think he's dead.

BETHANY: Why?

WYLER: Alexa told me.

KADEN: PUTZ!

ALEXA: His lifeless body. The wrists gashed with shaving razors and—

WYLER: You think he's still living?

BETHANY: If he exists at all.

ALEXA: The wedding was part Jewish owing to the groom and—

WYLER: He's in England maybe.

KADEN: Says her. Try New York.

ILLYA: I never bought that Indian princess crap.

BETHANY: Indian? Indonesian.

KADEN: Or Iranian.

BETHANY: Ah, she's probably American and so's her probably living dead husband. Or girlfriend.

KADEN: Try New York, then try London.

ILLYA: And then Denmark. Maybe. (*All, save* ALEXA *and* WYLER *leave the stage.*)

ALEXA: Dear God. Well, Michael.

WYLER: (*He is now on the phone with* MIKE.) Michael Stabinsky?

ALEXA: Mr. Michael Stabinsky. (MIKE *appears.*) That name.

MIKE: Mike.

ALEXA: And Michael, the Jewish husband of convenience—

WYLER: But Stabinsky?

MIKE: Right, what can I do for you?

WYLER: Are you the Michael Stabinsky—I'm sorry I'm just trying to track somebody down and you're in New York and this person is probably in London but—God. By any chance, are you the Michael Stabinsky that knew—or do you know—Alexa Vere de Vere?

MIKE: Yeah, sure.

ALEXA: An ugly, unattractive, generous man who gave me my life and I destroyed him. (ALEXA *disappears.*)

MIKE: Wait. Oh God. You get taken?

WYLER: Yeah. I can't believe that—

MIKE: Oh. I'm sorry. And how did I die this time?

WYLER: Oh my—Are you—In a bathtub. Suicide.

MIKE: Bathtub. (*A moment as he thinks.*) *Death of Jean-Paul Marat* by David. Right. She tends to kill me off as great works of art. I've gone down on a ship, *Raft of the Medusa,* died in her arms, the *Pietà.* I think it's only a matter of time before I get struck by arrows like St. Sebastian. Listen, I'm sorry. I don't know anything about her whereabouts. I have absolutely no contact with her—haven't for years.

WYLER: Could I—

MIKE: Sorry?

WYLER: Could we . . . talk about her.

MIKE: Why would you want to do that?

WYLER: I just would like to know the truth.

Scene 4

(MIKE*'s loft.*)

(*The eighties.*)

(*First, the loft.* WYLER *sips a cup of coffee handed to him by* MIKE. *A shudder runs up his spine and then he smiles.*)

WYLER: Hmmm.

MIKE: Good?

WYLER: Sure. Coffee?

MIKE: Bless you for noticing.

WYLER: No, it's good, it's— (MIKE *takes a sip from his own cup and immediately spits it back into the mug.*)

MIKE: It's tar. Sorry, it's been on all day.

WYLER: It's OK.

MIKE: No, it's not.

WYLER: You're right, it's not.

MIKE: Then why did you say it was?

WYLER: I was being charming.

MIKE: Oh. Well. I don't do charm.

WYLER: Got it.

MIKE: I'll put new coffee on.

WYLER: So, tell me how you met Alexa.

MIKE: What did she tell you about me?

WYLER: Oh. Uh— (*He looks in his composition book.*) That you
were older. Than—well her.

MIKE: I am. So far, so good.

WYLER: Old money. European.

MIKE: Sorry, no. Pennsylvania. Po' white trash.

WYLER: Jewish.

MIKE: Close. Catholic.

WYLER: Unattractive.

MIKE: Your call.

WYLER: No, you're cute.

MIKE: Really, how cute?

WYLER: Don't . . . milk it, you're cute.

MIKE: Fair enough. Anything else?

WYLER: Uh. . . . You were married. To each other.

MIKE: No.

WYLER: Lovers?

MIKE: Not likely. I'm queer.

WYLER: Yeah well, that's not exactly a brick wall ending for her.

MIKE: So—

WYLER: More just a speed bump.

MIKE: You're queer?

WYLER: Yeah.

MIKE: Oh. So. And you think I'm cute?

WYLER: Let's not—I'm not pursuing that right—You really don't do charming. You're direct.

MIKE: That's 'cause I tell the truth. Only people who are deceitful have to be charming.

WYLER: Well maybe a little charm—

MIKE: Probably right. I'm overcompensating for lessons learned young. What else did she tell you about me?

WYLER: Uhm . . . (*He looks in the book again.*) —impossible Polish last name which is—

WYLER and MIKE: Stabinsky.

MIKE: True.

WYLER: And that you discovered her and created her which is probably—

MIKE: True.

WYLER: False. True? Really?

MIKE: Yeah.

WYLER: But you—I thought you just said—about not being charming but truthful and—

MIKE: Overcompensating for lessons learned young.

WYLER: Got it. So—what do you mean, you created her?

MIKE: Why do you want to know?

WYLER: I'd like to know what makes a person this way—

MIKE: And you want revenge?

WYLER: Maybe. Or get my money back. Make sure she doesn't do it again.

MIKE: Revenge strikes me as such the colossal waste of time. Look. What do you do?

WYLER: I'm a writer.

MIKE: Why don't you just go off and write something. Forget about Alexa.

WYLER: I can't write.

MIKE: (*Sarcastically as he gets the coffee.*) Yeah yeah, you can't write.

WYLER: I mean I can't write.

MIKE: Are you serious? (*He is taken aback.*)

WYLER: It isn't just the money that Alexa stole from me. She stole my arrogance. The arrogance it takes to just shamelessly write something and assume someone, anyone might read it. The gall to think I might be a success. It's gone. Killed. I can't. I'm blocked. I cannot write.

MIKE: Oh God. I had no idea. I'm so sorry. I—

WYLER: Just tell me about Alexa. Or, maybe I should leave. I mean, if you—

MIKE: No. No. Don't leave. I'll tell you.

WYLER: Really?

MIKE: Why not? My painting is going slowly. You're cute. You think I'm cute.

WYLER: I'm not—

MIKE: Enough tar?

WYLER: Thank you.

MIKE: OK, Alexa Vere de Vere.

WYLER: Where'd her name come from?

MIKE: We'll get to that later. Before Alexa it was Brenda.

WYLER: Brenda?

MIKE: Brenda Gelb. (ALEXA *appears as* BRENDA. *A younger girl with long blonde hair and a rough edge or ten. She is in the eighties.*)

ALEXA: Brenda Gelb and Mike Stabinsky. WE are soul mates, got it?

MIKE: I had graduated from Philadelphia College of Art and had gone back home to West Reading, Pennsylvania, to earn money for—

ALEXA: New York City.

MIKE: And had taken a job working tables in some Amish all-you-can-eat nightmare and. And also working there was a waitress.

ALEXA: Mike, we gotta get to New York City. We can save enough money if we really scrape till September and we can get a big loft in Soho and you can paint and I can—

MIKE: She was just out of high school and she had dreams.

ALEXA: —be a writer.

WYLER: To be what?

MIKE: A writer.

ALEXA: I can be really great.

WYLER: (*Laughing.*) Of course. A writer.

ALEXA: I mean my insights are so uncanny and my vocabulary is just so whatever, it's so huge.

MIKE: So we scrounged and saved and got ourselves to New York.

ALEXA: Us. Living in New York. Total everything of it all!

MIKE: It was a great time. We found a hole-in-the-wall space and just, you know, homesteaded. I painted. Brenda wrote. We worked graveyard shift at a diner. It was—it was OK, you know?

ALEXA: Mike, we gotta get some money quick.

MIKE: But nothing good lasts long.

ALEXA: I just heard that our beloved day job is going belly up.

WYLER: What happened?

ALEXA: They're turning our greasy spoon into a trendy restaurant with models as waiters.

MIKE: Everything that was good ran away.

ALEXA: We need something fast or it's back to West Reading.

MIKE: And we all needed something fast to replace it.

ALEXA: Art. And fame.

MIKE: And we all found it. Art and fame.

ALEXA: Art is exploding, Mike.

WYLER: Art.

ALEXA: You can't see your way through the East Village without stepping over a million galleries.

WYLER: And fame.

ALEXA: Art art, everywhere you look.

WYLER: Of course.

ALEXA: And people are buying. And you're better than anybody else out there. How soon can you get a show together? We could make some money here. (MIKE *turns to her. They are in the scene together. They are in the eighties.* WYLER *watches.*)

MIKE: Brenda—

ALEXA: Mike, you're so good. Look, I know this guy who works down at the copy center and he's semi-dating this guy with a column and he says that when you get a show together, I told him about your work, he is way way intrigued, and he said that his demi-boyfriend would definitely be there. And write it up!

MIKE: I can't get a show together by—

ALEXA: Don't you get it? If you do it, someone will write about it. And if somebody writes about it, somebody else will read about it. And if somebody else reads about it, they figured if somebody wrote about it, it must be good and then they buy it! How many paintings do you have done?

MIKE: Seven. Really only one, but the last six I could rush and—

ALEXA: Why do you take so long? What about this one?

MIKE: That's only a color study.

ALEXA: They don't need to know that.

MIKE: Brenda!

ALEXA: It's a seller's market. And seller's markets don't last forever.

MIKE: Art is eternal.

ALEXA: Eternal isn't as long as it used to be.

MIKE: No gallery—

ALEXA: What gallery? We take all the furniture in this loft, right? We move it to one end? Put a drop cloth over it. We have a gallery. Some rancid cheese, some three-dollar wine, we've been to enough of these openings, I mean what's the over-head?

MIKE: What would we call it?

ALEXA: I don't know. Something big and foreign and grand and—can you have this done in a month?

MIKE: I mean if I rushed it could—sure, look finished and—

ALEXA: Foreign with a hyphen. The gallery should have a foreign name with a hyphen.

MIKE: I've also got some photographs from this class I took in—

ALEXA: Leibshen-Amore galleries.

MIKE: Art school, that I could—

ALEXA: Avanti-L'chat galleries.

MIKE: Now, Brenda, we just do this once, for the money then we—

ALEXA: Fjord-Chang galleries.

MIKE: Quit it. This is a take the money and run—

ALEXA: Pesto-Fraulein galleries.

MIKE: Brenda, just name the damn thing, we can sit here coming up with foreign hyphens till we're blue in the face.

ALEXA: Bluen-DiFace galleries. (MIKE *turns to* WYLER, ALEXA *is gone. We are back in the present.*)

MIKE: And the Bluen-DiFace Gallery was born. A quick coat of paint, all the furniture at one end, and I raced like a whirling dervish and managed to whip up six very attractive but entirely pointless paintings. Framed them. And we had the most unique way of pricing things. We'd just shout out a price. And whatever price was so absurd that we had to laugh, that's the price we'd put on it.

WYLER: What about Alexa Vere de Vere? When did Brenda become Alexa Vere de Vere?

MIKE: Right. Alexa. OK. Well. Xeroxed off about a hundred invitations and we made lists and we called and we—she— came up with a lot of resistance. (*At one end of the loft,* BRENDA *is on the phone trying to get some attention.* MIKE *walks over and sits near her and watches. We are back in the eighties.*)

ALEXA: Hi, this is Brenda Gelb of the Bluen-DiFace Gallery and we have an opening and stuff coming up and—it's on—and I know you're busy I can imagine but—maybe on your way to the whatever biennial you could stop by and—oh— there's gonna be wine and—sure I understand. (MIKE *looks to* WYLER.)

MIKE: It was—

WYLER: Not happening.

MIKE: Not happening. (*He's back with* BRENDA.)

ALEXA: This is not happening.

MIKE: Well—I hope you don't mind me—Maybe you sound a little too much like a girl from West Reading, Pennsylvania.

ALEXA: That would be maybe because . . . I am? Just thinking off the cuff.

MIKE: Well maybe if you sounded like—I don't know—

ALEXA: Say it.

MIKE: Like—OK, remember that woman at that gallery, the woman who ran the opening of the space on East Ninth? Like her.

ALEXA: Affected?

MIKE: Well—

ALEXA: Snooty?

MIKE: Flawless.

ALEXA: Like Alexis on *Dynasty*.

MIKE: Joan Collins is a little—

ALEXA: Hello, this is Alexis DiFace from the Bluen–DiFace Gallery.

MIKE: —repulsive. No, your name shouldn't be in the gallery. And Alexis is too—on the money.

ALEXA: Alexxxxxxa?

MIKE: Alexa from the Bluen–DiFace Gallery.

ALEXA: Alexa from the Bluen–DiFace Gallery.

MIKE: We'll see. A familiar sounding last name. But not a real name that people can trace.

ALEXA: Alexa Van Cleef. And Arpels.

MIKE: Traceable. Possibly.

ALEXA: And I gotta get flawless. How do I get flawless? (*The lights go out. Only* MIKE *in a spotlight.*)

MIKE: That weekend we did nothing but rent videos and Brenda learned about flawless. (*Lights out on* MIKE. *Lights up full on* BRENDA. *The blue light of a television is before her. She is talking along with a videotape of Rosalind Russell in* Auntie Mame.)

ALEXA: Help will be here 'ere long, darlings! Mamie Dennis!! *Voilà!* Now where is that divine bootlegger, he promises to bring more gin—Aww Raymond, *mon chou,* I cannot wait for you to—Eveline, you have not returned my last two phone calls—hello darling be with you in a minute, Gregor, I'm ever so glad you are here! Ha ha oooh. Oh you must hear his new symphony, the pastoral. It has motorcycle motors and live goats on the stage it's debilitating, positively debilitating. Terry!! Morris!! Now where in heaven's name!!

(*The blue light goes out quickly. The lights come up on* MIKE, *still trying to come up with a name.*)

MIKE: Alexa von Trapp? No. (*The light abruptly goes out on* MIKE *as the blue television light flashes on* BRENDA. *She is standing up and acting out the videotape of Sally Bowles in* Cabaret.)

ALEXA: Fraulein Schneider *Nix sum hou*—have you a cigarette? I'm desperate. (*Cigarette is lit.*) Divine decadence. Sally Bowles, here. Come on in Brian, darling. It's the most marvelous boardinghouse. Wonderful boarders. Nobody has any money, who does these days? To be honest, I'm never around. I tear about all day and then am up all hours at the cabaret. (*A tango is heard.*) I'm not the type with wisdom, Brian darling. I have instincts. (*She dances.*) I have ancient instincts and I have this uncanny, possibly spiritual, thatish feeling about you. That you're going to be my roommate. My roommate. OK? OK? (*She offers a toast.*) Prairie oysters! (MIKE *steps into the blue light and ejects the tape.*)

MIKE: Alexa Vanderbilt?

ALEXA: I like the V to go with the X. But no van.

MIKE: God. Beggars can be choosers. (*He puts another video in.*)

ALEXA: Look. I have to say the name, let me pick it.

MIKE: (*Points to the video and then watches her.*) Watch. And learn. (*Just like that she is Holly Golightly in* Breakfast at Tiffany's.)

ALEXA: Telephone is right there. No it's not, where did it get to? Oh, that's right. I put it in the suitcase so I wouldn't hear it when it rings. Where's cat? Poor cat. Poor slob. Poor no-name slob. One day I'm going to find someplace where he and me can belong. I'm not sure where that is, but I know what it's like. It's like Tiffany's. I'm CRAZY for Tiffany's. (*Bossa nova music plays.*) Nothing too awful can happen to you there. I'm sorry you wanted something—oh right.

Telephone. (*The rest of the room comes up along with the blue light.* MIKE *hands her the telephone. She doesn't take it yet.*)

MIKE: Alexa Farquar.

ALEXA: A "v." A "v" to go with the "x."

MIKE: You know what? Lower the voice. (BRENDA *looks at the set, the lights change, and she is suddenly Tallulah Bankhead in* Lifeboat.)

ALEXA: Did you see anything of Charcoal? Joe, the porter. He helped me onto the lifeboat. What part of the ship were you on, darling? (*The scene is abruptly over.* MIKE *shoves the telephone back at her.*)

MIKE: Alexa Vere de Vere.

ALEXA: Alexa Vere de Vere. (*They both laugh.*) We can't. No one in their right mind would believe a name like— (*An instant later.*) I can't.

MIKE: You can. Just talk.

ALEXA: They won't believe me.

MIKE: They'll believe you because they'll want to believe you. (*He is dialing a number.*)

ALEXA: But—

MIKE: After a day full of fucking bores who wouldn't want a call from Alexa Vere de Vere? (*He hands her the receiver.*)

ALEXA: I can't— (*She takes the receiver and puts it to her ear.*)

MIKE: Shhhhhhh. Leo.

ALEXA: Hello, Alexa Vere de Vere from Bluen-DiFace galleries for Leo. Leo, Alexa Vere de Vere, *Voilà!* I never see you anymore. I tear about all day and then am up all hours at the caba— (*A squeeze on the arm from* MIKE.) gallery. I think I saw you last at Tiffany's. I'm CRAZY for Tiffany's. Nothing too awful can happen to you there. Now darling, the most wonderful gallery. Wonderful artists. Nobody has any money, who does these days? New artist—Michael Stabinsky. His work—debilitating, positively devastating. It's Monday the third, I know you'll want to be there. I'll messenger over the invite and—Terry, Morris! What part of the ship were you on? Darling, I must tear. But I have this uncanny, possibly spiritual thatish feeling about you and this artist. See you then? How utterly, utterly cunning. (*She hangs up. She can't believe it.*) He says he'll come.

MIKE: Where did utterly, utterly cunning come from?

ALEXA: I made that one up. (ALEXA *is gone. A flash,* MIKE *is back with* WYLER.)

MIKE: Brenda took to Alexa Vere de Vere like a flame to oil. And soon Alexa wasn't just a name we made up, it was a game we played. Every chance we had we'd see who could out-Alexa the other. She'd say, "Are you going to the drugstore?" I'd say, "I'm about to pop off to the chemists."

WYLER: Out of control.

MIKE: She was. Completely.

WYLER: Not just her. You. You were out of control.

MIKE: Yeah. I guess I was. But that was the great thing about New York in the eighties. Out of control didn't stick out at all.

WYLER: So. Alexa. What happened next?

MIKE: We laughed a lot. And called an obscene amount of receptive people, who really should have known better until—

WYLER: The opening?

MIKE: Yeah. The opening. No. Just before.

WYLER: God, I'll bet you were excited.

MIKE: Yes. No. Mostly terrified.

WYLER: Terrified? (MIKE *walks into the bathroom. We see* ALEXA *bending over a sink, a towel over her head. We are back in the eighties.*)

MIKE: May I have the sink, I want to vomit.

ALEXA: Vomit in the toilet, you know, Michael—

MIKE: Mike.

ALEXA: Michael, you really must do something about your name. It is but so unruly. How is anyone to take an artist seriously when you end your name with a sky?

MIKE: Kandinsky?

ALEXA: The exception that proves the rule. Stop vomiting and relax.

MIKE: You don't get it. You are so wrapped up in the whatever of it all that—these people, the ones coming tonight are all— they're the people I hope to one day impress with my real work. And they're here because we've . . . conned them. We've lied to them. Christ, we've lied to ourselves. We have no business doin—

ALEXA: Oh Michael.

MIKE: Mike.

ALEXA: Michael. We have every bit of business doing this. And what the fuck is this impress others crap?

MIKE: Brenda, no—

ALEXA: You yourself have told me myriad—

MIKE: —no, not like—

ALEXA: —times that the only person an artist is required to impress is himself.

MIKE: No, Brenda.

ALEXA: Yes, we've conned others to get here but once they are here, they are on their own.

MIKE: You're right.

ALEXA: And as for the conning of ourselves, all I can say is—we both know who we are. And we know what we've done.

MIKE: You're . . . right. I'm sorry, just opening night jitters. (*She removes her towel. Her hair is in the* ALEXA *black pageboy cut.*)

ALEXA: What do you think?

MIKE: My God, what have you done?

ALEXA: I just—when I look in the mirror, I don't want to see Brenda. I want to see Alexa. (*She is gone.* MIKE *looks forward. The bathroom is gone.*)

MIKE: And we were off. The crowd from the beginning was . . . amazing. The room soon filled with people, and Brenda was . . . on fire. (*Early eighties dance music is heard.*) She knew everyone by their first name. And everyone seemed so touched that she had remembered them. Never mind she had never met them, it was just nice she remembered. And the people. It was easy for Brenda slash Alexa to say where she'd seen them. She'd seen them in magazines. One after the other. They marched in. As if someone had suddenly made an issue of *W* in 3-D. Warhol walked by and Alexa kissed him on the hand and said, "Andy Warhol, we are your children!" And Warhol said, "Wow." And for those of us looking for signs, and we were, this was a biggie. Of course later we found out that was pretty much Warhol's response to anything. You could say, "Andy, your toupee is on fire" and he'd—"wow." But. But I look back on that time and I am envious. I am nostalgic. I am—I'd like to do it one more time. But that is dangerous. For when it was all over and it was just the two of us— (MIKE *is holding a canvas. He is alone in the now empty loft.* ALEXA *staggers in with a bottle of champagne. She is wearing early eighties high-fashion gear.*)

ALEXA: Michael? Lamb?

MIKE: Mike.

ALEXA: Success. A ringing success. A . . . successful success. Have some champagne. Every painting sold. A miracle in the order of fish and loaves.

MIKE: Every painting. Except one.

ALEXA: All right, every painting except one. Your glass is metaphorically half empty, isn't it?

MIKE: Brenda, the one that didn't sell was . . . is—

ALEXA: What?

MIKE: The only one that's finished.

ALEXA: Did anyone like it? What did Warhol say?

MIKE: He said, "WOW." What the FUCK does he ever say?

ALEXA: Don't you bark at me. I will not be—I am SO VERY sorry that we've made thousands of dollars this evening selling everything you've ever touched. And that now you are free to create for the next year. And you are, you know? Michael. Lamb. You are free to create for another year and do what you really want to. And when we're broke, we'll just do another mocked-up show and we'll—we get to do what we want, is that such a crime?

MIKE: No. Of course not.

ALEXA: We get to be whatever we want to be in this life. And so we do take advantage of the art world. May I say? So fucking what? A world that values its creators more dead? A world of "wow"?

MIKE: Of course.

ALEXA: We've done it. We've fucked them over and they've said thank you. We've won.

MIKE: Of course, of course.

ALEXA: Champagne?

MIKE: Yeah. (*He takes a swig.*)

ALEXA: And it was fun.

MIKE: It was fun.

ALEXA: I love you.

MIKE: I love you. (*They kiss.*)

ALEXA: I love you. (*They look at one another. Not quite knowing what to do.*)

MIKE: I . . . love you. (ALEXA *closes her eyes and moves toward him for a more passionate kiss.*)

ALEXA: I love you . . . lamb. (MIKE *pulls away.*)

MIKE: Uh—Brenda. This is . . . just silly. No.

ALEXA: Come on.

MIKE: No.

ALEXA: You can be whatever you want to be.

MIKE: Oh I think even Norman Vincent Peale would throw his hands up on this one.

ALEXA: Quickly tear my clothing off. Only gently, I want to return this dress to Bergdorf's in the morning.

MIKE: (*With a laugh.*) No.

ALEXA: You can be—

MIKE: I can be whatever I want to be and I want to be a homo-sexual. Now—

ALEXA: And you feel—

MIKE: Now I—

ALEXA: —Nothing? NOTHING—

MIKE: —Think we should—

ALEXA: Toward me after I—

MIKE: Just cool off here and—

ALEXA: After all I've—

MIKE: Go to, you know, neutral corners and—

ALEXA: Fucking done for you?!

MIKE: Fucking done for me? Where did that—

ALEXA: You know what your problem is—

MIKE: I wasn't aware of having—

ALEXA: You have success issues.

MIKE: What the fuck—

ALEXA: Fucker. Stupid fucker. After all I've done for you. After all I've fucking done for you and this is how you just choose to fucking repay me?!

MIKE: Brenda— (ALEXA *throws money at him.*)

ALEXA: I hate you!! What would it have taken to just—

MIKE: Just—

ALEXA: Given me a little something in return?! Here!

MIKE: Hey!

ALEXA: Here's your fucking half of the money. We are over as of this instant! I never want to see you again. You are dead to me—

MIKE: Brenda—

ALEXA: Brenda and Mike are dead! Someday you'll fucking know what you lost! (*She is gone.* MIKE *casually picks up the money and continues to talk to* WYLER. *We slowly move into the present.*)

MIKE: And I never saw her again. Ever. About two years later I bumped into someone in a gallery who had been to my opening. And he fell. It seems Brenda (now exclusively Alexa) had told them that I was dead. Suicide. I had hanged myself from a street lamp outside of a brothel. My body was discovered swinging over a pack of prowling scavenger dogs.

WYLER: Jesus.

MIKE: *Suicide* by George Grosz. 1916. Oil on canvas. She'd managed to leave with a couple of my art books. (WYLER *looks at the canvas.*)

WYLER: This yours?

MIKE: Yes.

WYLER: It's good.

MIKE: The one that didn't sell. Thanks.

WYLER: What's it called?

MIKE: As bees in honey drown. (WYLER *laughs.*) What?

WYLER: Alexa says that all the time.

MIKE: Yet another parting gift for her from my game show of an art career. (WYLER *laughs again.*) You're smiling. You look good smiling.

WYLER: Thanks.

MIKE: It makes your eyes squint. Makes your whole face look like a cow jumped over the moon. (*A pause. They just stare at each other. They then both smile.*)

WYLER: Well. Again. Thank you. Thanks for the stroll through the Alexa archives and the . . . interesting moon image.

MIKE: Anytime.

WYLER: I . . . should get going.

MIKE: I have a better idea.

WYLER: Yeah?

MIKE: Take me to dinner. (WYLER *laughs.*)

WYLER: Uh . . . I don't know, I—

MIKE: Then just come by sometime when I'm painting and hang out—We'll have a nondate.

WYLER: This isn't what I want.

MIKE: What do you want?

WYLER: To find Alexa. What do you want?

MIKE: I want a place to go and paint. To be left alone for a while. And when I'm done painting, I want to get together with some friends, have a beer and talk about stuff. And we'll commiserate if my painting went poorly. And celebrate if my painting went well. That's what I want. Rolling Rock if possible. But I'll settle for a scary Japanese thing if that's all you have. (*A pause.*) That was a hint in case you were wondering what to bring to the nondate.

WYLER: Uh. Thank you. I'd really like to. But, I have—I just have.

MIKE: Right. (*Offstage we hear* GINNY.)

GINNY: Mr. Morelli.

MIKE: See ya.

GINNY: Mr. Morelli. Please don't cry.

WYLER: Uh. No. But thank you for everything. The tar. All of it. (MIKE *goes back to painting.* WYLER *goes to the door.*)

GINNY: Mr. Morelli.

WYLER: Thanks. I have to go. (WYLER *runs off.* MIKE *looks back. Sees that* WYLER *has left behind his composition book.*)

MIKE: Bye. Hey, you left your— (*The lights fade on* MIKE *as he picks up the composition book and the lights come up on—*)

Scene 5

(*A photographer's studio.*)

(*Two telephones.*)

(*First, the studio. A seamless. The same as the beginning of the play.* GINNY, *a young violinist, walks on timidly. Topless, she is covering her breasts with her crossed arms.*)

GINNY: Mr. Uhm . . . Mr. Morelli. Please don't cry. I'm sorry. I just—It's my mom, she's not what you would call, in any meaning of the word, worldly and she—she wouldn't understand me getting my picture taken without my shirt clutching myself with a vacant yet sensual look on my face. And what it has to do with my violin recitals. But if you think it's what I should do to—please stop crying—if you think it's what I should do to get some recognition and— take my picture. I have my shirt off. You can take my picture. See? (*A flash and the lights go down on* GINNY. *Then, a spotlight in the darkness. We see* ALEXA *putting down the magazine upon seeing* GINNY'*s picture. She picks up the yellow pages and a phone.*)

ALEXA: Hello! Am I speaking to Ginny Cameron? The violinist. Now darling, I just saw this barely clad photograph and now I've gone and realized. You must play the score to the film of the story of my life. I want something like *Schindler's List* only cheerier! (*With that, at another end of the stage, the lights come up on* WYLER. *At a newsstand, he is just putting down the magazine with a picture of* GINNY. *He picks up a phone.*)

WYLER: Hello, is this—Ginny? Ginny, you don't know me—but you are going to—wait, are you the violinist in the magazine without the shirt? Great. You are going to maybe be getting a phone call from a woman with the unlikely name of Alexa Vere de—Already? Geez. Well has she—are you planning to meet her— (*Lights up on* MORRIS KADEN.)

KADEN: Thursday 1:45, the lobby of the Four Seasons.

WYLER: Do not go to that meeting.

KADEN: Got it.

WYLER: She is a con artist, ready to rip you off.

KADEN: Afternoon tea.

WYLER: What do you think?

KADEN: You're a sick man. (*Lights up on* ILLYA.)

ILLYA: The Four Seasons, Thursday at 1:45?

KADEN: But not without your style.

ILLYA: It's devilish.

WYLER: She's expecting some young violinist for tea. (*Lights up on* BETHANY.)

BETHANY: The Four Seasons. It'll be so horrible. Of course I'll be there.

WYLER: The violinist won't be there, but who will be there—

KADEN: The place will be packed.

WYLER: All of us. (*Lights up on* SKUNK.)

SKUNK: The Four Seasons!

ILLYA: Morris Kaden, Illya Mannon.

WYLER: Thursday, 1:45, the lobby of the Four Seasons. Alexa Vere de Vere will arrive to meet someone new and hot and, sadly, hungry. What she will find will be a lobby filled with the victims of Alexa Vere de Vere.

ILLYA: Bethany Vance.

KADEN: Martel Grushkov.

BETHANY: Skunk.

WYLER: Cold austere revenge. (*An ocean of voices reciting names. And another ocean of voices saying yes. Onstage the next three lines overlap.*)

ILLYA: That composer with the animation, the actress with the accents, the investor from Milan, the actor with the great hair who can't act, David Bowie, Iman, Morris Kaden of Delta records, Iman, the Duke of Chichester, Skunk, Bethany Vance, the Pet Shop Boys, the singer with the six-note range.

KADEN: The singer with the six-note range, the poet who can't rhyme. Evan Wyler, Skunk, Morris Kaden, Illya Mannon, Bethany Vance, David Bowie, Iman, the Duke of Chichester, the Pet Shop Boys. Everyone. The composer with the animation, the actress with the accents. Martel Grushkov.

BETHANY: Martel Grushkov, the Duke of Chichester, the Pet Shop Boys, David Bowie and Iman. Skunk, Morris Kaden, and Illya Mannon, the composer with the animation, Martel Grushkov, the actor with the really great hair who can't act. Oh and Evan Wyler. The singer with the six-note range. And the investor from Milan. (*Silence crashes.*)

Scene 6

(WYLER's *apartment.*)

(*In the West Fifties, a four-story walk-up tenement. A mess.* WYLER *walks in. The closet is open. Hanging inside, his suit. On the inside of the door, a mirror.* WYLER *taps on the answering machine. As the messages play back, an electronic beep. He takes the jacket out and tries it on.*)

KADEN: (*Voice on the machine.*) All right Wyler Evan Wyler. We'll be seeing you in one hour. Can't believe we're going through with this. Just about everyone will be there— (WYLER *looks in the mirror. He smiles. Another electronic beep.*)

ILLYA: (*Voice on the machine.*) Mr. Wyler, I find your sense of revenge openly delicious. Of course we'll be there. I'm so excited I could—what am I saying—I should be heading uptown. It's in forty minutes. (WYLER *looks at himself in profile.*)

GINNY: (*Voice on the machine.*) Hello, Mr. Wyler. This is Ginny. Ginny Cameron and—oh God—I think I just messed things up. (WYLER *is suddenly attentive. He stands straight in front of the mirror.*) See, uhm, Alexa called, right? And just—what you said made me so mad and—Well she just wanted to confirm things and I guess she could sense something in my voice, 'cause—well she pushed me and— (WYLER *is panicking. He looks at the machine. With that the closet door slowly closes.* ALEXA *is standing behind it. The reflection of* WYLER *becomes the actual* ALEXA.) OK, I kind of blurted out what you were planning and—I hope this doesn't ruin things for you. (*The machine ends.*)

ALEXA: One of the all-time great entrances and for the life of me, I don't have a line to top it.

WYLER: Alexa, how did you—

ALEXA: Please, twenty dollars and a super and I could get into heaven. But no. Nothing. No sentence I could hope to assemble. . . . No configuration of words could possibly surpass the fact that I am here and you are there!

WYLER: You bitch, give me my money back.

ALEXA: Long gone. Don't have it to give. But then you knew that. So, why then have you pursued me?

WYLER: Revenge.

ALEXA: Please. No really, why? Because you're in love with me?

WYLER: Maybe I was.

ALEXA: You're a poofta, guess again.

WYLER: I know who you are and how you work and—

ALEXA: And now that you do have me again what will you do?

WYLER: I—I—I don't know.

ALEXA: (*She casually sits and lights a cigarette.*) As I had suspected. Planned confrontations are always anticlimactic. I'll smoke and talk to you. You'll learn things, it will be lovely. I shall hazard a guess. The reason you have pursued me so doggedly is because you are the first to know—

WYLER: Know?

ALEXA: My lamb. My dearest lamb. My only lamb. You know. You know that I am not a mirage, I am an oasis. You are the only, the first. To chase. Most feel the sting and snap their hand from the bees. You—you actually are stung and . . . appear to be homesick for the hypnotic hum of the hive.

WYLER: You've got it wrong.

ALEXA: I have it unspeakably right. The reason no one has ever chased me, is because they've always had their blessed little artistic endeavors to keep them busy. Writing, dancing, painting, even I would speculate, the fiddle. No one would think of putting this much energy and effort into finding me let alone exacting recompense. This is the defining act of someone who—gets it.

WYLER: I don't get any of—

ALEXA: Oh no. You get it. You get it good. You know that this. The hum, the buzz, the hype, the flash, the fame. This is the only thing that matters. And you miss it. Who wouldn't? There is something unmistakably glorious about having a velvet cord pulled back. And you know it. And that's why I come with an offer.

WYLER: I didn't want your fucking—

ALEXA: I know, an offer, it seems too generous.

WYLER: What? Money to go away?

ALEXA: Better.

WYLER: Better?

ALEXA: Join me.

WYLER: You're fucked up.

ALEXA: Beloved lamb, you have the instincts, why deny them? You know that if you live your life as a writer you will be popular for a decidedly finite time. Fast-paced American culture won't stand for it. If you write novels, sixteen years. Plays, six years. Screenplays . . . six months. And then suddenly you're . . . out of favor. Stay with me and always be popular. Fame without achievement, it is the safest bet I know.

WYLER: I'm a writer.

ALEXA: Funny, you're not writing now. And you'll probably never write again. Because you know, as I knew, that there are only two interesting times to be a writer. The moment you start a project, and the moment you end it. All the rest is just drudgery. Me, here, this way, I start a project every week. And it ends that same week. What could be more thrilling?

WYLER: Right. And what if I have the desire to express myself artistically?

ALEXA: Suppress it. It is every time you create that you run the risk of proving or chiseling at your reputation. Come with me, live with me, and always live this life. Never, ever be hungry, or thirsty, or doubt yourself. Or wait in line. Or talk to bores. Or—

WYLER: Why?

ALEXA: Because I need you. When we were together, we were a team. A machine, if you will. The two of us, we could hit higher grounds. Hollywood but beckons. I mean morality is REALLY on a bell curve there. We could make our fortune. Maybe stop living so hand to mouth. Or start living larger hand to larger mouth. Come. Come with me. We're a perfect match. And.

WYLER: And?

ALEXA: And I love you. I want you. I have from the moment I saw your shirtless picture in that magazine. And I saw a very Welsh name attached to a very Semitic face. I wanted you, and I knew that you—you would want me also. (*They kiss.*)

WYLER: Alexa— (*They kiss again.*)

ALEXA: My lamb. (*They kiss a third time, more passionately.*)

WYLER: I've missed you— (*He kisses her neck, she unbuttons his shirt.*)

ALEXA: And I—my love, I have missed you so. Not since—since—I haven't felt this horribly alone since my husband Michael died, the— (WYLER *freezes. Then pulls away.*) He— (WYLER *steps back and looks away.*) Christ, you are thorough.

WYLER: Mike is still alive, you didn't kill him.

ALEXA: Alive, you call that living? I haven't heard of him in years, and I read everything.

WYLER: I think you should just . . . leave. Now.

ALEXA: A minor glitch. A single *faux pas.* Don't let that stand in the way of our—

WYLER: Get out. Now.

ALEXA: Back to revenge? Well you can't have it. You have no power. You're a commodity, bought and sold. You're a—

WYLER: Get!

ALEXA: Suit!

WYLER: Out!

ALEXA: A suit. Bought this year and then out of fashion.

WYLER: Leave me!

ALEXA: Fine. I'll leave. Simpleton. But in eleven days. In a week. After staring at blank page after blank page, you'll be— what? Wishing. Hoping. Desperately beseeching to be with me. (*She goes to walk out. We hear offstage.*)

KADEN: Such a party!

WYLER: Never!

ALEXA: You're not a writer.

ILLYA: The event of a lifetime!

ALEXA: You're not particularly good at listening to people and figuring out what's going on in their minds.

KADEN: In your whole life.

ALEXA: Or summing up with a grand sweeping statement.

KADEN: Could you again see such a group.

ALEXA: And what good is a semicolon? (*We see* ILLYA *and* KADEN.)

ILLYA: Everyone was there!

ALEXA: Please. Call me. You'll know where to find me. How to reach me. The beginning of every month. In the magazines. In all those fresh, young, desperate faces. Call them. For I will have. You'll soon find. . . . You need me, lamb. (*She is gone.* WYLER *says to the empty room.*)

WYLER: I don't need you.

KADEN: Such the A-list group. (WYLER *runs over to the open door and shouts off to* ALEXA.)

WYLER: I . . . DO . . . NOT . . . NEED . . . YOU!!

Scene 7

(*The Four Seasons.*)

(ILLYA *and* KADEN *give us their report.*)

ILLYA: You should have been there—

KADEN: At the Four Seasons.

ILLYA: There must have been—

KADEN: You should have been there.

ILLYA: —Hundreds. It was fantastic.

KADEN: It was phenomenal.

ILLYA: Everywhere you looked, somebody as famous than the next.

KADEN: A large lobby filled with the victims of Alexa Vere de Vere.

ILLYA: The famous, the known, the hypeworthy.

KADEN: The renowned, the celebrities, the sub-lebrities.

ILLYA: Household names.

KADEN: Photo ops.

ILLYA: Faces.

KADEN: Names.

ILLYA: And every one of us knew.

KADEN: Every one of us knew—

ILLYA: —Knew.

KADEN and ILLYA: —It meant nothing.

ILLYA: Nothing at all.

KADEN: But we all—

ILLYA: Every one of us.

KADEN: (*A pause and a smile, then*—) Knew how to play it.

ILLYA: The hype.

KADEN: The buzz.

ILLYA: The hum.

Scene 8

(MIKE'*s loft.*)

(MIKE *is painting. A knock on the door. He answers it. It is* WYLER.)

MIKE: Hey, I know you.

WYLER: Yeah right. Uhm, I was just in the neighborhood, so I thought I'd stop by and—

MIKE: Sure. Listen, I've just got to finish this before the paint dries.

WYLER: Sure, sure. Go ahead.

MIKE: The color won't match if I do it later. (*He goes back to painting.*)

WYLER: I'm just in the neighborhood, so. I'm like walking around. And. Actually that's not true. I'm in the neighborhood because I wanted to see you.

MIKE: Oh.

WYLER: Not that way. It's just. Everybody else seems so . . . I don't know, caught up. I'm kind of lost. At sea. Like uhm. I don't know, would I be flotsam or jetsam?

MIKE: You got me. You're the writer.

WYLER: Nah. I—I think I gave that up.

MIKE: Oh. I'm sorry to hear that.

WYLER: It is just so—incredibly difficult, you know? To try to create something. And to know that there are so many people waiting to criticize or capitalize and all you want to do is make something that will connect with other people so that we all won't feel so profoundly alone. And we are all so profoundly alone. Why does it have to be so hard to try to cure that in some way? It . . . is . . . so . . . difficult.

MIKE: Yeah.

WYLER: Yeah?

MIKE: Yeah.

WYLER: Yeah.

MIKE: You know what else is difficult?

WYLER: What?

MIKE: Ears.

WYLER: Ears?

MIKE: Ears are real difficult. You've got these little pockets of shadow and crevices and folds and light bouncing off and. Ears are difficult.

WYLER: Yeah. I never really thought of that.

MIKE: But I'm getting better at them. The more I work at it. (*He looks at* WYLER. WYLER *looks away.*)

WYLER: Why do you even bother?

MIKE: Well. If I get it right. This could be a really tremendous ear. (*He goes back to painting.*)

WYLER: I'm sorry to barge in like. This is—I should go and—

MIKE: You left your uhm—

WYLER: Sorry?

MIKE: When you were here before. You left your composition thing—

WYLER: God, right. (*He picks it up.*) Well. Useless. You could have thrown it out. (*He opens it to a page.*) Garbage. (*He looks at another page.*)

Scene 9

(*Deus ex machina.*)

(*Immediately following, a* MUSE *appears behind* WYLER. *She speaks as* ILLYA.)

A MUSE: (*As* ILLYA.) I really don't know her. It was like, like one weekend and twenty-five grand. (WYLER *rips the page out of the book. He looks at the next page. A* SECOND MUSE *appears. She speaks as* BETHANY.)

A SECOND MUSE: Fucker rips you off and then claims you into a circle of friends. (WYLER *rips another page. The first* MUSE *is now* CARLA.)

A MUSE: You look resplendent. (WYLER *rips another page. The* SECOND MUSE *is now a* BACKUP SINGER.)

A SECOND MUSE: He's a Welshman, he is. (*He rips out one page after another with the next several lines. They are things* ALEXA *has said, but the two* MUSES *speak them.*)

A MUSE: If you absolutely had to sleep with one of the Three Stooges, which one would it be?

A SECOND MUSE: (*Coming in on the "Stooges" of the last sentence.*) I believe in cash, in this flighty world it's the only thing left with any impact.

A MUSE: (*Coming in on the "left" of the last line.*) A WELSHMAN. I shall trust anyway.

A SECOND MUSE: (*On the "trust" of the last line.*) The new becoming old almost before we find newer new.

A MUSE: (*On the "find" of the last line.*) We beat the path to Hollywoodland—

A SECOND MUSE: Hollywood—

A MUSE: Do we dare?

A SECOND MUSE: And look at your face light up.

A MUSE: (*Simultaneously with the next line.*) You will buy hundreds, nay thousands of suits.

A SECOND MUSE: (*Simultaneously with the last line.*) After work I needed, nay required a hot bath.

A MUSE: What care I?

A SECOND MUSE: Gore Vidal says that.

A MUSE: Calvin Klein fragrances.

A SECOND MUSE: I say it too.

BOTH MUSES: You're not the person you were born. Who wonderful is? You're the person you were meant to be. (*He rips the final page out and crumples it up. He then thinks for a moment. He flattens out the paper and reads it again.*) You're not the person you were born. Who wonderful is? You're the person you were meant to be. (*He absently takes out a pen and writes something. Then looks at it. This has his interest. He begins to write something else on the page. The MUSES leave. A moment of the two artists creating and then—*)

MIKE: What you writing?

WYLER: (*Absently.*) Nothing. (MIKE *is gone.* KADEN *is in his office. His* SECRETARY *walks in.*)

SECRETARY: Mr. Kaden.

WYLER: Nothing.

SECRETARY: Mr. Kaden, you have a call on line three—

KADEN: I'm going into a meeting.

SECRETARY: Mr. Kaden, on line three—

KADEN: I'm—

SECRETARY: On line three. Alexa Vere de Vere.

KADEN: You're kidding.

WYLER: (*With the great joy of realization.*) Everything. (ALEXA *is on the phone with* KADEN.)

KADEN: Alexa?

ALEXA: Morris, darling, he has really overstepped the bounds of libel.

KADEN: Alexa, to what do I—

ALEXA: And he uses YOUR NAME—that has got to be illegal!

KADEN: My name? Who is using my name?

ALEXA: I was walking down Fifth Avenue, in the Mid Forties, a light snow was falling, I merely looked for the reflection in a window to *trompe* up the *l'oeil,* darling, when there in the window— (ILLYA *is reading a book.*)

ILLYA: *As Bees in Honey Drown.*

ALEXA: A book. The author's name was unknown to me.

WYLER: A novel by Eric Wollenstein.

ALEXA: Of course I was intrigued. I burst into the store and grasped a copy. And there—

WYLER: In a V-neck pullover sweater and a button-down shirt, leaning on a stack of Proust.

SECRETARY: "About the author:"

ALEXA: Evan Wyler! (KADEN *laughs.*)

ILLYA: "Eric Wollenstein's debut novel, *Pig and Pepper,* was published under the pseudonym Evan Wyler. He has written short stories, and—"

ALEXA: I nervously flipped through to the front of the book.

ILLYA: "This is his second novel."

MIKE: "He resides in New York City with painter Mike Stabinsky."

ALEXA: And he's written it all!

ILLYA: "Chapter one."

SECRETARY: (*Turns to an unseen friend, and says of the book she is reading.*) He's very good at listening to people and figuring out what's going on in their minds.

ALEXA: All of our names and—Morris, we must sue. This is—

SECRETARY: And summing it up with a grand sweeping statement.

ILLYA: "Evan walked into the Paramount Hotel. He was going to meet Alexa Vere de Vere."

ILLYA and SECRETARY: "Alexa worked for Morris Kaden of Delta records. Morris and Alexa were very big deals." (KADEN *laughs.* ALEXA *is now crying.*)

ALEXA: Don't laugh, he—he's— (ALEXA *is sobbing.*) He's destroying—

MIKE: "Soon to be a major motion picture." (ALEXA *looks up, she is plotting away. Oh, the possibilities!* WYLER *walks over to* ALEXA. *He sits next to her. A moment.* ILLYA *reads from the book.*)

ILLYA: "Alexa took a sip of tea."

WYLER: Which tea are you drinking, the orange pekoe or the Sodium Pentathol?

ALEXA: Repartee! You are brilliant. God. I love writers. They always have the last word, because they know so many. I'm part Indian, I know things. Do you think David Bowie is dark enough to pull off an Indian? I mean a red-dot Indian not a woo-woo Indian. Try the boysenberry, it's a revelation.

WYLER: Have you ever thought of diagramming these sentences in your head before you speak them?

ALEXA: See.

ALEXA and ILLYA: That's what I mean.

ALEXA, ILLYA, and SECRETARY: Who else but a writer—

ALEXA, ILLYA, SECRETARY, and KADEN: —They know so—

ALEXA, ILLYA, SECRETARY, KADEN, and MIKE: —Much about life.

ALEXA: No one pulls the cashmere over the eyes of a writer. (ALEXA *looks at* WYLER. WYLER *looks out. And smiles. Ars Longa, Vita Brevis.*)

END OF PLAY

BE AGGRESSIVE

Annie Weisman

For my sister

Be Aggressive premiered at La Jolla Playhouse in La Jolla, California, on July 29, 2001. Directed by Lisa Peterson; set design by Rachel Hauck; lighting design by James F. Ingalls; sound design by Laura Grace Brown; costume design by Audrey Fisher. The cast in order of appearance was as follows:

LAURA	Angela Goethals
HANNAH	Daisy Eagan
PHIL	Mark Harelik
LESLIE	Jennifer Elise Cox
JUDY	Linda Gehringer
CHEERLEADER CHORUS	Tamala Horbianski, Carly Kleiner, Joy Osmanski

Prologue

(*In darkness, we hear the sound of the ocean, then the sound of the freeway, then the sound of a horrible car crash.*)

(*Silence.*)

(*Lights up. Bright sunshine. Vista Del Sol High-School-by-the-Sea.* CHEERLEADERS *in formation. The sound of pom-poms shaking.*)

CHEERLEADER #1: Did you guys hear?

CHEERLEADERS #3 AND #4: Dead.

CHEERLEADER #2: Who?

CHEERLEADER #1: Dead.

CHEERLEADER #2: Who?

CHEERLEADERS #1, #3, AND #4: Dead! (*Beat.*)

CHEERLEADER #3: Our maid's their maid's daughter.

CHEERLEADER #4: Our lawyer's their lawyer's son! (*Beat.*)

CHEERLEADER #3: My dermatologist lives on her cul-de-sac!

CHEERLEADER #4: My gynecologist lives next door!

CHEERLEADER #1: Dead. On impact.

CHEERLEADER #3: Nuh uh! Vegetable. All night.

CHEERLEADER #2: Fifteen feet it threw her.

CHEERLEADER #3: Fifty feet, I heard.

CHEERLEADER #1: The hole in her head was the size of a golf ball.

CHEERLEADER #2: Bocce ball!

CHEERLEADER #3: Honeydew!

CHEERLEADER #4: Cantaloupe!

CHEERLEADER #1: It was on Avenida Avocado.

CHEERLEADER #2: That's where my stepmom power walks!

CHEERLEADER #1: They said that her dad had to come identify her mom's mangled body. (*They gasp. Beat.*) It's gonna be open casket.

CHEERLEADER #3: NUH UH!

CHEERLEADER #2: YEAH RIGHT!

CHEERLEADER #1: They're gonna have an open casket!

CHEERLEADER #3: NO WAY!

CHEERLEADER #2: YOU LIE!

CHEERLEADER #4: Pieces of her body are strewn across the street. (*All look out. Pause.*)

CHEERLEADER #1: I heard it's at the Surfswell Plaza Freeway Project.

CHEERLEADER #3: I heard she got so crushed that they're gonna pave part of her right into the new road.

CHEERLEADER #4: I heard that too.

CHEERLEADER #3: I heard her head hit like a hackey sack on a handball court.

CHEERLEADER #2: Like boobs on a boogie board.

CHEERLEADER #4: Splat!

CHEERLEADER #1: They drove away.

CHEERLEADER #2: Who?

CHEERLEADER #3: The ones who killed her.

CHEERLEADER #4: They hit her into a hole and they drove away. (*Beat.*) Vista Del Sol is like, a dangerous place. (*Pause.*)

CHEERLEADER #1: K guys! Practice!

CHEERLEADER #2: Without her?

CHEERLEADER #1: Without her.

CHEERLEADER #4: Is she coming back?

CHEERLEADER #2: Yeah, can she cheer anymore?

CHEERLEADER #3: How long's it gonna take? We already made up our Game One greeting cheer! It's gonna be totally truncated without her!

CHEERLEADER #1: She'll be back. (*Beat.*) HANDS ON HIPS!

ALL: SMILES ON LIPS!

CHEERLEADER #1: (*A cheer.*) READY?

ALL: OK!

CHEERLEADER #1: H! (*Clap! Clap! Clap! Clap!*)

CHEERLEADER #2: E! (*Clap! Clap! Clap! Clap!*)

CHEERLEADER #3: L! (*Clap!*)

CHEERLEADER #4: L! (*Clap! They wait for the "O." It doesn't come. They continue.*)

CHEERLEADER #1: H! (*Clap! Clap! Clap! Clap!*)

CHEERLEADER #2: E! (*Clap! Clap! Clap! Clap!*)

CHEERLEADER #3: L! (*Clap!*)

CHEERLEADER #4: L! (*Clap! Clapping, stomping.*)

(*Lights shift.*)

Scene 1

(*Lights up on* LAURA *in her room with her little sister* HANNAH. *They are getting dressed.*)

LAURA: O.

HANNAH: What?

LAURA: Nothing. (*Pause.*)

HANNAH: It's not fair.

LAURA: I know.

HANNAH: I don't have a whole black outfit. And you do. I only have separates. My blacks don't even match. It's not fair!

LAURA: Then change.

HANNAH: Into what?

LAURA: I don't know. (*Beat.*)

HANNAH: Is everyone in all-black outfits, or just us?

LAURA: Um, I don't know. People wear brown too. I'm pretty sure. Earth tones. (*Pause.*)

HANNAH: Is our age group expected to wear dark sunglasses? 'Cuz I only have pink ones and purple ones and teal ones.

LAURA: Well, tough.

HANNAH: My new tortoise-tee has some black in the trim. Can I wear that?

LAURA: Why are you asking me?

HANNAH: Well who am I supposed to ask? (*Beat. Pause.*)

LAURA: OK, no. I don't think you should wear your tortoise-tee.

HANNAH: How come?

LAURA: DUH! It's COMPLETELY inappropriate!

HANNAH: How would YOU know! How would you know anything! (LAURA *throws an item of clothing at* HANNAH.)

HANNAH: Ow! Bitch!

LAURA: Oh, please!

HANNAH: You hurt me!

LAURA: Stop being a baby! (*Pause.*)

HANNAH: What's she gonna look like?

LAURA: We don't have to look at her.

HANNAH: How do you know? You're older. They'll put you in front. You'll have to look.

LAURA: No they won't.

HANNAH: They'll put you in front, and they'll put me in back, with Grandma. It's no fair! She gives me dirty cough drops from the bottom of her purse. She makes that clucking sound 'cuz we don't know the prayers. I don't see why you get to sit in front and look.

LAURA: It's just 'cuz I'm older. (*Beat.*)

HANNAH: Who's gonna make my waffle?

LAURA: Dad, I guess.

HANNAH: And my hot chocolate?

LAURA: Yeah.

HANNAH: He can't do the hot chocolate!

LAURA: He can too.

HANNAH: From scratch? No way! Mom doesn't use a mix. She starts with Ghirardelli bitter chocolate. I put my finger in it once and it was like dirt. Dog crap. It was awful tasting. You have to know how to make it.

LAURA: You just mix it with sugar and milk.

HANNAH: But you have to know exactly how much. And I don't know and he doesn't know and neither do you! (*She turns and looks at* LAURA.) When did you get boobs?

LAURA: Hannah . . .

HANNAH: When did they get so big?

LAURA: Hannah.

HANNAH: I swear you got them today! You're not supposed to have big fat boobs! (*Beat.*) Are you sexually active?

LAURA: Where did you hear that?

HANNAH: When are we going back to school?

LAURA: I don't know.

HANNAH: Are you going to cheer practice? (*Beat.*)

LAURA: I don't know.

HANNAH: Are you gonna be in the Game One greeting cheer?

LAURA: Of course!

HANNAH: Not if you don't go back to practice! (*Beat.*) If you're not in the Game One greeting cheer, you can forget about being a starter this year. You're gonna be an alternate again, senior year, the last cheer year of life!

LAURA: That's none of your goddamn business!

HANNAH: Are you still going to work?

LAURA: I don't know!

(*In silence they pick up brushes and brush their own hair. Lights shift revealing their dad,* PHIL. *Somewhere else. Just looking out.*)

LAURA: Everybody's gonna be looking at us! It'll be sort of like a pep rally, but quiet, and we're the pom squad. So we have to think about how we're gonna look! Come here.

(HANNAH *is making a mess of her hair.* LAURA *reluctantly goes to her and begins to comb it.*)

HANNAH: When's Dad coming back?

LAURA: I'm not sure.

HANNAH: I heard something from the other room. When Dad was calling everybody. He said something about the size of the hole it made in her head. When her head hit the ground! (*Panic. Builds.*) Are we gonna have to look at it? The hole? (LAURA *accidentally pulls* HANNAH's *hair.*)

HANNAH: Ow! Bitch!

LAURA: Fine! Then do it yourself! (LAURA *moves away from her.*)

HANNAH: Do you think the stuff from my old room is still in the storage facility? I'd like to get that mobile back I had over my bed. That circled around and played those stupid tinkly little songs? I bet Dad has it logged on a list on his computer. I want to get it back! (*Beat.*) You have humongous disgusting tits.

(*They hold a tableau. Hugging themselves. Lights shift.* PHIL, *still in a pool of light. A cop speaks to him, in voice-over.*)

COP: We're very sorry for your loss.

PHIL: Thank you.

COP: This is really just a technicality. We just have to clear up a few facts with you regarding your whereabouts on the afternoon of the eleventh of September.

PHIL: I was at work.

COP: You were at the office.

PHIL: No. I was out in the field, actually. At the survey site.

COP: So you were out at the wetlands. (*Beat.*)

PHIL: No. (*Beat.*)

COP: To have to answer these questions, sir, in light of your loss, must be very difficult, but we do need to verify—

PHIL: No. It's not that. It's that . . . (*Beat.*) They are not "wetlands." That's a myth generated by the environmental lobby. It is a man-made bog. We're draining and reclaiming it for the community.

COP: OK.

PHIL: I was doing a check-in at the survey site on Camino Del Mar. It was only the first day of our hydrology study and we're already at two weeks to public review. I walked the site, did a quick touch base with the team heads. Routine stuff. (*Beat.*) And when I got back to the office, the message light was blinking. So I pressed the button and the machine said, "You have one new message." And it was my daughter Laura's voice. "Dad come home. Mom is dead." Then there was a very long beeping sound and the machine said, "To erase press two. To save press three." (*Beat.*) You don't think you're ever gonna hear that. (*Pause.*)

COP: Sir, was your wife an avid jogger?

PHIL: She was very physically fit.

COP: She jogged routinely?

PHIL: After breakfast. That was her morning.

COP: And she was aware of the dangers of jogging on the old bluff road? The traffic diversions being caused by the Surfswell Plaza Freeway Project?

PHIL: We were always telling her. I would tell her.

COP: Because where her body was found . . . she was jogging in a very dangerous place. Any car doing fifty, particularly if they're not local and they don't know how to take the Caminito Curve . . .

PHIL: I told her! I bought her a treadmill and put it in the atrium where there's plenty of natural light. But she wanted to jog on the old bluff road. Look out at the ocean. I told her she was nuts. The traffic, the erosion. (*Beat.*) She's the one who found this neighborhood. We drove up the coast looking for a place to live, when she was pregnant with our first child. A place with ocean views, reasonable seafood restaurants, and good schools. Eighteen years, we've been here. That's a lifetime in this community. Got in on the first tract development they cut into the hill. The iceplant hadn't grown over the retaining walls yet. The cement dividers were still soft. We got a Spanish stucco ocean view unit for forty-five thousand dollars. It's worth ten times that now, as a teardown! (*Beat.*) She planted this eucalyptus seedling when we got here. It's a huge thing now. Towering over the breakfast nook. Dropping leaves into our Jacuzzi. (*Beat.*) I tried to tell her that things had changed.

COP: I think we have the information we need to pursue the matter. Thank you for coming in. I want to tell you how our hearts and prayers go out to you and your family.

PHIL: We're Jewish people actually. My family. We don't practice, not since we moved here. But just so you know, if you are gonna pray. Pray Jewish.

(*Lights shift. The sound of the freeway.*)

Scene 2

(LAURA's *house.* LAURA *is sorting through her dead mother's clothes with her dad.*)

LAURA: We're out of stuff. (PHIL *holds up a hat.*)

PHIL: Keep?

LAURA: I don't know.

PHIL: Give away?

LAURA: I guess. (*Beat.*)

PHIL: What stuff?

LAURA: (*Irritated.*) Stuff me and Hannah eat! Like, food!

PHIL: Didn't people leave all that . . .

LAURA: It's weird casseroles. And like, pies. It's not stuff we eat.

(*She holds up a jacket. He points to a pile. She throws it in.*)

PHIL: Well, then, you'll need to go to the market, I guess. Can you do that?

LAURA: Yeah.

PHIL: You know what to get?

LAURA: I used to push the cart sometimes. I know her pattern.

PHIL: What was it?

LAURA: What?

PHIL: The pattern.

LAURA: Just her way of going! The order of things?

PHIL: What order? What order was it?

LAURA: It was just the way she went, that's all! Produce, dairy, frozen stuff. Bread, drinks, checkout. And she tells Hannah "NO!" when she picks up a Snickers and then she pays, and that's all.

PHIL: How are you gonna pay?

LAURA: With the ATM card.

PHIL: You know the code?

LAURA: Yeah.

PHIL: How do you know the code?

LAURA: She told it to me.

PHIL: She did?

LAURA: Yeah. (*Beat.*)

PHIL: So you'll go to the market, and you'll get what she got. And you'll make something. You'll do that chicken she does.

LAURA: With sun-dried tomatoes?

PHIL: That's the one.

LAURA: I don't know how to do that.

PHIL: Why don't you look at her cookbooks, and figure that one out.

LAURA: She didn't use cookbooks.

PHIL: Well then just figure it out, somehow, and we'll sit down to a nice family dinner. I think it's important that we do that. For Hannah.

LAURA: Can't we just order something?

PHIL: No.

LAURA: But, that's gonna take all afternoon, and I just—

PHIL: You just what?

(LAURA *holds up a shirt to her chest.*)

LAURA: Keep?

(PHIL *looks at it for a long beat. A memory. He touches the shirt.*)

LAURA: Keep or give away?

(*He smooths the shirt over* LAURA*'s shoulders.*)

PHIL: Looks like you could wear this one. (*Beat.* LAURA *pulls away.*)

LAURA: Can't we get a nanny?

PHIL: I don't want some person in our house.

LAURA: What if she was here after school, only?

PHIL: I don't want a stranger here that I don't know.

LAURA: What about Grandma?

PHIL: Your grandmother lives far away from us, and it's going to stay that way. (*Beat.*)

LAURA: But I want to go back to my work.

PHIL: You don't have to work! We've told you that.

LAURA: I like my work.

PHIL: You need to be here.

LAURA: But . . .

PHIL: But, what?

LAURA: I want to go back to cheer practice.

PHIL: What?

LAURA: If I don't go back to cheer practice now I won't learn the Game One greeting cheer and if I don't know the Game One greeting cheer they'll cut me and I'll never make varsity!

PHIL: Varsity? For jumping up and down?

LAURA: That's not what we do!

PHIL: You jump up and down . . . and you yell?

LAURA: That's not what cheerleading's about!

(LAURA *opens the bottom drawer—the lingerie drawer. She holds up a sexy black nightgown. They freeze. A long sad silence.* PHIL *takes the nightgown and lays it gently on the bed.*)

PHIL: Your mother was planning a family trip to Israel. You didn't know that. After the project, she wanted me to take the family on a trip to Israel. I said, are you nuts? The violence, the heat. But she said, no. Not by the coast. The coast is temperate and mild. Like here. Which makes a lot of sense for the promised land. (*Beat.*) I have to work very hard and very late until the freeway opening. The project is at its most critical phase and your little sister and I will need you here!

LAURA: The freeway blows! Everybody says! It's gonna destroy natural resources!

PHIL: Do you have any idea what kind of population growth our county has seen in the last ten years? If we don't make a freeway to accommodate the Surfswell Plaza congestion then before long, every four-by-four in the Inland Empire is gonna be gunning through our formerly walkable and charming downtown shopping district. You couldn't park on Caminito Del Mango and walk to Krissie's Muffins without taking your life into your hands! And before we know it, they'll start bringing their inner tubes and their boom boxes full of John Cougar Mellencamp to our beaches. You won't be able to lay out on the sand anymore without some morbidly obese family eating their surplus cheese sandwiches and having a domestic dispute! Everything we have would be ruined! (*Beat.*)

LAURA: Krissie's Muffins is already closing. The plaza has a Breads Etc. megastore! (*Pause.*)

PHIL: I don't want you doing things. I want you here.

(*Lights shift.*)

Scene 3

(*Sound of a blender. Then two. Then six. Then all the blenders of the Southland, whirring at top speed. Lights up on the smoothie shop. LAURA with her hand on the top of a blender. Her body shakes. It stops.*)

LAURA: K. First you add the Basic Boost. (*Adds something to the blender. Puts on the top. Loud blending sound again. Her body shakes. It stops.*) Now the All-Pro Protein. (*Adds something.*) Then, ask if they've tried any of our "Smoothie Madditives," which are: Mood Lift, Memory Boost, Energina, Youth Jolt, and Mega-Cleanse. Then, tell them about this week's promotional madditive, which is—(*Checks a list.*) Moby Thick!—a fiber blend made from the baleen of humpback whales whose healthful benefits have been enjoyed by the Inuit people for centuries. And we guarantee these whales died naturally of old age and not by poaching or disease. (*Beat.*) Then, they pick their fruit. Oh, you're supposed to try to push the new fruits. Otherwise, people will just get like, strawberry and banana. There's a new hybrid of kiwi and cassava melon—it's called Kissava—and it has twice the mineral content of an average serving of fruit. You're supposed to say that. (*Beat.*) Oh, and the cool thing is, no matter what you put in, you always add our special smoothie starter at the end. That way, the color always comes out the same. The healthful rosy flush that customers want. If you forget this final additive the color will be a grayish brown. And when they see it, they won't like it. (*Beat.*) Oh, and if you mess it up, just throw it away and do it over. We never run out of anything. Somebody comes in at night and stocks it all, I guess. (*Pause.*) I don't know how. Some of the stuff is like, really heavy. (*Beat.*) K, that's it. That's all you need to know. (*Pause.*) Now blend! (*Noise of a thousand blenders.*)

(*Lights shift.*)

Scene 4

(*Transition. Cheer practice. Stomp stompstomp. Stomp. Stomp. Stomp. They come together into a tight Fosse clump and hit a solid frozen pose. Tight. Serious faces. On another beat, they smile. On another beat, they sneer. On another beat, they do a sexy, wild dance, then freeze. They do a bunch of military-style moves. They freeze.*)

CHEERLEADER #1: Ready?

CHEERLEADERS: OK! (*Beat.*)

CHEERLEADERS:

> GO!
> FIGHT!
> WIN!
> GO!
> GO! FIGHT! WIN!

(*Music stops.*)

LESLIE: I have an idea!

CHEERLEADER #1: Excuse me!

LESLIE: I made something up.

CHEERLEADER #2: YOU made something up?

LESLIE: Well, since we don't have Laura anymore, I thought I would make up a new Game One greeting cheer, that works without her. And I thought I would up the ante a little too, while I was at it.

CHEERLEADER #3: Up the what?

LESLIE: Make it BETTER! K?

CHEERLEADER #1: OK, Leslie. Show us your cheer.

LESLIE: (*Builds.*) Thanks. OK. It goes, "Seagulls, DOMINATE! This is our year—make it great! Victory! Is our fate! Our battlefield is your booty. Our field is your behind. We'll stomp you down we'll beat your butts and I SAID WE'LL BLOW YOUR MIND." (*Beat.*) And on "mind," we're gonna basket-toss Katie into a double "V" toe-touch jump, and while she's in the air, we're gonna turn out and do a fully extended "happy face with jazz hands," then melt into a sexy-face pivot, catch Katie, slap back to buckets, smile, sneer, and then here's the thing . . . (*Beat.*) Simultaneous standing back tucks. (CHEERLEADERS *gasp*.) K?

CHEERLEADER #2: Um, what?

LESLIE: Simultaneous standings! It's de rigueur among competitive squads. (*Beat.*) And we could get butt patches that say
stuff when we flip! (*Beat.*) K?

(*Silence. No one responds.*)

CHEERLEADER #1: Um, I'm glad you took the initiative to make
up a cheer, but . . . standing back tucks? Isn't that where you
like fling your body upside down? Backwards?

CHEERLEADER #3: You basically throw your head on the ground.
(*Beat.*)

LESLIE: Yes, it'll take some commitment. But together we can
conquer it. (*Beat.*) And it'll be thirty-two karat when we
nail it, I swear to you. (*Beat.*) K?

(*Silence.*)

(LAURA *walks out from behind the pack of* CHEERLEADERS. *She is not in
her practice uniform. Everybody except* LESLIE *sees her. They freeze. It's
her first time back since it happened.*)

LESLIE: I said . . . K? (*Silence.*) You guys? (*Beat.*) K?

(*The* CHEERLEADERS *exit.* LAURA *slowly approaches* LESLIE. *Long pause.*)

LAURA: K.

(*Lights shift.*)

Scene 5

(LAURA*'s house.* HANNAH *is hysterical.*)

HANNAH: A chainsaw! With a chainsaw!

LAURA: What kind of a chainsaw?

HANNAH: That kind that makes the loudest noise ever and cuts
down trees! He was cutting it down!

LAURA: When did he do this?

HANNAH: He said, "It could fall down on the house at any time." He said we were in danger. He said, "They're notoriously shallow-rooted trees." He researched it.

LAURA: What are?

HANNAH: Eucalyptus!

LAURA: Where did he get a chainsaw?

HANNAH: We had one in the garage.

LAURA: He did?

HANNAH: Under stuff. Under late-night television fitness machines. Recycling. It was there. (*Beat.*) It was SO LOUD! Like somebody making a smoothie out of a tennis racket! It sounded AWFUL! (*She cries.*)

LAURA: He cut down our eucalyptus tree?

HANNAH: It tipped over our property line and onto the Stevenson's Sports Court. And that's grounds for a lawsuit! And then he just sat down on the stump and he goes, "It's over. It's over. It's over."

LAURA: Like that?

HANNAH: Three times. (*Beat. Then hysterical.*) We have a murdered mom!

LAURA: It's not murder!

HANNAH: Murder happens here!

LAURA: It's not murder! It was a hit-and-run. A terrible accident.

HANNAH: But they said it was a death trap and she jogged right into it!

LAURA: Sh!

HANNAH: What killed her!

LAURA: Just, a car. Hit-and-run.

HANNAH: But what EXACTLY? What?

LAURA: The impact, I guess.

HANNAH: How? Did it crush her heart? Did her brain just pancake? Did it make a hole that made all her living parts come out and mix with the dirt in the road?

LAURA: No! She died instantly. She just closed her eyes and died.

HANNAH: Whose fault is it?

LAURA: It's not anybody's fault. It was an accident.

HANNAH: There's faults! There's always faults! Underneath us! Cracks in the earth that open up and shake and swallow things. (*Beat.*)

LAURA: Sh, no. She closed her eyes and died.

HANNAH: How do they make asphalt?

LAURA: I don't know.

HANNAH: Cement is one thing, and asphalt is a lot of things mixed, right? Gravel and cement and tar. How do they mix things that are so hard?

LAURA: They have to heat them up I guess.

HANNAH: When they're hot they're soft, and when they get cold they're hard!

LAURA: That's right.

HANNAH: Our mom got crushed in the road!

LAURA: No! Sh. Come here. It's okay. Come here.

(*She takes* HANNAH *into her arms, rocks her, strokes her hair. She sings the tune their mother used to sing to them. Sweet, soothing.* HANNAH *begins to calm.*)

LAURA: Sh. I'm here. I'm here.

(*Lights shift.*)

Scene 6

(*Cheer practice has just ended. It's just* LAURA *and* LESLIE.)

LESLIE: I'm so glad you're allowed to come back to practice now.

LAURA: Thanks.

LESLIE: We missed you. (*Beat. Serious.*) I missed you.

LAURA: I wasn't sure you knew me.

LESLIE: We're squadmates!

LAURA: Well, yeah, but. I just didn't think you could really tell me and Laura Lesterson apart sometimes.

LESLIE: Well, now I can. K?

LAURA: K.

LESLIE: I'm pregnant.

LAURA: Oh.

LESLIE: Sean Ashton, that needle-dick prick wank. He said he'd pull out right away. Well so did Nixon in Nam!

LAURA: Who?

LESLIE: You know, Sean. He drives the magenta Jetta! We hooked up at Kira Kartanian's Labor Day Weekend pool party on Friday night and then we cruised to TJ on the school day off. His mom LIVES in the Seabluff Bungalow Suites! I dumped him the day after. And Stacie said he bragged to the whole longboarding team that I swallow. (*Beat.*) And then I skipped my p and now I have to get the dustbuster!

LAURA: What a jerk. Are you telling your mom?

LESLIE: She'll just be SO "unconditionally supportive." She'll just hold my hand and be all, "I remember my first abortion." And then she'll "treat me" to that stinky Iraqi facialist on coast highway that I HATE. And then she'll buy me a "cozy" brown sweater.

LAURA: OK.

LESLIE: That's all?

LAURA: Yeah. (*Beat.*) OK. (*Pause.*)

LESLIE: I'm just kidding. Wanted to see how you'd react. Bravo. You were totally mellow. I knew you could be my best friend.

LAURA: I can?

LESLIE: Yes. I mean I did get pregnant last year and I got an abortion. But not by Sean Ashton. He asked for my number and I was like "1-800-AS IF!!" (*Pause.*) I knew you were my best friend. (*Long pause. They slump down. The sound of the ocean.*) There is absolutely fucking nothing to do in this stupid boring town. (*Beat.*)

LAURA: Do you want to go shopping?

LESLIE: I was just joking about joking. I am pregnant. But you are my best friend.

LAURA: K. Do you want to go to the beach?

LESLIE: I'm too white.

LAURA: Me too.

LESLIE: I'm chalk.

LAURA: I'm butt.

LESLIE: Let's get smoothies.

LAURA: Had one at work today.

LESLIE: Let's get wraps.

LAURA: K. Have you tried the sprouted cajun?

LESLIE: I get the cumin-scented barbeque tofu. No cheese, no sour cream.

LAURA: They have the new ocean-size sodas. We can get sixty-four-ounce Diet Cokes.

LESLIE: K. You work?

LAURA: Yeah. At Smooth Talk.

LESLIE: Oh. Are they hiring?

LAURA: You need to work?

LESLIE: If I want department store cosmetics! If my mom had her way I'd be the Maybelline monster that she is. I used to work at Krissie's Muffins but they're on the path of the Surf-swell Plaza Freeway Project. Everything's changing you know. We can't even park our own cars at our own beach anymore! They're putting in a PAY LOT with SEVERE TIRE DAMAGE and everything! We're all getting paved right under. (*Beat.*) At RJRJ—R. J. Reynolds Junior High School where I went in Winston-Salem—cheerleading was WAY more important than it is here. At RJRJ we had a weight limit and if you exceeded it, you were dismissed in a very solemn ceremony. With paddles and everything.

LAURA: Wow.

LESLIE: But these bitches are dedicated to nothing but fear and mediocrity. Won't practice basket-tossing on the quad just because it's kind of cement-y? We were gonna be spotting! Have they ever heard of TRUSTING their squadmates?

LAURA: I couldn't more totally agree.

LESLIE: We're never gonna convince these guys to care about cheer as much as we do. Not as long as we're in the Avocado Athletic League. They just don't have our commitment to the sport. (*Beat.*) We should go to a professional cheer training program. Like the Spirit Institute of the South.

LAURA: What's that?

LESLIE: It's actual professional cheerleading. The Competitive

Sport of Cheer. Cheer for cheer's sake. We're talking Bible Belt intensity, not this perky coastal shit. (*Beat.*) I have a brochure. It's very compelling. They have a standing back tuck. Pre-req. It's hard-core.

LAURA: Do you have a standing?

LESLIE: Not yet. Do you?

LAURA: Not yet. (*Beat.*) Wait, standing back tuck? Isn't that where you like fling your body upside down?

LESLIE: Backwards! (*Beat.* LESLIE *approaches* LAURA.) There is a stirring passage in the brochure from the founder of the Institute. She went from doing a dozen doughnuts and a fistful of quaaludes a day to being the first person to execute a flying heel stretch on an all-girl competitive squad. Today, she offers the skills and experience garnered on her journey to girls like us. (*Beat.*) It's two weeks. A thousand bucks. We should go.

LAURA: To S.I.S.

LESLIE: To their winter training intensive. We'd have to nail our standings. And get the cash. We could do it. It's a leadership seminar as well as a professional cheer training program. This year's spirit slogan is "Believe to Achieve." And they televise the final session. Let's pick weights. I say ninety-five 'cuz the camera adds ten so that's like really 105.

LAURA: So we should just say 105 then.

LESLIE: But the camera adds ten.

LAURA: OK so let's say eight-five, 'cuz that's like ninety-five, then.

LESLIE: Eighty-five pounds. Done.

LAURA: Um, why don't they have cheerleader anchors like they have sports anchors. People who are experts on who the cheerleaders are and what they're doing. Everyone likes to look at girls more than guys so looking at the cheerleaders at

professional sports events could become like the most popular spectator sport! (*Beat.*) God. I don't usually talk so much!

LESLIE: It's called spirit! We should go.

LAURA: But we'd have to train. We'd have to get good. Maybe we
should get private coaching!

LESLIE: Yeah!

LAURA: Like the little gymnasts do.

LESLIE: Yeah! But they start when they're like, three. And the
good ones are all from countries with harsh dictators. But
no, we have to live in "America," land of the "rugged individual"! What a fucking joke!

LAURA: We'll just have to do it ourselves!

LESLIE: My mom is part of the coalition fighting the Surfswell Plaza
Freeway Project. They raised money by selling this promotional cellulite cream called "Firm Up Against the Freeway."
We could raise money to get a private coach to teach us our
standing, and the flying stunts and the double mounts! (*Beat.*)

LAURA: Um, I heard we need the freeway. 'Cuz otherwise fat
people are gonna clog up our charming downtown shopping district.

LESLIE: The freeway blows! It's gonna destroy natural resources!
(*Beat.*) I know. I'm gonna make my mom get me fake
boobs. Only instead, I'll use the money for S.I.S.!

LAURA: But won't she know when you don't get the boobs?

LESLIE: I'll just tell her they're subtle. Like yours. (*Beat.*)

LAURA: I don't have fake boobs!

LESLIE: We're squadmates. You can say you had your tits done.
Gillian did.

LAURA: She did?

LESLIE: Why do you think she always votes for the halter top spring uniforms? She doesn't have to worry about straps showing!

LAURA: I didn't know that.

LESLIE: You can just say!

LAURA: But I didn't! (*Beat.*) They feel fake sometimes. I swear. They're kinda hard. Kind of high up. They're like, aggressive. (*Beat.*) But I swear to God they just came out of my own skin. My body just made them. Fast!

(*Beat.*)

LESLIE: My mom is totally flat. That's one of the reasons I hate her.

LAURA: Yeah.

(*Long pause. The sound of the ocean.* LAURA *stares out. She closes her eyes and throws her head back. Feels it.*)

LAURA: Standing back tuck.

LESLIE: Pre-req.

LAURA: Hard-core!

(LESLIE *and* LAURA *do one loud simultaneous clap, their hands in prayer pose. They turn and stare at each other, thrilled.*)

LAURA: OH MY GOD!

(*Transition. From the* CHORUS, *we hear "Got to go! Uh-huh! Got to go! That's right! Got to go!"*)

Scene 7

(LAURA*'s house. Dinner. From the outside, the* CHORUS *continues.*)

CHORUS: BIG N! LITTLE O! The Surfswell Freeway's got to go! Uh-huh! Got to go! Say what? Got to go! (etc.)

(PHIL *slams the window shut. Sits.*)

HANNAH: Who are they?

PHIL: They're wealthy women with nothing better to do.

HANNAH: How come?

PHIL: Because they have teenagers who . . . drive themselves.

HANNAH: How come?

PHIL: Because time passes! I don't know. They are bored women. They have nothing to do. So they've decided to take a swing at the freeway development.

LAURA: They're sponsored by the Earth Watch coalition. It's national.

PHIL: Is that right?

LAURA: They're a fully accredited environmental group.

PHIL: They're a bag of hammers. They've already cost taxpayers three hundred thousand dollars with this sham of a class action lawsuit. They're suing on some special breed of gopher that Surfswell will make no more. Well I'll tell you something, this woman, the "leader" of the "coalition"—I'll tell you where her sympathy for the gopher comes from. Have you seen the woman's overbite? This girl could eat an apple through a picket fence! (*He chuckles. They don't. Beat.*) They are suing on behalf of some pellet-crapping pests. (*Pause.*)

HANNAH: I thought . . . Remember, Yosemite? When She took us there. And we stayed in a cabin. And we had that nature guide who was her old friend from her Berkeley days? Who had the longest hair ever and the guitar with stickers on it? And remember how She talked different with her old friend from her Berkeley days? She called things "far out." Remember? Well didn't She say something like, how gophers do something super important, really? Remember?

LAURA: Pockets of air in the soil. They give the ground its very life.

HANNAH: Remember? (LAURA *and* HANNAH *share a moment*.) I like gophers.

PHIL: What's in this rice?

LAURA: I need some money. Our cheer team, we're raising money to go to this special cheer training camp. We want to get really good.

PHIL: So?

LAURA: So, I want to go.

PHIL: How long?

LAURA: Two weeks. They have a "land-a-standing-pre-req." (*Beat.*) That means something.

PHIL: What about school?

LAURA: It's two weeks.

HANNAH: Where's North Carolina?

PHIL: What?

HANNAH: That's where it is, right?

PHIL: It's WHERE?

LAURA: I know you think it's nothing but it's not. We really want to go.

PHIL: Who's we?

LAURA: (*Beat.*) Our squad.

HANNAH: No, it's just her. And her one friend. They're the only ones that—

LAURA: It's our squad! (*Pause.* PHIL *takes a bite of his food.*)

PHIL: What's in this?

LAURA: Miso broth. I cooked it with miso broth.

HANNAH: What's a miso?

PHIL: It's related to the gopher!

HANNAH: Ewww! Laura!

LAURA: No, honey. It's made from a soybean and it's very good for you. He's teasing.

PHIL: Miso broth?

LAURA: I got it at the supermarket. They have this new "World Cuisine" section? The package said that since ancient times the Japanese people have recognized the healthful benefits of miso broth. All the heartiness and none of the fat. I just, got it.

PHIL: And you put it in our rice?

LAURA: She used to put stuff in it.

PHIL: She never put stuff in it. It was rice. She made us our rice.

LAURA: She put stuff in it. You don't know. I was making it. I didn't even know I could. My hands just put in the olive oil and browned the onions and toasted the rice and then I reached up like her to the cupboard above the stove. And there was the beef broth. She used to put in a can of beef broth instead of water and it would simmer in and soften it and make it rich. That's how she did it. OK. All this time.

PHIL: I don't want it different. I liked it before.

(*Long pause.*)

HANNAH: I love these wrinkly tomatoes, they're so weird. It looks like eating your ear or something.

PHIL: Your sister wouldn't put a—wait, uh-oh, my ear is gone! Laura came in my room, while I was sleeping, and she cut it off and threw it in the pasta sauce! Oh no!

(PHIL *chases* HANNAH *around the table with a sun-dried tomato, she squeals and laughs. They spill out into the living room.* PHIL *returns. To* LAURA, *final.*)

PHIL: Um, no.

(*He exits. Sounds of chasing, playing, laughter.* LAURA *lifts the window, we hear:*)

CHORUS: Oh Yeah! Got to Go! That's right! Got to Go! You know it! Got to Go! Now show it! Got to Go! (etc.)

(*Lights shift.*)

Scene 8

(*Cheer practice.*)

CHEERLEADER #1: READY!

CHEERLEADERS: OK!—

(*Loud clapping sound, first from the* CHORUS, *and then louder, like a hundred kids stomping in a gymnasium.* LAURA *and* LESLIE *stand together. The other* CHEERLEADERS *surround them. Sweet, light.*)

CHEERLEADERS:

B-E-A-G-G-R-E-S-S-I-V-E!

SO BE!

AGGRESSIVE!

BE! BE!

AGGRESSIVE!

LAURA and LESLIE: (*Loud, tough.*) AGGRESSIVE!

CHEERLEADER #1: You guys, what was that?

CHEERLEADER #2: That was loud.

CHEERLEADER #3: And wrong.

CHEERLEADER #2: It was totally loud and wrong!

CHEERLEADER #1: You guys are supposed to spot.

CHEERLEADER #3: What were you guys doing?

LESLIE: We were being what we're saying! FOR ONCE!

(CHEERLEADERS *look at each other. Puzzled. Pause.*)

CHEERLEADER #1: We don't do the being. We do the cheering.

LESLIE: But—

CHEERLEADERS: Yeah?

LESLIE: I want more. (*Beat.*)

CHEERLEADER #1: It's gonna get cloudy out!

CHEERLEADER #2: Yeah, k'wee just cheer?

CHEERLEADER #3: You guys? Spot us?

LAURA: No! We're not spotting!

CHEERLEADER #1: What?

LAURA: We're not! No!

CHEERLEADER #2: Why?

LAURA: 'Cuz, um, I mean, oh, I'm sorry. I don't know. I'm sorry.

(LESLIE *glares at* LAURA *for a long moment.* LAURA *shrugs and joins the squad. The* CHEERLEADERS *go back to building their stunt.*)

CHEERLEADERS:

> B-E-A-G-G-R-E-S-S-I-V-E!
> SO BE! AGGRESSIVE!
> BE, BE! AGGRESSIVE!

(LAURA *moves into a spot position.* LESLIE *refuses.*)

(*Loud sounds of clapping, stomping.*)

(*Lights shift.*)

Scene 9

(*Lights up on* LESLIE's *house. Smoke. Dinner.*)

LESLIE: You smoke!

JUDY: Smoke put food on your table.

LESLIE: Well I want boobs.

JUDY: You have boobs.

LESLIE: No, I don't

JUDY: You've got plenty.

LESLIE: I'm a B!

JUDY: That's fine. That's good.

LESLIE: That's shit. B is for below the radar. I need a C.

JUDY: How much?

LESLIE: Five grand.

JUDY: Five grand? That's too much. It should be cheaper.

LESLIE: Well I'm sure I could get it done for a sixer of Dos Equis in a Tijuana parking lot. But do you WANT me to look like a thrift shop water bed?

JUDY: It can be done for less.

LESLIE: Not with the skill I deserve and the discretion you desire.

JUDY: Discretion?

LESLIE: I'll tell unless you get me them.

JUDY: Tell what?

LESLIE: Tell why we have this pile of money now after you resigned from R. J. Reynolds. And even in a white-collar prison for women, I assure you, nobody likes a tattletale.

JUDY: You are way out of line. (*Beat.*) Four grand is the going rate.

LESLIE: I've done research. It's five grand. Five installments. One thousand up front. That's less than the lease on your Lexus. All you gotta do is say yes.

JUDY: Why don't you eat?

LESLIE: You know. I hate. (*Holds up a green leaf.*)

JUDY: No daughter of MINE, doesn't like cilantro!

LESLIE: I hate being in the same room as cilantro. It smells like burnt eyebrows and it tastes like potting soil.

JUDY: You're just trying to upset me. You know I chose it as the patio ground cover. Next you'll tell me bougainvillea is ugly.

LESLIE: Tacky! It looks like the front of a Mexican groomsman's polyester tuxedo shirt.

JUDY: I bought this condo at the top of the market, bankrupted myself for you, so we could have a bougainvillea-covered stucco wall and the aroma of fresh local herbs wafting in through an ocean breeze. I got us out of the dead air of the humid shitty south, and I found a house, a semidetached home, so we could make a fresh start. (*She lights another cigarette.*) Will you please eat something tonight? At least your crust.

LESLIE: I don't eat crust anymore.

JUDY: You used to only eat the crust.

LESLIE: I'm off carbs!

JUDY: But I made the fat-free chedderella mexipizza. I thought you'd eat it. I know it's a little bland, that's why I added the cilantro!

LESLIE: I eat cheese and meat only now. No carbs, no sugar. I eat the top.

JUDY: But it's a honey corn crust, from the *Sauce of the Southwest* magazine I've been getting. And I used the low-fat preparation option. (*Beat.*) You used to slide off the whole top, no matter what I put on it, and just eat the bottom. Even in front of company. It looked like the underside of skin. (*Beat.*) When I had my face-lift, I looked.

LESLIE: I eat the top now.

JUDY: You've become more and more like your father.

LESLIE: That's because, like him, I hate you!

JUDY: You've gotten that lip thing. That ugly lip thing.

LESLIE: It's called an adolescent sneer!

JUDY: No, it's him.

LESLIE: I smoke you know. I smoke and then I suck Certs before you get home. And I ash in your tiger orchids. That's why they've lost their spots. It wasn't Santa Ana winds. It was me.

JUDY: It's him. (*Beat.*) I spent a thousand dollars on that low-fat lifestyle cooking class. And now it's "no carbs"?

LESLIE: For now. I'm flirting with the lifestyle of all engineered nutrition. Powders, bars, and shakes. Smoothies and wraps. That's it. Laura and I are losing weight for cheer.

JUDY: Why do you hate me?

LESLIE: Because you're old and ugly.

JUDY: I'm forty-three.

LESLIE: He left you.

JUDY: He left us.

LESLIE: Get me my boobs. Or I'll go too.

JUDY: Where?

LESLIE: To my father.

JUDY: You don't even know where he is.

LESLIE: Yes I do.

JUDY: You're a little liar.

LESLIE: We have an epistolary relationship!

JUDY: You heard that on Sally Jesse!

LESLIE: He writes me all the time. I can smell him on the paper. Obsession For Men. I write him all about my feelings. And all about you. He loves me.

JUDY: Your father wouldn't piss on your burning ponytail! He always thought you were a worthless ugly little girl from the time you were born till the time he walked out our sliding glass doors. (*Beat.*) No offense, sweetie. He hated me too.

LESLIE: You'll never fit in here, Mother. You can't master the local vernacular like I have. You've got dirt under your pastel french tips and everybody knows it.

JUDY: What do you want from me?

LESLIE: Tits.

(*Lights shift.*)

Scene 10

(*The Phone Zone.* LESLIE *and* LAURA *talk on the phone. Late at night.*)

LESLIE: So?

LAURA: Yeah?

LESLIE: My mom's in.

LAURA: How?

LESLIE: Blackmail.

LAURA: What?

LESLIE: Told her I'd alert the media to her tattletaling against the tobacco company. It was such a bluff. I mean I know she's an asshole, but I wasn't sure she was a professional one. Now she's margarine on my toasted sesame bagel. (*Beat. Then angry.*) You can just say!

LAURA: What?

LESLIE: I've been let down before! You can just say you're not in anymore. I knew you couldn't cut it anyway. You're just not Ginsu, like me. YOU'RE A FUCKING BUTTER KNIFE! You believed that crap about "We're not being, we're cheering!" You swallowed their horse pill of lies!

LAURA: No, no, no. I swear. I just didn't know how to do it. To my dad.

LESLIE: I thought you were gonna cash the death card!

LAURA: I couldn't do it. (*Beat.*) He just sits in the backyard, on this stump that used to be our eucalyptus tree. I have to walk over and say "Dad, come inside. I already put the fajitas into the tortillas and they're getting all gummy." I have to make him come in and eat. Or he just sits there.

LESLIE: OK. (*Beat. Calm.*) Then, what vulnerability does your father have left? We went through everything else. Does he have any sexual dysfunctions? Missing testicle? Does he fuck too fast?

LAURA: How should I know?

LESLIE: What does he do for a living?

LAURA: He's a development consultant.

LESLIE: What does he do?

LAURA: He, consults.

LESLIE: Who?

LAURA: Developers!

LESLIE: Of what?

LAURA: Of, lots of stuff. Places. Things. You know.

LESLIE: No, what?

LAURA: Well, at this particular point in time, of the Surfswell Plaza Freeway Project.

LESLIE: Your dad's building the freeway over the endangered wetlands and through our second-favorite muffin place?

LAURA: He's not building it, he's consulting! He is mitigating its harmful environmental impact through the implementation of certain standards. Or something.

LESLIE: This could be perfect.

LAURA: How?

LESLIE: We find some flaw in his study, or make one up. Then we blackmail him to reveal it to the press. I'll pretend my aunt is an investigative broadcast journalist.

LAURA: What does your aunt really do?

LESLIE: She's a whore.

LAURA: Oh, OK. (*Beat.*)

LESLIE: You have to think of yourself as powerful. Like . . . an interior decorator! You just fan out the fabric swatches and go, "HERE THEY ARE." (*Beat. Serious.*) You think I know how to do stuff? I don't. I just do it. (*Beat.*) Sneak over tonight and stretch my middle splits for me. And spot my standing?

LAURA: You have your standing?

LESLIE: Almost. You?

LAURA: Um. I'm closer.

LESLIE: Come over!

LAURA: I can't leave. Yet. (*Beat.*) Sometimes I wonder . . . no it's stupid.

LESLIE: What?

LAURA: It's just, I wonder sometimes. Sometimes I think that I don't know what I look like. That I don't really have any . . . traits. That I might look at a picture I'm in and not know it's me. (*Beat.*) Ever think that?

LESLIE: You have low self-esteem.

LAURA: I do?

LESLIE: There's a whole-day self-esteem seminar at S.I.S.

LAURA: Do you have low self-esteem?

LESLIE: Yes! I hate myself! Duh!

LAURA: Oh. (*Pause.*)

LESLIE: There's three kinds of cheerleaders, Laura. There's flyers, bases, and spotters. Flyers and bases make stunts. And spotters, they get to stand around with their hands up making sure Laura Lesterson doesn't fall on her tennis elbow again! Spotters. IS THAT WHAT WE'RE GONNA BE FOR THE REST OF OUR LIVES!

LAURA: Um, No.

(*Lights shift.*)

Scene 11

(*Lights up on dinner at* LAURA's *house.* LAURA *lights a candle at the empty place at the table. It burns silently.* PHIL *and* HANNAH *eat.* LAURA *tries to get up the nerve to say something to her dad, but can't.*)

(*Lights shift.*)

(*Lights up on dinner at* LESLIE's *house.* LESLIE *uses her silverware to do little cheers, while she mouths the words. Her mother eats. She looks up.* LESLIE *continues to silently cheer.*)

(*Lights shift.*)

Scene 12

(LAURA's *room.* LAURA *and* HANNAH *on the bed.* LAURA *sits behind* HANNAH, *brushing her hair.*)

HANNAH: (*Gently.*) Ow! Bitch!

LAURA: Sorry!

HANNAH: How come it was so quiet at dinner?

LAURA: I was thinking.

HANNAH: About what?

LAURA: I have a lot of stuff to think about now.

HANNAH: Are you ovulating?

LAURA: Where do you hear these things?

HANNAH: ARE you?

LAURA: No! I don't know. Maybe.

HANNAH: I think you're ovulating. That would explain it. Can I go with you to cheer camp?

LAURA: It's not cheer camp. It's the Spirit Institute of the South.

HANNAH: Are the rest of the cheerleaders going?

LAURA: I didn't say I was going!

HANNAH: Well, are they?

LAURA: No.

HANNAH: Why not?

LAURA: Because they don't care like we do.

HANNAH: Like you and Leslie?

LAURA: Yes.

HANNAH: Are you guys same-sex lovers?

LAURA: Hannah!

HANNAH: Kelly Kembrook said you guys are total lezzies. I think it's OK if you are. I would be your ally. How come you don't hang out with any of the other cheerleaders? How come you and Leslie are never in the stunts? How come you guys are always on your knees, with your hands in the air?

LAURA: The girls on the squad are jealous of us because we have Bible Belt intensity. They're just perky coastal pep girls who want to hang at the games to get guys. They knock us 'cuz we dare to care for cheer for cheer's sake, and we have our sights set high! (*Beat.*)

HANNAH: Dad wants you to start co-coaching my soccer team. She was going to.

LAURA: When?

HANNAH: Now, tomorrow. Two days a week. And he wants you to supervise my piano lesson. He doesn't want me alone with that Hungarian woman. So that's another day a week. And I might start taking classes to learn the ancient language of our people.

LAURA: Latin?

HANNAH: Hebrew!

LAURA: Where do they have Hebrew lessons?

HANNAH: At Temple Del Sol. It's the temporary temple in the coastal civic center. There's this Israeli woman, Shoshana Levis, and she's starting a Hebrew school class and Dad says I should go and learn it, and you should drive me there, and read a beauty magazine in the car until it's over, and then drive me home. Like the others.

LAURA: I don't think it's "Levis." (*Pronouncing it like the jeans.*)

HANNAH: Oh.

LAURA: I think it's "Levy." (*Rhyming with "heavy."*)

HANNAH: Oh.

LAURA: Since when are we Jewish?

HANNAH: Since ever.

LAURA: Well yeah but, Hebrew?

HANNAH: Dad says it will be meaningful to me. (*Beat.*) So that's every day of the week. That means no sneaking away to cheer anymore and leaving me here to cover for you. (*Beat.*) Besides, you don't have a thousand dollars, or the balls to ask Dad for it!

LAURA: Who said it's a thousand dollars! Are you spying on me?

HANNAH: Yes. Somebody has to. Ow! You're pulling my bangs too hard!

LAURA: Sorry.

HANNAH: You better not leave for that place!

LAURA: I'm sorry.

HANNAH: The mobile doesn't work anymore. The tinkle stopped. (*Beat.*) I need you to stay where you are!

(*Lights shift.*)

Scene 13

(*LAURA and LESLIE at the freeway. At night. Alone. The sound of the freeway. They practice.*)

LESLIE: Ready?

LAURA:

OK! WE'VE GOT SPIRIT!
YES WE DO!

> WE'VE GOT SPIRIT!
> HOW 'BOUT YOU?

LESLIE:

> WE'VE GOT SPIRIT!
> YES WE DO!
> WE'VE GOT SPIRIT!
> HOW 'BOUT YOU?

LAURA:

> WE'VE GOT SPIRIT!
> YES WE DO!
> WE'VE GOT SPIRIT!
> HOW 'BOUT YOU?

LESLIE:

> WE'VE GOT SPIRIT!
> YES WE DO!
> WE'VE GOT SPIRIT!
> HOW 'BOUT YOU?

LAURA and LESLIE:

> WE'VE GOT SPIRIT!
> YES WE DO!
> WE'VE GOT SPIRIT!
> HOW 'BOUT YOU?

(*A loud, strange sound answers them.*)

LAURA: Hello?

LESLIE: Hello?

(*The sound continues, building into a stomping, drumming, tribal rhythm. In voice-over, we hear a chant, the girls dance along.*)

CHORUS: (*Voice-over.*)

> CAN YOU HEAR IT? CAN YOU HEAR?
> DEEP INSIDE OUR POM-POMS

SOMETHING SHUSHES WHEN WE CHEER
IN THE CRACK OF OUR LIGAMENTS
WHEN WE HIGH KICK
THE SOUND OF OUR FINGERNAILS
GROWING FROM THEIR QUICKS
OUR SHOES COULD MAKE A SQUEAK
THAT COULD SHATTER GLASS
WE COULD SHAKE THE BLEACHERS
UNDER EVERYBODY'S ASS!
IN OUR FACE IN OUR FISTS
IN OUR KNEES IN OUR KNUCKLES
IN OUR BRAS IN OUR JAWS
IN OUR TEETH THERE ARE MUSCLES
WE COULD THROW OUR BODIES UP TOTALLY
    HIGH
WE COULD TURN OUR SNEAKERS
INTO PIECES OF THE SKY!

(*Music stops. Freeway sounds. Pause.* LAURA *and* LESLIE *catch their breath, entranced.*)

(*Lights shift.*)

Scene 14

(*Lights shift. Sound of a thousand blenders. The smoothie shop.* LAURA *has her hand on top of a blender. Her body shakes. It stops.*)

LAURA: K. This month's smoothie madditives have a spiritual theme. We have Buddhaberry, Messianic Mango, and Kabbalah-Cran. (*She goes to add one. Stops. A pause.*) You're supposed to know this prayer. The Kaddish? You say it at people's funerals. He was faking it. He put his head down, so the rabbi couldn't see his mouth. He didn't know the words to say. Not any of them. I could tell. He was embarrassed. There are words you're supposed to say and he didn't know them. (*Beat.*) We never run out of anything here! Everything gets filled right back up. They put it all back! (*Beat.*) It doesn't matter what goes away! K? (*Beat.*) THEY JUST REFILL IT! (*Sound of a thousand blenders.*)

(*Lights shift.*)

Scene 15

(*Lights up on the Phone Zone. Late at night.* LAURA *and* LESLIE *in their respective rooms.* HANNAH *leaning against the wall overhearing.* JUDY *and* PHIL *in their respective beds, alone.* LAURA *and* LESLIE *whisper ferociously.*)

LESLIE: READY?

LAURA and LESLIE:

> OK! B–E–A–G–G–R–E–S–S–I–V–E!
> SO BE! AGGRESSIVE! BE, BE AGGRESSIVE! (*Beat.*)

LAURA: We're going! As soon as they go to sleep. (*Pause.*)

LESLIE: Can you hear your dad sleeping yet?

LAURA: I'm not sure.

LESLIE: I hear my mom.

LAURA: She snores?

LESLIE: She just breathes. And I hear it. (*Beat.*) How did she die?

LAURA: Hit-and-run.

LESLIE: Is it true about her body?

LAURA: What?

LESLIE: They said her parts are mixed with the pavement where the freeway's gonna be!

LAURA: We're going. As soon as they're asleep.

LESLIE: What killed her?

LAURA: Hit-and-run.

LESLIE: But what, what killed her?

LAURA: The impact, I guess. (*Beat.*) There was a logo from a car in the skin of her back. A brand-name fingerprint.

LESLIE: What kind of car?

LAURA: A Lexus.

LESLIE: What do you guys drive?

LAURA: A Cherokee Chief.

LESLIE: And?

LAURA: A Lexus. (*Beat.*) I hear him!

LESLIE: Breathing?

LAURA: Snoring.

LESLIE: It's time. I told you you could do it!

LAURA: What?

LESLIE: Get the money! From your dad.

LAURA: Right. (*Beat.*) Got yours?

LESLIE: Got it.

LAURA: Got the brochure?

LESLIE: Zipped in my duffel!

LAURA: Got the car keys?

LESLIE: Warm in my pocket!

LAURA: Which car?

LESLIE: The Lexus. My mom can drive my Jetta for once. (*They giggle, then silence.*) Ready? (*Beat.*)

LAURA and LESLIE: OK.

(*Blackout.*)

END OF ACT 1

ACT 2

Scene 1

(*Loud, loud music. The music resolves itself into a loud, loud sucking sound.*)

(*Lights up.* LAURA *and* LESLIE *in the car.* LESLIE *drives. They both have harnesses around their waists into which are fitted sixty-four-ounce Diet Cokes. The music stops. The loud, loud sucking sound continues, then breaks into two individual sputters. Then stops.*)

(*Long pause.* LAURA *and* LESLIE *breathe, very full of air and liquid.*)

LAURA: Did you know that sea horses are the only animal species in the oceanic kingdom or otherwise, in which the male carries the babies? (*Beat.*) And the males are nesters, too. They can stay on one blade of sea grass for like, three whole years. Hence, their vulnerability. (*Pause.*)

LESLIE: You're not gonna be one of those people who fills the quiet spaces with like, metaphors, are you?

LAURA: Guy! I was just . . . thinking.

(*They both slurp their drinks, then sputter to a stop. Empty. Pause.*)

LESLIE: So, what else?

LAURA: (*Pouting.*) What?

LESLIE: About the sea horses.

LAURA: Well, Chinese herbalists use their desiccated and pulverized corpses to heal many injuries and ailments. Like gout, rheumatism . . .

LESLIE: What are those?

LAURA: Diseases.

LESLIE: Oh. (*Long pause.*) What else?

LAURA: That's all I remember. (*Beat.*)

LESLIE: Where are we?

LAURA: We're getting closer.

LESLIE: How much longer?

LAURA: (*Refers to the map.*) Like, eight inches.

LESLIE: Good. We'll be there soon.

LAURA: But in the last eight hours we went like, half.

LESLIE: Laura, I'm the one who remembered to steal my mom's Triple A card, I'm the one who got the maps with it, I'm the one who split the line into threes and picked the stop points. So, if you have a better plan than mine for getting us there then say so. K?

LAURA: Well, I got the ATM card.

LESLIE: I know, and I'm grateful for that. That was a good call on your part. (*Beat.*) What's the code? I need greens bad. Let's stop and get cash and get salads.

LAURA: Um.

LESLIE: Oh my god.

LAURA: No, I know it. I know it.

LESLIE: You don't know the fucking code.

LAURA: No, no. I knew it. I swear. Fuck.

LESLIE: We were relying on that card. I got the car, you got the cash. What the hell are we gonna do?

LAURA: I know it, I swear. I'm just nervous, I'm not thinking right. Just be quiet and I'll think of it. It's something. It stands for something. It's my sister's middle name, no that's our security system disarmer. Shit. I know it stands for something. It's some important thing in our lives. Fuck! What is it?

LESLIE: This is just great. Great! The one thing I ask you to take care of, and you don't have the courtesy to follow through. You are totally careless, you know that? (*Beat. Stunned.*) That was my mother!

LAURA: I'm sorry, it's just that somehow it's out of my head, out here. I look out and see all these, like, the lands, and somehow, that code, just, isn't there anymore.

LESLIE: You didn't get any extra cash? No spending money?

LAURA: I just got the tuition. Eight hundreds, two fifties, and five twenties.

LESLIE: You didn't even get any ones?

LAURA: I didn't think about it.

LESLIE: What about tipping? Huh? How are we gonna tip?

LAURA: I don't think you tip at like, motels.

LESLIE: We're gonna have to live off the Mobil card.

LAURA: You got the Mobil card?

LESLIE: Yes, of course I got the Mobil card. I said I was going to, and I did. That's how I work. Great. We're going to have to eat off the gas station now. This is just great. For three days. What are we gonna eat? Microwave mini-burgers? Corn dogs?

LAURA: They have yogurts there. Sometimes.

LESLIE: Yeah, like whole-fat banana flavor. We're gonna have to make do with pretzels and candy corn. I guess.

LAURA: What about protein?

LESLIE: Well if you can think of a low-fat protein source they might have at a Mobil station, then by all means, let me know.

LAURA: Well they have those turkey things don't they, those triangle sandwiches?

LESLIE: You're kidding, right? Those cat food quality cold cuts, on Wonder bread, with iceberg and mayonnaise? (*Beat.*) Why don't we just get a brick of pork lard and a couple of soup spoons?

LAURA: Well maybe we could separate the turkey, that's all, and wipe off the mayo. And just eat the slices. (*Beat.*) K?

LESLIE: (*Beat.*) OK.

(*Long pause. They have reached an open place. There are fields.*)

LAURA: What do you think they're growing?

LESLIE: I don't know. Corn. Cotton. Hay. Something.

LAURA: Hay?

LESLIE: I don't know.

LAURA: When do they pick, you think?

LESLIE: I don't know.

LAURA: How many corns on a plant? Like three? Or like twenty? Do they rip 'em out and redo 'em every year, or do the corns just wait under the weather and come back in the sun?

LESLIE: I don't know. (*Pause.*)

LAURA: How many jog bras did you bring?

LESLIE: Eight. You?

LAURA: Eight. How many books?

LESLIE: None. You?

LAURA: One.

LESLIE: What?

LAURA: *Roots.*

LESLIE: *Roots?*

LAURA: It's African American Week in World Lit. (*Beat.*) Have you ever tried the corn wrap?

LESLIE: Already talked about that!

LAURA: Who's your favorite trainer at—

LESLIE: Already talked about that, too!

LAURA: K.

(*Silence. More fields.*)

LAURA: Why don't we open the windows?

LESLIE: I have the AC on.

LAURA: Yeah, but why don't we try it for a bit. Let something in.

(LESLIE *opens the windows. Long silence.* LESLIE *closes the windows.*)

LESLIE: That's enough.

LAURA: What did your dad do?

LESLIE: A spokesmodel. She sold resistance training rubber bands gym to gym. He moved away with her. He hasn't communicated with me in a calendar year. (*Long pause.*)

LAURA: Elastercizers?

LESLIE: Yeah, those.

LAURA: Nobody uses those anymore. Now that there's the new latex bands.

LESLIE: I know. They're twice as supple without compromising any of the strength. (*Beat.*) I don't know what he does now. (*Pause.*) Are we in Utah, yet?

LAURA: I haven't seen a sign.

LESLIE: My neck hurts.

LAURA: Well, pull over. It should be my turn to drive by now.

LESLIE: I'm not pulling over until we get to Utah.

LAURA: There should be an automatic neck adjustment. Our Lexus has a weight-sensitive neck support.

LESLIE: So does Tracy's mom's Lexus. So does Stacie's mom's Lexus. But my mom has to get the stripped model, of course! Everybody else gets the turkey, and my mom gets the carcass! (*Beat.*)

LAURA: Is Utah . . . on the way to the south?

LESLIE: Look, I've skied there. Do you have a plan?

LAURA: No.

LESLIE: (*Final.*) Then, Utah.

LAURA: K.

(*Lights shift.*)

Scene 2

(LAURA*'s house.* PHIL *practices a speech in front of* HANNAH.)

PHIL: It's a draft.

HANNAH: Don't apologize. Just read it!

PHIL: OK. (*Beat.*) My fellow Vista Del Solians. (HANNAH *shakes her head.*) Solites? (HANNAH *shakes her head.*) Soltans? (HAN-NAH *shakes her head.*) People of Vista Del Sol? (HANNAH *nods.*) People of Vista Del Sol. We live in paradise. Not a tropical place. There are no coconuts falling onto beds of moist ferns. This is a paradise of geological variety. We have high desert bluffs, deep sandstone canyons, a soft, shifting ocean floor. This is tectonic territory. There are fractures beneath it, that make it violently slip, and change. Our temperamental paradise has been created by eons of constant destruction. (*Beat.*) What a shock and a revelation it must have been for our ancestors to encounter this stunning topographic diversity after crossing endless miles of flat dusty empty plains in their covered wagons. (*Beat.*) Well, not my ancestors. My ancestors were busy fleeing the Balkan pogroms.

HANNAH: Digression!

PHIL: Sorry. But nevertheless, that's why these people who talk about losing something when the Surfswell Plaza Freeway Project comes cutting through the bluff and into our town, they don't have a clue what they're talking about. Destruction is what the edge of the world is made of. These people, the "coalition," they don't understand that. What we're doing is not just important, it's inevitable. These people don't know shit about losing anything! (*He stops, agitated.*)

HANNAH: Well it's edgy.

PHIL: That last part, that's not gonna be part of it.

HANNAH: That's probably good.

PHIL: Isn't her practice over by now?

HANNAH: She probably just stayed late.

PHIL: How late?

HANNAH: She'll be back soon.

PHIL: What about dinner?

HANNAH: I'll make something.

PHIL: You will?

HANNAH: I know how. I've watched. (*Beat.*) She'll be back soon!

(*Lights shift.*)

Scene 3

(*The Mobil station.* LAURA *reads from the back of a bag of pretzels.*)

LAURA: Yep. Palm oil

LESLIE: Jesus Christ! Even in the pretzels! And the only crackers they have are "savory flavored"! Do you know what that means, "savory flavored"?

LAURA: No.

LESLIE: Me neither, but I'm sure it's horrible.

LAURA: I think I'm starving.

LESLIE: I'm not.

LAURA: I think I'm really really hungry.

(LESLIE *grabs packages, two, three at a time.*)

LESLIE: "Covered in creamery butter." Mother of God!

LAURA: Does caffeine make you more or less hungry?

LESLIE: More. Less. More. I can't remember!

LAURA: My head is hurting. From hunger. We have to eat something here. We just have to find something that we can eat.

LESLIE: My head hurts too. But it's not hunger. I'm just pissed at you 'cuz you're such a useless dumb ass. Just think of the goddamn code and we could at least get the dinner salad at Denny's with the dressing on the side. Can't you think of it? It has to be part of something. (*Beat.*) Caffeine-Free Regular Coke. WHERE ARE WE?

LAURA: My head hurts. We have to get something.

LESLIE: What? What are we gonna get? Huh? Yes, excuse me, I'd like a tall, cold BACON CHEDDAR SODA PLEASE!

LAURA: WE HAVE TO GET SOMETHING HERE. (*Beat.*)

LESLIE: What?

LAURA: Something we want.

LESLIE: Want?

LAURA: OK. What do you feel like?

LESLIE: Feel?

LAURA: Let's just close our eyes and try to think about what we feel. What. Feels?

(LAURA *closes her eyes.* LESLIE *reluctantly closes hers. Then, immediately:*)

LESLIE: I want a corn dog.

LAURA: What?

(LESLIE *opens eyes.*)

LESLIE: I used to eat them at the Winston County Fair, when I was a kid. With my dad. (*Beat. Closes eyes again. Opens them.*) Orange soda. Do they still have that?

LAURA: Yeah. It's on the thing. It's always on the thing. It's right next to the Diet Coke.

LESLIE: I'd like the regular-size one of those. The regular-size.

LAURA: OK. Let's get in line. I think I might want to get us another map. I think there might be a better map than the one we've got. I'm gonna take a look.

(*Lights shift.*)

Scene 4

(HANNAH *standing in a pool of light. A* COP *speaks to her in voice-over.*)

COP: We're very sorry about this.

HANNAH: OK. Can I go now please?

COP: I'm sorry, but I need to clarify, you said, she . . .

HANNAH: I just said they take things more seriously than the other girls.

COP: Like what?

HANNAH: Like cheer! She said they take it more seriously than the other girls, that's all.

COP: Did she say why?

HANNAH: She said that the other girls are interested in the football guys and they're not. They're interested in achieving together.

COP: Did she say what they were interested in achieving?

HANNAH: Cheerleading! They were interested in achieving in cheerleading!

COP: I'm sorry. What does that mean?

HANNAH: They were sick of how mediocre their peers were. She wanted to go to a better place.

COP: Did she use those words—"a better place"?

HANNAH: Yeah. Can I go now? 'Cuz, my friend's mom is taking me home.

COP: Did she make any other comments that you thought were a little strange?

HANNAH: Strange?

COP: Did she say anything about her connection to Leslie? Did she use any other words that you might remember?

HANNAH: Other words?

COP: Like, "love" or . . .

HANNAH: OH! You think this is some kind of inscrutable Sapphic suicide pact? (*Beat.*)

COP: How old are you?

HANNAH: Look, she and Leslie are . . . different. The other cheer-leaders don't ever invite them to their pre-parties. They don't ever get to stand in the middle. They're terminal flanks. And they always carry other people's megaphones to the cars after the games. They call them the spot sisters, 'cuz they never mount or base. They're never allowed to call a cheer. I listen to them talk on the phone. I hear what they say to each other. I take my hair dryer and stick it up to the wall. The heat coils conduct vocal sound waves with surprising clarity. Sometimes it's so quiet, for so long. And sometimes it's just like hours of "uh-huh" "uh-huh" and "totally." And sometimes they say things that are very frightening indeed.

COP: Hannah Rachel Green, your sister has committed theft. Do you know where she is?

HANNAH: You know how if you look at a picture just one year later, you can look back and see exactly what kind of hair-cut you really had? Well that's what I think she's doing. But with space instead of time. (*Beat.*) I'm eleven years old.

Scene 5

(*Motel room.* LESLIE *is alone. The TV flickers in her face.*)

(*Rhythmically, every six seconds, she laughs along with a laugh track, then stops. Every fourth time, she sighs. Then the laugh track stops. She still laughs, every six seconds, three more times. Then sighs.*)

(LAURA *enters.*)

LESLIE: What did you say?

LAURA: It's done.

LESLIE: Yeah?

LAURA: It totally worked.

LESLIE: What did you say?

LAURA: You don't have to worry about it. I took care of it.

LESLIE: Well I'd like to know the plan. What did you tell the guy?

LAURA: I told him you were pregnant and that my mom died and I totally cried, I couldn't believe it, I was just crying and crying. I think he just wanted me out of there. I said our dad was coming tomorrow and paying and couldn't we just stay here till he came tomorrow.

LESLIE: You played the death card.

LAURA: Yep.

LESLIE: He bought it?

LAURA: Cash-and-carry, baby! Look what they had in the lobby! (*She holds up a Twinkie.*)

LESLIE: I can't believe they didn't insist on an imprint. Don't they have to have an imprint? Isn't there some kind of law? The center of a Twinkie is made with lamb lard!

(LAURA *devours the Twinkie.*)

LAURA: This is the best best food I've ever had. Why haven't I had this before? This is . . . exquisite.

LESLIE: What if they catch us?

LAURA: We sleep and we scram!

LESLIE: But . . . did you look at that man in the lobby? He had more piercings than teeth!

LAURA: We have to keep going.

LESLIE: Did you look underneath the desk? Did you see his lower body? On one leg. His entire calf was gone. He had a leg bone, and no calf! He had no calf! (*Beat.*) I'm cold.

LAURA: Shh, it's gonna be okay. Here. (LAURA *throws a sweater at* LESLIE.)

LESLIE: Ow! Bitch!

LAURA: I'm sorry.

LESLIE: You hurt me!

LAURA: I'm sorry, shh . . .

LESLIE: I don't like it here.

LAURA: Shh. It's gonna be okay. Just, Shhh. . . .

LESLIE: I don't want to wear this stupid fucking sweater!

LAURA: Be quiet!

LESLIE: I hate being away from my stuff!

LAURA: Shh! Just be quiet, OK! Just, Shh!

LESLIE: I want to go home and be with my stuff!

LAURA: Shut up.

LESLIE: I have a corn dog inside me. I want to go home!

LAURA: I SAID, SHUT UP!

(*Lights shift.*)

Scene 6

(LAURA's *house.* PHIL *and* JUDY *sitting in the living room, where nobody ever sits.* JUDY *has tea,* PHIL *doesn't.*)

PHIL: It's not too strong?

JUDY: It's fine, think you.

PHIL: I don't usually make tea. Or, really, never. I've never made tea. (*Beat.*) Ever.

JUDY: Well, it's lovely. (*Pause.*) Is this one of those antique door tables? I've seen these.

PHIL: Yes, yes. It's a table made of an old door.

JUDY: They're so clever. What they think of. I have a mirror that's made from an old window. It has a sill still. (*Pause. She doesn't drink her tea.*)

PHIL: You're sure that's not too strong—

JUDY: No, no it's just right. (*Beat.*) What kind is it?

PHIL: Um, Chinese. I believe. Or Irish. No, it's Indian. Well, it's from somewhere else, I can't remember.

JUDY: Well it's lovely.

PHIL: We have so many teas.

JUDY: Then this was a very nice choice. (*Pause.*) What do you do for a living, Phil?

PHIL: I am an environmental impact consultant.

JUDY: Oh! (*Beat.*) What is that exactly?

PHIL: I consult on issues involving the impact to the environment of various development projects. And yourself?

JUDY: I was a consultant, too. A marketing consultant for a large corporation in the South. You know, there's a familiar smell here.

PHIL: I'm sorry.

JUDY: No, no. It's not an odor. It's not unpleasant at all. Just, a smell. That's familiar. That's all. (*Beat.*) I'm sorry. Sometimes I just say things. (*Pause.*)

PHIL: The girls—

JUDY: Yes.

PHIL: What are we going to do?

(*Lights shift.*)

Scene 7

(*Motel room.* LAURA *and* LESLIE *stand next to twin beds, holding their thin motel bedspreads.*)

LAURA: Just pull it off.

LESLIE: Won't we be cold?

LAURA: You don't sleep with these. They're universally yucky. Just strip 'em off.

LESLIE: But I'll get cold.

LAURA: You should have brought more sweaters.

LESLIE: How many did you bring?

LAURA: Five.

LESLIE: How did you get five sweaters in your bag?

LAURA: I made it a priority. It's cold in other places.

LESLIE: There's no way you fit five sweaters in that one bag.

LAURA: Yes I did. (*Beat.*) I left my whole hair care product pouch on the bed. All of it. Conditioner, retexturizer, straightening balm, pomade, paddle brush, round brush. Comb. It was so heavy. So I chucked it onto my comforter. (*Beat.*) Tomorrow I'm gonna have to use whatever complimentary product they have in the shower here. I'm gonna have to just wash it and let it be. (*Beat.*) I have no idea what it is going to actually look like. (*Beat.*) Now stuff the spreads in the corner and help me move the twins to the wall. Let's spot each other's standings.

LESLIE: But this carpet . . .

LAURA: So?

LESLIE: It's like, government surplus.

LAURA: Yeah?

LESLIE: It could sand our faces off. (*Beat.*)

LAURA: In the tuck section of the brochure, it describes how a girl landed face-first trying to nail her standing, and she swelled so high she couldn't see for a week. Now help me.

LESLIE: You don't have any hair product?

LAURA: Not an ounce.

LESLIE: But I have coarse, dry, chemically treated hair and you have limp, fine, oily hair so you can't even borrow mine! There's a whole-day competitive grooming seminar at S.I.S. It's a big part of the point system if you wanna win the spirit stick at the final award ceremony. You're gonna look, I don't know what you're gonna look like!

LAURA: So?

LESLIE: Well it's just . . . I think maybe we should turn around and go home. My mom . . .

LAURA: Yeah?

LESLIE: She's probably freaking by now.

LAURA: You hate her.

LESLIE: Well yeah, but . . .

LAURA: There's a picture in the brochure of a girl named Jolene. She and her team just won the all-girl squad professional nationals. She's the only one smiling with a closed mouth. Why? Because in the first flying stunt her mounter kicked her coming down from a heel stretch and knocked her two front teeth clean out. They flung across the gym like a couple of peppermint Chiclets. And while her mouth was welling with blood, Jolene nailed that routine to the final tumbling pass. She took that intensity and used it. (*Pause. A plea.*) Remember?

LESLIE: Yeah. It's just that she's my mom.

LAURA: And I'm your squadmate. I'm squatting for my standing. Spot me? (LAURA *turns and squats into a prep position for a standing back tuck.* LESLIE *doesn't move.*)

(*Lights shift.*)

Scene 8

(LAURA's *house.*)

JUDY: Do you sit in this room a lot?

PHIL: It's the living room.

JUDY: But do you really, LIVE here?

PHIL: The TV's in the other room.

JUDY: So for you this is sort of a, parlor.

PHIL: I suppose.

JUDY: That's what I would call it. This is lovely. Your house. I enjoy this whole development. I have a friend in this subdivision with this very same model of home. I enjoy her. Her living room looks much smaller than this. But she has a tendency to overfurnish.

PHIL: Actually, this area is unique in that the homes, although built in a tract style, are each, in themselves, uh, unique. It's unique in that way. And they're unusually large.

JUDY: Yes, it's very spacious here. (*Beat.*) My friend actually uses this as an office.

PHIL: Really?

JUDY: Yes. It's an unconventional choice. But she runs a gift placement service out of her home so she likes an open office area.

PHIL: Where is her living room?

JUDY: Right through that hall and to the right.

PHIL: That's my office!

JUDY: Isn't that funny? Opposites. She says she likes the living room to feel confined. Makes her feel like she's in the mountains. (*Pause.*)

PHIL: Does your daughter cook?

JUDY: Leslie! My daughter wouldn't know a saucepan if you used it to split open her tiny little head!

PHIL: Does your daughter eat?

JUDY: None of them eat today. Don't you watch prime-time news magazines? They all "suffer" from low self-esteem. I try to work around it. Does yours puke? Now that I won't tolerate. Vomit erodes the porcelain. I have a friend with four teenage daughters and she has had to revarnish their toilets every summer.

(*She notices the silver family picture frames on a piece of furniture. She stops to look. She puts down her tea cup. Beat.*)

PHIL: Yes.

JUDY: I used to have a deep fat fryer. I put everything into that. I'd make tempura and serve it with chop suey and water chestnuts. I'd have to slap her little hand 'cuz she'd try to eat it off the serving platter. I remember that deep bubbling sound. The oil sound. I haven't heard that in years. That was just their favorite thing. They just loved my Oriental night. (*Beat.*) I had a husband at the time.

PHIL: The neighbors sometimes make bacon. We can smell it from our breakfast nook. They're from Chicago. It reminds me of grad school. (*Beat.*) I have a master's. In public policy.

JUDY: Oh. (*Beat. A sound. They both jump.*) Was that?

PHIL: No. Just the security system. Every few hours it checks on us. It beeps. How did I let this happen?

JUDY: We're doing everything we can. You made sure the ringer's on "high"?

PHIL: Yes.

JUDY: We're doing everything we can. (*Pause.*) There's that smell again. What is it? It's so familiar. But I can't quite place it. (*Long beat.*)

PHIL: Eucalyptus.

JUDY: Eucalyptus! (JUDY *looks out the window. Sees the stump.*) Oh!

PHIL: I had to cut it down. It was time.

JUDY: Oh yes. They can fall right onto the house at any time. They're supposed to be very shallow-rooted trees.

PHIL: That's what I've heard too.

(*Lights shift.*)

Scene 9

(*The car.* LAURA *drives.*)

LESLIE: We give the money back. And say sorry.

LAURA: No!

LESLIE: It'll be snap crackle pop! I give the money back to my mom, and you give the money back to your dad, and we just cry, and say that our blood sugar was low, and our hormones were high and . . . we were menstruating, and all that blood loss was really depleting our ethical stores. We play the period card!

LAURA: We're not going back! (*Beat.*)

LESLIE: What about the ground-breaking? Aren't you supposed to be there? Don't you have to be there, for your dad? He needs you there. (*Beat.*) You're going ninety! You're not supposed to go ninety!

LAURA: Look, if we're gonna get into an accident, we might as well get into a big gnarly one and die. If we're gonna go, we're gonna go SMOOTHIED! NO TRACE!

LESLIE: Please slow down! I'll be your best friend!

LAURA: You ARE my best friend.

LESLIE: Fuck. (*Beat.*) You're going a hundred! I don't think Lexuses go a hundred! It's gonna break!

LAURA: You can go a hundred and fifty in a Lexus and not feel a thing! IT'S A LUXURY SEDAN! (*Beat.*)

LESLIE: OK, this isn't cheer anymore.

LAURA: This is just starting to be cheer!

LESLIE: I don't know who you are. (*Beat.*)

LAURA: Know what? I didn't get the money from my dad. I stole it. From the Smooth Talk smoothie shop. I committed an actual crime. With actual consequences.

LESLIE: You stole?

LAURA: You blackmailed!

LESLIE: Yeah, my MOM! You stole from one of the pillars of the community.

LAURA: You talk a lot of shit. You know that? (*A scary pause.*)

LESLIE: You STOLE?

LAURA: Yep. I have focus and intensity!

LESLIE: You don't even have your standing!

LAURA: Yes I do!

LESLIE: You threw yourself onto the bed.

LAURA: I am so close! We just have to "Believe to Achieve"!

LESLIE: We also have to be able to do it, though. And we can't. We can't do standing back tucks. Our CARTWHEELS are for shit! We don't weigh eighty-five pounds! And, your hair! It's like, alive! It's like a . . . living thing!

(LAURA *screeches to the side of the road. Stops.*)

LAURA: I'm doing it. I'm showing you. I can. You watch.

(*Lights shift.*)

Scene 10

(LAURA*'s house.* PHIL, JUDY, *and* HANNAH *in the family room.*)

HANNAH: Theft.

PHIL: What?

HANNAH: That's what he said. Grand theft. Or maybe petty. Where did I hear that? Petty? (*Beat.*) He knew my name. He pulled right up after soccer practice and it was so embarrassing. I died. Crishelle Kravitz's mom was taking me home and she had to wait! He talked to me against his car. He said he needed to talk about my sister. Laura. And he knew my name. He had three long hairs gooed on the shine of his head.

PHIL: He said, theft?

HANNAH: Grand or petty or something. He said theft.

PHIL: What did you tell him?

HANNAH: I just said she left. I just said what's true.

JUDY: Are you sure it was a cop?

HANNAH: Yes. He showed me his I.D. card.

PHIL: You mean badge.

HANNAH: No, it was a card. In his wallet.

JUDY: Was he driving a black-and-white squad car? With a light bar?

HANNAH: No, it was more like a . . . Honda.

PHIL: A Honda.

JUDY: A light blue Honda sedan?

HANNAH: Yeah.

JUDY: Was it a laminated yellow card that he showed you?

HANNAH: Yes.

JUDY: Vista Del Soldiers. The private security force. What did he say was stolen?

HANNAH: Money. He said Laura stole money from the smoothie shop. Lots of it. They're looking for her.

PHIL: Go to your room.

HANNAH: I'm in trouble?

PHIL: Go to your room. That's where you go.

HANNAH: We're supposed to have dinner.

PHIL: Oh. Well, have dinner. And then, go to your room. (*Pause.*)

HANNAH: Daddy, what does this mean?

(HANNAH *exits.* JUDY *and* PHIL *face each other.*)

PHIL: Theft?

JUDY: It's not REALLY theft.

PHIL: She said—

JUDY: They won't contact the police. They'll handle it within the jurisdiction of the mall. They're at fifty-percent capacity and this is the last thing they'd leak. They're looking for sushi and dry-cleaning tenants, not pawnshops and check cashers. You need to eat. Sit down at your table. I'll cook you something. We'll have dinner.

PHIL: I'm not hungry.

JUDY: What is that sound?

PHIL: What sound?

JUDY: From outside. It sounds like some kind of chanting. Hear that? Let me open your window.

PHIL: No! Please. I think I'm hungry after all.

(*Lights shift.*)

Scene 11

(*The side of the road.* LAURA *is in the prep position to do a standing back tuck.* LESLIE *spots, tentatively.*)

LESLIE: Don't do it!

LAURA: I'm gonna. I know I can.

LESLIE: You're gonna get hurt!

LAURA: SO?

LESLIE: So this isn't what cheer is about!

LAURA: This IS what cheer is about. We're only seventeen years old. Seventeen! We're not supposed to have to take care of other people. We're not supposed to have to drive them to their piano lessons and their Hebrew lessons and make them their chicken and rice! We're seventeen! We're supposed to be reckless and careless! We're supposed to do stupid dangerous shit and learn from it!

LESLIE: No we're not! Just stop it. Why don't you look around where we are right now. Look! See how it's all dead flat here?

Well some of us have actually lived in shitty places like this! You've lived your whole life where it's all nice and new but we had to work our butts off to get there! We lived in places that were dead, dead flat! Like my mom. And me! (*Beat.*)

LAURA: It's not nice and new where we live! They just pave over what's there! There's big ugly holes and they pave on top of them, that's all! (*Beat.*) I'm doing it!

LESLIE: I'm not spotting! I'm not gonna spot!

LAURA: I don't need a spot!

LESLIE: Please, don't. Please? Oh my god!

(LAURA *preps to flip, and just at the point of no return . . .*)

(*Lights shift.*)

Scene 12

(PHIL *and* JUDY *in the Phone Zone.*)

JUDY: What did they say?

PHIL: Nothing. Still.

JUDY: You're sure you have the call-waiting activated?

PHIL: Judy, you've—

JUDY: Asked you that ten times already. Sorry.

PHIL: It's okay. I understand.

JUDY: They're looking. They have the number. You have call-waiting. We're doing everything we can. (*Beat.*) We only have three days left you know.

PHIL: Three days?

JUDY: Until the Surfswell Plaza Freeway Project ground-breaking.

The end of our town as we know it. The coalition is kicking into high gear. They're picketing the house of Mr. X, some bigwig in the project. I've got the graveyard shift tomorrow night. We all need to do our part.

PHIL: Oh God. Oh God.

JUDY: Sh, sh. (*Beat.*) I know. (*Pause.*)

PHIL: Do you like your daughter?

JUDY: No. Do you?

PHIL: No. Wait. Which one? The older, or the younger?

JUDY: The older.

PHIL: No. She scares me.

JUDY: She scares you?

PHIL: She makes me scared.

JUDY: But we love them so much.

PHIL: Yes.

JUDY: And we know them so well.

PHIL: Yes. (*Beat.*) There's something I have to tell you.

JUDY: Yes?

PHIL: I've never said it before.

JUDY: Yes. I know. (*Beat.*)

PHIL: But I can't. I haven't yet.

JUDY: You can. (*Beat.*) READY?

PHIL:

OK!
SHE'S D-E-A-D
AND SHE AIN'T COMIN BACK TO ME.

JUDY: UH-HUH. THAT'S RIGHT. AND SAY IT ONE
       MORE TIME.

PHIL:

    MY WIFE IS DEAD
    SHE HIT HER HEAD
    I'LL NEVER SMELL HER ON MY BED.

JUDY: UH-HUH. YOU GOT IT. A LITTLE LOUDER NOW.

PHIL and JUDY:

    WE GOT OUR HOUSES
    IN THE SUN!
    BUT OUR SPOUSES
    HAD TO RUN!
    WE'RE LONELY!

JUDY: SAY WHAT?

PHIL:

    WE'RE L-O-N-E-L-Y
    AND WE AIN'T GOT NO ALIBI!
    WE'RE LONELY!

JUDY: UH-HUH!

PHIL: WE'RE LONELY!

JUDY: THAT'S RIGHT!

PHIL and JUDY: WE'RE SPENT! (*Long pause.*)

PHIL: What was that?

JUDY: A cheer.

PHIL: For what?

JUDY: For ourselves.

(*Lights shift.*)

Scene 13

(*Lights bump up on* LESLIE *and* LAURA. LAURA *lies face down on the road.*)

LAURA: I did it.

LESLIE: You fell on your face!

LAURA: I DID IT!

LESLIE: Let me see!

(LAURA's *head pops up. She's bloody. She spits. A gasp.*)

LAURA: OCEAN!

LESLIE: Oh my god!

LAURA: It's ocean!

LESLIE: There's road on your face!

LAURA: How could I be so stupid!

LESLIE: You're bloody!

LAURA: It's O-C-E-A-N!

LESLIE: What is?

LAURA: The ATM CODE! It's the ATM code! Of course she picked that, because that was her place. She used to take us there to play, and walk around, and DO stuff. Before we started just laying on the sand to get tan. There was this one time, I was throwing these rocks at a post under the old pier. They tore the old pier down. It's something else now.

LESLIE: The Seabluff Bungalow Suites. I know.

LAURA: I was throwing these rocks hard against the posts, just enjoying how it made a cracking and smacking sound. And my mom yelled at me, "Stop it!" And she grabbed me by the wrist and led me under the pier and showed me the mussels. There were mussels that made their home there. I thought they were just shells, or rocks or something. Things. But she said, "Look!

Look close!" And I saw what came out. It was little pieces of flesh. Living tissue from a living thing. (*Beat.*) I felt like a terrible awful person, the worst. But she said, it's okay. Someone just has to teach you that you have impact. Someone has to teach you about impact. (*Beat.*) We used to swim for hours in the ocean and when it got cold, we would run out and my mom would have a wide, white towel open and she would clutch us up in it and rub us warm and dry. She'd call us her baby burritos. That was before we had wraps. (*Pause.*)

LESLIE: My dad used to take me onto roller coasters. That was our thing. I would ride the scariest loopiest roller coaster when I was legally way too little. He used to call me Ironside. That means I'm really fucking strong. (*Beat.*) Oh my god! Do you smell that?

LAURA: What?

LESLIE: Don't you smell it? (LAURA *sniffs.*)

LAURA: Yeah. What is it?

LESLIE: It's tobacco! It's a crop that we grow here. In the South. I can't believe it. (*Beat.*)

LAURA: We made it.

LESLIE: Oh my god!

LAURA: Get in the car!

LESLIE: We're here!

(*Lights shift.*)

Scene 14

(LAURA's *house. Dinner.* PHIL, HANNAH, *and* JUDY *quietly eating.*)

PHIL: This is lovely.

HANNAH: What is it?

JUDY: I had to work with what was here. You have quite a few sun-dried tomatoes.

HANNAH: (*Trying to revive the joke.*) Oh no! Wrinkle tomatoes!

(PHIL *gives her a token chuckle.*)

JUDY: They're very high in sodium. And there were quite a few dusty cans of beef broth in the back there. I used one in the rice.

PHIL: I can tell. It's very hearty.

JUDY: We almost never cook with beef anymore. It's mostly chicken and the fresh fish I get from Hattie's heart-friendly butcher on Camino Del Mar. My friend Hattie opened that place after her husband had a massive infarction three years ago. That shop saved their life and their livelihood. Of course, they're right on the path of the Surfswell Plaza Freeway Project. She's the one who got me involved with the coalition to fight the freeway. It's been very fulfilling for me. (*Chanting is heard.*) There's that noise again. What is that?

PHIL: Pass the rice please.

HANNAH: You have the rice.

PHIL: Then pass something else!

JUDY: What is that sound? (HANNAH *opens the window. We hear the protest.*)

CHORUS:

> H (*Clap! Clap! Clap! Clap!*)
> E (*Clap! Clap! Clap! Clap!*)
> L! L! (*Clap! Clap!*)
> N–O!
> SURFSWELL PLAZA FREEWAY PROJECT (*Clap!*)
> HELL NO! (*Etc.*)

HANNAH: My dad did it.

JUDY: Pardon me?

HANNAH: It's Dad's freeway.

JUDY: Is that so?

PHIL: I'm consulting.

HANNAH: It's my dad's project.

JUDY: You're Mr. X?

PHIL: I'm a development consultant, which means I'm mitigating its harmful environmental impact through the implementation of certain civic standards.

HANNAH: There's a ground-breaking ceremony in two days. Did he invite you?

JUDY: A ground-breaking?

HANNAH: Yeah. They're tenting the whole area. They're already setting up the grandstands and the carnation arch and the beer garden. There's gonna be complimentary muffins courtesy of Breads Etc. There's gonna be news vans and roving photographers and man-on-the-street opinion polls. And my dad is gonna cut the ribbon. Aren't you, Dad?

PHIL: That hasn't been determined.

HANNAH: (*To* JUDY.) Did he invite you to come? (*Pause.*)

JUDY: I will be there. (*Beat.*) Hannah, more broccoflower?

HANNAH: I've consumed quite enough.

JUDY: Phil?

PHIL: Yes. Thank you. (*He doesn't take any.*)

(*Lights shift.*)

Scene 15

(*An abandoned schoolyard.* LAURA *and* LESLIE *run in.*)

LESLIE: Nobody.

LAURA: Did you run around the back again?

LESLIE: Four times!

LAURA: Me too!

LESLIE: I looked under rocks! I looked under leaves! There's no one here.

LAURA: What happened?

LESLIE: Let's look at the brochure again. Maybe we got it wrong.

(LAURA *looks at the brochure.*)

LAURA: Where did you get the brochure?

LESLIE: I found it.

LAURA: Where?

LESLIE: In the library. I went to the mag rack at recess to put on some perfume from a *Mirabella*. And I saw it poking out of a shelf.

LAURA: When?

LESLIE: A while ago.

LAURA: Do you see what this says at the bottom? Right here? In solid black ink? (*Beat.*) Copyright 1971. 1971! See how the print's all weird? How the letters are like, all, flared at the bottom?

LESLIE: I thought it was retro.

LAURA: Oh my god. (*Long pause.*)

LESLIE: My mom says everything comes back. Shoulder pads, every-thing. She says you just keep it in your closet and you hold on tight. 'Cuz everything comes back! My mom says it does!

LAURA: No, it doesn't. In 1971, my mom was alive, and she's dead now. In 1971, my mother was alive, and today, she's gone.

LESLIE: But she's always in your heart.

LAURA: Is that all you have to say? 'Cuz that doesn't mean anything. (*She stares at the brochure.*) In 1971, I wasn't even around yet. But that's when she was really alive, I think. She had a gray streak in the front of her hair. Premature gray. She had it for years until she finally got sick of the giggles and stares and she dyed it like the rest of them. I don't even remember barely. I was so little. She used to tell us things, but I barely remember and I can't ask her again! I can't say, hey Mom, tell me things I never listened to! Tell me how to do things! Tell me how to bake sugar cookies so they're soft in the middle! Tell me how to sweep my hair up so it holds with just a pin. Tell me what it feels like when your water breaks and a baby comes out! I don't have anybody to tell me that! (LAURA *starts to tear the brochure.*) I hate my dad! I'm sorry, but I hate him so much! How could he just keep going? I don't understand how he could just keep going! (*Beat.*) Is that what happens? You're young, and you believe in things, and then you, what? You get married, you have kids, you move into a Spanish stucco ocean view unit and you forget? One day you wear your white streak like a peacock's tail, and the next day you're letting them paint it with bleach and toner and wrap it in tinfoil and sitting under a hair dryer to cook for an hour while you learn lip-lining tips from a beauty magazine! Like everybody else! When you sit under those dryer domes, you can't see or hear a thing. You just have to sit there quietly and let all that stuff soak into you. (*Beat.*) She's really kind of been gone for a long long time. (LAURA *finishes tearing the brochure and starts to scatter the pieces.*) I don't want to be a dead girl. I want to be a person who's alive. (*She turns and starts to slowly walk away.*)

LESLIE: Where are you going? (LAURA *turns. A beat.*)

LAURA: I'm going home.

(*Lights shift.*)

Scene 16

(HANNAH's *room.* JUDY *sits on* HANNAH's *bed, brushing* HANNAH's *hair.*)

JUDY: They're not wetlands. That's a myth generated by the environmentalists' lobby. It's a man-made bog. They're draining and reclaiming it for the community.

HANNAH: What about the gophers!

JUDY: There's been a gopher agreement. In the settlement. There's a gopher provision in the project!

HANNAH: What are they gonna do to them?

JUDY: They're building a temporary burrowing facility.

HANNAH: They're gonna build gopher condos?

JUDY: It's only temporary.

HANNAH: Out of what material will they build these condos? Are they gonna protest big-time? Are they gonna hang my dad in effigy? Is he gonna have to testify?

JUDY: No, there's been a settlement. That means they've dropped the lawsuit. It's over.

HANNAH: They're gonna build them out of tar and gravel. The gophers have to settle for the gravel! (*Beat.*)

JUDY: Here's something I can teach you. You'll learn that you can live with almost anything. You can find a way to make it work and move on. Do you hear me? You can make it work and keep going.

(PHIL, *isolated in a pool of light.*)

PHIL: The bluffs crumble to the beach. The waves wash the sand away and for a while there are jagged rocks and trash all over the shore. But the city comes in with trucks and deposits a fine layer of sand over the broken glass and the discarded feminine hygiene products and replenishes the smooth recreational surface we've come to know and rely upon. With just a little help from man, nature's cycle continues. In a year, this very ground upon which we stand will be racing with high-speed cars. Today we move forward. We don't look back. We proudly pave our way to tomorrow.

Scene 17

(*Lights up on the ground-breaking ceremony.* PHIL *is flanked by* JUDY *and* LESLIE. *He holds a ceremonial shovel.*)

PHIL: Thank you. Thank you. I played only a small part in this. I consulted, only. But I thank you. For your support.

(*He goes to dig, but stops. He can't.* JUDY *approaches, and helps him dig. They wait for applause, none comes. They look to* LESLIE. *She gets the crowd to applaud. By cheering.*)

(*The sound of applause.*)

(*Lights shift.*)

Scene 18

(*Lights fade out on everyone but* HANNAH *and* LAURA, *who stand at the beach, using their toes to write in the sand.*)

LAURA: What does yours say?

HANNAH: I'm not done, wait!

LAURA: Let me see!

HANNAH: Wait! There.

LAURA: What does it say?

HANNAH: You first.

LAURA: OK. Mine says, "LYING." I lied about stuff. What does yours say?

HANNAH: Forgetting. I'm afraid I'm forgetting her. I can't remember what it tasted like when she leaned over to kiss good-night and some of her hair would get in my mouth. (*Beat.*)

LAURA: We're not going to forget her.

HANNAH: Well, Shoshana said whatever you want to wash away. You can write it. (*Beat.*)

HANNAH: We should go! We're supposed to meet them in ten minutes. We're supposed to cheer for Dad.

LAURA: It's over.

HANNAH: What's over?

LAURA: The ground-breaking. It was over an hour ago.

HANNAH: Why didn't you take me there? We're gonna get into trouble! We were supposed to cheer for Dad.

LAURA: I kind of quit cheering. I'm gonna try to do something else.

HANNAH: What?

LAURA: I don't really know yet. What else does Shoshana say? (*Pause.*)

HANNAH: She says . . . wait! Here comes a wave. (*They grab hands.*)

LAURA: Here we go.

HANNAH: Here it comes! (*Beat.*)

LAURA: Ready?

HANNAH: OK.

(*As they run back, the sound of the freeway is overwhelmed by the sound of a wave crashing, then the sound of Pacific Ocean. Lights fade.*)

END OF PLAY

NONE OF THE ABOVE

Jenny Lyn Bader

None of the Above was originally produced by New Georges (Susan Bernfield, Artistic Director; Sarah Cameron Sunde, Managing Director) at the Ohio Theatre in New York City on March 15, 2003. It was directed by Julie Kramer; the set design was by Lauren Helpern; the lighting design was by Tyler Micoleau; the costume design was by Veronica Worts; the sound design was by Jill B. C. DuBoff; the production stage manager was Alison Dingle; the production manager was Samuel C. Tresler; the props were by Faye Armon; the casting was by Bernard Telsey Casting/Jaclyn Brodsky. The cast was as follows:

JAMIE	Alison Pill
CLARK	Kel O'Neill

ACT 1

Scene 1

(*November 1994. At rise of curtain,* JAMIE, *seventeen, in a lavish bedroom, somehow smokes a cigarette and does her nails at the same time, while dancing to electrifying pop music. She blows cigarette smoke on her fingernails to dry them, then dances across the room. A completed game of solitaire looms on her computer screen. There is a knocking on the door that gets louder and more insistent until* JAMIE *realizes someone is at the door. She puts out the cigarette, lowers the music, grabs a purse, and answers the door. She sees* CLARK, *early- to mid-twenties.*)

JAMIE: You're late!

CLARK: What?

(*She turns the music off.*)

JAMIE: You're late.

CLARK: Actually, I'm five minutes early. Hi, I'm Clark.

JAMIE: Your *name* is Clark?

CLARK: Is that a problem?

JAMIE: You're not early, you're late. I believe you were supposed to be here at 5:30 and it's 5:55. But let's not argue over details. Have you got everything?

CLARK: I'm supposed to be here at 6:00 and I don't know what you mean by "everything." I've got the books.

JAMIE: Books?

CLARK: Let's start again. You're Jamie. I'm Clark, your SAT tutor.

JAMIE: Oh shit. I totally forgot.

CLARK: You mean you "utterly" forgot.

JAMIE: I thought you were someone else. Utterly. You want a beer?

CLARK: No, thanks. I usually don't "imbibe" on the job.

JAMIE: Right. Wouldn't want to get—er—"inebriated"?

CLARK: Very good!

(JAMIE *rolls her eyes.*)

Did you know, too much beer can be "dehydrating"?

(*She takes out a bottle of Evian.*)

JAMIE: Well, I always have water around.

CLARK: (*Surprised.*) You know "dehydrating"!

JAMIE: It's a rather common word.

CLARK: You got it wrong on your PSAT.

JAMIE: Did I? Funny. (*Pause.*) Wait. How the hell do you know that?

CLARK: Well, for an appointed sum of money, you can request the exact answers and questions of a given student and . . .

JAMIE: And my father bought it.

CLARK: Yes he did.

JAMIE: (*Suddenly curious.*) How much is he paying you?

CLARK: I'm not at liberty to say. So—you know the word "dehydrating," yet you got it wrong on the test. Explain why in fifty words or less.

JAMIE: (*Smiles.*) I was wasted out of my mind during the test. My friend Justine, she was mad about there being a test? So she like rented out the 21 Club the night before. . . . I think that was less than fifty words.

CLARK: It was thirty-three words. Very nice.

JAMIE: You just made that up. You could *not* have counted.

CLARK: (*Rapidly.*) "I was wasted out of my mind during the test." Ten words. "My friend Justine she was mad about there being a test." Eleven words. "So she like rented out the Twenty-one Club the night before." Twelve words, including "like" used incorrectly but we'll throw it in. Ten plus eleven plus twelve last I checked is thirty-three. So no, I didn't make it up.

JAMIE: Where did you learn to do that?

CLARK: Unfortunately, I always knew. So— (*Still grappling with this.*) your friend Justine rented a *room* at the 21 Club?

JAMIE: No. The whole restaurant. After-hours. Private party. So yeah we stayed out late that night.

CLARK: Wow. And you were hungover during the test?

JAMIE: Not sure. No, I think I never went to bed. I think I was still drunk.

CLARK: That's great!

JAMIE: It is?

CLARK: You could raise your score immediately, just by taking the SAT sober.

JAMIE: Maybe.

CLARK: Maybe? Jamie. You didn't know that *this* was one-third!

(*He shows her a pie chart. She laughs.*)

JAMIE: I hate those pie things.

CLARK: They're called pie charts. And they're just circles. Perfect circles, divided into precise, vivid morsels. Each one unique. What is there to hate about them?

JAMIE: (*Mystified.*) How can you care so much about circles?

CLARK: How can you not?

JAMIE: Have you considered getting help for that? What might it mean that you're so into circles?

CLARK: It might mean I like abstract renderings of fractions.

JAMIE: Look, it's nice you appreciate the pie things. Charts. Whatever. But studying is not a good context for me to meet people in. Studying is just not "me." So why don't you leave?

CLARK: *What?*

JAMIE: I'll tell them you came and tutored me. And you can just take the money and run.

CLARK: I can't leave. I have a job to do.

JAMIE: Consider it done.

CLARK: But I want to do it. I care about doing it.

JAMIE: Right. You're here because you care deeply about me.

CLARK: I care "profoundly" about your test score. I hope that we can "augment" it in our sessions together.

JAMIE: "Augment" it? Do you always talk like this?

CLARK: I talk like this with my students.

JAMIE: You know what I think? I think you always talk like this—with your students . . . with your friends, if you have any. I think you couldn't stop if you wanted to. And I think you always count words too. No matter who you're talking to. You can't help it. (*Pause.*) How many was that?

CLARK: Forty-nine.

JAMIE: See what I mean?

CLARK: While you, on the other hand, don't even bother counting when you're supposed to. Your Math PSAT—480. I know you were drunk at the time, but it's still not encouraging.

JAMIE: Math isn't my favorite subject.

CLARK: What do you mean by that?

JAMIE: Is that a trick question? It's boring.

CLARK: Take this problem. Greg and Hilda are grading papers. There are forty students in their class. Eighty-five percent of the students do not receive As. How many receive an A?

(*She pauses, as if about to answer.*)

JAMIE: The question is ridiculous. It's not like it's a situation you're going to run into very often. Who are Greg and Hilda? Especially Hilda. No one today is named Hilda. No one would dare name their child Hilda. And why do two people have to grade papers for only forty students? Schools are understaffed enough as it is. One teacher should be able to handle forty papers. And eighty-five percent of the kids not getting an A? That means like what, fifteen percent As? That's unusual. It's not a lot. Why are they giving so few As? They don't seem like very nice people.

CLARK: Why don't you just tell me the answer?

JAMIE: Twelve.

CLARK: That's not the answer.

JAMIE: It isn't?

CLARK: (*Interested.*) Why do you say twelve?

JAMIE: (*Profoundly.*) Because the answer tends to be twelve. Believe me. If you answer twelve often enough you do pretty well.

CLARK: Do you know how to calculate fifteen percent?

JAMIE: I don't think you appreciate how right I am about the nature of twelve. My friend Bill and I figured it out in the sixth grade, and it has helped us through many a trying time.

CLARK: Well, I'm in linguistics graduate school, and I can promise you the answer is never twelve.

JAMIE: That's your fault for studying linguistics. (*The phone rings.*) Excuse me. Hello? Hi! Yeah, Friday. The Clash Club. Only rule is you have to wear something that clashes. Well of course it can be designed by Jane's mom, just don't tell her. (*To Clark.*) The children of all New York City fashion designers attend Billington. It's very stressful. (*Back to Sheila.*) No one. Family friend. So what I want to know is did you actually get academic credit for baking those cookies? What did you tell Madame Vernelle? *French* cookies? Oh my god from Proust?! Too much. Mmm-hm. All my love. Later. (*Hangs up.*) That was Sheila Martin. A horrible, vindictive, superficial girl, with no spiritual values or social graces, and the biggest moron ever to roam the earth. Sorry. You were saying?

(CLARK *stares at* JAMIE*'s bracelet. He gestures toward it.*)

CLARK: What kind of triangle is that?

(JAMIE *glances at it.*)

JAMIE: What kind of triangle? It's a bracelet.

CLARK: Yes, and . . .

JAMIE: And . . . it's a silver triangle.

CLARK: Is it—equilateral? Scalene?

JAMIE: Looks like sterling silver.

CLARK: It's an isosceles triangle. Do you know why?

JAMIE: Because of its shape.

CLARK: Right! Can you explain that?

JAMIE: I don't need to explain it. I just need to fill in the circle. Right? They don't want explanations.

CLARK: I want explanations.

JAMIE: Um, two sides are the same, the third side is different.

CLARK: Good!

JAMIE: (*Changing the subject.*) I have triangle earrings too, with all the sides different.

CLARK: (*Returning to the subject.*) And your earrings are . . .

JAMIE: They're copper with a cubic zirconium stone?

CLARK: But are they . . . isosceles?

JAMIE: (*Exhausted.*) No.

CLARK: They are . . .

JAMIE: Clip-ons.

CLARK: They're *scalene.* If you see triangles that look like your copper clip-on earrings on the test . . .

JAMIE: I fill in the circle that says scalene.

CLARK: Does any of this seem at all familiar to you?

JAMIE: Sure, I just don't know why anyone would care.

(*A knock on the door.*)

Excuse me. (*Opening the door and addressing someone offstage.*) You're late. You sure it's good? Cool. Right. Later. (*Returning with a wad of bills and a paper bag.*) Sorry.

CLARK: Great. So you're on drugs too.

JAMIE: Are you kidding? I've totally quit. I don't even smoke anymore. Besides cigarettes.

CLARK: So what was that?

JAMIE: I deal a little. I need the money.

CLARK: (*Looking around the palace that is* JAMIE's *room.*) You? Need the money?

JAMIE: My parents won't give me money anymore. Not since this party I gave where I . . . broke this Ming vase thing and they said it would come out of my allowance and I wouldn't see my trust fund till I'm thirty. So I looked at my savings and thought, hey, in not many communities would a few hundred dollars be serious cash flow, but in a high school? I could be the connection girl. I can advance it, then take a little cut.

CLARK: What's a little cut?

JAMIE: Fifteen percent.

CLARK: (*Incredulous.*) We just had a problem with fifteen percent!!

JAMIE: Did we?

CLARK: Okay. Solve this. Guy sells you some weed. He charges you forty dollars. You sell it to the next guy and take your usual cut. How much do you earn?

JAMIE: (*Quickly.*) Six bucks.

CLARK: Yes! And it's not twelve bucks is it? It's six bucks.

JAMIE: Why would it be twelve?

CLARK: You said it's the answer to everything.

JAMIE: On *tests.* Not in business. When you talk about Greg and Hilda I start to zone out. It's not the same as doing a deal.

CLARK: You'd prefer if the questions on the SAT involved illegal transactions?

JAMIE: Oh come on. You know drugs should be legalized. You're a graduate student.

CLARK: Actually, I don't think drugs should be legalized. You should be more careful.

JAMIE: What do you mean? Like, safe sex?

CLARK: I mean scheduling your deal during your tutoring session. It's desperate behavior. It's as if you want to be caught.

JAMIE: No, wanting to be caught is for hardened criminals. This was more a case of being double-booked.

CLARK: Double-booked.

JAMIE: Don't you ever schedule two activities at once? The school play, the weekend class trip to France.

CLARK: You had a "weekend class trip" to France?

JAMIE: I've been plagued by double-booking from the age of eleven. Please don't mention this to my parents. I really thought you would be cool about it. Just from your general . . . coolness?

CLARK: You know I have no general coolness.

JAMIE: Sure you do. Well. You have glimpses. Of coolness.

(CLARK *takes out a copy of* The New York Times.)

What are you doing? *The New York Times* is a conspiracy. I never read it.

CLARK: Do you see any words on page one you don't know?

JAMIE: I see words everywhere I don't know. That's not why I don't read it. It's dirty, it comes off on your hands. (*Beat. Fascinated.*) You really do care about my score. Don't you?

CLARK: Yeah.

JAMIE: Wait! My father's paying you on a sliding scale isn't he? Depending on how well I do. He's paying you more the higher I score. Isn't he? Just tell me that.

CLARK: Jamie, I need to warn you against fixating on the dollar as your only way of interpreting situations and making decisions. It's a mistake I've made, and it ends badly.

JAMIE: So he *is*! He *is* paying you on a sliding scale! And that's why you're doing it. It's okay, I'm just trying to understand.

CLARK: Has it occurred to you I might enjoy tutoring you? Or you might *enjoy* taking the test? Derive pleasure from it?

JAMIE: No. The test means doing something you hate in order to do something you love.

CLARK: What do you love?

JAMIE: *That* is none of your business.

CLARK: But you love something?

JAMIE: Doing something you hate in order to do something you love goes against my loving nature. And I am very loving. Usually. But with stuff I hate, frankly, I'm very *hating*. Even more hating than loving. I warn you.

CLARK: You're warning me.

JAMIE: I admit I'm in no position to warn you, because now that you know I deal drugs, you could blackmail me, you could destroy me.

CLARK: Do you often give people the tools to destroy you?

JAMIE: You must know my ex-boyfriend. Have you ever tutored anyone at Billington before?

CLARK: No. I've never had a private student.

JAMIE: Oh my god! You're not even qualified to teach me!

CLARK: I didn't say that. I said I'd never had a private student.

JAMIE: That's it. I have to discuss this with my parents. (*She presses the intercom button.*) Mom. Mom are you home? Mom can you pick up the intercom? (*Silence. She picks up the phone. Dials.*) Hi is Caroline there please? It's her daughter. Sure. Yes she has my number. Thanks. Bye. (*Hangs up, dials again.*) Hi. It's Jamie. Is my dad there, please? Sure I can hold. (*To* CLARK.) My dad likes to put people on hold. That's like, his thing. Now they're playing the remix of "Message in a Bottle." (*To phone.*) Can he get back to me *tomorrow*? Oh right.

He's still in Singapore. Thanks. (*Hangs up, seeming upset.*) Dammit! He didn't tell me he was going to Singapore. Shit, I hope Mom knows.

CLARK: But you just said . . .

JAMIE: You think I'm going to let some idiot secretary know that I have no idea where my father is?

CLARK: Right.

JAMIE: Okay. My mom's on an international conference call. My dad *is* an international conference call. No one is present to confirm that you're my tutor and not, say, some axe murderer.

CLARK: Your housekeeper had instructions to let me in.

JAMIE: Martita doesn't speak English and isn't so good with instructions. She let in the IRS once. You're not from the IRS are you?

CLARK: I'm from the SAT.

JAMIE: Do you have some ID?

(*He takes out a driver's license.* JAMIE *scrutinizes it.*)

Nice license. You photograph well. You have a car?

CLARK: Yes. No.

JAMIE: Which is it? You have a car or not?

CLARK: Did have a car. Sold it.

JAMIE: Why?

CLARK: Long story.

JAMIE: How did my dad find you?

CLARK: Longer story.

JAMIE: What qualifies you to tutor me?

CLARK: I used to work at Kaplan.

JAMIE: You worked at Stanley Kaplan?

CLARK: Yeah, I taught a special class for a few kids who were already scoring 1300 or above.

JAMIE: And what happened?

CLARK: Their scores went up.

JAMIE: Up from 1300? How high?

CLARK: I thought you didn't care about the SAT.

JAMIE: I don't. I'm just curious. I mean, I should know if my tutor is qualified.

CLARK: They all got perfect scores.

JAMIE: Perfect?

CLARK: Sixteen hundreds. Each one of them.

JAMIE: Are you making this up?

CLARK: No.

JAMIE: Wow. So you must have a lot of private students now.

CLARK: No.

JAMIE: How many?

CLARK: Just you.

JAMIE: You must have had a lot of offers.

CLARK: Uh-huh.

JAMIE: Why did you take this one?

CLARK: It seemed . . . like the biggest challenge.

JAMIE: You're saying I'm stupid.

CLARK: No—

JAMIE: Because there are a lot of people who are stupid. And I happen not to be one of them. Screwing up and being stupid are not the same thing.

CLARK: That's nice that you take pride in screwing up.

JAMIE: (*Intensely.*) My screwups are beholden to no one. They're completely mine. You could teach me algebra, geometry, hell, you could probably explain trig. But then I could still refuse to put the right answers on the thing. And *that* would be mine.

CLARK: Oh god. No, it wouldn't, Jamie! Your screwup would be my screwup. Because I'm your tutor. I'm there with you in the test.

JAMIE: You're coming with me to take the test?

CLARK: No, I'll be there in spirit. I'll be thinking of you.

JAMIE: Yeah right. Why would you care?

CLARK: Is this your attitude in school too? Or is it me?

JAMIE: Hmm. I can't think of a single example of anyone who has ever cared about me, one-on-one, in a classroom, or in my extended family. So why you, who are being paid to teach me about absurd little triangles and vivid morsels of pie and ridiculously long words that no one ever uses in conversation, would suddenly care, I can't imagine.

CLARK: Oh man. That's sad.

JAMIE: Fuck you it is not.

(*An awkward pause.*)

CLARK: (*Slowly.*) How about we do . . .

JAMIE: (*Assuming he's being sexual.*) What? How about we do what?

CLARK: A reading comprehension question. How about we do a reading comprehension question. Here. (CLARK *shows* JAMIE *a page. As she looks, she starts humming a song.*) Try not to hum while you read. (*She stops humming but is still moving to the music.*) And look for the important words. . . . A word is important if it catches your eye. If it means more than one thing. Or if it stops you.

JAMIE: This whole sentence stops me.

CLARK: Read it to yourself three times.

JAMIE: (*Sarcastic.*) Oh that will help. "Dysfunction begets dysfunction." "Dysfunction begets dysfunction." "Dysfunction begets dysfunction." (*Surprised.*) Huh. It almost makes sense.

CLARK: What does it mean?

JAMIE: Um. It means if your family is screwed up now, they'll always be screwed up?

CLARK: Good.

JAMIE: I don't like this passage.

CLARK: Okay. But notice how the repetition helps you make sense of it. Now. The two people in the passage—do you think they could become friends?

JAMIE: That's not one of the questions!

CLARK: I'm changing the questions. See, I want you to read every word. Love each word. And remember: If a word catches your eye, if it can mean more than one thing, if it stops you—read it to yourself three times.

JAMIE: Be careful with what you tell me to do. I'll read it to myself three times. But I will *never* love each word.

CLARK: Do you think they could become friends?

JAMIE: Definitely not.

(*Lights down.*)

Scene 2

(*Six weeks later. January. It is* JAMIE *and* CLARK's *fourth tutoring session.* JAMIE *is in bed, sleeping in the clothes she wore the night before: shirt, miniskirt, back-seamed pantyhose, one black pump; the other shoe is on the floor.* CLARK *knocks on the door several times.*)

JAMIE: Come in!

(CLARK *enters.* JAMIE *rolls over in bed.*)

Hello?

CLARK: Jamie? You okay?

JAMIE: Schmangover.

CLARK: We have a tutoring session today.

JAMIE: I have a hangover today. (*Looks up at him, playful.*) I promised to study. I didn't promise not to go out the night before. Clark. It's *Saturday*. (*She pulls the covers over her head.*)

CLARK: Jamie you're going to have to get out of bed.

(*The bed shakes its head "no."*)

I'll be right back.

(*He exits.* JAMIE *rolls over, tosses and turns. He returns with a hangover concoction.*)

Here. Drink this.

(*She does. It perks her right up.*)

JAMIE: What did you put in that?

CLARK: Secret recipe. I'll tell you if you do really well on your SAT.

JAMIE: Who taught you to make it?

CLARK: Margaret.

JAMIE: Who's Margaret?

CLARK: She was my SAT tutor.

JAMIE: No, seriously.

CLARK: Girl I used to go out with.

JAMIE: Was she hungover?

CLARK: She was an alcoholic. Now get out of bed and tell me you've learned the area of a circle like you promised.

JAMIE: That must've been hard. Did you date her a long time?

CLARK: The area of a circle, Jamie.

JAMIE: Was she pretty?

CLARK: She was beautiful. Probably still is. Area of a circle.

(JAMIE *rolls her eyes.*)

JAMIE: Um. Pi. Wait. Yes. Pi–R–squared.

CLARK: Very good! We dated two years. I made her go to AA. She met another guy there and married him.

JAMIE: Very good! I mean. Wow. Did you sleep with her again after you found out?

CLARK: Area of a triangle.

JAMIE: Base times height over two.

CLARK: Good for you! I didn't sleep with her again.

JAMIE: Good for you! Are you drinking hangover juice too?

CLARK: No. Plain orange juice.

JAMIE: Did Martita make you breakfast again? She likes to make breakfast. What are those?

CLARK: Grape Nuts. You want some?

JAMIE: You're always snacking when you're here.

CLARK: I've told you, I'm a starving graduate student.

JAMIE: Yeah, but my dad must be paying you a lot. At least enough for breakfast.

CLARK: He's not.

JAMIE: Do you want me to talk to him?

CLARK: No. Don't. (*Beat.*) Don't.

JAMIE: I want to talk to him. Or, maybe my mom's still home and I could ask her right now! (JAMIE *runs to the intercom and presses the button.*) Mom? Mom, can you hear the intercom? Mom if you're there, will you pick up the intercom? (*To* CLARK.) I know it probably looks bad, how I try to talk to my mom on the intercom and she never picks up, but she used to be more into it. I swear. She used to love talking to me on the intercom.

CLARK: I believe you. I just think she's not home.

JAMIE: Yeah.

CLARK: They're not home much, are they?

JAMIE: Don't pity me.

CLARK: I'm not pitying. I'm empathizing.

JAMIE: I don't want your sympathy.

CLARK: Empathy isn't the same as sympathy. Empathy implies a personal identification . . .

JAMIE: Stop teaching me words!

CLARK: I'm not. I'm saying, I know what you're going through.

JAMIE: Right. So . . . what, your parents neglected you?

CLARK: Mine were worse than most. What's staggering is that yours are worse than mine.

JAMIE: Oh, so you're pathetic, and I'm more pathetic?

CLARK: No. I'm just—surprised. I was expecting to see your father around here—

JAMIE: What made you think that?

CLARK: He seemed so concerned about you. . . . I guess I was expecting a nice Upper East Side apartment, nice Upper East Side family. Something a little more close-knit.

JAMIE: We're close-knit! My mom even gave me her new cell phone number. *That's* where I'll call her! I'm going to call her right now and ask her what she's paying you. (JAMIE *picks up the phone and starts dialing.*)

CLARK: Stop.

(*She hangs up.*)

Your mom's not paying me anything.

JAMIE: Oh my god are you her lover?

CLARK: Of course not.

JAMIE: Good. (*Gasps.*) Are you my father's lover?

CLARK: No.

JAMIE: Then what's going on? Stop being so . . . so . . .

CLARK: What? Give me a word for it!

(JAMIE *comes up with the word, triumphant.*)

JAMIE: (*Enunciating with pleasure.*) "Ee-lip-ti-cal"! You—are being—"elliptical"! Just tell me. We're in this together. Like two variables in an equation.

CLARK: Don't push it.

JAMIE: We're like—an arc and a tangent.

CLARK: You may be like a tangent. Speak for yourself.

JAMIE: Are you kidding? You are so the tangent. Clark. Include me. On what scale is he paying you that you don't have food but you've given up all your other students?

CLARK: There is nothing you can do that would make me tell you that.

JAMIE: Oh yeah? I can get you fired so fast it would make your head spin.

CLARK: I signed a very long contract describing my dedication to this job. I can't quit, and you can't fire me.

JAMIE: (*Sensual.*) Contracts can be declared "null" and "void." (JAMIE *slowly unbuttons the top button of her shirt.*)

CLARK: What are you doing?

JAMIE: Unbuttoning. (*She unbuttons the second button.*)

CLARK: Jamie stop that. Put that button back where it was.

JAMIE: No. (*She unbuttons the third button.*)

CLARK: Lord Jesus.

JAMIE: Are you going to tell me or not?

CLARK: Not. I'm going to not. Jamie. Stop unbuttoning. As the head of this class, I officially order you to stop unbuttoning.

JAMIE: Except there's no class. Just you and me babe. (*She finishes unbuttoning, revealing a bra, and throws her shirt at* CLARK. *He brings it back.*)

CLARK: For god's sake put this back on.

(*She throws the shirt back at him.*)

JAMIE: Actually, I think I'll just go into the kitchen and chat with Martita.

CLARK: You wouldn't! It's not your nature. You're a manipulator, but you're not a liar.

JAMIE: I prefer "manipulatrix."

CLARK: You wouldn't tell her I took your shirt off.

JAMIE: I wouldn't have to. She may not speak English, but she understands flesh. That's the beauty of it. I don't have to lie. I just have to walk into the kitchen in my undergarments while you're here. My housekeeper will have to conclude either that we're having a lurid affair or that I'm a closet exhibitionist.

CLARK: You're an *overt* exhibitionist!

(JAMIE *turns the door handle.*)

Stop!

(*She starts to open the door.*)

You wouldn't. You would not. I'm a good judge of character. And *you* would *not*.

JAMIE: You seem like you might be right, but there's a little percent chance that you're wrong. And then what? (*Beat. Playful.*) What do I have to lose, Clark? *Tutoring.*

CLARK: My respect. My approval.

JAMIE: Your respect. Your approval. Your *tutoring.*

CLARK: (*Taking charge.*) Shut the door.

(JAMIE *does.*)

Put your shirt back on.

(*As she puts it on, but does not button it:*)

You're right about that little percent chance. The slimmest chance is the one that can get you into trouble.

JAMIE: You in trouble?

CLARK: I want you to button it.

JAMIE: I want you to tell me.

CLARK: (*Beat.*) Your mother hasn't paid me anything. Neither has your father. At this moment they are paying me: Nothing.

(*She buttons the bottom button.*)

JAMIE: So you're like indentured! They're starving you so you'll be forced to teach me. It's like Russia under Stalin. No, under the czar. Where the tutor is always the poorest person, exchanging wisdom for scraps of bread.

CLARK: (*Eyeing the buttons.*) They're paying me nothing, unless . . .

JAMIE: Unless what?

(*He nods toward the shirt. She buttons another button.*)

CLARK: One more button, please.

(*She touches the third button, but doesn't button it.*)

JAMIE: Unless what?

CLARK: Now.

JAMIE: Unless. What?

(*He nods at the button. She buttons it. A beat.*)

CLARK: Unless: You get a perfect score.

(*She lets go of the shirt, which has only three buttons fastened, so her bra is still visible.*)

JAMIE: A perfect score?? Like, 1600?

CLARK: (*A little beleaguered.*) Could you please button the rest of your shirt?

JAMIE: And what do you get if I get a perfect score?

CLARK: I'll tell you if you button it all the way.

JAMIE: Tell me now.

CLARK: All the way.

(*She buttons the fourth button.*)

JAMIE: Okay. How much?

CLARK: I said all the way.

JAMIE: No one buttons the top one. That's a fashion mistake.

CLARK: I don't care what anyone else does. I want your shirt completely fastened to your body.

(*Slowly, she buttons the top button. He smiles.*)

That doesn't look half bad. You could start a trend.

JAMIE: How much?

CLARK: Did you learn the quadratic formula?

JAMIE: I learned it.

CLARK: Tell me the quadratic formula.

JAMIE: Tell me the size of your bonus. Your perfect score bonus.

CLARK: You first.

JAMIE: X is equal to minus B plus or minus the square root of B squared minus four AC all over 2A.

(CLARK *nods, amazed.* JAMIE *indicates her shirt.*)

I look like a dork.

CLARK: Yes, but a dork who knows the quadratic formula.

JAMIE: Yeah, maybe there's a connection! Miles Gardner buttons his shirts like this and he sure knows the quadratic formula. Come on, Clark. You promised.

CLARK: If you get a perfect score, all of my graduate school tuition and debts will be paid. Plus a hundred grand in cash.

(JAMIE *whistles.*)

JAMIE: You have like a six-figure deal for tutoring me!

CLARK: It all adds up. To about a quarter million.

(JAMIE *takes this in. Then:*)

JAMIE: I don't get it! If my dad wants me to get into a good college so badly, why doesn't he just take the money and donate it to Princeton?

CLARK: I asked him that. He doesn't want you to get in that way. He wants you to get in because you're perfect.

JAMIE: We established earlier I'm not perfect.

CLARK: He doesn't believe in institutional giving because the donor can't control where the university spends the money. He would rather give to a person in need, or a deserving individual.

JAMIE: I'm a deserving individual! He never gives me anything!

CLARK: Deserving in the sense of hardworking. Your father's a venture capitalist. A professional risk-taker. He can afford to pay me. He'd even be happy to pay all that money if you got a perfect score. But there is a distinct chance he won't have to pay me anything. And you'll still do quite well. He knows that, and I know it.

JAMIE: A distinct chance, huh? You both think I'm a loser.

CLARK: Fewer than one percent of kids who take the test get a perfect score.

JAMIE: Yeah but your whole class from Stanley Kaplan did.

CLARK: That was last year. This year, they're changing the format, adding questions that aren't multiple choice. And they're changing the curve. Recentering it. Under the new system, most scores will go up. But there will be fewer perfect scores. So with the new test, and the new curve, the odds are . . .

JAMIE: (*Shocked.*) The *odds*? You and my dad are gambling! Over how well I do!

CLARK: No, this isn't really gambling. This . . .

JAMIE: Sure it is. He not only thinks I'll probably fail, he's put money on it. My own father is betting against me.

CLARK: (*Softly.*) He's not betting against you. He's hoping for a miracle . . . and then . . . hedging.

JAMIE: A miracle?

CLARK: A very unlikely probability. One-twentieth of one percent get a perfect score. Do you know how small that is? He's hedging against that. It's . . . portfolio diversification. A lot of Wall Street guys think that way.

JAMIE: But it's not human. It turns me into a probability. It forgets about me.

CLARK: It's nothing against you. Believe me. It's just—a way of thinking about what's likely.

JAMIE: How can you talk this through so calmly when you have just been added to the legion of people who lie to me, conspire against me, and worship the dollar.

CLARK: I don't worship the dollar. I need it.

JAMIE: How desperate are you for the money?

CLARK: I didn't say I was desperate.

JAMIE: Maybe you are. You should've just taught your class again. I could flake on you. And then you'd be nowhere.

CLARK: I hate to see you being so self-destructive.

JAMIE: And why is that? Because you feel so close to me? I have one question: Do you ever get this close to your poor students who don't have parents with whom you can make Faustian bargains?

CLARK: Give me a break. I've only worked at private SAT schools, I've never *had* a poor student.

JAMIE: *That's* comforting. You don't even mix with the lower class!

CLARK: I *am* the lower class!—And it worries me that you can make jokes about Faustian bargains and class warfare and operate a small illegal business out of your room and yet you are baffled by the simplest of logic problems on the test.

JAMIE: It wasn't a joke. You made a Faustian bargain.

CLARK: Faust was a doctor and an alchemist. He made a bargain with the *devil* . . .

JAMIE: (*As if this is obvious.*) My dad!

CLARK: He was trying to acquire supernatural knowledge.

JAMIE: And you are trying to get a Ph.D. in linguistics!

CLARK: Jamie, where do you come up with these things?

JAMIE: I'm creative. That's why I don't test well.

CLARK: And how do you know about Faust?

JAMIE: We did the play in fourth grade. I was Gluttony.

CLARK: So what's the end result of your analogy? Ultimately, we wind up in hell?

JAMIE: *Princeton!*

CLARK: You're very adept at analogies when you're not taking practice tests.

JAMIE: I've told you, I don't test well.

CLARK: That's just a false belief that you need to let go of. You believe you don't test well, so you panic and you crack under pressure. It's not just you. Your whole school's under pressure. The whole city is. Last year, one of my students fed his baby sister one of the practice tests. Put it in her applesauce. He thought he would get rid of the test and the sister at the same time.

JAMIE: What was he doing with a baby sister? Second marriage?

CLARK: Same marriage. Accident.

JAMIE: What happened to your student?

CLARK: Stanford.

JAMIE: So, like, even your weirdest ones end up at really good schools.

CLARK: The weirder, the better. There's hope for you!

JAMIE: But what if people point at me in the hallway? "There goes Jamie, the girl who's so dumb her parents bought her a million-dollar tutor."

CLARK: You're not dumb. It's not a million. And no one knows you have a tutor.

JAMIE: My friend Katya knows. But she has one too. Hers is two hundred bucks an hour. Same as her shrink. . . . So. You really want to tutor me after this whole "brouhaha"?

CLARK: Hey, nice use of "brouhaha." Of course I want to tutor you.

JAMIE: But you have incentive. The pure driving force of financial incentive. (*Pause. Then it occurs to her:*) Hey. How about you give me a cut? We could make an arrangement . . .

CLARK: An "arrangement" . . . ? This is unbelievable!

JAMIE: I don't see how it's any more unbelievable than your original arrangement. Which was *unbelievable.*

CLARK: My original arrangement was money for *teaching*, a profession that customarily generates an income! Your arrangement would be money for *studying*, an ancient art that usually doesn't bring in a competitive salary.

JAMIE: This wouldn't be money for studying. I wouldn't get it just for studying. It would be money for doing really well on the test. Like prize money. You believe in prize money, right?

CLARK: (*Deadpan.*) All Americans believe in prize money.

JAMIE: Clark, the cash would just help push me along. My parents have so much and they don't give me any of it. Ever since—

CLARK: Ever since you broke the Ming vase thing.

JAMIE: Is it my fault that I live in this place where everything is fragile and worth a gazillion dollars? How was I supposed to know what to hide before the party?

CLARK: I don't know. You could have started with things a hundred years old and worked your way back.

JAMIE: What am I, a curator?

CLARK: Don't you think you should take responsibility for what happened?

JAMIE: Sure. But for how many years? There's no justice here. No correlation between the crime and the punishment. My parents . . . leave me alone for weeks at a time and then they expect to come back and find not a single thing broken.

CLARK: So you broke the vase to get their attention?

JAMIE: That is such a loser interpretation, I wouldn't expect it of the school shrink! Believe me, their attention is not that exciting.

CLARK: So you just broke it because it was there.

JAMIE: Excuse me?

CLARK: At least if you had broken it to get their attention, it might have been a cry for help. But you don't even want help. You broke it out of carelessness.

JAMIE: You don't know what you're talking about.

CLARK: I knew people who went to Billington when I was in school. It was a different time. The people were different. But they all have one thing in common. An absolutely infuriating sense of entitlement. You're only, what, seventeen, but you've got it already.

JAMIE: I do not.

CLARK: Sure you do. You assume you'll always be surrounded by privilege, so what's one Ming vase more or less? You can see one in the Metropolitan Museum, you can knock one off the coffee table, there'll be others.

JAMIE: That's not true.

CLARK: You don't have to be careful, you don't have to work hard, right? It's not even cool to work hard, is it? It's only cool to have things come to you, be handed to you. Right?

JAMIE: You are talking about some friends of yours who graduated from Billington when it was—as you have mentioned—totally different. You're not talking about me at all.

CLARK: I'm talking about entitlement. Entitlement is the reason you want me to give you part of my salary. You feel you deserve it. It's the reason you don't study. You feel it's beneath you. And it's the reason you just carelessly, without thinking about any of the things or people involved, broke a 400-year-old vase.

(JAMIE *falls dead quiet. Then she bursts out, almost crying.*)

JAMIE: It wasn't me who broke the vase! Okay? I didn't do it!

CLARK: But you said—

JAMIE: What I *said* doesn't matter. I didn't break the vase. Someone else broke it and I took the blame. So please stop trying to fit me into your little theory of entitlement. Because I do *not* go smashing up precious antiques; that is not my idea of a fun time. I have never broken anything in my life.

CLARK: Then why did you say . . . ?

JAMIE: Just drop it, all right?

CLARK: Couldn't you just tell your parents who broke it?

JAMIE: You know, for a genius you can be pretty dense.

CLARK: I was just wondering, who could've—

JAMIE: It was my boyfriend! Roger Auerbach. And I knew if I told them that he broke it they would make it a rule for me not to see him and it would be really tricky to violate that because they are like really good friends with the Auerbachs. And I thought I loved him. So I told them I broke it. That's when they came up with the unique punishment of no allowance for thirteen years.

CLARK: And was Roger grateful?

JAMIE: No, he left me the following week for Sheila Martin. The nonentity who called the other day. The new girl in school. At this point everyone has been at Billington since nursery school and we usually don't take new people after seventh grade? So to have a new girl junior year is like a revelation. All of the men just melted. Also, she's richer than Donald Trump, and she buys him presents, which of course I had to stop doing when my funding was cut off. I have to discuss every potential purchase I make with my mother. So this cramps my style a little bit.

CLARK: Your style doesn't seem that—cramped. You still manage to get to the right clubs and parties.

JAMIE: Yeah, and if it weren't for the dealing I do? I wouldn't be able to afford the cabs. I'd be in dangerous neighborhoods. Alone. Dependent on the charity of insane adolescent men. The business itself is pretty dangerous. No one used to care, but now the mayor is cracking down on small-timers. We're living in a fascist state.

CLARK: So you'd like to give up dealing?

JAMIE: Would I like to retire? Absolutely. Not just that. I would be a new person.

CLARK: How so?

JAMIE: If you gave me this chance, I would be so dedicated to the SAT, it would blow your mind. I mean, I've been paying basic attention, but it would be more. Like the way I'm dedicated to My Life now? I would be dedicated to The Test.

CLARK: Are you saying you would study?

JAMIE: More than that. I would develop *study habits*! I wouldn't stay out all night. And I would be able to afford the basics of growing up in New York. Which I can't now. Just the pressure to buy the right brand of sneaker is beyond description. Last month if you didn't have Top-Siders you were nowhere. This month it's Reebok and only Reebok.

CLARK: So the money could help with these crucial sneaker purchases.

JAMIE: Not just sneakers. My whole existence. The chaos of this household. My parents . . . like me better when I don't have money. Then they can relate to me by giving me money. But with a cut, I'd be able to handle it all. I just need a little freedom. A little spending money.

CLARK: And how much is "a little spending money"?

JAMIE: (*Hesitates.*) Just my usual cut.

CLARK: Fifteen percent.

JAMIE: Yeah. Fifteen thousand. I wouldn't want your tuition money, I understand that's . . . specifically for your schooling. So you'd still have that, plus eighty-five thousand. Clark, they've cut me off. I know it's hard to believe but I'm like you. I need it.

CLARK: No, Jamie. *I* need it. I have serious bills to pay. You don't need it. You want it.

JAMIE: Okay. I want it. And in a small emotional way you don't understand because you're from somewhere else, I need it.

(CLARK *sees that she means it. He considers what she is saying and takes it seriously. Then:*)

CLARK: No. I'm supposed to be your *tutor*! You're not supposed to be manipulating me.

JAMIE: Think of it like a problem on the test. Clark and Jamie start a business. Clark earns $100,000 plus perks. He wants Jamie to do a good job. Should he pay her: A) $100,000, B) $15,000, C) Five cents, or D) None of the above?

CLARK: I give up.

JAMIE: B! Fifteen thousand. A's too big, C's too little, and "None of the above" is always a boring, and wrong, answer.

CLARK: "None of the above" is sometimes the answer.

JAMIE: Not in this case. Doing "None of the above" is no way to run a business.

CLARK: This is not a *business*! It's a *tutorial*!

JAMIE: (*Excited.*) But it could be like a business! We already have meetings, and agendas. . . . Now all we need is profit-sharing!

CLARK: How about you give me an analogy. A persuasive analogy.

JAMIE: Okay. Though they don't make you write analogies on the SAT, just recognize them. This is like extra credit.

CLARK: Fifteen thousand dollars is also like extra credit.

JAMIE: Um . . . Tutorial is to Profit-sharing as Tutor is to Genius!

CLARK: How?

JAMIE: Well, it's *rare* to find profit-sharing in a tutorial, just as it's rare to find genius in a tutor. But when you do—wow.

CLARK: Flattery will get you nowhere. But that was actually a very strong analogy. And I like how hard you work when you want something. How about . . . (*Beat.*) I give you twelve.

JAMIE: Twelve thousand? Why?

CLARK: You told me yourself the answer tends to be twelve.

JAMIE: Okay! (*She goes to her desk and gets a pen and notebook.*) Now we just need a contract!

CLARK: Do you know how much trouble we would get into for that?

JAMIE: You have a contract with my father. . . . Without a written agreement, how can I trust you to stay and tutor me? What if you decide tomorrow you'd rather tutor Sheila Martin?

CLARK: I won't.

JAMIE: Her parents could offer you a million dollars for a perfect score. Then where would I be? Nowhere. Of course you'd be nowhere too because she is dumber than a doorbell. She's one of the dumbest people ever to buy her way into the Billington School. You couldn't get her score to go up ten points.

CLARK: Why would I want to tutor her if she's really a . . . doorbell?

JAMIE: What was the word you used with me? The . . . "Challenge." You want challenge? Forget about me. *Sheila Martin.*

CLARK: If I gave you a contract, would you agree to stop dealing drugs while you study for the test?

JAMIE: This means giving up a steady income.

CLARK: I gave up mine.

JAMIE: (*Curious.*) What are these debts of yours anyway?

CLARK: Answer my question.

JAMIE: Yes.

CLARK: Good. I'll draw up the contract. (*Starts writing the contract.*) "I promise to be a perfect student . . ."

JAMIE: You gonna define perfect?

CLARK: Define it?

JAMIE: As a term.

CLARK: Since when are you an expert on contracts?

JAMIE: My mom's a lawyer.

CLARK: Don't show her this. (CLARK *scribbles, adding more details to the contract, as* JAMIE *watches.*)

JAMIE: You are writing every tiny thing down! You are so *aggravating.*

CLARK: Irritating.

JAMIE: What?

CLARK: I'm irritating. Not aggravating. Aggravate means to make worse. I thought you knew the As already. (*Signs the contract and hands it to her.*) Sign here.

(*She signs. They shake hands. Lights down.*)

Scene 3

(*The following week.* JAMIE *is jogging in place and reading her SAT book. A knock at the door.* JAMIE *bounds across the room and swings the door open. She hugs* CLARK.)

CLARK: Jamie? You okay?

JAMIE: I'm more than okay! I'm rapturous! That means wildly ecstatic. Over the weekend, I quit dealing. I mean, I "desisted" "trafficking" in "narcotics." Paul was upset. Paul "chastised" me. (*Sexy.*) He "blandished" me!—But *Arthur* asked me out! *Arthur* is—*pulchritudinous*!

CLARK: Pulchritudinous means beautiful.

JAMIE: I know! He said he never asked me out before because he doesn't like girls who sell drugs, and I said *he* sold drugs and he said he did it for the money, and I said I had done it for the money too and he laughed and laughed.

CLARK: He laughed at you?

JAMIE: That's the one thing about Arthur. He doesn't understand people who live on Fifth Avenue, and how we actually can be broke on a lot of levels? But I told him about his pulchritude and he was psyched. He loves it when girls use big words. Even when he doesn't know what they mean.

CLARK: Ah! And then when you realized that this beautiful guy likes girls who use big words you started learning them!

JAMIE: Are you kidding? I wouldn't learn words for some guy!

CLARK: Oh right. We've established that.

JAMIE: I did it for me. I memorized the whole book. This weekend.

CLARK: That's impossible.

JAMIE: I *did*! Ask me anything.

CLARK: Okay. (*Curious.*) What happened with Arthur?

JAMIE: I meant ask me anything from the vocab guide.

CLARK: I know what you meant.

JAMIE: He kissed me.

CLARK: Just all of a sudden?

JAMIE: We were talking on the terrace by this little potted spider plant. And he knocked over the plant—he is such a klutz I love that in a man—and there were ferns with bits of dirt spilling out on the flagstone and the air was all of a sudden warm . . . and our housekeeper mysteriously vanished just as the sun was lowering itself into Central Park and the sky was changing moods and turning colors and Arthur was kissing me.

CLARK: You really like this guy.

JAMIE: It's odd. I don't usually kiss men in my grade. I usually date men twice my age. I usually date men twice *your* age.

CLARK: You do?

JAMIE: Sure. Normally, you would be way too young for me. It's not about age, it's about emotional maturity.

CLARK: What happened then? After he kissed you?

JAMIE: Get your mind out of the gutter! Nothing. I told him to get lost so I could study vocab and he looked at me like that was the hottest thing! I think the vocab-sunset-kiss combo went to his head. Then I studied all weekend.

CLARK: (*Skeptical.*) You did?

JAMIE: You don't believe me? Ask me a word. Any word.

CLARK: All right. Mendacious.

JAMIE: Telling lies.

CLARK: Unctuous.

JAMIE: Smug or moralistically oily. Obsequious in a slimy way. You know who's totally unctuous? Peter Fratton. He sucks up to all the teachers at Billington, saying he loves their assignments—but then he copies Miles Gardner's home-work.

CLARK: I know the type.

JAMIE: What were you like in high school?

CLARK: (*Scanning the book for the next word.*) Maudlin.

JAMIE: Really?

CLARK: Define maudlin.

JAMIE: Oh. Adjective. Sentimentally depressed. Or exhausted from drinking too much. "Sheila Martin gets so maudlin at after-parties." After-parties! Plural noun. Festivities held in unmarked lofts after the regular parties are over.

CLARK: (*Trying to stump her.*) Temerarious.

JAMIE: Um. No one ever uses that word. I'll remember in a second. Wait.

CLARK: So you didn't memorize the whole book . . .

JAMIE: Will you calm your cookies! Give me a moment, I am concentrating! (*Remembers and takes a flying leap onto the bed.*) Temerarious: reckless or rash. "The after-party was full of temerarious freshmen."

CLARK: (*Stunned.*) You really learned the book.

(JAMIE *jumps up on the bed.*)

JAMIE: I did—and now— (*She falls on the bed sideways and lies still.*) I may need a nap—

CLARK: (*Realizing.*) Jamie. Did you not sleep this weekend?

JAMIE: You said you didn't want me to sell pot. You didn't say I couldn't take uppers.

CLARK: (*Horrified.*) Are you on speed?

JAMIE: Of course not. (*Bolts up in bed, suddenly manic again.*) Did you know there is speed in Dexedrine? Rocky Gerstein once mashed a Dexedrine into Miles Gardner's lunch and Miles got so high he started reciting his chemistry notes in pig latin.

CLARK: What are you on?

JAMIE: NoDoz.

CLARK: NoDoz?

JAMIE: (*Points to the bottle.*) Caffeine pills. You're in graduate school and you've never heard of NoDoz? I thought everyone in higher education took NoDoz. Like No-Doze. Get it?

CLARK: (*Looks at the bottle.*) Do you know how much caffeine is in one of these pills?

JAMIE: A bunch?

CLARK: There's 200 milligrams of caffeine in just one of these pills. If you take just three of them, they can be *addictive*. Do you know what addictive means?

JAMIE: In the book, addictive means "tending to cause a psychological need for a habit-forming substance."

CLARK: No, that's not what addictive means! It means you forget what you care about. It means . . . (*Deep.*) What it *means* is not in a book.

JAMIE: Clark. They're not drugs. They're OTC. Over the fuckin' counter. They're like, sleeping pills except they're for waking. I'm not an addict. I took like, twelve of them.

CLARK: Twelve?

JAMIE: Approximately. Who's counting?

CLARK: Me. I'm counting. (*He pours the pills out and counts instantly.*) Thirty-six in the bottle, twenty-one left. You took fifteen. So over three days, you ingested . . . 3,000 milligrams of caffeine. That's like having thirty-five cups of coffee!

JAMIE: So? Don't you know anyone who drinks ten cups a day?

CLARK: No! (*He runs into the bathroom and flushes the rest of the pills down the toilet.*)

JAMIE: What are you doing?

CLARK: An intervention.

JAMIE: I bought those pills out of my clothing budget . . .

CLARK: My heart bleeds for you.

JAMIE: You don't have to be so mean.

CLARK: But I do. Because you have an addictive personality. I see how you party when you feel like partying. I see how you study when you feel like studying. You don't let up.

JAMIE: I let up.

CLARK: You get wired. I bet that's why you stopped doing drugs and started selling them, right? You know once you start something you can't stop.

JAMIE: I can stop.

CLARK: Then you shouldn't mind that I threw the pills out. Best way to quit is to go cold turkey.

JAMIE: Cold turkey?? What did this alcoholic do to you anyway? It's like you're obsessed!

CLARK: Do to me?

JAMIE: Yes. Your alcoholic girlfriend—what did she do to you? They can do things. I know, I dated one myself in the sixth grade.

CLARK: In the sixth grade?

JAMIE: He used to steal my mom's jewelry. And Charlene dated an alcoholic sophomore year. He made her pregnant and she went on *Nightline* in their segment "Girls from Rich Private Schools Get Knocked Up and Have Abortions" but they made her face all blurry so you couldn't tell it was Charlene and her hair looked like electric worms.

CLARK: Is there anything that doesn't happen at that school of yours?

JAMIE: Sure. Love. Warmth. Decency. Traditional values. So what did Margaret do to you? Borrow money? You can tell me. Roger borrowed money from me and never paid me back and he didn't even have a drinking problem. Where did you meet her anyway?

CLARK: Why, where did you meet Roger?

JAMIE: We met in fifth grade in our Early Church History class. Also known as Popes for Dopes. Where did you meet Margaret?

CLARK: Not in Popes for Dopes. It was more like just plain dopes. They teach you Early Church History in grade school?

JAMIE: It was an elective. We had a choice between that, Chinese calligraphy, and medieval Armenian architecture. (*Beat. Then, suddenly realizing:*) You know who gets wired?

CLARK: I just told you. You do.

JAMIE: Not. (*Putting it together.*) The one who gets wired—is you. (*She is triumphant in her discovery, but still struggling with the clouding aftereffects of the pills.*) I've seen you. (*Figuring it out, in sudden lucid flashes.*) You're . . . wired on—numbers. Like my—parents. Oh my head.

CLARK: You're falling apart. Why don't you try to get some sleep before our next session? You can't just study day and night.

JAMIE: (*Crawling into bed.*) I thought the point was to study day and night! Thomas Edison did. He said that whole thing about sweating.

CLARK: Edison said, "Genius is one percent inspiration and ninety-nine percent perspiration." He didn't say sweating. And he didn't say you shouldn't sleep.

JAMIE: But I learned so many words.

CLARK: Yes. Short-term memory is a remarkable human talent.

JAMIE: Are you saying I won't remember them later?

CLARK: I don't know. I hope you do.

(*He starts to leave. She closes her eyes and sinks into a blissful rest.*)

JAMIE: Clark?

CLARK: Yes?

JAMIE: I'm asleep.

CLARK: Yes.

(*He starts to leave again.*)

JAMIE: Clark?

CLARK: What?

JAMIE: You know I just took those pills because I thought I needed to. To be better.

CLARK: (*Looking at her with compassion.*) I know.

(*He starts to leave again.*)

JAMIE: Clark?

CLARK: Jamie?

JAMIE: I learned a lot of words. And now I'm asleep.

CLARK: (*Moved.*) Yes you did. Yes you are.

(*Beat.*)

JAMIE: Clark.

(JAMIE *looks at* CLARK *and then closes her eyes.*)

CLARK: Jamie. (*He leaves.* JAMIE *falls into a deep sleep. Lights down.*)

ACT 2

Scene 1

(*The next day,* CLARK *is scanning the vocabulary book, testing* JAMIE.)

CLARK: All right, how about . . . mendacious. Define mendacious.

JAMIE: Damn I knew this yesterday. Don't you dare say I told you so!

CLARK: Did I . . . say anything? I asked you a word. You just don't remember it because you're not wired on caffeine today.

JAMIE: (*Curious.*) What do you get wired on?

CLARK: Girls who do their homework.

JAMIE: Oh, right.

(*She gives him her homework. He checks it quickly.*)

CLARK: How did you get twelve here? And don't tell me that the answer is always twelve.

JAMIE: I multiplied? You know, you never told me how you met Margaret. I tell you everything, and then you completely withhold from me.

(CLARK *stands, determined.*)

CLARK: Jamie. You are never going to get a problem like this one wrong again.

JAMIE: That's impossible.

CLARK: I know it seems impossible to you right now. But it's like . . . climbing a mountain. What appears to be completely impossible at first, the rock face that looks vertical from below, the steepest part of the incline—that face always looks different when you're at the top, looking down, doesn't it? And you can only see, after you've done it, how you did it.

(JAMIE *looks at him blankly.*)

You have climbed a mountain, haven't you?

JAMIE: I'm from New York. Where would we find a mountain?

CLARK: Upstate, maybe?

JAMIE: Is that where you're from?

CLARK: Yes. That's where I'm from.

JAMIE: So you were raised, like outdoors? Scaling mountains?

(CLARK *stares at her.*)

I'm just asking, because, it's interesting. Exotic. I mean there's nothing to scale here.

CLARK: Sure there is. You just have to be more inventive.

JAMIE: You mean like the rock wall at the Reebok club?

CLARK: Like that. OK. Take this problem. What are the main numbers here?

JAMIE: Where are you from exactly in the mountains? A farm?

CLARK: I'm from a small town. You've never heard of it.

JAMIE: How small?

CLARK: So small, there were no nightclubs!

JAMIE: Wow, so where did people hang out?

CLARK: The bar.

JAMIE: *The* bar? There was only one bar in your town?

CLARK: Yup. That's how small it was.

JAMIE: But what if you got carded? Where could you hang out?

CLARK: No one got carded. Everyone just drank from a young age. Are you looking at the problem?

JAMIE: You must be glad you moved here.

CLARK: That's debatable. What are the main numbers here?

JAMIE: A small town, huh? Did you call yourself townies?

CLARK: Townies don't call themselves townies.

JAMIE: So what drove everyone to drink from a young age?

CLARK: I don't know. Maybe the despair of having only one bar?

JAMIE: You must have had an interesting childhood.

CLARK: Not as interesting as yours.

JAMIE: So how old were you when you realized that you count words and numbers compulsively?

CLARK: Seven.

JAMIE: Were you on a mountain?

CLARK: (*Remembering.*) I was under a table. Hiding. Listening to my parents argue. I thought if I could count the number of words, they couldn't be infinite. It would have to end.

JAMIE: Did it work?

CLARK: You can't count to infinity, right? So it would have to work.

JAMIE: (*Understanding it didn't.*) Right.

(*A beat.*)

CLARK: What are the main numbers here?

JAMIE: Clark? Do you just think about the SAT all the time so you won't have to deal with your real problems?

CLARK: What are the main numbers?

(JAMIE *stares at* CLARK, *mesmerized. He is completely focused in a way she has never seen before.*)

JAMIE: Well, there are three kumquats. And there are four pineapple wedges. So: three and four.

CLARK: What's three plus four?

JAMIE: Seven.

CLARK: What's three times four?

JAMIE: Twelve.

CLARK: Good! Now we eliminate the seven and twelve as answers! See, a lot of students just add or multiply. But *the obvious answer is never right.*

JAMIE: Are you serious!? They put the seven and twelve there to trick people?

(CLARK *nods.* JAMIE *looks at the test.*)

Oh my god! These all have phony answers!

CLARK: They're not phony Jamie, they're—

JAMIE: They're attempts by the people in New Jersey to fuck with us!

CLARK: People in New Jersey?

JAMIE: Do you realize Educational Testing Services is in New Jersey? That's why they do this. They resent being in New Jersey.

CLARK: Jamie, they're in *Princeton*. Why would they resent being in Princeton? It's quite beautiful.

JAMIE: Not if your father wants you to go to school there. Then it's just like the rest of New Jersey, except with eating clubs.

CLARK: Look these over. I want you to cross out the two obvious wrong answers. Quickly. Go!

(*She starts crossing out answers.*)

Don't hesitate. Follow your gut. Look for the trick. Yes. Good. Keep going.

JAMIE: How'm I doing?

CLARK: Do you know, you've never asked me that?

JAMIE: I never knew the test people were trying to trick me! This is outrageous! I'm gonna show *them*!

CLARK: Circle the ones you think are right.

(*She keeps going.* CLARK *paces, coaching.*)

The obvious answer is never right. The right answer is never obvious. Would you rather be impulsive or right?

JAMIE: I don't know! I love being impulsive! But I want to be right.

CLARK: Great. Now let's try it with Verbal.

JAMIE: (*Horrified.*) There are fake answers in Verbal too??

CLARK: There are fake answers everywhere.

(JAMIE *looks miserable.*)

What's wrong?

JAMIE: (*Tearful.*) Analogies. The ones where I don't know half the words. They make me want to crawl into bed. Quit school. Quit everything.

CLARK: I can get you through it.

(JAMIE *shakes her head.*)

"Walk is to Perambulate as" . . . "A) Pedestrian is to Stroll"?

JAMIE: Um. Yeah. They both have to do with walking. It looks right.

CLARK: That's why it's wrong!

JAMIE: Oh no!

CLARK: Look. Walk *is the same thing* as perambulate. Is pedestrian the same thing as stroll?

JAMIE: (*Bitterly.*) No.

CLARK: So we eliminate it! Anything else to cross out?

JAMIE: Um, "D"? As "Run is to Canter"?

CLARK: Yes! Why?

JAMIE: (*Triumphant.*) Because run isn't the same thing as canter. A canter is a slow run! (*Beat.*) I went to horse camp.

CLARK: These tests are actually designed for people who went to horse camp. It's amazing you haven't scored higher.

JAMIE: You don't have to be so rude about this social class stuff. You have a lot more earning potential than I do, so the tables will be turned in no time.

CLARK: Will they?

JAMIE: Yes. And then you'll still hate me. There will be no other option. So let's return to the problem, where we do have options: "B) Mordant to Sarcastic" or "C) Ephemeral to Permanent." Wait! Perambulate and permanent start with the same sound!

CLARK: But the words aren't actually related—

JAMIE: Clark. Kumquat. Pineapple wedge. Sweetie. The words are unrelated—so what? They *look the same*! So I am expected to *think* they're related and dive like a lemming to my death! But, no—I just learned that anything that *looks* Right is Wrong! I go back to B—I still don't know what mordant is, but now I know how to fuck with the test. I pick B, I win, and I even learn a new way to say sarcastic. (*She grabs another problem set.*)

CLARK: What are you doing?

JAMIE: Cross them out. Kill them off. D. O. A. (*She rapidly does another page as* CLARK *watches.*) C. Done. I can do that. Give me another exercise.

CLARK: Okay. (*Takes out a pile of vocabulary cards.*) The blue cards have words. Yellow cards, definitions. Watch. (*He swirls the cards in the air, with the technique of a professional magician as she watches, amazed. The cards land faceup. He hands her a stopwatch.*) Time me. I'm going to match words and definitions. Go! (CLARK *sorts the cards at a dazzling speed.*)

JAMIE: I don't know a lot of these words—I hope you don't expect me to— (*He finishes.*) Thirteen seconds!

CLARK: Now study the cards. I want you to match my time.

JAMIE: But—

CLARK: Don't worry about getting them right. Just follow your impulses.

(JAMIE *quickly glances at the cards.*)

JAMIE: When you were throwing cards in the air just now, you reminded me of the magician at my tenth birthday party. He wore a black cape and a top hat and a mask and he turned balloons into letters and numbers. He made cards glide through air and climb walls . . . (*She looks over the cards some more.*) But there was one trick he did that outclassed all of the others.

CLARK: A card trick?

JAMIE: A human trick. He disappeared. Ran down the hallway and never came back. A few minutes later we opened all the doors looking for him. But there was just my dad, taking a nap.

CLARK: (*Smiles.*) Taking a nap, huh?

JAMIE: None of my friends figured it out. They thought he scaled the building. Seventeen flights. Their mothers would call and ask for the name of the magician and my mother would say he retired. The girls who were at the party talk about it to this day—the magician who disappeared. I think it set a standard for the men in their lives for years to come.

CLARK: Did you ever ask him?

JAMIE: No. I knew. No one would want to scale this building.

CLARK: Nice story. But I think you're just buying time to study the words.

JAMIE: Are you going to disappear?

CLARK: (*Beat.*) You ready to start sorting? (JAMIE *nods.* CLARK *hurls the cards in the air.*) Go! (JAMIE *sorts the cards rapid-fire as* CLARK *times her.*) Keep going.

JAMIE: Done!

CLARK: My god! They're all right. Except for these. Here. (*He rearranges four pairs.*) Study them. Now sort just the ones you got wrong. Go! (*He throws the cards and she sorts them manically.*) Four seconds! You got them all.

(JAMIE *picks up the cards and starts playing with them, doing small versions of his elaborate card-juggling.*)

JAMIE: Where'd you learn to handle cards like that?

CLARK: Where did *you* learn?

JAMIE: By playing. And I had books. About card games, card tricks.

CLARK: Your father didn't mention that.

JAMIE: Why would he?

CLARK: I like to know what games my students play. Tells me how their minds work. I asked your father what games you like. He said he didn't know.

JAMIE: Really? But I love card games. I know forty kinds of solitaire. (*She hurls the cards in the air. They land. With the stopwatch, she times herself as she re-sorts the cards. Smiles at* CLARK. *He stares at the cards.*)

CLARK: You're at a hundred percent.

JAMIE: I never thought I'd hear you say that!

CLARK: Jamie. What you said earlier isn't true.

JAMIE: Which part?

CLARK: The part about me hating you. (*With love.*) I don't hate you.

JAMIE: Oh yeah? Prove it.

(*Beat.*)

CLARK: You know I can't.

(*Lights down.*)

Scene 2

(*Two months later. March 1995, the day before the SAT. It is six p.m., the beginning of* JAMIE's *final tutoring session. She lets* CLARK *in.*)

JAMIE: I called you last night.

CLARK: Sorry I got in too late to call you back.

JAMIE: It's never too late to call me back! When did you get in?

CLARK: Two a.m. Which is definitely too late to call you back two nights before your SAT date. You should have been getting on a good sleep schedule in time for the test tomorrow.

JAMIE: Did you see the article in the *Times* today about the SAT people? I always knew they were fuckups.

CLARK: You mean the one about the Justice Department investigating whether there are enough test dates for disabled students? Wait, I thought you didn't read the *Times*.

JAMIE: I read it when no one's looking. But only if there's a good headline. I think the headline was "SAT people fucked and in serious trouble." (*Beat.*) So you were out till two a.m.? Where were you?

CLARK: I . . . had a date.

JAMIE: You? Had a date?

CLARK: It's not outside the realm of possibility!

JAMIE: I just meant I didn't think you were quite ready to date yet. I thought Margaret had turned you off of women for a while.

CLARK: What did you have to tell me?

JAMIE: How was your date?

CLARK: Good. It was just a first date.

JAMIE: What did you do?

CLARK: We went to a lecture at the Museum of Natural History. And then to dinner.

JAMIE: A lecture? About what?

CLARK: Rational Choice Theory. It was her idea.

JAMIE: This girl is totally wrong for you. Everyone knows you don't go on a first date to a lecture. Second date maybe. First date you go to a movie. You go bowling. Not a lecture. And if you're in the Museum of Natural History, my god, there is a whole new set of dinosaurs just crying out for a first date. Where did you take her to dinner?

CLARK: She took me. To the um, Couscous Café.

JAMIE: She took you?

CLARK: To pay me back. I did her a favor. Helped her get access to a private research library.

JAMIE: Private research library? What does she do?

CLARK: She's an economist.

JAMIE: What a nightmare.

CLARK: Why?

JAMIE: Because you already live in your head. You need someone who gets you out of your head. A danceriser. A violinist. A ski bunny.

CLARK: A ski bunny?

JAMIE: Don't get me wrong, I have nothing against economists! They can be totally sexy. But for you—it's like putting strawberry sauce on strawberries. If you went out with an economist, all you would talk about would be theory!

CLARK: That's not true.

JAMIE: What did you talk about?

CLARK: Um. Rational Choice Theory. Keynesian Theory. Game Theory.

JAMIE: Uh-huh.

CLARK: Vindala happens to be a very nice woman.

JAMIE: And her name is Vindala! She sounds like an appetizer.

CLARK: You're the one who kissed Arthur. Who sounds like a raincoat.

JAMIE: And Couscous Café is a very unimaginative choice. It has nothing to recommend it except it's next to the museum. Otherwise on obvious disaster.

CLARK: It wasn't a disaster!

JAMIE: And the girl should never pay on a first date.

CLARK: Surprisingly, I agree with you. But she insisted. And I'm having financial difficulties. I'm broke.

JAMIE: I'm broke too. So what? You put it on a credit card and deal later.

CLARK: (*Stunned.*) You have got to be the most infuriating, spoiled, self-absorbed ingrate I have ever met and I've met many infuriating spoiled self-absorbed ingrates so that is saying a lot.

JAMIE: (*Hurt.*) How can you say that to me? Anyone can get a charge card. Homeless people have them. I have a friend on scholarship—on real scholarship, like welfare family, and her nephew is four and *he* got an offer for a credit card. They'll offer credit cards to anybody.

CLARK: They'll also take them away.

JAMIE: So you get an emergency one. I may be spoiled but I'm not an ingrate. I have never been ungrateful. Every day of my life I thank God I am so lucky to have been born into comfort.

CLARK: You believe in God?

JAMIE: Of course not. But I thank him. I have to thank someone. Even when I'm miserable I know I'm lucky.

CLARK: Well, in my day no one sent real scholarship kids any emergency credit cards. But I played it so now I have even less of a chance of one.

JAMIE: You were a real scholarship kid?

CLARK: That's irrelevant.

JAMIE: Your credit cards were taken away? Why?

CLARK: Not important. So why did you call me last night?

JAMIE: Oh my god. Was Vindalia there when I left the message?

CLARK: Vindala. No.

JAMIE: Were you at her place? Because you shouldn't go to a girl's place on the first—

CLARK: I'm sorry I missed your call. But that doesn't give you the right to criticize my date.

JAMIE: I just want to help you.

CLARK: How could you possibly help me?

JAMIE: I understand relationships. Everyone at Billington comes to me for love advice. The way that I need to study for the SAT? You need to study women.

CLARK: I do?

JAMIE: Yes. This chick is not sensual enough for you. Just her choice of restaurant and lecture shows it. Couscous Café. Rational Choice Theory. I can't think of a worse combination.

CLARK: Jamie, you wouldn't know what Rational Choice Theory was if it fell on you.

JAMIE: Not likely it would fall on me, since it's not a thing. It's an interdisciplinary movement that predicts human behavior based on universal principles. But that's not even my point.

CLARK: Jesus. What else do you read when no one's looking? Did you learn about Rational Choice Theory in sixth grade too?

JAMIE: Eighth I think. Same year I lost my virginity.

CLARK: What does that have to do with Rational Choice Theory?

JAMIE: A lot, actually. (*Beat.*) I lost it to Ramsay Michaelson.

CLARK: (*Stunned.*) The Nobel Prize–winning economist?

JAMIE: Hello. How many Ramsay Michaelsons do you think there are?

CLARK: Where did you meet him?

JAMIE: At the Limelight.

CLARK: Ramsay Michaelson goes clubbing?

JAMIE: He went through a clubbing phase. He was really into that Rational Choice thing too.

CLARK: I bet he was.

JAMIE: Yeah it helped convince me actually.

CLARK: My head is spinning.

(*Beat.*)

JAMIE: You should have called me last night. I had something important to tell you.

CLARK: I'm sorry. What was it?

JAMIE: I took a practice test!

CLARK: (*Confused.*) We ran out of practice tests last week.

JAMIE: Yes but Paul Devine had gotten ahold of a bootleg copy of last year's *10 SATs* which had the 1982 test in it, which I'd never taken. And gave me a pretty good price.

CLARK: What is wrong with that school of yours? Doesn't anyone *borrow* anything anymore? Where did you all learn to buy and sell each other like this?

JAMIE: Paul probably learned from his dad, who's comptroller of the city of New York? (*She shows him the test.*)

CLARK: Jamie! You've checked all of these. You didn't miss a one.

JAMIE: Made good time too. Oh Clark! If only I had been a junior in 1982! (*Teary.*) I'd be so happy. I'd be so smart. And I'd have twelve thousand dollars.

CLARK: You still can do it.

JAMIE: Oh, why weren't you there when I wanted to talk to you?

CLARK: I'm sorry. I'm here now. And it's. Incredible. Congratulations. You still can do it tomorrow. Right?

JAMIE: You sound unsure. You sound nervous.

CLARK: (*Nervous.*) No, I don't.

JAMIE: Do you realize, tomorrow morning I could go in there and screw up my entire life?

CLARK: No, you couldn't. You could screw up my entire life, but that's a whole other story.

JAMIE: What are you talking about?

CLARK: I'm just kidding.

JAMIE: (*Agitated.*) I still have a few hours left to study! Let's focus!

CLARK: Jamie. What's up. (*Beat.*) What's wrong with you today?

JAMIE: The SAT is tomorrow. What could be more wrong than that?

CLARK: It's not the SAT. Something is affecting you. And as your tutor I should warn you to try to resolve any personal problems before the test.

JAMIE: Since it's tomorrow, why don't we focus on problems that might be *on* the test!

CLARK: Maybe it's time to relax. You got a perfect score.

JAMIE: In 1982! This is 1995.

CLARK: Calm down. What's the square root of forty-seven?

JAMIE: (*Upset.*) Uh . . . it doesn't *have* a square root.

CLARK: That's right! See how prepared you are?

JAMIE: Well, it doesn't have a whole number square root. But I guess the square root would be . . . plus or minus 6.86.

CLARK: You're messing with me! (*He rapidly checks her calculation.*) Six point eight six times 6.86 . . . 47. How did you just do that?

JAMIE: I noticed they had an irregular square root on the test in 1985 so I did them all out the other day and memorized them?

CLARK: Jamie, will you promise me that after the test is over you will maintain this enthusiasm for your education?

JAMIE: No. (*Beat.*) Ask me another question.

CLARK: Are you sure there isn't something wrong?

JAMIE: I guess there's a reason you're the top tutor in America, Clark. Something's bothering me. Happy now?

CLARK: Do you want to talk about it?

JAMIE: Definitely not.

CLARK: If something is upsetting you it can affect your test performance. And if it would help to talk about it, I'm here.

JAMIE: Maybe it wouldn't help to talk about it!

CLARK: Okay.

(*Beat.*)

JAMIE: It's my dad. I think he's having an affair.

CLARK: Why?

JAMIE: He called last night and said he was still in Singapore. He doesn't know I have caller ID. For a guy who works in high-technology financing he can be really out of it. But he was actually in New York. Probably at some woman's house.

(CLARK *looks at the caller ID box.*)

CLARK: Your father isn't having an affair.

JAMIE: How do you know?

CLARK: I know that number. It's the number of a private business. I can't tell you where exactly, but I know.

JAMIE: Tell me.

CLARK: I can promise you, your dad was at a place of business.

JAMIE: It's funny, Clark. I used to think the right answer was enough. But someone—was it you?—recently taught me that I want more. I want the explanation behind the answer.

CLARK: But—

JAMIE: And now you're unteaching me what I learned. Aren't you. You're like . . . the anti-tutor!

CLARK: You shouldn't have to worry about this. It's nothing to worry about. You need to rest tonight.

JAMIE: Rest? Do you have any idea how stressed out I am? I have to know. If you don't tell me, I'm calling the number. Now. (*She gets up and picks up the cordless phone.*)

CLARK: All right. Sit down.

(*She sits, still holding the phone.*)

JAMIE: So what's this about, Clark? What's this "business"?

CLARK: It's the number of a private club. A betting parlor. A place where people play cards for money. Your father plays cards there, usually on Thursdays. Sometimes all night.

JAMIE: My father is a gambler?

(CLARK *nods.*)

How do you know this?

CLARK: (*Confessing.*) I met him there. At the blackjack table. I was card-counting. So was he.

JAMIE: Card-counting?

CLARK: It's a betting system used by professional gamblers.

JAMIE: You're a professional gambler??

CLARK: I was. I retired.

JAMIE: Retired? You mean, you lost?

CLARK: I won for a time. A long time. But I'd play all night and miss the day. So I went to Gambler's Anonymous. That's where I met Margaret.

JAMIE: Margaret's a gambler too?!

CLARK: No, just an alcoholic. But part of the twelve-step philosophy is that you can attend each other's meetings.

JAMIE: And find more addictions?

CLARK: Yeah. When we met we became sort of—addicted to each other.

JAMIE: Ew. Gross.

CLARK: When we moved in together, I started gambling again. She started drinking again and stopped going to AA. I made her go back, you know the rest. After she moved out . . . I started playing new games. Against the guys I saw beating the house. Against your dad.

JAMIE: So you owe him money! That's why you took the job!

CLARK: I took the job because I believed in you.

JAMIE: Bullshit. You didn't even know me.

CLARK: But I know your dad. And I figured genius could run in the family.

JAMIE: You think I'm a genius?

CLARK: I think you may have genius in you.

JAMIE: People don't talk to me like this. They don't talk to me about genius. They talk to me about nail polish.

CLARK: They don't know you.

JAMIE: How does it work? Card-counting?

CLARK: That's not important.

JAMIE: You are upsetting me the night before the test. I want to know what it is. How does it work?

CLARK: You just, um, keep track of the cards as you go along. You calculate how many cards of each category have been played, get a sense of the whole deck. A casino might use up to seven or eight decks of cards so it can take a long time. But you keep counting to increase the odds of busting the house more of the time.

JAMIE: Show me. I want to understand where my father goes on Thursdays. Can you show me?

CLARK: Could I show you? Of course not. No. This is not what I teach.

JAMIE: I know it isn't, but—

CLARK: Teaching is how I overcome this. So I can't *teach* you *this*—

JAMIE: It would just be so I can understand. It wouldn't be for money.

CLARK: Doesn't matter what it's for. It's the rush, the high . . .

JAMIE: We wouldn't be gambling. Just playing cards. Just for a little bit.

CLARK: I'm sorry. I—

JAMIE: Remember you once asked me what it is I love? I think I know. I think it's—playing. I never really get to play. (*Beat.*) Please, I'm so nervous. I think it would help.

CLARK: Okay. But only a few hands. You need to sleep.

(*He deals the cards. Lights down.*)

Scene 3

(*Four weeks later. Lights up on* CLARK *and* JAMIE *as they enter. She's holding an envelope that has a plastic window. He can see it is the letter from Educational Testing Services. The envelope is sealed.*)

CLARK: You haven't opened it yet?

JAMIE: No. (*Beat.*) When you said I could screw up your entire life in one morning, what did you mean?

CLARK: I told you I was kidding.

JAMIE: Now tell me the truth. I want to know what you've been protecting me from.

CLARK: Why do you think I've been protecting you?

JAMIE: I know you.

CLARK: I just didn't want you to feel—any more pressure than was already on you. While you were studying. Do you understand?

(*She nods, close to tears.*)

JAMIE: So.

CLARK: So. Your father's not the only person I owe money to.

JAMIE: I *knew* you were in trouble. So that's why you accepted this deal.

CLARK: Yes. I made a mistake. Borrowed money from the wrong people. This deal looked like the only way to get out of the trouble in time. It's fine. If it doesn't work out, I'll just have to—leave town.

(JAMIE *starts crying*.)

   Sssh. It's okay. Are you ready to open it?

JAMIE: I can't.

CLARK: Do you want me to open it?

JAMIE: That would be . . . so great. (*She hands the envelope to* CLARK. *He opens it*.)

CLARK: Wow. Congratulations!

JAMIE: Did I do okay?

CLARK: Better than okay.

JAMIE: Better than okay doesn't sound like perfect. It has to be perfect.

CLARK: It doesn't have to be anything.

(*She tears the score out of his hand. She is overwhelmed*.)

JAMIE: 1590! Clark I got a fuckin' 1590!

CLARK: It's incredible.

JAMIE: Just ten points away from—oh god. Are you mad at me?

CLARK: Of course not.

JAMIE: I got an 800 Verbal! He has to give you the money for that. And a 790 Math! Are you sure you're not mad at me?

CLARK: Why would I be mad at you? You did great.

JAMIE: I wonder what it was. Which question I got wrong. I felt like I was getting them all—

CLARK: Let's see. (*He opens another envelope.*)

JAMIE: What's that?

CLARK: You can order your test with answers two weeks from now but I know a guy at ETS who could get it to me early. (*Looks over the answer sheet.*) It's this one. The answer was twelve! Why did you say "None of the above"? You love twelve!

JAMIE: Oh god. I did think it was twelve at first. But then when I checked over the test I noticed there wasn't a single other "None of the above" on the whole test!

CLARK: So?

JAMIE: So I used to think "None of the above" was never the answer. But you said it sometimes was. And then I realized, it's a crucial option. "None of the above." It's huge. It's vast. It's one of the most important answers there is!

CLARK: Sure it is. (*Beat.*) —If you have a completely negative outlook on life!

JAMIE: That's not fair! You taught me it could be the answer.

CLARK: I can't believe I signed this contract. (*He throws the contract at her. She looks at it.*)

JAMIE: Is this *it*? Wow this is like reading comprehension from hell. Clark I wasn't trying to be negative. I was just trying to remember everything you taught me.

CLARK: (*Cold.*) Don't blame me for your mistake.

(JAMIE *stares at* CLARK, *stunned. She rips up her score.*)

Hey. Hey I'm sorry.

(*She throws the pieces of paper at him.*)

JAMIE: Not as sorry as I am.

CLARK: You've been—a wonderful student.

(*She looks sad. He stares at her, moved.*)

JAMIE: When do you have to leave?

CLARK: Tomorrow.

JAMIE: How much money do you owe?

CLARK: Fifty thousand.

JAMIE: Let me help you.

CLARK: How?

JAMIE: Any way. You know I would do anything to help you.

CLARK: You don't have to. Especially now that I've been such a jerk.

JAMIE: That just confirms that you're my type! I'm really into jerks. (*Beat. Then she sees the cards and it hits her.*) Maybe we could find a place for me to—

CLARK: (*Understands.*) We can't. You're underage.

JAMIE: My fake ID is really good. (*She shows him the ID.*)

CLARK: Where the hell did you get this?

JAMIE: Best place in the city. Wasn't cheap either. Look, I could get in with this. But then I look young enough—they'd never suspect I can count cards. They won't know what hit them.

CLARK: No.

JAMIE: It could work.

CLARK: I know it could work. That's why I say no. I can't let you—

JAMIE: It would just be this one time. *I* know how to stop.

CLARK: "Just this one time" is what people say before they start!

JAMIE: I know you think I have an addictive personality, but I can do this just once—I can do pretty much anything once. Then I get bored.

CLARK: Except this isn't boring.

JAMIE: Look. I'm going to try it one day. When you're not there to stop me. Why not try it now? I'm fresh. I've just learned the system. And you can completely supervise.

(CLARK *considers this, then looks at the fake ID.*)

CLARK: We could get you in with this. But after we get in, you'd have to look innocent. Not too sophisticated.

JAMIE: I have just the thing.

(*She goes into her walk-in closet. Noises are heard.*)

CLARK: Are you okay in there?

JAMIE: I'm fine. I just have to get to it. I have one outfit that is so not sophisticated.

CLARK: Just one?

JAMIE: I know it's hard to believe. We waste so much time at school trying to look older. But I do have this one—Oh Clark, I need to reorganize this closet.

(*Crashing sounds come from the closet.*)

CLARK: Maybe this isn't a good idea.

JAMIE: No! I found it!

(JAMIE*'s shirt flies out of the closet door.* CLARK *catches it and backs away.*)

CLARK: Jamie, why don't I meet you in the lobby?

JAMIE: No, no, I'll only be a moment.

(*Now the pair of pants she was wearing flies out.*)

I really hate the stereotype that women take a long time to get ready. That's so not true about me.

CLARK: (*Smiles.*) No stereotype is true about you.

JAMIE: So this is a dress I bought for Charlene's stepmother's wedding in Southampton. Maybe it could work.

(*She emerges from the closet in a pink floral dress.* CLARK *stares at her, at a loss for words.*)

CLARK: Let's go.

(*They exit. Lights down.*)

Scene 4

(*Lights go up on the bedroom, empty. Early dawn light pours into the dark room. Music.* CLARK *and* JAMIE *enter, both in high spirits.*)

CLARK: You were so great!

JAMIE: No, you were! You taught me.

CLARK: Just sitting there in that stupid pink dress—

JAMIE: You told me to wear it!

CLARK: —And looking so silly and naive but underneath I can see how wise you are. How profoundly beautiful and wise. You are so wise underneath all the playing dumb.

JAMIE: Really? (*He nods.*) I had no idea New Jersey could be so wonderful. (*Beat.*) I still think we should've stayed overnight.

CLARK: You can't move to Atlantic City just because you're having fun playing cards.

JAMIE: It's not like anyone would've noticed.

CLARK: They would've noticed. It might have taken them a day or two, but they would have noticed. They should watch you more closely.

JAMIE: They should.

CLARK: I was watching you. You were magnificent.

JAMIE: So you still haven't told me.

CLARK: The number doesn't matter.

JAMIE: Of course it does.

CLARK: The dealer was catching on to you—even though you kept saying, "Aren't I lucky?" (*He cracks up.*)

JAMIE: We can go to another dealer. Another casino.

CLARK: No, Jamie. I brought you there to make the money. But . . . you were starting to *enjoy* it.

JAMIE: How much did I make?

CLARK: You made $14,000. (*He stares at the cash. Then he hands it to her.*)

JAMIE: But you need it. You're broke.

CLARK: As you have pointed out to me you're broke too. In more ways than I can understand. Take it.

JAMIE: But you're broke and in debt. (*She hands him the money back.*)

CLARK: You earned it. (*He returns it. She counts out some bills.*)

JAMIE: Just take this much for—for when you go.

(CLARK *accepts some of the money, stares at it.*)

CLARK: Jamie.

JAMIE: You are going, right?

CLARK: Yes. You know I am.

JAMIE: Yep. I know. (*Pause.*) Hey.

CLARK: What?

JAMIE: Could you wait a couple of days?

CLARK: For what?

JAMIE: Before you leave?

CLARK: I can't.

JAMIE: But if you did—

CLARK: You're not thinking this through.

JAMIE: I know I'm not. But I am. If you waited—just a couple of days—

CLARK: Then?

JAMIE: Then we—I—if you waited— (*Pulls herself together.*) I bet I could get some card games started at school and have the rest of the money for you!

CLARK: No!

JAMIE: But—

CLARK: Taking you to that place—on the list of all the wrong things I have done in my life or even thought about doing, it was the worst.

JAMIE: (*Flirting.*) What have you thought about doing?

CLARK: I don't want you counting cards at home, at school, or even in your daydreams. Promise me.

JAMIE: Can we backtrack to the part where I looked beautiful?

CLARK: Don't try to find me. Don't talk to anyone about me. Not even your doorman. They love paying off doormen to find people. I know one guy who owed money, got turned in by his own doorman.

JAMIE: But—if you're scared of the doorman, how will you come visit?

CLARK: I don't know. (*An admission.*) I won't.

JAMIE: Clark? Do you realize you're not my tutor anymore?

CLARK: Yes. So?

JAMIE: So maybe now you can show me you don't hate me.

CLARK: It's not right.

JAMIE: It's not right *or* wrong. It's . . . it's "None of the above."

CLARK: Jamie. You know how much I wish—but I'm going away.

JAMIE: So what? Everyone goes away.

(*He stares at her.*)

CLARK: (*Sad.*) Come here. (*He holds her.*) Good-bye, Jamie.

(*Lights down.*)

Scene 5

(*A couple of weeks later. May. Evening.* JAMIE *is on the phone, while she is putting things away around her room and in her desk.*)

JAMIE: Justine. You're way too good for him. And it's definitely beneath your dignity to keep breaking into his e-mail account. (*Beat.*) No I haven't heard from him. (*Finds the contract.*) Oh, look, here's the contract he signed with my father. What was he thinking? Lawyers are such bad writers! I would get a D minus if I turned this in. "Wherewhichfore the party of the first part" . . . who are these schmucks? . . . "should Jamie Silver answer enough questions correctly to merit a 1600, thus . . ." (*Beat. Looking at the signature on the contract.*) You know another thing about Clark? He had terrible handwriting. I should have known he would leave. Just from his handwriting. (*Beat.*) Dr. Lorin says even though I'll never hear from Clark again I'll always have a part of him inside me. What? No, I'm not pregnant! He meant—actually I have no fucking clue what he meant, but it seemed comforting at the time. (*Beat.*) Saturday? I was thinking of going to this lecture at the New School. No I am not geeking out on you Justine. It's about probability. Chance. I think chance is cool. All right. Later. (*Hangs up, stares at the contract, reads to herself.*) "Should Jamie Silver answer enough questions correctly to merit a 1600 . . ." Should Jamie Silver answer enough questions correctly to merit a 1600. Should Jamie answer enough questions correctly to *merit*— (*She freezes. Picks up the phone.*) Hi, is my dad there? Oh. Tell him to call me as soon as he gets back. (*She hangs up. The phone rings. She answers swiftly.*) Hello? Oh, hi Mrs. Hargraves. Maybe. I'd need to talk to her. Hi Peggy! What did you do this weekend? What did you buy? Oh I love Gaultier. How much was it? Tell me what you think the tax was. Estimate. Just follow your gut. Good! That was very close. Put your mom on. Mrs. Hargraves? I can work with Peggy. I charge a hundred an hour and I'd have to meet with her at least two hours a week if she's going to take the SAT in the next . . .

(*A loud crashing sound is heard from the balcony.*)

Gotta go!

(*Another crash.* CLARK *enters, in mountain-climbing gear.*)

Jesus! You scared the hell out of me! What the fuck.

CLARK: I missed you too.

JAMIE: You scaled the building! (*Moved.*) It's never been done before.

CLARK: It's only seventeen flights.

(*Beat. They stare at each other.*)

JAMIE: So you really are scared of the doorman.

CLARK: I can't stay long. I just had to see you.

(*They move toward each other, but then she remembers the contract.*)

JAMIE: Wait I have to show you something. You know how this winter they recentered the test? They completely changed the curve?

(CLARK *nods.*)

When did you sign this contract?

CLARK: October.

JAMIE: Yes. Before the recentering! (*Showing him the contract.*) And see what it says here?

CLARK: (*Looks and realizes:*) This would have to hold up in court.

JAMIE: Oh can we go to court? I've always wanted to sue my parents! (*The phone rings. She looks at the caller ID box.*) That's him.

CLARK: Who?

JAMIE: Your gambling partner. (*Answers phone.*) Dad. We need to talk about your exploitation of my tutor. I saw the contract and I think it sucks. I also think it has a key loophole. Where it says "answer enough questions correctly to merit a 1600"? Well, under the old curve, before recentering, I would have gotten a 1600. See, recentering helped most students who took the test, but at the very top of the curve, where I am, in Math, the scores got lower. Yesterday's 800s became today's 790s. What? (*Beat.*) The test was recentered, Dad, they changed the shape of the curve this winter. (*Beat.*) I don't know why! Because—sometimes, things just need to be recentered!! (*Beat.*) Of course it's a great loophole. No!! I found it myself. Bye.

CLARK: What did he say?

JAMIE: He said he's not sure it's legally valid but it's the most creative reading of a contract he's ever heard. He's faxing his attorney. Oh my god. Should I call her?

CLARK: You know his attorney?

JAMIE: I don't know if I *know* her. But she's my mom.

CLARK: Your mom is your dad's attorney?

JAMIE: That's how they met. Isn't that cute?

CLARK: Isn't that a conflict of interest?

JAMIE: Maybe. It's actually the cutest thing about them. (*Picks up phone and dials.*) Hi, it's Jamie. Is my mom there? (*Beat.*) But this is urgent. Do you know where she is? Bye. (*She gets off the phone, wipes a tear away.*)

CLARK: Are you okay?

JAMIE: It's just my contact lens.

(*Beat.* CLARK *goes to* JAMIE *to comfort her. He puts his arm around her. Then suddenly a rush of intercom static can be heard. And then* JAMIE's *mother's voice can be heard over the intercom.*)

INTERCOM: Jamie.

(*Momentarily confused by hearing her mother's voice,* JAMIE *rushes to the intercom.*)

JAMIE: Mom?!

INTERCOM: Yes.

JAMIE: Mom, you're upstairs!

INTERCOM: Yes. Jamie. My office said you just left an urgent message.

JAMIE: I did.

INTERCOM: And I also just received a fax from your father. I'm surprised at you, Jamie.

JAMIE: You are?

INTERCOM: Where did you learn to read a contract like this? It's ingenious, original, and surprisingly legal.

JAMIE: Really?

INTERCOM: I'm wiring his fee to his bank account now. And I'll send the tuition to Columbia in the morning . . . (*Sounding a little anxious.*) It's best to settle these things immediately, before they escalate!

JAMIE: Thanks, Mom!

INTERCOM: Listen, Jamie, I should run, but—I have some free time this weekend. Do you want to have lunch?

JAMIE: Sure.

INTERCOM: Good. We can talk more then. Bye!

JAMIE: Bye. (*She turns to* CLARK.)

CLARK: I don't believe it.

JAMIE: So after you pay me the twelve thousand and those friends of yours the fifty thousand (*Calculating:*) you'll have thirty-eight thousand left! To invest for the future.

CLARK: Since when do you think about the future?

JAMIE: Two months ago all anyone at school talked about was the SAT. But now all they talk about is the future. It's getting late. We have to move fast.

CLARK: If no one talks about the SAT, why all the new books? You planning on taking it again for the other ten points?

JAMIE: I'm a tutor now.

CLARK: Really.

JAMIE: I only have three students so far. (*They stare at each other.*) Clark?

CLARK: Yeah?

JAMIE: My mom wants to have lunch with me.

CLARK: (*Saddened. Softly.*) Have I ever told you that every time I see you, you break my heart?

JAMIE: No! You've never told me anything! Somehow you use so many words but don't tell me anything. How many was that?

CLARK: (*It hits him.*) I don't know! I've—I've stopped counting! Jamie?

JAMIE: What?

CLARK: Have you stopped anything?

JAMIE: (*Smiles.*) I've stopped everything. Clark?

CLARK: What?

JAMIE: You're not going to go away again are you?

CLARK: No. I'm sorry I went away before. And I— (*A confession.*) I don't think about the perfection of circles as often as I used to.

JAMIE: Really?!

CLARK: Yeah. (*He begins to embrace her again, then pulls back.*) Jamie? I'm not the . . . tangent. Anymore. Am I?

JAMIE: Oh my god I am so sorry I ever called you a tangent. You—are *so* not the tangent. You are so much more than that. *Arthur* was the tangent. If there was one.

CLARK: Good. He sounded like one.

JAMIE: Were you jealous?

CLARK: You know I was. (*He starts to hold her again. Now she pulls away.*)

JAMIE: Clark?

CLARK: What?

JAMIE: You . . . you don't think I'm . . . an addiction? Do you?

CLARK: No. You are so not an addiction. You—are to "addiction" as "life"— (*Beat. He stops before finishing the analogy.*) Jamie?

JAMIE: (*Grins.*) *What?*

CLARK: No more words.

(*He takes her into his arms and kisses her. They draw close to each other and kiss as lights fade.*)

(*Curtain.*)

REFUGE

Jessica Goldberg

Refuge was produced by Playwrights Horizons (Tim Sanford, Artistic Director; Leslie Marcus, Managing Director; Lynn Landis, General Manager) in New York City on November 18, 1999. It was directed by Neil Pepe; the set design was based on a concept by Scott Pask; the lighting design was by Tyler Micoleau; the sound design was by David Carbonara; the costume design was by Sarah Edwards; the production manager was Peter Waxdal; and the production stage manager was Karen Shepherd. The cast was as follows:

AMY	Catherine Kellner
NAT	Chris Messina
BECCA	Mandy Siegfried
SAM	Chris Bauer

CHARACTERS

AMY: Mid-twenties. The caretaker. No-nonsense.
NAT: Amy's brother, twenty. The survivor of two massive brain tumors. He is handicapped.
BECCA: Amy's sister, sixteen. A club kid.
SAM: A guy, mid- to late-twenties. A drifter.

TIME

The present.

PLACE

The play takes place in a rundown lower-middle-class home. The house looks like it has been lived in for years.

Scene 1

(*A small bedroom—books, a bed, not much decoration, clothes strewn about.* AMY, *in her mid-twenties, sits on the bed smoking. She holds a ton of stuff inside. She looks sad but acts her happiest.* SAM, *in his late-twenties, moves about the room looking at things.*)

SAM: Nice room.

AMY: You think?

SAM: Yeah. Lots of books.

AMY: Yeah.

SAM: Reading feeds the mind, huh?

AMY: Supposed to.

SAM: Yeah, small.

AMY: The room?

SAM: Yeah.

AMY: Big enough.

SAM: Sure. (*He approaches her, looks at her cigarette.*) You gonna put that out?

AMY: Sure.

SAM: You're pretty.

AMY: Nah, I got hips.

SAM: That's a good thing.

AMY: A butt.

SAM: That's good too. (*He kisses her.*) Taste nice.

AMY: Thanks. (*He kisses her again, longer now.*)

SAM: You wanna turn the lights off?

AMY: How do you want 'em?

SAM: Most ladies don't like it with the lights on.

AMY: I don't care. (*He kisses her hard, real. She pulls his belt.*)

SAM: Ow! You're a wild thing, aren't you?

AMY: Nah.

SAM: It's okay. Don't mind. (*She undoes his belt. They fall on the bed kissing.*) You got a bag?

AMY: What?

SAM: A safe?

AMY: Rubber?

SAM: Yeah.

AMY: No.

SAM: Shit. Let me check. (*He goes to his wallet, looks in.*) Got one.

AMY: Great. (*He comes back to* AMY, *puts the condom on the bed, begins to kiss her. They get into it. They begin rolling around on the bed.*)

SAM: Can we turn a light off?

AMY: Sure.

SAM: Got a candle?

AMY: Doubt it.

SAM: It's romantic.

AMY: I don't have one.

SAM: Okay. (*He gets up, turns the light off.*) You do this a lot?

AMY: What?

SAM: This.

AMY: No.

SAM: Shouldn't, it's not healthy.

AMY: I don't. (*He kisses her more and more . . . They get into it, they are into it. A sound in the house, unheard, then outside the door, then a knock, a voice.*)

NAT: Ames, Amy Ames.

SAM: Who's that?

AMY: Shh . . . What?

NAT: (*Unseen, behind the door.*) I can't sleep.

AMY: Lay on your side.

NAT: Hurts.

AMY: Try your back.

NAT: It hurts everything. C'I come in?

AMY: C'mon.

NAT: Someone in there?

AMY: Go to bed.

NAT: You okay?

AMY: Fine, go to bed.

NAT: (*Whining in pain.*) Everything hurts, my head, my back, havin' dreams.

AMY: (*To* SAM.) Shit. (*To the door.*) Go in your room, I'll be in in a sec.

NAT: I could come in.

AMY: I'll be right there, please. (*Quiet. They wait, then the sound of* NAT *shuffling away.*) Sorry. My brother.

SAM: Oh.

AMY: He's been sick.

SAM: Yeah.

AMY: Gotta go, I'll be back.

SAM: Right.

AMY: You don't have to wait.

SAM: It's okay.

AMY: You sure?

SAM: How long?

AMY: Quick, I'll be quick. (*She goes.* SAM *sits on the bed, smokes, looks around the room, moves around, turns things over, takes off his shoes, gets up, moves, uneasy.* AMY *returns.*) Sorry.

SAM: He okay?

AMY: Yeah. He gets nightmares, had an operation, doesn't have a bone back there.

SAM: That's gotta be hard.

AMY: Yeah.

SAM: You take care of him?

AMY: Yeah.

SAM: Must be hard.

AMY: You took your shoes off?

SAM: Just him and you?

AMY: And my sis.

SAM: Where's your parents?

AMY: That mean you're staying?

SAM: Yeah. Did they die?

AMY: No.

SAM: My brother died, few years back, car accident. Family, you can't replace 'em, hardest thing to lose, ya know? People are full of sorrys. Think they understand, they don't. We were close, real close. After he died—

AMY: I'm tired.

SAM: What? (*She approaches him.*)

AMY: I'd just like that, if you stayed. (*Blackout.*)

Scene 2

(*Lights up in the kitchen the next afternoon.* BECCA *dances around the kitchen. She wears huge headphones and bops her head to the music. She is sixteen, thin, pretty, dressed to club.* AMY *enters. She is reading.*)

BECCA: Wanna hear about my dream?

AMY: What?

BECCA: My dream, wanna hear about it?

AMY: Sure. (AMY *reluctantly closes the book.*)

BECCA: Dreamt I was a baby again, in one of those baby things, you know, on Mom's back, right? And anyway thing is, it was stuck, you know, she couldn't get it off, right? She was freaking, but I was just happy shaking my rattle.

AMY: Wonder what it means? (BECCA *makes a face as if to say,* "Duh." *She snorts.*)

BECCA: Where's Nat?

AMY: McDonald's.

BECCA: By himself?

AMY: We're on a plan.

BECCA: Oh yeah, what kind of plan?

AMY: It's on the fridge. (BECCA *gets up, looks at the fridge, reads the plan:*)

BECCA: One: get up, have coffee. Two: walk to McDonald's for an Egg McMuffin—try to talk to someone. Three: watch TV. Four: read half an hour. Five: walk with Amy, twice around the house. Six: more TV—eat a vegetable. Seven: write in journal before dinner. He writes in a journal?

AMY: Think it will be good for him.

BECCA: Yeah, right. (BECCA *pulls out a bag of heroin. She cuts a line on a book that's lying on the table.*) Have some of this shit left over from a few days ago, just want to get rid of it, you know? Don't like to keep it around. You never know, you could get searched or something, so it's probably better to do it, 'cause you never know, right?

AMY: Nat'll be home soon. It'll freak him out. (BECCA *snorts.*)

BECCA: Want some?

AMY: I don't do that shit. You got any coke? I'll do some coke.

BECCA: Nah. I'm quittin' soon anyway, all the shit. (BECCA *puts the heroin away, lights a cigarette.* AMY *takes one, lights up as well.*) You love me, so I don't touch the needle. If you want me to stop, just tell me, you can tell me to stop.

AMY: As long as you don't shoot up—Nat's here. Let's not talk about this anymore. (NAT *enters. Twenty, he is heavy, stiff, awk-ward. He carries his McDonald's bag. He stands in the doorway a little lost, like a sleepwalker.*)

BECCA: Sit, Nat, right here, c'mon.

NAT: Hey.

AMY: How was the walk?

NAT: All right.

AMY: Talk to anyone?

NAT: C'mon.

AMY: Gotta try.

NAT: I ordered the McMuffin.

AMY: Gotta try, only way.

NAT: (*Sits at the table, opens his Egg McMuffin.*) You don't understand.

BECCA: It's not like you're mute, you know.

AMY: Can we not—

NAT: I hate her. She doesn't get it, not at all, selfish—

BECCA: I'm so sick of you complaining.

NAT: Maybe people look at me, but they don't care. They don't give a shit—

BECCA: Like they give a shit about me, but I don't care.

AMY: Let's be nice.

NAT: Drug addict.

AMY: Stop, please stop. (NAT *eats.*)

NAT: I could be a fly, I am a fly.

AMY: You're not a fly, Nat.

BECCA: Could be.

AMY: You stop it.

NAT: She's so selfish. You don't spend every day alone. You don't have to know that no one will ever want you, that you'll never have a girlfriend, that you'll be alone, always alone, and your body will ache when you get up, and sometimes you can't even piss—if the piss comes, that'll be your friend for one second, then it's in the toilet, gone.

BECCA: Amy's a fly.

NAT: No she isn't.

BECCA: I'm a fly too, even in a club or at a rave with hundreds of people around me. I'm dancing, and dancing, so hard, but still, it's just me, you know, only me. My arms, my legs, my head, movin', up and down, up and down, up and down. (BECCA *closes her eyes. The heroin has hit.*)

NAT: Ame?

AMY: Yeah?

NAT: I got those shooting pains again, through my hand.

AMY: I'll get your pills.

BECCA: C'I borrow some cash money, Amy?

NAT: And lie down with me, rub it.

AMY: It's not time yet, wanna finish this book, day's just begun. Why don't you watch some TV, relax, and I'll be in soon. No, Becca, we're broke.

NAT: Wish you could feel the pain.

AMY: Me too—

BECCA: I feel the pain.

AMY: —sometimes I wish it was me.

NAT: No you don't. You're too good, gotta take care of us.

BECCA: Please, Amy.

AMY: How much?

BECCA: Ten, twenty, thirty bucks?

AMY: I don't know. (AMY *lights a cigarette.* NAT *eats slowly.* BECCA *just stares off into space. The doorbell rings.*)

AMY: Who's that?

BECCA: I don't know. Could you get it? (AMY *goes to the door, she opens it.* SAM *stands in the doorway.* NAT *and* BECCA *stare at him.*)

SAM: Hi, I was wondering if you wanted to go out?

AMY: Now?

SAM: Yeah, it's a nice day. (AMY *looks out.*)

AMY: I'm kinda busy. Where?

SAM: I don't know. Can I come in?

AMY: I guess. (*She lets him in.*)

SAM: How many rooms in this house?

AMY: What?

SAM: How many bedrooms?

AMY: Three.

SAM: Any extra space?

AMY: Why?

SAM: Lost my job.

AMY: So?

SAM: Need to rent, cheap, thought maybe the extra cash would do you good.

AMY: You wanna move in?

SAM: Sort of.

BECCA: Who's he Amy? What's he say he wants? (AMY *looks at* SAM.)

AMY: What do you want?

SAM: A place to stay, that's all.

NAT: No space here.

AMY: The living room.

NAT: The living room? That's my room.

AMY: You have a room.

NAT: What about the TV?

AMY: We'll put it in here.

NAT: In the kitchen?

AMY: Why not?

NAT: He can't live here. Who is he?

AMY: Who?

NAT: Him, who is he?

AMY: Who are you?

SAM: I'm just Sam, need a place, lost my job. I do carpentry stuff, odd jobs. Met you, you seemed nice. It's a calm house. I like a calm house. Thought I'd ask, give it a shot.

BECCA: Amy, can you get me a glass of water?

NAT: Nope, sorry, no room here. (NAT *closes the door in* SAM's *face.*)

BECCA: Water, Amy, water.

NAT: What kinda shit person thinks he can live here, no room here. (AMY *opens the door,* SAM *is still standing there.*)

BECCA: How much he gonna pay?

SAM: What do you think?

BECCA: Fifty a week.

SAM: Sounds good, sounds doable, I could do that, if it's cool
    with you.

AMY: I guess, couldn't hurt, the money.

SAM: I like you. (*Blackout.*)

Scene 3

(*The next day.* NAT *is watching wrestling on TV in the kitchen.* SAM
*enters, a beer in one hand, a quart of Breyer's in the other. He sits, starts
to watch the television.*)

(NAT *looks at* SAM *and looks away.* SAM *tries to smile. Silence.* SAM *clears
his throat.*)

SAM: What's up?

NAT: Nothin'. (NAT *watches the TV again. Silence.* SAM *tries again.*)

SAM: Huh, this is great, funny.

NAT: Scum of the earth.

SAM: Yeah, lowest of the low.

NAT: Got a problem with scum?

SAM: Nah.

NAT: 'Cause you are?

SAM: What?

NAT: Scum.

SAM: You think I'm scum?

NAT: Didn't say that, you did.

SAM: When?

NAT: Said you were scum.

SAM: Who?

NAT: Forget it. (*Quiet.* SAM *tries again.*)

SAM: Wanna beer?

NAT: I don't drink.

SAM: No?

NAT: What? That bothers you? Huh? Can't stand a guy who doesn't drink, not cool, huh?

SAM: I don't care.

NAT: Course you don't care. Nobody does. I don't need drinks, I don't need drugs, they're stupid. Never did, even before this. You're outcast if you don't do that stuff, you know? I went to college one year and I was like this, this outcast 'cause I never took a sip of beer. People like you making me a outcast. I can't move my neck.

SAM: I didn't go to college.

NAT: So? Do what you want. Drink, drink eighty beers, I don't care. (*Silence.*)

SAM: What happened to your parents?

NAT: I drove them crazy.

SAM: Huh . . . really?

NAT: Yeah.

SAM: Okay. (*They watch the TV.*)

NAT: So, you're a bum, huh?

SAM: Sort of.

NAT: She doesn't need another bum.

SAM: Amy?

NAT: You staying in her room? At night?

SAM: I've only been here one night.

NAT: Did you stay with her?

SAM: Yeah, uh, yes.

NAT: I'll never be with a girl, never, I want to, but I won't.

SAM: I can get you a girl.

NAT: I don't want a girl. I want a wife.

SAM: Right.

NAT: (*Calling.*) Ame, Amy Ammmyyy!!! (AMY *comes.*)

AMY: What?

NAT: Can you get me a green apple and a glass of water?

SAM: I coulda got it.

AMY: I'll get it. (*She leaves.*)

SAM: I coulda got it.

NAT: Nah, that's her job.

SAM: Can't get your own?

NAT: I get dizzy when I stand up. How are you gonna pay the rent without a job?

SAM: I'll get a job, tomorrow.

NAT: Nothin' I hate more than freeloaders. People just don't know what they've got. (AMY *returns. She gives* NAT *his water and apple.*)

AMY: (*To* SAM.) Are you gonna be around for supper?

SAM: I don't think so.

AMY: Okay. (*She leaves.*)

NAT: I used to play sports, you know. Run, all that. I mean, mentally I was off, but physically I was okay. Look at my body now.

SAM: Can't you work on it?

NAT: What good would that do? It hurts too much anyway.

SAM: You could go to one of those places, you know, like a gym with doctors.

NAT: Yeah. I got the back of my head cut open twice, and all I got was one month of that therapy shit, only enough to get me off the couch. Gotta have money to be normal in this shit country, America, the rich get richer and the poor get drunk.

SAM: I think I'm gonna go out.

NAT: Am I driving you crazy?

SAM: No.

NAT: Sure.

SAM: I just gotta go. (*He gets up, moves out of the room.*)

NAT: I drive everyone crazy.

Scene 4

(AMY *and* SAM *in bed, afterwards.*)

SAM: C'I ask you a question?

AMY: Depends.

SAM: You have an orgasm?

AMY: What?

SAM: You cum?

AMY: Why?

SAM: Just wondering.

AMY: Didn't I act like I did?

SAM: I was just wondering if maybe you don't feel, like the way you walk through this house, not feeling, not yelling, like that's what makes you safe. So I was wondering if you feel me, you know, in there.

AMY: What?

SAM: Am I gettin' to you?

AMY: You really think you'd be here if I didn't feel anything?

SAM: You using me?

AMY: No. Just talking back.

SAM: Hey, I'm no one's gigolo.

AMY: C'mon.

SAM: Then, talk to me.

AMY: What about?

SAM: Normal things, you ask questions, learn stuff about the person, you know.

AMY: Fine. You start. Go ahead, ask a question.

SAM: Okay, your brother really drive your parents crazy?

AMY: No. Where you from?

SAM: C'mon, gotta give a better answer than that. He really drive your parents crazy?

AMY: Nah, just left, said they were goin' to Florida, vacation. They were kinda fucked anyway, never came back. Got a postcard once: "We're so sorry just couldn't do it anymore,

so little time left, please try to understand, love Mom and
Dad."

SAM: I'm from Cleveland.

AMY: What are you doing here?

SAM: Like to move around, never felt tied to anything.

AMY: That's lucky, I guess.

SAM: I guess. Hey, you ever want to get out of here?

AMY: Nah.

SAM: What were you doing before they left?

AMY: Was gonna go to school, I don't really like talkin' about
this.

SAM: Maybe I was tied to my brother before he died. He used to
get beat up and shit on the playground. I was in the car
when it crashed—

AMY: Please. I'm not good at, I can't hear about . . . it makes me
nauseous.

SAM: Hell Amy, you're like a . . . a . . . shook-up beer. It's unhealthy.
(AMY *turns away from him, on her side, and stares at the wall.*)

Scene 5

(BECCA *dressed to go out and* NAT *playing checkers in the kitchen.* AMY
leans against the fridge reading. She smokes. She is somewhere else.)

NAT: I met a Christian.

BECCA: Cool.

NAT: They're interesting, those Christians.

BECCA: Really.

NAT: I'm in McDonald's, and this Christian says, "You're not well, something's not right, I can tell."

BECCA: Yeah.

NAT: He was sick too. That's how he knew, sick like you, going to Dead shows, doin' acid. He found Jesus—

BECCA: That's scary.

NAT: He talked to me, about things, 'bout how we suffer, that was good. I don't get to have deep conversations much. Amy?

BECCA: I have lots of deep conversations. (SAM *enters with a black eye. He gets a beer.*)

AMY: What happened to your eye?

SAM: Job interview.

BECCA: Really?

SAM: This fuck, he's taking me round the site. We're shooting the shit. Everything's going great, I'm the man for the job, then, pow, six-fifty an hour for fucking construction. Construction! I told him to suck my asshole.

NAT: Six-fifty's better than freeloading.

BECCA: It's good to stand up for your rights.

AMY: You need some ice?

SAM: Punches me, pow, in the eye. Six-fucking-fifty an hour, my ass, my fucking asshole—you know? I smashed out all the lights on his car, front window too. (AMY *comes to* SAM, *touches his eye.*)

AMY: Doesn't look so good. (SAM *holds her hand there. She tries to retract it.*)

BECCA: It's walk time, isn't it?

NAT: What's that supposed to mean?

BECCA: It's time for you and Amy to take your walk.

AMY: That's right, let's go, once around the house.

NAT: "It's walk time, it's reading time, it's talking time," I just friggin' . . . yuhh . . . (*A guttural noise.*)

AMY: I know. I know.

BECCA: Better walk, or you'll get fat.

NAT: Fuck off.

BECCA: Hey Sam, Nat's getting brainwashed by the Christians.

NAT: What?

BECCA: He was in McDonald's and some Christian starts talkin' to him and he's so weak he starts talkin' back. Now he's getting brainwashed. They like people like him, you know. Fuckin' scary those Christians, always tryin' to save you, making life all serious.

SAM: Hey, I'm a Christian.

BECCA: Life is fun.

NAT: We talked about suffering. I like talking about suffering.

AMY: We'll walk. You'll tell me about it. (NAT *and* AMY *leave.* BECCA *pulls a couple of pills out of her purse, pops them, drinks water.*)

SAM: What's that?

BECCA: Ex. Slow hit, kick in on the ride, peak by the time I get to Baltimore.

SAM: You're going to Baltimore?

BECCA: Rave.

SAM: What d'ya do there?

BECCA: Dance, get high. Wanna come?

SAM: Maybe.

BECCA: You should.

SAM: Amy go?

BECCA: Yeah right.

SAM: C'I get one of those?

BECCA: Ex?

SAM: Yeah.

BECCA: It'll cost you.

SAM: How much?

BECCA: Thirty bucks.

SAM: Isn't there a family discount?

BECCA: What? You?

SAM: Sure.

BECCA: 'Cause you're fucking Amy?

SAM: Hey.

BECCA: What? You like her?

SAM: Sure. Why? What do you think?

BECCA: Think you need a place to stay.

SAM: I'll give you ten now, twenty when I get a job.

BECCA: You coming to Baltimore?

SAM: Maybe.

BECCA: Okay.

SAM: You shouldn't do all those drugs.

BECCA: I'm only sixteen.

SAM: So.

BECCA: Got plenty of time to straighten out. (AMY *and* NAT *come back in the house.*)

AMY: Journal time.

NAT: Ughhh . . . (*Guttural sound.*)

BECCA: Journal time, journal time! (NAT *gives* BECCA *the finger.*)

AMY: C'mon. Write one half hour, then you can watch TV.

NAT: Okay. (NAT *shuffles out of the kitchen.*)

BECCA: Sam's coming to Baltimore. He thinks he's family.

AMY: Are you?

SAM: I don't know.

BECCA: He wants to.

SAM: That okay with you?

AMY: What do I care?

BECCA: (*Hands* SAM *a pill.*) Here, you better take it now.

SAM: Thanks.

AMY: You gonna take that?

SAM: Maybe. Wanna do it, together?

AMY: No.

SAM: You be mad if I do it?

AMY: I said I don't care.

BECCA: She cares, wow.

AMY: No I don't. Do what you want, whatever you want.

SAM: Okay. (*He puts the pill in his pocket.*) Wanna go to Baltimore?

AMY: No. No, I don't, okay.

SAM: Sorry.

BECCA: Did I piss you off, Ame?

AMY: No.

BECCA: 'Cause I feel like I did.

AMY: You didn't.

BECCA: (*To* SAM.) Give it back.

SAM: What?

BECCA: The Ex, give it back.

SAM: Why?

AMY: You didn't piss me off, okay.

SAM: I'll give it back.

AMY: Look, I don't care. Both of you do what you want, okay.

BECCA: Fuck, see what you did.

AMY: He didn't do anything, nothing happened.

BECCA: It did, Amy. I don't have to go, if you don't want, or I could come home, like with a curfew.

AMY: It's fine, Bec, fine, everything is fine.

BECCA: Really?

AMY: Yes, go.

BECCA: Amy?

AMY: What?

BECCA: I got bruises.

AMY: What?

BECCA: I got bruises on my arms and legs, big black and purple hard ones, wanna see?

AMY: What d'ya mean?

BECCA: See. (BECCA *pulls up her sleeves. There are large purple and blue bruises covering her arms.*)

AMY: Oh my God. (SAM *gets up, looks at the bruises.*)

SAM: You been shooting up?

BECCA: No.

AMY: Have you? Have you? I'll kill you.

BECCA: No, I swear, got 'em on my legs too.

AMY: Oh my God, has she been shooting up? (SAM *examines* BECCA*'s arms.*)

SAM: I don't see any marks.

AMY: Well why does she have bruises?

BECCA: I don't know why. They come, they go, you know.

AMY: Maybe you're sick, are you sick?

BECCA: No.

SAM: She's gotta go to a doctor.

AMY: Why didn't you tell me, huh? Why?

SAM: Hey, just relax, probably from all that dancing, right? She'll go to the doctor, don't get worried till then, okay? Fuck, acting all crazy about a few bruises, hey. Okay, Amy? Okay?

AMY: Right.

BECCA: I didn't want to tell you, didn't want you to get upset. Hug me.

AMY: Okay. (AMY *hugs her.*) We'll go to the doctor.

BECCA: Ow, Amy, you're squashing me. (AMY *lets go.*)

SAM: See everything's all right, right? (*The sound of a car horn.*)

BECCA: That's my ride to Baltimore. (BECCA *looks to* AMY, *waits.*)

AMY: Have fun, Bec.

BECCA: If you don't want, I don't have to go. You could make me go to bed early, sleep in the bed with me if you need to.

AMY: It's okay, have a great night.

BECCA: Yeah, bye. (BECCA *leaves.* AMY *sits.*)

AMY: What is it?

SAM: Don't worry about it. You'll go to the doctor.

AMY: I hate the doctor. (SAM *throws the hit of Ex in the garbage like he is making a basket.*) Didn't have to do that for me.

SAM: Wasn't gonna do that shit anyway. (NAT *shuffles in.*)

AMY: Can't talk about it in front of him, everything's fine.

NAT: What? What?

AMY: Nothing, time to cook. (AMY *gets up to cook.* NAT *sits at the table.* SAM *and* AMY *act particularly okay.*)

NAT: Get me a carrot, Amy?

SAM: I'll get it.

AMY: Would ya?

SAM: Yeah. (*He gets up to get the carrot. He brushes by* AMY *at the stove making sauce. On his way back to the table, he bites her neck.*) Look at us, like a family, me getting Nat a carrot. (*He kisses her again.* AMY *smiles.*)

NAT: I can get my own carrot.

SAM: Look at that, Amy smiling. You see that, Nat?

NAT: What? (SAM *brings the carrot to* NAT, *holds it out in front of him.*)

SAM: It's good having me here, isn't it, Amy? (*She doesn't answer.*)

NAT: Amy?

SAM: It's good, right?

NAT: Is it? Amy?

SAM: Is it?

AMY: I'm not saying it's not good, okay.

SAM: Yessss . . . (NAT *snatches the carrot out of his hand, eats.*) We could rent a movie or something later.

AMY: That would be nice.

SAM: Yeah . . . would be. Amy cares . . .

AMY: Please.

SAM: Tell you how I really got this black eye.

AMY: I thought you had a job interview.

SAM: Didn't make it, went to a bar. This guy asks me where I'm living. I say here, with you. He says this family's crazy, bad luck, messed up, called you a slut.

AMY: What?

SAM: Said you were a wild teenager—

NAT: Amy's not a slut.

SAM: Always goin' to bars taking guys home.

AMY: It's not true. God, people, they've got no . . . it's not true.

SAM: Look, doesn't matter, long as you're my slut.

AMY: Shut up. I'm nobody's nothing, okay—nobody's nothing!

NAT: You should get outta here.

SAM: Hey, sorry, Amy knows I'm just joking.

NAT: Nobody has to get mad. Amy's happy. Amy's good. This Christian, right, he said that God or Jesus or someone is gonna come back, come down, and you know, he's gonna judge who's been good, who's been bad, and the good go to Paradise, the bad go to hell, right? Amy'd go to Paradise. Where would you go? Huh? She'll go to Paradise.

AMY: What'd he say it was 'sposed to be like, paradise?

NAT: Didn't say. I'll ask him tomorrow.

SAM: This is Paradise. Right here, baby. This is it.

AMY: Yeah. Yes it is. This is paradise. Hallelujah! (AMY *turns back to the stove. She begins to stir her sauce furiously. Blackout.*)

Scene 6

(*A rave in Baltimore.* BECCA *moves through flashing lights. The music throbs.* BECCA *dances. Her face is flushed. She moves, alone, wild . . .*)

Scene 7

(AMY *and* SAM *in the bedroom.* SAM *tries to turn* AMY *on.*)

SAM: What?

AMY: Not in the mood.

SAM: Why?

AMY: Pissed at you.

SAM: Why?

AMY: I hate going to the doctor.

SAM: What'd I do?

AMY: Called me that word.

SAM: What?

AMY: You know, that word, 'bout me sleeping with people. It's not true. You know, I left one year, before all the shit came down and Mom and Dad motored . . . got back here and God . . . it was so . . . quiet.

SAM: Nobody really called you that.

AMY: What?

SAM: Just wanted to know why you picked me up that night in the bar.

AMY: 'Cause I'm a slut. Duh. You're an asshole. Why'd you come home with me?

SAM: Nice hips.

AMY: Already know you're a liar. Fuck, you're probably not even from Cleveland.

SAM: Cleveland, Ohio, my brother died, went to Mexico.

AMY: Read, reading all the time, started this book about this woman who gets lost in Morocco, got sick of reading, couldn't turn another page of a goddamn book. You went to Mexico?

SAM: Yeah, drove. Long ride you know, 'specially from Cleveland. Broke down in Kansas. Big fucking country, lotsa states, some of 'em fuck bigger than others. Lots of road, lotsa color, lots of rest stops, lots of cigarettes, drank too much, listened to the Stones. "I can't get no, no satisfaction." Met a girl even, Nomie from Israel. She was wild. We had fun . . . turned out she was a bitch. Anyway, kept driving just had to get there—

AMY: And?

SAM: Couldn't find a place though. Kept driving. Days of driving, days and days. Nothing . . . more of fucking nothing, and no one. Too many nights sleeping in the car. Kept driving, came through here, first steady bed I've had in years.

AMY: What was it like? (SAM *tries to kiss her.*) Tell me what Mexico was like.

SAM: It wasn't like anything.

AMY: It was. It was beautiful and warm and you were really far away, tell me, tell me, c'mon pleeze. See, I was reading this book about Morocco and there's sand, warm sand on your feet, and sometimes there's thunder, only it's not scary, and there's this woman, this woman who gets lost, well, once she gets lost she can't get back, you know.

SAM: But you can, see. I think you can get back. That's what happened to me, here, meeting you. A secret, Amy?

AMY: About Mexico?

SAM: I want a safe place.

AMY: Tell me more about Mexico.

SAM: Your eyes look funny. I'm gettin' hard. C'mhere.

AMY: Tell me about the states you drove through.

SAM: C'mhere, kiss me, maybe you'll taste 'em.

AMY: Yeah?

SAM: It's all there inside. You can smell 'em. (*She comes to him, inhales deeply, smells.*)

AMY: Oh God. (*They begin to make love.*)

Scene 8

(*The kitchen, the next evening.* NAT *writes in his journal.* BECCA, *back from Baltimore, pours herself a glass of water.*)

BECCA: Watcha writin' about?

NAT: Myself.

BECCA: What?

NAT: Personal.

BECCA: I'm starved.

NAT: You look sick.

BECCA: Feel great. I need food. Where's Amy?

NAT: At the store. I could tell you about what I'm writing about, how I'm trying to change myself, if you want.

BECCA: Sure.

NAT: You have a soul, Bec?

BECCA: Amy say something about me last night?

NAT: No.

BECCA: She didn't?

NAT: No. (AMY *enters with the groceries. She's pretty flustered.*)

AMY: Where's Sam, you seen Sam?

NAT: Not today.

AMY: He wasn't here, when I woke up—

BECCA: I'm feeling much better today, Amy.

AMY: You think he's gone?

BECCA: Who?

AMY: Sam.

NAT: He's got nowhere else to go.

BECCA: I took an aspirin, and they're going away.

AMY: I think maybe I scared him, last night.

BECCA: How?

AMY: I, oh, never mind.

BECCA: But I'll go to the doctor if you want me to.

NAT: He'll be back.

AMY: Why? You think he likes me?

BECCA: He gives me the eye.

AMY: Really?

NAT: She's full of shit.

AMY: Where is he? Oh, what do I care, right?

NAT: Exactly.

AMY: I don't care. He was just a pain in the ass.

NAT: Exactly. You could do better.

AMY: I could find a rich man.

BECCA: A rich man.

AMY: You think? Really?

BECCA: I don't know.

NAT: I'm hungry.

BECCA: Yeah me too, Amy. (BECCA *puts her arms around* AMY.)

NAT: I'm gonna put my journal away, Amy, 'less you want me to read it to you.

AMY: Not now.

NAT: I'm writing about Cleveland, and Mexico. (AMY *looks at him.*)

BECCA: I felt sad today, this morning, you weren't here.

NAT: You're like a lesbian, Becca. You don't have to always be touching her.

AMY: (*Confidential.*) C'I ask you a question, Bec?

NAT: You could ask me.

BECCA: I had the coolest night. There was this—

AMY: You think it would scare someone off if you made their back bleed with your nails?

BECCA: Huh?

AMY: You know, while doing it, you know.

BECCA: Thing is, I don't want to go to the doctor.

NAT: Why she have to go to the doctor?

AMY: He can move, see states, I probably wouldn't even like him anymore if he came back. He coulda asked if I wanted to go. I wouldn't've, but he could've asked.

NAT: What Amy?

BECCA: Remember Aunt A? (AMY *falls into a chair.*) Remember we went to visit her, right, she had all those bruises, so Mom is like you gotta go to the hospital, you gotta go, so she goes, then she's dead, you know?

AMY: Yeah.

NAT: What's she talking about Amy? Amy?

BECCA: Then there was Nat, and he was just having a little trouble walking before he went to the doctor.

AMY: Right.

BECCA: Then Mom, she wouldn't have freaked out if she didn't start going to that group. And Grandma, and Grandpa, and Uncle Freddy—

NAT: She's so crazy, yuhhh . . . (*A guttural noise.*) I'm gettin' a friggin' headache. Tell her to shut up—(AMY *covers her ears.*)

BECCA: You don't want me to be sick, do you Ame? Amy? Amy? AMY!!! (AMY *stands. She begins to move slowly out of the kitchen.*)

NAT: Amy?

BECCA: I'm hungry.

AMY: I have to go to the bathroom. I'll cook in a bit.

BECCA: I could cook, don't know how to make anything, but I could cook.

AMY: That would be good, maybe.

NAT: You okay, Amy, you look weird.

AMY: Oh I'm fine, just fine, I just need to pee, to pee, to pee. (AMY *is out of the room,* BECCA *sits at the table with* NAT. *The sound of a door slamming, then a sound, muffled, the sound of steady sobbing, gasping, far away.* NAT *and* BECCA *sit in silence.* SAM *comes in the kitchen. He carries a shoe box. His shoes are filled with sand. His shirt is unbuttoned and there is sand in his nails and hair. He looks tired and excited.*)

SAM: Hey!

NAT and BECCA: Hey.

SAM: What's going on? Isn't it dinnertime? Where's Amy? (*No one answers. He hears the sound.*) Sounds like a horse is dying, what's the noise?

NAT: Amy.

SAM: What's she doing?

BECCA: I think she's crying.

SAM: She is?

NAT: Amy never cries.

SAM: Why's she crying?

BECCA: I don't know. Maybe one of us should go in there?

NAT: (*To* SAM.) Probably you.

SAM: She's in the bathroom?

NAT: Yeah.

BECCA: Shit, what if we have to pee?

SAM: Oh. I was gonna . . . why's she crying?

BECCA: I don't know. I'm not going in there.

NAT: Me either.

SAM: Okay. I was gonna . . . (SAM *sits at the table.*)

NAT: Amy never cries. (*They all remain seated, not moving, silent,
        listening to the sound of* AMY *broken open, as the lights fade. Pause.
        The rhythms of techno fill the house as the night moves on, and
        morning comes . . .*)

Scene 9

(*Morning in the kitchen.* BECCA *and* NAT *are asleep with their heads on
the kitchen table.* BECCA*'s headphones lie on the table. Techno drifts out
of them.* SAM *just sits, stares forward, plays with his shoe box.* NAT
wakes up, looks around, remembers slowly, looks at SAM. SAM *looks
away.* NAT *stands. He's stiff. He tries to stretch. He aches. He mumbles.
He goes to the cabinet to attempt to make coffee.* SAM *watches him.* NAT
fumbles with the coffee can, drops it on the floor.)

SAM: I can do that.

NAT: I got it. (NAT *drops the can again.* SAM *gets up, picks it up, begins
        to make the coffee.*) Didn't go in there, huh? (SAM *ignores him,
        makes coffee.*) I said, you couldn't go in there, huh?

SAM: I was gonna . . .

NAT: Yeah.

SAM: Look.

NAT: What?

SAM: Nothing. You want milk?

NAT: Yeah. (BECCA *wakes up, looks around, puts her headphones on, bops to the music for a few seconds, looks at* NAT *and* SAM, *remembers, pulls the headphones around her neck.*)

BECCA: No Amy?

NAT: No.

BECCA: What'd she say when you went in?

NAT: He didn't.

BECCA: He didn't go in?

SAM: No.

BECCA: Shit. Someone should, 'specially if she doesn't come out. (*She notices the box.*) What's in the box? (SAM *grabs the box.*)

SAM: Hey, nothing.

BECCA: What is it?

SAM: A present, for Amy.

BECCA: You should go give it to her.

SAM: Yeah, after breakfast. I'll cook. What do you guys eat?

BECCA: Huh?

SAM: Like if I made breakfast, what would I make?

BECCA: You could made eggs, or just cereal.

NAT: You don't have to make us anything.

SAM: That sounds good, cereal. (AMY *enters quietly. She sees* SAM *first.*)

AMY: Sam?!?

SAM: Morning.

AMY: Thought you left?!?

SAM: No.

NAT: You okay, Amy?

AMY: Fine. When did you come back?

SAM: Last night.

AMY: Oh.

SAM: I'm making the coffee.

AMY: So?

BECCA: Think we should make that appointment with the doctor today?

AMY: Yeah. Where'd you go?

SAM: Built a roof, construction, job.

AMY: Really?

SAM: Yeah, basically.

AMY: When'd you get back?

SAM: Get back?

AMY: Yeah, when'd you get back here?

SAM: Oh, around, dinnertime.

AMY: Dinnertime huh? Sure you left. I would've.

NAT: What?

SAM: Disappointed?

AMY: Whatever.

BECCA: Maybe we could go out for a sundae or something, after the doctor.

NAT: Why's she have to go to the doctor?

BECCA: Might be sick.

NAT: You're not sick.

BECCA: Might be.

AMY: What'd you do when you got back?

SAM: Hung out.

AMY: Where?

SAM: Here.

AMY: In the kitchen?

BECCA: We should have pancakes today.

AMY: (*Quietly.*) Did you hear me?

SAM: What?

AMY: Nothing. If you'd've left, where would you of gone?

SAM: Nowhere, wanna stay here.

AMY: Please.

SAM: Wanna help you out.

AMY: Make yourself a doctor's appointment, Bec.

BECCA: Okay. (BECCA *leaves to call the doctor.*)

AMY: I'm not in the mood for pancakes. Who wanted pancakes?

NAT: Bec did.

AMY: Wish I had a car.

SAM: You could use mine.

AMY: I'm just so sick of having nothing. I've been wearing the same clothes for five years. I want new clothes.

SAM: I'll buy you clothes.

NAT: You look good.

AMY: No one heard.

SAM: Heard what, Amy?

AMY: Forget it, just fucking forget it.

SAM: I'da come if I heard.

AMY: You hear, Nat?

NAT: What?

AMY: You hear me?

NAT: Uhmmm . . .

AMY: Did he? Did he hear? (NAT *looks at his feet*.) Bec!! BECCA!

BECCA: Got us a doctor's appointment, tomorrow, three o'clock.

AMY: You hear anything weird last night?

BECCA: Heard something, didn't know what it was.

AMY: Fuck. I just need to get out of here.

BECCA: We got an appointment, did you hear me? Three o'clock tomorrow.

NAT: What d'ya mean, Amy? What?

AMY: I don't want to go to the doctor. I don't have anything to wear to the doctor. My shoes got holes—

SAM: I told you I'll take her to the doctor.

BECCA: I'm only going to the doctor with Amy.

AMY: Nothing to read.

NAT: I don't know what's going on here, what's going on? (*To* SAM.) You shoulda gone in, yughhh . . . I told you.

AMY: Great, fucking, great, great!

SAM: Look, Amy, got a gift for you—

AMY: What? Not "safe" enough?

SAM: Hey.

AMY: I'm not feeling very "safe" right now. Pussy.

NAT: What's safe?

AMY: This is safe, right here, me, I'm safe. Right, Sam? Right? Safer than fucking Mexico, right, Sam? Right?

SAM: Hey.

BECCA: You're acting like Mom, Amy.

SAM: Calm down, Amy, c'mhere. I'm gonna take you out tonight, special, you and me. (*Silence.*)

NAT: Amy?

AMY: You are?

SAM: Yeah, want to talk . . .

AMY: You're gonna take me out later?

SAM: Yeah.

AMY: Out?

SAM: Yeah.

AMY: Now?

SAM: Not now. (*He comes to her, puts his hands on her shoulders, rubs.*) First you gotta finish cooking, then you gotta take Nat for his walk, then I'll take you for a ride, got some things I wanna talk over with you.

NAT: Where you gonna take her?

SAM: Want some privacy, want to talk to Amy.

NAT: You'll bring her back?

BECCA: Duh, course he will. We got to go to the doctor tomorrow, me and Amy. It'll be fun.

AMY: Will you?

SAM: Hell, of course I will, you'll see, you'll see what I wanna talk to you about. (AMY *cooks.*)

AMY: I'd like to go out.

SAM: Yeah, you'll like this. (*He kisses her at the stove.*) Like to watch you make breakfast, like man of the house, hell, get me a beer, Bec. (BECCA *gets him a beer.*)

BECCA: You could come to the doctor too, but only if Amy comes, three of us.

NAT: Why's she going to the doctor?

SAM: I'll take you both to the doctor, pick up some ice cream. We'll celebrate, paradise, Morocco.

AMY: I'd like to go out. (*Blackout.*)

Scene 10

(SAM *and* AMY *outside. They walk.*)

AMY: Where we going?

SAM: Up this hill, nice spot, we'll talk.

AMY: I know this hill. (AMY *looks out. There is a view. She breathes deep.*) Smell that? That tree?

SAM: I smell something.

AMY: That's sumac, smells like sperm. We used to park under it, in high school, just to smell, in amazement.

SAM: That's weird.

AMY: Yeah. We were teenagers. It made us laugh. So nice out here.

SAM: Yeah.

AMY: So?

SAM: Amy.

AMY: Yeah, Sam.

SAM: You look real good.

AMY: Really?

SAM: I'm gonna buy you new shoes.

AMY: It's okay, so nice out here.

SAM: Yeah.

AMY: So?

SAM: What?

AMY: My nerves are all jumpy.

SAM: Me too.

AMY: Got scared 'bout what I did to your back.

SAM: Fuckin' hurt.

AMY: I can be crazy, huh?

SAM: Yeah, but that's okay, now.

AMY: Now?

SAM: Yeah.

AMY: Why?

SAM: Because, because . . . I wanna do something, you and me.

AMY: Oh.

SAM: Yeah.

AMY: I don't know.

SAM: You don't.

AMY: Shit, my heart's going so fast. The other night when I smelt you, Sam, smelt all that—

SAM: Mine too.

AMY: What about them?

SAM: I think they'll like it.

AMY: No, no they won't. They might die without me.

SAM: Without you?

AMY: You think I'd be able to stop thinking about them? I don't know, I don't know if I could live with that, but maybe you could help me? I'd have to forget everything. Maybe you could make me forget.

SAM: They'll have both of us, I'll be good to them. I want it, a family, a fucking family. If it's something bad with Becca we'll take care of it together. (*Silence, as* AMY *tries to figure out what he has said.*)

AMY: A fam . . . what?

SAM: C'mon, don't make me say it.

AMY: Say what? Say what?

SAM: Wait. (*He goes to the car, comes back with the shoe box.*) Here, for you. (AMY *opens the box. It is full of sand. She reaches her hand in, elated, scoops up handfuls of sand and lets it fall through her fingers.*)

AMY: Oh, Sam!

SAM: I woke up, other morning, and I knew before, but now I really knew, went out, built that roof, bought it, no big deal, small, but hey, it's in there somewhere. (AMY *picks up a handful of sand, it falls through her fingers till she's left with a ring. She stares at the ring.*) So, wanna marry me?

AMY: (AMY *stares at the ring, realizes.*) Oh.

SAM: We could even have our own kid, you know. I'll get a job. I'll buy you clothes. Clothes and shoes.

AMY: (*Still staring at the ring.*) Oh.

SAM: What do you think?

AMY: Well, I was starting to get ideas, in my head, ideas, I was starting to . . . (AMY *is having trouble breathing.*)

SAM: All those books, all those ideas, something I really like about you, Amy.

AMY: (*Hyperventilating a bit.*) Oh well, it's very, well, what do you mean, get married?

SAM: I mean you put on a nice white dress and I put a ring on you, and we make something together, you know, with our lives, something with a lot of meaning, you know.

AMY: Where will we live?

SAM: 208 Flat Lane, your house, our house.

AMY: Right.

SAM: Yeah. I figured, you know, it's time, why the hell not. We could get married on the weekend.

AMY: This weekend?

SAM: Look Amy, we'll have this house right, and it'll be a lot realer than I ever been. You'll have a lot more time to, you know, do what you like, you know, read and stuff, and it'll be like it's 'sposed to, you know. Tomorrow we'll take Bec to the doctor. (AMY *starts to laugh.*) What? What? Why you laughing? That mean yes?

AMY: How could I ever of thought . . . they need me so bad, you know, our parents when they left, shit, shit, shit. (AMY's *body goes limp.* SAM *holds her in his arms.*)

SAM: Amy, Amy, this is life, real life; see, I got an idea in my head too.

AMY: Yeah.

SAM: Sounds good, doesn't it, you and me, right?

AMY: Sure, sure it does.

SAM: C'mon, let's go home. (AMY *pushes him away.*)

AMY: I don't know Sam, I don't know if I can do that. I don't know.

SAM: Fuck, Amy, here I go putting myself out there, shit.

AMY: I didn't say no. I just said I don't know.

SAM: All right, all right, you'll think about it. Hey, I know, I know it's right. You'll know it too. I got no doubt of that, so I'm fine, see? (*He holds his arms out, smiles at her.*) You like me, Amy, don't you?

AMY: Yeah.

SAM: I like you. (*Blackout.*)

Scene 11

(*The kitchen the next day, late afternoon, early evening.* NAT *sits at the table.* AMY *enters in a slightly ill-fitting wedding gown that she wears over her day clothes. She stands behind* NAT, *her hands on his shoulders, staring out.*)

NAT: Sometimes, sometimes when I'm alone in this house I can't find things, like I forget where things are, then I think maybe something, something happened, like a UFO came and took me away for ten years and I had this whole other life, and they brought me back here, and I'm having trouble remembering this life, even though I can't remember that life at all. I wonder what it was like. Maybe I looked different, maybe I had a family, maybe I was the mayor or something, maybe it was easy to move, to get out of bed. Then you come in, Amy, and I know where things are 'cause you show me. (AMY *strokes his shoulders and arms.*) Wish I could feel that, but my body is numb. (AMY *moves so she is facing* NAT.)

AMY: Whadd'ya think?

NAT: Why you wearing that?

AMY: Sam asked me to marry him.

NAT: Oh.

AMY: What do you think?

NAT: It looks good, pretty.

AMY: 'Bout me getting married?

NAT: He gonna take you away?

AMY: No, he wants to live here, all of us, a big happy family.

NAT: You want to?

AMY: Maybe. It's pretty weird, you know, never would of thought—

NAT: If he promises never to take you away from us.

AMY: This dress was Mom's.

NAT: Yeah. (*Beat, as if* NAT *and* AMY *have traveled somewhere else.*) What's she look like again?

AMY: Who?

NAT: Mom, what's Mom look like again?

AMY: Brown hair.

NAT: Eyes?

AMY: Brown.

NAT: Skin?

AMY: Just skin.

NAT: Small.

AMY: Yeah.

NAT: And Dad?

AMY: Do you hate them?

NAT: Try not to.

AMY: Think you could forget what I look like?

NAT: Nah. Would you have a baby?

AMY: God, I don't know.

NAT: I wouldn't mind a baby.

AMY: I'd like to go on a honeymoon.

NAT: Why?

AMY: Gotta celebrate, 'specially if you get married, you know?

NAT: Where you go?

AMY: Some beach or something, I don't know.

NAT: What are we gonna do?

AMY: You can take care of yourselves for a few days, can't you?

NAT: How long does it take to starve?

AMY: You won't starve.

NAT: Sure we will.

AMY: Only if the car crashes on the way.

NAT: Oh, no, that wouldn't happen.

AMY: Or if I got kidnapped or something.

NAT: That wouldn't happen to you.

AMY: But if it did, you wouldn't starve.

NAT: Course we would.

AMY: It's just sometimes, I miss something . . .

NAT: What?

AMY: I don't know. I don't know. (*She does a quick turn in the dress.*) C'mon really, m'I a sight for sore eyes?

NAT: It's a little big.

AMY: Too big to wear?

NAT: Nah, you look beautiful.

AMY: I do?

NAT: Yes, Amy. (*Beat.*)

AMY: Think I'll take it off now, before they get home. (*She takes the dress off, folds it carefully, returning it to a big, beat-up box . . .*)

NAT: Amy?

AMY: Yeah?

NAT: What's love like?

AMY: What?

NAT: What's it like, to be in love?

AMY: Oh. It's great.

NAT: Wish I could feel it.

AMY: You're in love with me, aren't you?

NAT: But that's different.

AMY: No, it isn't. It's exactly the same. (SAM *and* BECCA *enter with a Friendly's ice cream cake.*)

SAM: Hey guys. Celebration time!

NAT: That Christian, you know, he talks about how people are put on the world for a reason, and you're lucky 'cause you've got this reason that makes sense. The Christian, he wants to come over and meet you. He thinks you sound great.

BECCA: (*Getting plates and forks.*) How come he doesn't want to meet me?

NAT: Not ready.

BECCA: I could be sick.

NAT: Yeah right.

BECCA: I've got blood clots, isn't that right? Amy? Sam? We went to the doctor.

SAM: That's right.

AMY: Thanks for takin' us.

BECCA: Amy was so scared she couldn't get out of the car.

AMY: I told you, I hate the friggin' doctor.

NAT: She's not sick, no way.

BECCA: I'm gonna have a test. Maybe I got a virus.

NAT: Nah.

BECCA: My blood is thin.

NAT: Unh-uh.

BECCA: It's true, it's true, lah di, dah dah dah. (AMY *plays with the cake.*)

AMY: I prayed in the car. (SAM *comes to her, kisses her.*)

NAT: I'll talk to the Christian.

BECCA: I can have tests, and whatever happens, you can take care of me, and it's probably nothing.

SAM: I know all about that, prayin' in the car.

AMY: (*To* SAM.) What'd you think life was gonna be like when you were a kid?

SAM: I don't know.

AMY: I mean when you were little and you imagined yourself now?

SAM: Thought it would be better. There'd be a girl like you.

AMY: (*Smiling.*) C'mon.

BECCA: Awww, sweet.

SAM: What'd you think?

AMY: Oh I don't know, some kinda movie or something. No one got sick, and no one disappeared. You did things 'cause you wanted to, not because you had to. Now I don't know. People, they get sick, they disappear, they die, and the thing to do, the only thing that won't kill your insides is to do this.

BECCA: I'll bet Mom's insides are like a real heavy bowling ball.

AMY: Sam?

SAM: Yeah, baby? (AMY *gets up. She begins to move out of the kitchen.*)

AMY: Guess I'll marry you. (*Everyone stops eating, looks up.* AMY *leaves the room.*)

SAM: What? (*He follows her out of the room,* NAT *and* BECCA *sit there.*)

BECCA: Wow. (BECCA *pulls a joint out of her pocket, lights it.*) I can't wait to get married.

NAT: You have to smoke that?

BECCA: It's just a special cigarette.

NAT: C'mon. You know, Amy talked this whole thing over with me, asked me what I thought, when you guys were out.

BECCA: Sam talked it over with me. Makes sense though, you know, I've always been sort of psychic, right? The other night I had a dream the four of us lived on a seashell floating in the ocean. It was such a nice dream.

NAT: I never dream when I'm sleeping.

BECCA: Fucking beautiful.

NAT: You're on drugs.

BECCA: Duh.

NAT: Maybe Amy will have a baby?

BECCA: No. At the end of my dream the shell got really heavy and started to sink, but I forgot that part. (*Blackout.*)

Scene 12

(*Colored lights flash. A rave, another night, another city . . .* BECCA *dances, something like Moby's "Feeling So Real." The dance is slow at first. It grows and grows until* BECCA *is dancing wildly, punching her arms and legs with her fists, beating herself. The music fades and* BECCA *falls in a heap on the dance floor.*)

Scene 13

(AMY *and* SAM *in the bedroom, the eve of their wedding.*)

SAM: Tomorrow you're gonna be Mrs. Sam.

AMY: I could be dead tomorrow.

SAM: What?

AMY: Just kidding.

SAM: You make stupid jokes, Amy.

AMY: You ever been in love, Sam?

SAM: What kinda question is that?

AMY: What's it feel like?

SAM: I'm in love with you.

AMY: What's it feel like?

SAM: You feel it, don't you?

AMY: Sure. Just want to know what it's like for you.

SAM: It's like . . . I don't know. It's like paradise.

AMY: What's paradise like?

SAM: Like, like being a little buzzed all the time.

AMY: What's that like?

SAM: I don't know, Amy.

AMY: Aren't you gonna miss driving, goin' places?

SAM: No.

AMY: We'll go on a honeymoon, won't we?

SAM: Course, after we settle down, get some money together.

AMY: Not right away?

SAM: It's hard to just take off. I like it here.

AMY: We could go to Florida.

SAM: Yeah.

AMY: Bump into Mom and Dad.

SAM: That would be a hoot.

AMY: Not gonna happen though, is it?

SAM: We could go to Florida, couple months, or so.

AMY: Danger is, we could have a car accident on the way.

SAM: Not with me behind the wheel.

AMY: I could get shot.

SAM: Relax, Amy, we're just getting married. You're a nervous
    wreck.

AMY: Yeah I'm nervous.

SAM: C'mhere. (*She comes.*) Mrs. Sam.

AMY: Tell me about Mexico.

SAM: No. (*He kisses her.*) Fucking husband and wife, hell, say it.

AMY: Husband and wife. (*He laughs. He kisses her.*) Sam?

SAM: Yeah, baby.

AMY: That night when I cried, and you heard, you couldn't come in, right?

SAM: You won't cry anymore.

AMY: You couldn't come in. You can't take me away. You want a family.

SAM: We've got a family.

AMY: Fuck you, Sam.

SAM: Hey, I'll learn, I'll learn what to do if you cry.

AMY: Fuck you, Sam.

SAM: What?

AMY: Just said fuck you.

SAM: I'll take care of you. I'll keep you safe, and me, you'll do that for me, 'cause you don't know about the road, Amy, you don't know.

AMY: Did you ever get to Mexico, Sam? (*He doesn't answer.*) Sam? (*He doesn't answer.*) Where's the keys to your car?

SAM: On the drawers. (AMY *goes to the dresser, picks up the keys, holds them.*) Amy.

AMY: I could take 'em and I could go, I could go to Florida, I could drive to Florida, right now—

SAM: Amy.

AMY: —'Cause it all fucking sucks, all of it. I'm totally sick of it,
    I'm gonna leave you behind, with all this, huh, see, how'd
    you like that? You, you totally stupid person! Shit I don't
    know how to get to Florida!

SAM: You could buy a map!

AMY: I could buy a map. A map, yes.

SAM: Go ahead!

AMY: Yeah, I'll buy a fucking map! 'Cause you ever think about
    it, Sam, who I'd be without all this shit, who else I'd be?

SAM: You wouldn't be anyone! (*Beat.*)

AMY: I hate you, I hate all of you. (*Blackout.*)

Scene 14

(*The kitchen.* NAT *and* BECCA *playing checkers.*)

NAT: Couldn't sleep.

BECCA: Dreamt our house was on fire, but it was okay. There was
    a new house waiting down the street.

NAT: Afraid I won't make the walk down the aisle.

BECCA: I could do it for you.

NAT: I'm gonna give her to him, if anyone is. (SAM *enters.*)

SAM: Morning family.

NAT and BECCA: Morning.

SAM: I'm cooking this morning. (*He puts on* AMY's *apron.*)

BECCA: Feel like eggs.

SAM: Eggs, huh. (*He goes to the fridge, takes out eggs. He proceeds to crack and scramble, making a mess.*)

NAT: I'm still writing, writing about my life on the UFO. (BECCA *takes out a joint, lights it.*) Not again.

BECCA: Gonna celebrate tonight, celebrate for you guys, Pennsylvania, Amish country, if it's okay, Sam.

SAM: You could call me Dad.

BECCA: (*Winks at him.*) I can't call you Dad.

SAM: Why not?

NAT: What's in Amish country?

BECCA: Rave.

NAT: In Amish country?

BECCA: Yeah, cool.

NAT: Nothin', nothing goes untouched, disgusting. C'I have a glass of water?

SAM: Sure.

BECCA: Me too. Any munchies?

SAM: Not before breakfast, gotta start the day right, you know, eggs, bacon, toast. Can I have a hit of that? (BECCA *passes* SAM *the joint.*)

NAT: Where's Amy?

SAM: Shower.

BECCA: Nervous?

SAM: Yeah. (AMY *enters, in the wedding gown, in all its glory.*)

AMY: Morning.

SAM: Morning, baby.

AMY: How do I look?

NAT: You look beautiful.

SAM: You do.

AMY: Really?

NAT: Wish I was marrying you.

BECCA: Ewww . . .

AMY: (*Reaches out her hands to* NAT *and* BECCA.) Mom and Dad had some great kids.

BECCA: Now they're yours, isn't that funny.

AMY: Yeah. (*She smiles, a slow, slow smile, and turns to* SAM.) You cooking?

SAM: That's right.

AMY: Making a mess.

SAM: I'll get better at it.

AMY: I'll do it.

SAM: You sure?

AMY: Yeah. (SAM *takes off the apron, hands it to* AMY. *She puts it on very slowly.* SAM *helps her. The kids watch.* SAM *sits at the table, takes another hit of* BECCA's *joint.* AMY *moves to the stove.*)

NAT: What's it gonna be like now that you guys are married? (*No one answers.*) Ame, Amy, Ames, what's it gonna be like?

AMY: It'll be the same, 'cept there'll be two of us. We'll take you for your walk. We'll eat. You'll watch TV. Becca will dance. I'll read. Sam will have a beer. We'll see the doctor again and again if we have to. We'll deal, we'll go on, we'll keep going, and we'll do it together, keep going, together, because we are a family. We are a family. Maybe someday, when we die, we'll go to Paradise and we'll look back on this, we'll watch everything we did here, and we'll smile. 'Cause this is life, real life, this, doing this, keeping each other safe, that's what we'll do. It's all we can do. (AMY *cooks, turns to the table.*) Breakfast is ready. (AMY *serves the breakfast. She watches as* SAM, NAT, *and* BECCA *salt their eggs, reach for the ketchup, etc. Finally* AMY *joins them . . .*)

END OF PLAY

THIS IS OUR YOUTH

Kenneth Lonergan

The world premiere of *This Is Our Youth* was originally presented by The New Group (Scott Elliott, Artistic Director; Claudia Catania, Executive Producer).

This Is Our Youth was produced by Second Stage Theatre (Carole Rothman, Artistic Director; Carol Fishman, Managing Director; Alexander Fraser, Executive Director), by special arrangement with Barry and Fran Weissler and The New Group in New York City, in November 1998. It was directed by Mark Brokaw; the set design was by Allen Moyer; the costume design was by Michael Krass; the lighting design was by Mark McCullough; the sound design was by Robert Murphy; the fight director was Rick Sordeler; and the production stage manager was William H. Lang. The cast was as follows:

DENNIS ZIEGLER	Mark Rosenthal
WARREN STRAUB	Mark Ruffalo
JESSICA GOLDMAN	Missy Yager

CHARACTERS

DENNIS ZIEGLER: Twenty-one years old.
WARREN STRAUB: Nineteen years old.
JESSICA GOLDMAN: Nineteen years old.

TIME

March 1982.

PLACE

Dennis's one-room apartment on the Upper West Side of Manhattan.

ACT 1

(*A cold Saturday night in March 1982, after midnight. A small, impersonal pillbox studio apartment on the second or third floor of a somewhat rundown postwar building on the Upper West Side of Manhattan between Broadway and West End, lived in by* DENNIS ZIEGLER. *There are a TV and stereo, a lot of records, some arbitrary furniture, a little-used kitchenette, and a mattress on the floor in the corner. Scattered around the room are piles of the* New York Post, *sports magazines, and a lot of underground comic books. There is sports equipment in the apartment, if not actually in view. The room looks lived-in, but aside from a wall of photographs from* DENNIS's *life, no effort whatsoever has been made to decorate it. It looks like it could be packed up and cleared out in half an hour.*)

(DENNIS *is watching an old black-and-white movie on TV. He is a grungy, handsome, very athletic, formerly long-haired kid, just twenty-one years old, wearing baggy chino-type pants and an ancient polo shirt. He is a very quick, dynamic, fanatical, and bullying kind of person; amazingly good-natured and magnetic, but insanely competitive and almost always successfully so; a dark cult god of high school only recently encountering, without necessarily recognizing, the first evidence that the dazzling, aggressive hipster techniques with which he has always dominated his peers might not stand him in good stead for much longer.*)

(*The buzzer buzzes.* DENNIS *is too cool to answer it right away. It buzzes again. He gets up and goes to the intercom.*)

DENNIS: Yeah?

WARREN: (*Over the intercom.*) Yo, Dennis. It's me, Warren.

DENNIS: What do you want?

WARREN: (*Over the intercom.*) Yo, lemme up.

(DENNIS *hits the buzzer. Sits down and watches TV. There is a knock at the door. Again, he doesn't answer it right away. Another knock.*)

WARREN: (*Off.*) Yo, Denny.

(DENNIS *gets up and unlocks the door without opening it, then plops down again to watch TV.*)

(WARREN STRAUB *comes in the front door. He is a skinny nineteen-year-old—a strange barking-dog of a kid with large tracts of thoughtfulness in his personality that are not doing him much good at the moment, probably because they so infrequently influence his actions. He has spent most of his adolescence in hot water of one kind or another, and is just beginning to find beneath his natural eccentricity a dogged self-possession his friends may not all share. But despite his enormous self-destructiveness, he is above all things a trier. His language and wardrobe are heavily influenced by* DENNIS—*but only up to a point, and he would be a good-looking kid if he eased up on his personal style a little.*)

(*He comes into the apartment lugging a very big suitcase and an overloaded heavy-duty hiking backpack.*)

WARREN: Hey.

DENNIS: What's with the suitcase?

WARREN: Nothing . . . What are you doing?

DENNIS: Nothing.

(WARREN *closes the door and puts down his stuff. Sits down next to* DENNIS *on the mattress and looks at the TV.*)

WARREN: What are you watching?

DENNIS: Lock the door.

(WARREN *gets up and locks the door. He sits down as before.*)

WARREN: What are you watching?

(DENNIS *flashes off the TV with the remote control.*)

DENNIS: Nothing. What do you want?

WARREN: Nothing.

DENNIS: I don't have any pot.

WARREN: I don't want any. I got some.

DENNIS: Let me see it.

(WARREN *produces a ziplock plastic bag carefully wrapped around a small amount of dark green marijuana.* DENNIS *opens it and smells it.*)

DENNIS: This is good. Where'd you get it?

WARREN: From Christian.

DENNIS: Can we smoke it?

WARREN: I'm saving it.

DENNIS: For what?

(DENNIS *takes the pot out of the bag and reaches for a record album. He starts to crumble the pot onto the album cover.*)

WARREN: Just half.

DENNIS: Shut up.

WARREN: Just *half*, man.

(DENNIS *looks at him and crumbles the rest of the pot onto the album.*)

DENNIS: You got papers?

WARREN: You're a fuckin' asshole.

(*He gets up.* DENNIS *laughs.*)

DENNIS: There's some papers on the table. Gimme one.

(WARREN *does not comply.*)

DENNIS: (*Sharply.*) Hey! Give me a *rolling* paper. Do you know how much *money* you owe me?

(WARREN *takes out a small wad of bills, peels off a few, and drops them on the bed.*)

DENNIS: Where'd you get this?

WARREN: What do you care?

DENNIS: Well if you're so rich then you can get more pot from Christian tomorrow, so give me the fucking rolling papers before I beat the shit out of you.

(WARREN *goes to the table and throws a packet of Club or Zig-Zag rice papers to* DENNIS.)

DENNIS: What happened, Jasonius kicked you out?

WARREN: No, man, I left.

DENNIS: You can't stay here.

WARREN: I don't want to stay here.

DENNIS: Why'd he kick you out? What'd you do?

WARREN: Nothing. I got stoned and he comes home and he's like, "This apartment smells like pot *all the time*." And I'm like, "Yeah, 'cause I'm always *smoking* it." So then he's like, "I want that smell out of this house." And then he's like, "No, actually, I want *you* out of this house." Then he throws a few bills on the floor and is like, "There's some cash, now pack up your shit and get out before I beat your fuckin' head in." And I was like, "Whatever." So he went on a date with his whore, and I packed up my stuff and left.

DENNIS: Where are you going to stay?

WARREN: I don't know. Maybe I'll stay with Christian. I don't know. Maybe I'll stay in a hotel. Who the hell knows?

DENNIS: How are you going to stay in a hotel?

WARREN: I got money.

DENNIS: How much did he give you?

WARREN: He gave me some money.

DENNIS: Why? Like to thank you for leaving?

WARREN: I guess.

DENNIS: How much is this?

(*Putting the beautifully rolled joint in his mouth,* DENNIS *counts the money* WARREN *threw on the bed.*)

WARREN: Two hundred.

(DENNIS *finishes counting. From under the mattress he pulls a beat-up school composition notebook and flips through it till he finds* WARREN's *name.*)

DENNIS: "Warren."

(*He writes something in the book.*)

DENNIS: (*Writing.*) "*Cleared,* with stolen funds."

WARREN: They're not stolen, man, he gave it to me.

(DENNIS *closes the book, finds a match, and lights up.*)

DENNIS: (*Holding in the smoke.*) Where did Christian get this from?

WARREN: I don't know.

(DENNIS *slaps* WARREN *in the face, playfully but hard.*)

DENNIS: Don't fuckin' lie to me—where'd he get it?

(WARREN *tries to hit* DENNIS *back. They scuffle, but* DENNIS *is much bigger and stronger and stops him.*)

WARREN: Don't fuckin' hit me—

DENNIS: Where did he get it from?

WARREN: Why don't you ask him?

DENNIS: Did he get it from Philip?

WARREN: No, he said he got it from some fuckin' Rastafarian.

DENNIS: That guy Wally?

WARREN: I don't know.

DENNIS: That guy Kresko?

WARREN: I don't know. I don't keep track of where you guys perform your criminal activities. Who cares? Gimme that.

(DENNIS *doesn't move. He keeps smoking.* WARREN *reaches for the joint.* DENNIS *allows him to take it.*)

DENNIS: How much money did you steal?

WARREN: A lot.

DENNIS: Let me see.

(WARREN *opens his backpack and takes out a felt shoe bag stuffed with thousands of dollars in small bills. He loosens the ties and shows it to* DENNIS.)

DENNIS: That's a lot.

WARREN: It's fifteen thousand dollars.

DENNIS: Are you *fucking* crazy? (*Pause.*) Give me half.

WARREN: No.

DENNIS: Give me five.

WARREN: I'm not giving you anything.

DENNIS: No. Give me five, we'll go to *France*, and we'll mail the rest back to your dad with a note. "Took five. Went to *France*."

WARREN: I'm keeping it.

DENNIS: Are you kidding? He'll send large men after you with *guns.*

WARREN: He doesn't even know I have it.

DENNIS: What do you mean?

WARREN:	DENNIS:
I mean he—	Where did you *get* it from?

WARREN: It was in his room.

DENNIS: It was in his *room*?

WARREN: Yeah.

DENNIS: Your father keeps fifteen thousand dollars cash in his *room*? For what? *Tips*?

WARREN: I don't know. I guess he's got some kind of illicit lingerie deal in the works or something, I don't know.

DENNIS: Your father is so heavy, man . . .

WARREN: Yeah, so after he threw me out and went to *supper,* I was just roaming the house looking for liftable objects, if that was gonna be his attitude. So I go in his bedroom and there's this sinister looking *brief*case just *sitting* on his *bed.* So I jimmied open the lock and there's like rows and rows of cash just starin' at me. Like totally full of money.

DENNIS: *Jason.*

WARREN: Yeah! So I'm like, "*Dad* . . . !" And then I'm like, "Should I take this? This is some serious money." And then I'm like, "Fuck yeah. Make him *pay.*" So I take out the cash, and I fill the briefcase with all these old *National Geographic*s and lock it up again. So it'll probably sit there for the weekend, and then when he goes to deposit it, or bribe whoever he was planning on bribing, he'll open it up and hopefully he'll think like one of his *cohorts* ripped him off. Or like, his *slut* did it.

DENNIS: No he *won't*.

WARREN: Why not?

DENNIS: Of *course* he won't.

WARREN: Why not?

DENNIS: Because he's not a *moron*.

WARREN: Yes he is.

DENNIS: You really think after he throws you out of the house he's gonna open his briefcase and find twenty copies of his own *National Geographic*s where his *money* should be, and he's not gonna know you did it? You're a fuckin' moron. Now get that shit outta here.

WARREN: I'm telling you—

DENNIS: Take it over to Christian's house and let your father's bodyguards break *his* fuckin' legs.

WARREN: He doesn't *have* any bodyguards.

DENNIS: The guy who drives his car is not a bodyguard?

WARREN: No, he's a *driver*.

DENNIS: That guy like shows me his *gun*, like every time I *see* him.

WARREN: Yeah, because he's *insane*. But my father is not a *criminal*. He's just in *business* with criminals.

DENNIS: I don't give a shit *what* he is. I can't believe you cart that kind of money across town and like bring it to my *doorstep*. No—no—I mean you are so stupid, man, you are so incredibly stupid. He kicks you out so you steal fifteen thousand *dollars* from him?

WARREN: I was pissed.

DENNIS: OK: Get it out of here. Take it to Christian's house.

WARREN: He's not home.

DENNIS: Take it to Yoffie's house; go to Leonard's house. I don't care.

WARREN: Nobody's home. Everyone's parents are home. I'm not allowed in their houses. Come on. I don't want to be wandering around the streets with all that money. Come on.

(*Pause.*)

DENNIS: This is so typical of you, man, I mean this is like . . .

WARREN: Yeah yeah yeah.

DENNIS: This is like the prototype moronic move we've all come to expect from your corner. You drive the guy *crazy* because you're such a sniveling little obnoxious punk, you *grate* on the guy until he finally throws you out—arguably the most dangerous lingerie manufacturer in the *world*— And then you steal his money and bring it to my *house*, and expect me to like *hide* you or something?

(WARREN *starts to speak.*)

DENNIS: No—no— That's why nobody likes you, man, because you're always provoking people. OK, now everybody's provoked, only *you're* the one they all fuckin' hate! Listen to me. I'm trying to tell you something. This is good for you.

WARREN: Oh, yeah.

DENNIS: No it is. It's good for you. Listen. You're a fuckin' *idiot*. You never have any money. Nobody can stand to have you around. And you can't get laid. I mean, man, you cannot get laid. You *never* get laid. Like the last girlfriend you had was in like ninth grade and it lasted for two weeks, and that bitch probably still hasn't recovered.

WARREN: She hasn't. I freaked her out.

DENNIS: What kind of *life* do you lead? You live with your father—a psycho. He beats the shit out of you on like this regular *basis*, you habitually owe me hundreds of dollars, you never pay me—until now, but we won't even discuss that— Nobody can stand to have you around because you're such an annoying loudmouthed little creep, and now you're like some kind of fugitive from *justice*? What is gonna happen to you, man?

WARREN: What's gonna happen to anybody? Who cares?

(DENNIS *shrugs, sits. Relights the joint, which has gone out.*)

WARREN: Like you're so independent?

DENNIS: Yeah, because my parents *pay* for this apartment. They don't throw me *out* of it. Because they're so grateful I don't wanna live with them. Because I don't *goad* them into *making* me dependent. I'm just like, "*Don't* send me to college. Just spring for my rent, I'll be a fuckin' *bike* messenger till I decide what I wanna do, and we'll never have to deal with each other." And they're like, *"Fine."*

(*Pause.*)

WARREN: Why do you say that shit?

DENNIS: Because it's true.

WARREN:	DENNIS:
Why do you—	Because you deserve it.

(WARREN *is close to tears.*)

DENNIS: Are you *crying* now?

WARREN: No. (*Pause.*) *I* don't know what to do (*Pause.*) *I* don't know where to go.

DENNIS: Well—for one thing you should give me five thousand dollars and then you should return that money.

WARREN: I'm not giving you five thousand dollars.

DENNIS: I'm telling you. *France.*

(*Pause.*)

WARREN: You want some money?

DENNIS: No, I don't want any money.

(WARREN *opens the bag and holds out two bricks of cash.*)

WARREN: Take some money. Go to fuckin' France.

DENNIS: I don't wanna go to France. Like I want your father *stalking* me for the rest of my life? Now put that shit back in the bag and take it back to where you found it. It *scares* me.

(WARREN *puts the money back and closes the ties.*)

WARREN: I can't return it because he's home by now. He's *asleep.* The shit is in his bedroom and he's gonna be home all day tomorrow because he's having some associates over for *brunch.*

DENNIS: Brunch. (*Pause.*) That's a wild concept: It's not breakfast and it's not lunch. It's *brunch.* (*Rolls the word around in his mouth.*) "Brunch." "Let's serve *brunch . . .*" It's something you *serve.* (*Long pause.*) This is strong pot.

WARREN: I know.

DENNIS: All right: You know what you should tell your father?

WARREN: It doesn't matter what I do. He's gonna kill me anyway, so what's the difference?

DENNIS: No. Let's figure this out. It's gonna be OK. I'm a total mathematical genius. Now how much of this cash did you spend?

WARREN: Not much. I paid you back . . . I took a cab . . . I ate sushi . . . Two hundred and fifty bucks. But he gave me fifty.

DENNIS: OK. So don't spend any more, hang out till Monday, and then return it on Monday when he goes to work. If the briefcase is already gone, then just like, leave the cash in his bedroom with a note of explanation—and like, leave town.

WARREN: I don't know.

DENNIS: That's a sound plan. And if he still hasn't even opened the briefcase you're like home free. Except for two hundred bucks.

WARREN: Can I get the two hundred back from you?

DENNIS: No, man, that's like, *paid*. I can't release that cash.

WARREN: Where am I gonna stay?

DENNIS: Stay with Christian.

WARREN: Why can't I stay here?

DENNIS: 'Cause I don't want you.

WARREN: It's just two days.

DENNIS: I don't care.

WARREN: Come on. Nothing is gonna happen. He's not gonna know I came here. He definitely won't open the briefcase till Monday, and I'll be gone by then.

DENNIS: You are so stupid, man. I mean this definitely crowns your career as an idiot.

WARREN: Just let me stay here for Christ's sake! I do shit for you all the time—

DENNIS: Like what?

WARREN: Like when your girlfriend kicked you out, you stayed at my house for two *weeks*—

DENNIS: That was your *father's* house.

WARREN: So *what*?

DENNIS: This is *my* house.

WARREN: And I got in a lotta trouble for that, too. I hang out with you whenever you want, I play sports with you all the time, I buy pot from you, I take all your fuckin' abuse and I'm a good fuckin' friend. So why can't you help me out when I'm in trouble and not be such a fuckin' asshole?

DENNIS: 'Cause you're *always* in trouble. You have like no sense of *differentiation*.

WARREN: It's just two days!

DENNIS: All right, all right, shut up.

WARREN: Thanks.

DENNIS: But if your father shows up here I'm givin' you up immediately.

WARREN: I'm sure you will. But he's not gonna.

(*Silence.*)

WARREN: So what's up? What do you wanna do?

DENNIS: No, I don't wanna *do any*thing. Don't *needle* me, Warren. If you wanna stay here you can stay here, but you gotta shut up.

(DENNIS *turns on the TV and watches it wholeheartedly.*)

WARREN: Hey, where's that chick Jessica? (*Pause.*) Denny. Have you seen that chick Jessica recently?

DENNIS: No. What about her?

WARREN: I'm into her.

DENNIS: She's out of your league, man.

WARREN: I think she likes me.

DENNIS: No she doesn't.

WARREN: I think she does.

DENNIS: Shut up.

WARREN: She's really cute, man.

DENNIS: She is cute. That's why it'll never happen.

(WARREN *wanders over to the fridge.*)

DENNIS: There's nothing in there.

(WARREN *opens the fridge and looks in. It's pretty bare.*)

DENNIS: Get *outta* there, Warren! I just told you there's nothing
in there.

WARREN: How come you never have any food in here?

(DENNIS *doesn't answer. He watches TV.*)

WARREN: Let's go play football.

(DENNIS *doesn't answer.*)

WARREN: Where's your girlfriend?

DENNIS: We had a fight.

WARREN: Why?

DENNIS: Because she's a cunt.

WARREN: Tell her to come over and bring that girl Jessica.

DENNIS: Tell her yourself.

WARREN: (*Going to the phone.*) Where's she at?

DENNIS: You can't call her. We had a fight.

(WARREN *picks up* DENNIS's *football and makes phantom passes.*)

WARREN: Let's go outside and play.

DENNIS: Forget it.

WARREN: Let's call your girlfriend and tell her to call that girl
Jessica, and we'll take a few thousand bucks out of the
shoe bag and rent a really nice hotel suite and get a lot of
champagne and shit and have a wild party. What do you
think?

(WARREN *throws* DENNIS *the football.* DENNIS *throws it back.* DENNIS *knows how to throw a football.*)

DENNIS: You can't spend that money.

WARREN: I'll spend some of it. Big deal.

(*They toss the football back and forth.*)

WARREN: Come on, I'll get laid. It'll be good.

DENNIS: Let's just get a couple of prostitutes.

WARREN: OK.

DENNIS: You want to? We can call this Japanese place Philip goes
    to, and they'll send over like two incredibly beautiful and
    obedient Oriental hostesses to entertain and delight us.

WARREN: Let's do it.

DENNIS: How much will you spend?

WARREN: I don't know. How much is it?

DENNIS: Like two hundred apiece.

WARREN: I'd be into that.

DENNIS: What'll you tell your dad?

WARREN: Fuck my dad. I took his *money*!

DENNIS: You *robbed* him!

(WARREN *throws a hard pass that goes wide and smashes into some
breakables.*)

WARREN: Whoa. Sorry.

DENNIS: What is your problem?

WARREN: I lost control of the ball.

(DENNIS *gets the ball out of the smashed shelfware.*)

WARREN: Yo. Denny. Toss it back.

DENNIS: You broke my girlfriend's sculpture!

WARREN: Whoa . . . Really? I'm sorry.

DENNIS: What is your *problem*?

WARREN: I don't know. I really broke it?

DENNIS: *Yeah,* you really *broke* it.

(WARREN *comes over and examines the broken clay sculpture.*)

WARREN: What was it?

DENNIS: It was two girls, makin' out.

WARREN: Intense.

DENNIS: Now it's like, half of two girls.

WARREN: I'm really sorry, man, it was an accident.

DENNIS: It's a piece of shit anyway.

WARREN: Yo, lemme see it. Maybe I can glue it back together.

DENNIS: Get away from it.

WARREN: Lemme see.

(WARREN *tries to get a hand on the broken sculpture.* DENNIS *roughly blocks him out with his body and elbows.*)

DENNIS: Go sit in the *corner*, Warren, you're a fuckin' menace. Look what you *did*.

WARREN: Let me repair it.

(DENNIS *can't do anything with it. He lets* WARREN *look at it.*)

WARREN: No problem. You just get some Krazy Glue and glue it together. Do you have any?

DENNIS: No I don't have any *Krazy* Glue.

WARREN: I can fix this.

(DENNIS *wanders away from the shelves.*)

DENNIS: I'm *wasted* . . .

WARREN: Look. See?

(*He has propped the two halves of the broken sculpture together so it looks whole.*)

WARREN: Just glue it like that and it'll be fine. You probably don't even need a clamp.

(WARREN *picks up the football and makes phantom passes at* DENNIS.)

WARREN: Yo, heads up. Yo, Denny—go out.

DENNIS: Would you put that *down*?

WARREN: Go long!

DENNIS: The fuck am I gonna go *long*?

WARREN: Yo, go out!

(WARREN *throws the football hard, a little out of* DENNIS*'s reach, and it smashes into a bunch of other stuff.*)

DENNIS: What is *with* you, Warren?

WARREN: Come on, you *had* it!

(DENNIS *grabs the football, rears back, and wings a viciously hard pass at* WARREN*'s head.* WARREN *ducks and the football smashes into the sculpture again, totally demolishing it.*)

DENNIS: *Catch* it, you *moron!* Don't *duck!* This is my *house!*

WARREN: You tried to kill me, man!

DENNIS: What is the matter with you?

WARREN: I didn't *do* anything!

(DENNIS *stalks into the room toward* WARREN, *grabs him in a headlock, and flings him down on the floor. They are both half-laughing.*)

DENNIS: Get outta my *house!*

WARREN: Come on, man, I didn't do anything!

(DENNIS *rains open-handed blows down on* WARREN's *head and body.* WARREN *covers up.* DENNIS *drops onto his gut, knee first.* WARREN *groans in pain.* DENNIS *gets up and looks at the wreckage.*)

DENNIS: Look what you did.

WARREN: Oh my stomach.

DENNIS: Oh, forget *this* . . .

(*He starts tossing the pieces of the sculpture, basketball-style, into the wastepaper basket across the room. He's a good shot. Most of them go in.*)

DENNIS: She's gonna freak out.

(*The last piece goes into the wastepaper basket.* DENNIS *walks over to it and boots it into the wall. He goes to* WARREN, *who is covering his head.*)

DENNIS: You all right?

(WARREN *uncovers his head.* DENNIS *slaps him in the face.*)

WARREN: Cut it out.

DENNIS: That's for breaking her shit.

WARREN: You murdered my stomach.

(*Long silence.*)

WARREN: I'm restless.

(DENNIS *gives him a look.*)

WARREN: So, you don't wanna call any Japanese hostesses?

DENNIS: You couldn't handle it. You'd go limp and be depressed about it for like a year and a half.

WARREN: Let's call 'em!

DENNIS: Shut up. It's two hundred dollars apiece. You wanna spend that cash?

WARREN: No, man, I can't.

DENNIS: What are you gonna do about the two hundred bucks?

WARREN: I don't know. I'll sell something.

DENNIS: What, from like your little faggot memorabilia collection?

WARREN: Yeah.

DENNIS: So why don't you ever sell any of that shit to pay *me*? You should let me call Adam Saulk's brother, man. He makes a fortune buying and selling that shit.

WARREN: I pay you.

DENNIS: You do not.

WARREN: Besides, paying you isn't like life and death. Anyway, you make so much money off all of us already it's like completely ridiculous.

DENNIS: Yeah, and I always smoke pot with you, all of you, *my* pot, all the time, like hundreds and hundreds of dollars' worth. So why shouldn't I make some money offa you? You fuckin' guys like *gripe* at me all the time, and I'm providing you schmucks with such a crucial service. Plus I'm developing valuable entrepreneurial skills for my future. *Plus* I'm like providing you with precious memories of your *youth*, for when you're fuckin' *old*. I'm like the basis of half your personality. All you do is imitate me. I turned you on to *The Honeymooners*, Frank *Zappa*, Ernst *Lubitsch*, *sushi*. I'm like a one-man youth culture for you pathetic assholes. You're gonna remember your youth as like a gray stoned haze punctuated by a series of beatings from your fuckin' dad, and like, *my* jokes. God *damn*! You know how much *pot* I've thrown out the *window* for you guys in the middle of the night when you're wandering around the street like *junkies* looking for half a joint so you can go to sleep, because you scraped all the *resin* out of your pipes? And you bitch about the fact

that along the way I turn a little profit? You should thank
God you ever *met* me, you little fuckin' hero–worshipping
little *fag*.

WARREN: You are out of your mind, man.

(DENNIS *laughs.* WARREN *opens his big suitcase and starts removing the
first items in an extensive collection of toys and memorabilia from the
1950s and '60s: mint-condition mid-'60s Mattel toys, first-release
albums, a 1950s toaster, etc.*)

DENNIS: Don't take that stuff out in here.

WARREN: Why not? I wanna see what I can sell.

DENNIS: No—no— Don't take that stuff out in my apartment. It
depresses me.

WARREN: Why?

DENNIS: Don't take all that cutesy kitschy fuckin' retro-sixties
bullshit out in my apartment. I don't wanna look at it.

WARREN: I can get a couple of hundred bucks for any of these
albums.

DENNIS: Lemme see.

(WARREN *hands him an obscure early Frank Zappa album.*)

DENNIS: Where'd you get this?

WARREN: From this buddy of mine in Seattle.

DENNIS: This is an amazing album.

(DENNIS *looks through some of the stuff.*)

DENNIS: What is this shit? What's with the little *spacemen*? You
are weird, man.

WARREN: This is Major Matt Mason. Don't you remember this?

DENNIS: No.

WARREN: They had these when we were little. They're really cool, and these are in really good condition. I could get like a hundred fifty, two hundred bucks for this.

DENNIS: Seriously?

WARREN: Yeah.

DENNIS: So how do you always owe me money?

WARREN: 'Cause I don't wanna sell them.

DENNIS: You are a depressing little man. Now put that shit away.

WARREN: (*Holding it out to him.*) Look, he's got a little space helmet. The visor moves up and down.

DENNIS: Get that shit *away* from me!

(*The phone rings.* DENNIS *lets it ring twice, then picks up.*)

DENNIS: (*Into the phone.*) Yeah? . . . Because you're bein' a cunt.

(*The line goes dead.* DENNIS *hangs up and laughs, suddenly energized.*)

WARREN: You're intense, man.

DENNIS: I'm the best! I don't let people freak me out. I freak *them* out.

WARREN: You're an amazing man.

DENNIS: Hey—listen: That girl you like: what's her name?

WARREN: Jessica.

DENNIS: She's friends with that other girl, Natalie. You know her?

WARREN: Yeah?

DENNIS: OK, check it out: That girl Natalie likes me, OK? Last summer when Valerie was in Sweden with her family, I was like making out with her all the time, but that's all she ever let me do. But I saw her last week and she was coming on to

me all over the place. So look: new plan: We'll take a thousand bucks out of the shoe bag, cab it over to Philip's house,
pick up an ounce of blow, call Natalie, tell her and Jessica to
come over here, we'll get them wired, I'll fuck Natalie—
you do your best to fuck Jessica—then tomorrow we make a
few calls, sell the rest of the blow, turn a tidy little profit,
and return the whole fifteen grand to your psychotic father
intact on Monday. That's a great plan.

WARREN: How do you figure?

DENNIS: Because we extract a quarter ounce for ourselves, throw
back in a quarter ounce of cut, sell it for like a hundred
twenty-five a gram, clear around thirty-six hundred bucks,
return the thousand-dollar investment to the bag along with
the two hundred you already owe him, and you're still gonna
end up making like six hundred dollars.

WARREN: (*Slowly.*) . . . All right . . .

DENNIS: OK?

WARREN: Yeah.

DENNIS: (*Grabbing the phone.*) OK—

WARREN: But like . . . what's the basic margin of profit?

DENNIS: Like eighteen hundred each.

WARREN: So but . . . if we're making eighteen hundred each,
how come I only end up with *six*?

DENNIS: (*Still holding the phone.*) You *don't* end up with six: you
end up with *eighteen*, minus the thousand you're investing
and two hundred you already *owe*. Plus a free eighth of blow,
which you can snort or sell as you see fit. Get it?

WARREN: Um, not really. But whatever.

DENNIS: What don't you get?

WARREN: I don't really get the whole thing.

(DENNIS *hangs up the phone.*)

DENNIS: Look: We're buying a Z for a *thousand dollars* . . .

WARREN: No, I get *that* part. I just—I mean, theoretically, we're making a joint investment, right?

DENNIS: Yeah . . . ?

WARREN: Only in terms of the actual cash outlay, it's all coming from my area. Right? So in a way, I'm the only actual investor.

DENNIS: Yeah . . . ?

WARREN: So then why aren't I making all the money?

DENNIS: Because it's my connect and my customers and I'm gonna have the shit in my house.

WARREN: Yeah, but—

DENNIS: What do you *mean* why aren't you making all the money?

WARREN: I'm not saying I *should*. But you're saying we should split the profits *before* I put back the thousand dollars, and I'm saying like, why aren't we doing it *afterwards*?

DENNIS: Because it's my *connect*. I'm providing the *connect*.

WARREN: I'm providing the *cash*.

DENNIS: So what?

WARREN: . . . So I figure the odds be fifty-fifty.

DENNIS: You do, huh? All right. Whatever . . . But that's fucked up, because I'm doing all the work, and all you did was steal some money from your father which you're getting back in like ten *minutes*.

WARREN: All right, so what do you want to do?

DENNIS: I don't know. I just—I should definitely get some kind of *service* fee. So look—we'll split the twenty-six hundred net: thirteen hundred each. And then you pay me two hundred more for doing all the *work*—that leaves me with fifteen and you with eleven hundred. Out of which you can pay your father back the two hundred dollars or not. Whatever you want. OK?

WARREN: I guess.

DENNIS: Is that all *right* with you? Can I *call* him now?

WARREN: Yeah. Call him up.

DENNIS: Don't *ever* try to out-Jew me, little man. I'm twice the Jew you'll *ever* be. I'm like a Jewish *god*. I'm like—*Jooooo*lius *Caesar*!

WARREN: You're a fuckin' *mental* case, man.

DENNIS: Way to take care of *business*, little Warren!

(DENNIS *pinches* WARREN *very hard*.)

WARREN: Ow!

(DENNIS *dials the phone. Waits*.)

DENNIS: (*To* WARREN.) He's not there. (*Into the phone*.) Philly. Dennis. Call me. I'm looking for some fun.

(*He hangs up*.)

DENNIS: Shit.

(*The phone rings. He lets it ring twice, then picks up*.)

DENNIS: (*Into the phone*.) Yeah? . . . No! . . . 'Cause I don't know! . . . 'Cause I don't *give* a shit . . . Yeah . . . Yeah, OK . . . (*To* WARREN.) Go in the bathroom.

WARREN: Come on . . .

DENNIS: Go in the bathroom!

(WARREN *goes in the bathroom*.)

DENNIS: (*Into the phone.*) I'm sorry, baby. I know I messed up . . .
I know! As soon as I start arguing, I immediately snap into
attack mode and just become as insanely brutal as I possibly
can. It's because of my fuckin' *mother* . . . All right, why
don't you come over? . . . Warren's here, but I'll get rid of
him . . . Yeah . . . Oh, *really*? . . . No, totally *bring* her: Warren's
like, in *love* with her . . . Would she be into that? . . . What
if we got some blow? . . . She might. All right. See if she'll
come over. I'll work on it.

(DENNIS *hangs up.*)

DENNIS: Hey!

(WARREN *comes out of the bathroom.*)

WARREN: What's up?

DENNIS: Nothin'. I got good news for you, so get your little
boner ready, 'cause my girlfriend's on her way over with
your favorite teenage prostitute.

WARREN: What do you mean?

DENNIS: What do you think I mean?

WARREN: She's with Jessica?

DENNIS: Yeah.

WARREN: They're coming over here?

DENNIS: That's right, my little love machine.

WARREN: Excellent.

DENNIS: Only I told 'em we'd get drugs, so shut up for a second
and let me think.

(*Pause. He picks up the phone and dials.*)

WARREN: Who are you calling?

(DENNIS *ignores him.*)

DENNIS: (*Into the phone.*) Stuey. Hey. What are you doing? . . . You are too much, man. You shoulda been like, a Roman *senator.* Let me ask you something: Have you seen this weed Christian's been selling? It's like an olive-colored dark green heavy sense with like a medium amount of fuzz, very wet and sticky, in like long oblong-shaped little buds, shaped like beef sate . . . Oh you got some? . . . Do you know where he got it? . . . All right: Let me ask you something else. Do you know where Philip is? . . . Yeah. Have you seen it? . . . How is it? . . . *Really.* How much did you get? . . . What's he asking? . . . I did. He's not home . . . No, I just *tried* him, you fat fuck, he's *not home.* Why do you have to aggravate me all the time?

WARREN: What's up?

DENNIS: (*Into the phone.*) So listen. Stuey. Baby: If I can't get ahold of Philip in like twenty, I'm comin' over there and taking an eighth offa you, all right? . . . No, *Stuart,* I'm not *buying* it from you, I'm *taking* it, at cost. I'll give you cash up front, whatever you paid Philip, and you can get more from him tomorrow . . . *Yeah,* as a *favor* . . . Because I'm *asking* you to, that's why. Because I fuckin' *introduced* you to him in the first place, you fuckin' *globulous fuck.* You wouldn't even *know* him if it wasn't for me: you'd still be dealing commercial pot outside some Long Island mall to a bunch of dyed-blonde Great Neck *bimbettes,* you fat fuckin' asshole. I *created* you, Stuey, and I can destroy you just as easily! I don't care how many syphilis-ridden Dutch backpackers are blowing you, man. Why do you always have to like, try to have some mincing little bullshit *advantage* over me all the time? So you don't feel like such a fat, ugly *man* or something? . . . No, man, because you're like totally uncivilized. You have like no sense of protocol, like whatsoever . . . All right all right. I'll call you back.

(*He hangs up.*)

WARREN: What's up?

DENNIS: Nothin.' He's sitting on his waterbed doing *speed*balls with some naked Dutch *hitch*hiker he picked up at the *bus* stop, and he wants to like *dicker* with me over the price of an eighth of coke, like I can't go over to Philip's myself tomorrow and pick it up for *less* than what *he* paid, and like I haven't turned him on to tons of business and tons of my own customers—just so he can be holding some kind of *cards* on me or something. Plus he's so stoned out of his mind to begin with you can't understand a word he's saying anyway.

WARREN: So . . . what are we gonna do?

DENNIS: I don't know. See if Philip calls back, and if he doesn't, we'll just have to deal with the Fat Man. Maybe we should just forget it. It's late anyway. I don't wanna be lying in bed grinding my teeth all night. Unless you wanna just stay up and watch *H.R. Pufnstuff* at 5:30 in the morning.

WARREN: I can't watch that show, man. It freaks me out.

DENNIS: So what do you wanna do?

WARREN: Well . . . Are they coming over?

DENNIS: Yeah they're coming over.

WARREN: I'm into it.

DENNIS: All right. Should we get heroin? No, too much, right?

WARREN: Let's do speedballs.

DENNIS: Shut up. Do you even *know* what a speedball *is*? No.

WARREN: Yeah I know what a speedball is. It's like half heroin half cocaine. Right?

DENNIS: Yeah, but we can't give these girls *speed*balls. What are you, a maniac? Anyway, Valerie won't do heroin. *You* won't do heroin. So what are you talking about?

WARREN: I've done it.

DENNIS: Yeah, *once.* You'd be throwing up all night. That'd make a good impression. Speedballs are *sick*, man. They get you so fucked up you're like, really sorry.

WARREN: Let's do it!

DENNIS: Shut up.

(*Long pause.*)

WARREN: What's up?

DENNIS: No, nothing's *up.* How can you sit in a room with somebody for hours with nothing going on, and keep asking "What's up?" every ten minutes like something *new* happened all of a sudden that you didn't know about?

WARREN: I don't know. It's just an expression.

(WARREN *is walking around the room, picking things up and looking at them.*)

WARREN: So what's up? Where are they?

DENNIS: They're coming. Take it easy. And get away from my shit.

(WARREN *keeps looking through* DENNIS*'s stuff.*)

WARREN: But do they know I'm here?

DENNIS: Yeah, yeah, I told 'em you're here, I totally set it up for you. Just don't get weird and bizarre and start talking about your dead sister, and you'll do fine.

WARREN: I'm not gonna talk about anything.

(*Pause.*)

DENNIS:	WARREN:
Yeah, just don't be like—	You're really harsh, man.

DENNIS: *I'm* harsh?

WARREN: Yeah.

DENNIS: Why? You should *face* that shit.

WARREN: I face it all the time.

DENNIS: Well why do you have like her childhood *pictures* up all over your room, and like articles about her *murder* in your fuckin' *drawer*, like ten years after the fact? You're gonna let that shit dominate your life? You gotta like, get *on* with it.

WARREN: I am getting on with it. That's why I have her picture up. So I can get on with it. (*Pause.*) She's fuckin' lucky she's dead anyway.

DENNIS: She is not. Shut up.

(*Pause.* DENNIS *gets up and goes to his stereo and puts on a record. It is a slow song, e.g., Frank Zappa's "Any Way the Wind Blows," from* Ruben and The Jets. *He holds out his arms and walks toward* WAR-REN *singing along to him loudly.*)

WARREN: Get away from me.

(DENNIS *keeps coming, looming over* WARREN, *who tries to escape.*)

WARREN: Get away from me, man.

(DENNIS *falls on top of him, crushing him with his body, still singing.*)

WARREN: Get *off* me, man!

(DENNIS *laughs, screams.* WARREN *struggles to get out from under him.* DENNIS *gives him a loud wet kiss on the cheek and sits back.* WARREN *pushes him over and sits up.* DENNIS *flops onto his back.* WARREN *walks around.*)

DENNIS: I love Warren, man. He plays with me all day and all night for as long as I want and he never complains.

(*He sits up, grabs the phone, and dials.*)

DENNIS: (*Into the phone.*) Stuey. It's me. I'm comin' over: What are you telling me? . . . OK, *forget* it.

WARREN: What's up?

DENNIS: (*Covering the phone.*) He'll only sell us an ounce for fifteen hundred if you give him the cash up front. So I'm not doing that. I don't buy retail. But you can, if you want. But I'm not paying this *pork* loin fifteen hundred bucks for an ounce of blow. It's not worth my while.

WARREN: So let's—

DENNIS: *Unless*, we just keep an *eighth* for ourselves, instead of a quarter. That way you still make your eleven hundred and I make my fifteen. We just keep less blow for ourselves. (*Into the phone.*) HOLD ON A SECOND! (*Covers the phone.*) So what do you want to do?

WARREN: I'd go for it.

DENNIS: (*Into the phone.*) All right, I'm comin' over. Get dressed.

(*He hangs up and starts looking for his sneakers.*)

WARREN: So should we get some champagne or something?

DENNIS: All right. But I'm not payin' for that either.

WARREN: Nobody's asking you to.

DENNIS: What do you want, like Dom Perignon?

WARREN: There is no other brand.

DENNIS: How many should I get? One bottle? Two?

WARREN: Let's get two.

DENNIS: They're expensive.

WARREN: That's no problem.

DENNIS: All right.

WARREN: So . . . how much do you need?

DENNIS: Gimme fifteen hundred for the blow and like two hundred for the champagne.

WARREN: The champagne's not gonna cost two hundred dollars.

DENNIS: Just gimme enough to cover it. Or let's just forget the whole thing. I don't wanna do any coke. It's a terrible drug. It's for chumps. It sucks. I'll fuck my girlfriend and go to sleep, and you can go sleep in the park.

(*Pause.* WARREN *goes to the shoe bag and starts counting out the money.* DENNIS *starts putting on his sneakers.*)

WARREN: So but . . . should I come with you, or what's the deal?

DENNIS: No, you gotta let Valerie in. She threw her key down the trash chute.

WARREN: No, man . . . I don't wanna deal with your girlfriend.

DENNIS: It's all right. We made up. Just stay here. I won't be long.

WARREN: Whatever.

(DENNIS *finishes tying his sneakers and looks at him.*)

DENNIS: See—this is no good. You're already like freaked out and nervous. Forget it. That girl's gonna smell it the minute she comes in. What is the *matter* with you?

WARREN: What do you mean?

DENNIS: What are you, like, worried about what to *say*? Don't say *anything*. Just sit there and look handsome, you Greek *god*. She should be worried about *you*. You're a handsome guy. You're like an intelligent fuckin' interesting guy. You don't have to *do* anything. Just don't get freaked out. We're gonna break this stupefying losing streak of yours wide open. Now gimme the money.

WARREN: All right. (*Pointedly.*) This is *seventeen hundred*.

DENNIS: (*Mocking his grave tone.*) "All right."

(DENNIS *takes the money and shuffles into his coat.*)

DENNIS: So just let 'em up and I'll be back in like twenty.

WARREN: Cool.

DENNIS: Be *glad*, man! She's really cute and she's got a great body and maybe you can actually fuck her.

WARREN: I'm gonna give it the old college try.

(DENNIS *goes out.* WARREN *locks the door after him. Steps back into the room, alone. He looks at himself in the mirror. He tries to make his appearance more casual, but it's a challenge. He untucks his shirt, musses his hair, etc. He finds the half-smoked joint, lights it, and takes one huge hit.*)

(*He sits there without moving.*)

(*The buzzer buzzes. He waits for it to buzz again before getting up to press the intercom button.*)

WARREN: Hello?

JESSICA: (*On the intercom.*) It's Jessica.

WARREN: OK.

(WARREN *buzzes her in and moves away from the intercom. He waits. There is a knock on the door. He goes to the door, opens it, and steps back.*)

WARREN: You may enter.

(*Enter* JESSICA GOLDMAN. *She is the same age as* WARREN—*around nineteen. She wears effective makeup, big shoes, and a slightly pricey little dress that shows off her figure to good advantage. She is dressed up for the night, not down, and definitely looks a little out of place in* DENNIS'*s grunge palace. She is a fairly cheerful but very nervous girl, whose self-taught method of coping with her nervousness consists of seeking out the nearest available oasis of self-assurance and entrenching herself there with a watchful defensiveness that sweeps away anything that might threaten to dislodge her, including her own chances at happiness and the opportunity of gaining a wider perspective on the world that might eventually make her less nervous to begin with. Despite her prickliness, she is basi-*

cally friendly, definitely interested in WARREN, *and trying to make a good impression.*)

JESSICA: Hi, Warren. How are you?

WARREN: I'm OK.

(*He hesitates, then leans in to kiss her hello, on the cheek. She is not expecting this, so it's a little physically embarrassing.*)

WARREN: Um . . . Where's Valerie?

JESSICA: She went with *Dennis*. We ran into him downstairs, and they said I should just come *up*.

(*She stands by the door, not sure where to go or what's appropriate.*)

WARREN: So how you doing, Jessica? You're looking very automated tonight.

JESSICA: What the fuck is *that* supposed to mean?

WARREN: Nothing. It's just a fashion concept.

JESSICA: What?

WARREN: Um—nothing. You wanna come in?

(*She steps into the room. He closes the door.*)

JESSICA: So how long do you think they're gonna be?

WARREN: I don't know. Maybe a half hour.

JESSICA: What? What do you mean? Where do they have to go?

WARREN: Like, the East Fifties.

JESSICA: Well . . . OK. (*Pause.*) I don't mean to be paranoid. I just don't want to be the victim of some teenage matchmaking scheme.

WARREN: Noted.

JESSICA: You know? If I'm gonna get set up, I'm gonna do it myself.

WARREN: Well nobody's setting you up, so why don't you calm down?

JESSICA: Oh you can't see why I would *think* that?

WARREN: I don't know or care what you think, Jessica. I'm just staying here because my *dad* threw me out of the *house*. But go *home*. It's fine with me.

JESSICA: (*Not an apology.*) OK, *sorry.*

(*She comes in.*)

JESSICA: You probably think I'm like a total bitch now, right?

WARREN: I don't think anything. I don't even know what you're *talking* about.

(*He locks the door.*)

WARREN: And now . . . you're *mine*!

JESSICA: No *way*!

WARREN: I'm kidding! Calm *down*!

JESSICA: (*On "calm."*) That's not funny at *all*!

WARREN: Noted.

(JESSICA *sits down and takes out her cigarettes and lighter.*)

JESSICA: Is it OK if I smoke in here?

WARREN: Go ahead. It's not my house.

JESSICA: Well is there an ashtray or something I can use?

WARREN: I'm sure there's one somewhere.

(*He looks for an ashtray and finds one at the same time she finds an empty soda can.*)

WARREN: Here you go.

JESSICA: No, it's OK. I can use this. Thanks, though.

(WARREN *puts down the ashtray and sits down across the room from her. She smokes.*)

(*Long silence.*)

WARREN: So are you like a really big cigarette smoker?

JESSICA: I guess so.

WARREN: How many cigarettes would you say you smoke in the average day?

JESSICA: I don't know. Like a pack and a half a day, on a really heavy smoking day. Maybe like a half a pack a day if I'm like, in the country.

WARREN: . . . Yeah . . . I never really got into the whole cigarette scene myself. But I hear great things about it.

JESSICA: Well, but if you smoke pot all the time, it's much worse on your lungs than cigarettes.

WARREN: I guess my lungs are pretty severely damaged.

JESSICA: I'm sure they are.

(*Long silence.*)

JESSICA: So did those guys go to get, um, to get coke?

WARREN: That's the plan.

JESSICA: I don't want to do very much.

WARREN: Well, we're getting like, a *lot.*

JESSICA: I'll do *some* . . .

WARREN: And we're getting some Dom Perignon to top it off. So it should be pretty good.

JESSICA: Sounds good . . .

(*Long silence.*)

JESSICA: So why'd your dad throw you out of the house? What did you *do*?

WARREN: We just had a slight policy dispute. It's no big deal.

JESSICA: Are you staying here? Where are you gonna sleep?

WARREN: I don't know. It wasn't like a really detailed plan. I was just planning to crash on the floor for a few days till I figure out what I'm doing.

JESSICA: What *are* you gonna do?

WARREN: I don't know. I was thinking I might just buy a bus ticket and head out west. I have a buddy who lives in Seattle, so I might just do that . . . I definitely wanna get out of *this*—pit. That's for sure.

JESSICA: You mean New York? You don't like living here?

WARREN: What's to like? You go outside and it *smells* bad. You know? And I live on Central Park *West*.

JESSICA: Well—

WARREN: I like the *out*doors.

JESSICA: I know, but—

WARREN: Like last winter I went to visit this buddy of mine who lives in Jackson Hole? In Wyoming? And we'd just *ski* every day, you know? And bus tables at night. And when you get up in the morning and open the front door it's like, *silent*. You know? You go outside and it's like, the *mountains*. And *snow*. And nobody around for *miles*. And like the whole . . . *sky* over your head. You know? So what the fuck am I doing languishing on *this* trash heap for? The intellectual stimulation? I'm not getting any. All I do is smoke pot. I can do that anywhere. I can just bring that *with* me, you know?

JESSICA: Yeah . . . I don't really take advantage of the city's facilities either, and it just seems like such a total waste.

WARREN: Yeah. I mean . . . yeah.

(*Pause.*)

JESSICA: But—you're not planning on going to school at all? Didn't you *go* to school somewhere or something?

WARREN: Um, briefly.

JESSICA: So . . . ?

WARREN: I . . . It just wasn't happening.

JESSICA: Where were you?

WARREN: Ohio.

JESSICA: Where, Oberlin?

WARREN: Whatever. You're at F.I.T., right?

JESSICA: Yeah. I really like it there. It's a little Jappy for me, but there's a lot of really great people there if you know where to look for them. But it's kind of weird, because I'm living at home—which is great: like my mom and I get along incredibly well—but a lot of my formerly closest "friends" are out of the city now, and sometimes I wonder, you know, if I should've . . . I don't know.

WARREN: So are you heavily into fashion development?

JESSICA: Yeah. I've been doing a lot of designing. I've always done it. It's what I want to do.

WARREN: Well . . . My basic philosophy about clothes is that they should be comfortable, and not look like too many people had to slave over their creation. But then again, I'm not very fashion-oriented.

JESSICA: Yeah, but, you know, you will be someday.

WARREN: I doubt it.

JESSICA: Yeah, but you will. Your whole personality'll be different.

WARREN: You think?

JESSICA: Sure. What you're like now has nothing to do with what you're gonna *be* like. Like right now you're all like this rich little pot-smoking burnout rebel, but ten years from now you're gonna be like a plastic *surgeon* reminiscing about how wild you used to be . . .

WARREN: Well, I don't want to make any rash predictions at this point . . . but I seriously doubt I'm gonna be going in for plastic surgery.

JESSICA: Well, OK, whatever, but you'll definitely be a completely different person. Everything you think will be different, and the way you act, and all your most passionately held beliefs are all gonna be completely different, and it's really depressing.

WARREN: How do you figure?

JESSICA: Because it just basically invalidates whoever you are right *now*. You know what I mean? It just makes your whole self at any given point in your life seem so completely *dismissable*. So it's like, what is the point?

WARREN: I don't really know about that . . .

JESSICA: Well it's *true*.

WARREN: Maybe so, but I don't really *agree* with it.

JESSICA: Well, I've thought about this a lot.

WARREN: So have I.

JESSICA: I mean look who our *president* is now if you don't believe me.

WARREN: I'm not sure I follow you.

JESSICA: No, like the classic *example* is all those kids from the sixties who were so righteous about changing the face of civilization, and then the minute they got older they were all like, "Actually, you know what? Maybe I'll just be a *lawyer.*"

WARREN: I guess that's one interpretation . . .

JESSICA: But it's totally true! And now like Ronald *Reagan* is president of the United States. I mean, how embarrassing is *that?*

WARREN: It's pretty embarrassing . . . Although I have to say, I definitely know some people who are still seriously into civic activities. Like my mother does a fair amount of volunteer work for some kind of grape-picking civil-liberties organization in California . . .

JESSICA: I know people who do that too. But I'm not talking about the last pathetic remnants of—Upper West Side Jewish . . . *liberalism.* I'm talking about the *main*stream, and it is such a *joke.* I mean, I definitely feel that *evil* has like, triumphed in our time.

WARREN: So do I. But I still don't know if I would really ascribe all that to the theory that people's personalities undergo some kind of fundamental *alteration* when they get older.

JESSICA: Well, they do. And it's a big factor.

WARREN: I mean they obviously do to a *degree*—

JESSICA: Yeah!

WARREN: And things definitely happen to alter your general *trajectory*—

JESSICA: Yeah! And no matter—

WARREN: (*On "And."*) But I think that . . . you basically get a set of characteristics, and then they pretty much just develop in different ways. Like—

JESSICA: But can I just—

WARREN: (*On "can."*) Like the last year of high school, I suddenly realized that all these weird kids I grew up with were like well on their way to becoming really weird *adults.* And it was pretty *scary,* you know? Like you see a crazy kid, and you realize, he's never gonna grow *out* of it. He's a fucked-up crazy kid and he's just gonna be a fucked-up crazy adult with like a ruined life.

(*Pause.*)

JESSICA: Are you done now?

WARREN: I'm done with *that* thought.

JESSICA: Well can I please say something?

WARREN: Go ahead.

JESSICA: Thank you: I'm not saying anything about whether you're quote unquote "fucked up" or not. I don't mean it as a *moral* issue—

WARREN: Neither do I.

JESSICA: I just—

WARREN: *I* think that personality components are like protons and electrons. Like in science: Every molecule is made of the same basic components, like the difference between a hydrogen molecule and a calcium molecule is like *one proton* or something . . .

JESSICA: Yeah? That's wrong, but yeah?

WARREN: So my theory is that people's *personalities* are basically constructed the same way. None of them are exactly the same, but they're all made of the same thing.

JESSICA: That's interesting.

WARREN: Thank you.

JESSICA: Unfortunately it has nothing to do with what I'm *talking* about . . .

WARREN: That is unfortunate.

JESSICA: I'm not talking about the chemical structure of your *brain*, I'm talking about— It's like, when you find an old *letter* you wrote, that you don't remember writing. And it's got all these thoughts and opinions in it that you don't remember having, and it's written to somebody you don't even remember having ever written a letter *to*.

WARREN: I've never found a letter like that.

JESSICA: Well I have. Like, a lot of them. And it just makes you realize that there's just these huge swaths of time in your life that didn't register at *all*, and that you might just as well have been *dead* during them for all the difference they make to you now.

WARREN: That seems like a fairly nihilistic viewpoint, Jessica.

JESSICA: Well, I am so completely the opposite of nihilistic it's amazing that anyone could even *say* that about me.

WARREN: Well—

JESSICA: But we don't agree. So that's OK. You think what you think, and I think what I think, and there's no way we're ever going to convince each other, so my suggestion is we just drop it.

WARREN: All right.

(*Silence.*)

JESSICA: Hey, is there anything to drink in here? I've got this really bad taste in my mouth.

WARREN: (*Getting up.*) I think there's some water.

JESSICA: (*Starts to get up.*) I can get it.

WARREN: That's all right. "Chivalry is not dead. It just smells funny."

(JESSICA *does not know how to respond to this, so she just looks at him. He gives up and goes to the fridge, finds a juice jar full of cold water, pours some in a glass, and brings it to her.*)

JESSICA: Thanks a lot.

(*She takes the glass and drinks.*)

JESSICA: God, I was so thirsty.

(WARREN *sits down, this time right next to her on the bed. He is sitting next to her, but not looking at her. It's making them both very nervous.* JESSICA *gets up and goes to the wall of photographs.*)

JESSICA: So who are all these photos of? Are you on this wall?

WARREN: Yeah, I'm represented.

(*He follows her to the wall. She finds a photo with him in it.*)

JESSICA: Wow, is this *you*?

WARREN: Yep.

JESSICA: God, what a little *stoner.* You look so different with long hair . . .

WARREN: Yeah. Everybody definitely went for the traditional post-high-school chop.

JESSICA: Valerie says you just cut your hair when Dennis cut his hair.

(WARREN *does not respond.*)

JESSICA: Well, you definitely look better with it short.

WARREN: That seems to be the general consensus. But it makes me wanna like *instantly* have long hair.

(JESSICA *scans the photographs.*)

JESSICA: Wow. What a great picture of Dennis. I mean, he definitely has a slight cleanliness problem, but if he didn't, he'd be seriously gorgeous.

WARREN: You think?

JESSICA: Oh my God, are you *kidding*?

WARREN: I guess.

JESSICA: So his dad's like a really famous painter, right?

WARREN: I guess he's pretty famous.

JESSICA: Wow. So is that like, really hard for Dennis to deal with?

WARREN: I have no idea.

JESSICA: And his father's really sick or something?

WARREN: Uh . . . He's definitely having some pretty dire prostate problems.

JESSICA: His mom is beautiful . . .

WARREN: It's an incredibly attractive family.

JESSICA: What does she do?

WARREN: She's like a big-city social-worker administrator of some kind. She's always like installing swimming pools for the poor or something.

JESSICA: What?

WARREN: Nothing. She runs these programs for the city government or something. She designs social-work programs for street kids and drug addicts and stuff like that. But she's a fuckin' psycho.

JESSICA: (*Bristling.*) Why do you say that? Just because she's a social worker?

WARREN: No—because of her *behavior.*

JESSICA: Why? What does she do?

WARREN: I don't know. She's just really *strident.* She's like a bleeding-heart dominatrix with like a *hairdo.* She—

JESSICA:	WARREN:
"Bleeding heart?"—	I don't know. Yeah!

JESSICA: What are you like a big *Republican* or something?

WARREN: Not at all. I'm a total Democrat. I just—

JESSICA: So why do you *say* that about her?

WARREN: Because that's what's she's *like*. But I don't really *care*. Maybe she's really nice. I don't really want to get into an argument about it.

JESSICA: No, it's just—my sister is a social worker, and I really—

WARREN: I didn't say anything *about* your sister.

JESSICA:	WARREN:
I know you didn't. I just th—	I didn't know you *had* a sister.
I know—but I just think it's like a really good thing to do with your life and I j— OK, I *know*! I just admire people who dedicate themselves like that, and I—	And I was not attempting to vilify the entire social-worker community!

WARREN: So do *I*. What she *does* is fine. It's just how she *is*. I think it's totally brave to do that kind of work. Unless you're just—

JESSICA: Unless what?

WARREN: Unless you just have no sense of people. No— Like if your *mission* overrides your actual moral *opinion*, but—forget it. It's not—it doesn't matter.

JESSICA: All right. I certainly didn't mean to offend you.

WARREN: I'm not offended.

(*A moment.* JESSICA *looks at the stuff in* WARREN*'s open suitcase.*)

JESSICA: Hey—what's this stuff?

WARREN: Those are just some of my belongings.

JESSICA: (*Looking through.*) What are these?

WARREN: It's just some fuckin' shit.

JESSICA: What are these, like antique toys or something?

WARREN: Um, for the most part . . .

JESSICA: These are really cool.

WARREN: You think?

JESSICA: Yeah, they remind me of the stuff my cousins had when I was a little kid. I always wanted to play with their toys, and they were like, "Go play with dolls, you little bitch." And I was like, "Fuck *you!*" . . . I *love* old toys.

WARREN: I have a fair amount of this kind of thing.

JESSICA: Do you know how many toys I had—I mean how much, of the stuff I had when I was little, I wish I had now? Like, I think of some of those toys and I just look back on them with this *longing* . . . You know?

WARREN: Definitely.

JESSICA: (*Takes out the Major Matt Masons.*) Who are these guys?

WARREN: That's my Major Matt Mason collection. You know Major Matt Mason.

(*She shakes her head.*)

WARREN: Come on, Major Matt Mason, when we were kids— Aw, he's the best! Check him out, he's like, ready for his *mission.* I have a complete set, all in prime condition. I could actually sell them for a lot of money, but I'm hanging on to them.

JESSICA: Really cool.

(*He shows her his heavy-duty 1950s toaster.*)

WARREN: And this is my amazing toaster. Toaster Amazing, I call
it. Look at this. It's really something. (*She looks.*) Yeah, G.E.
made only like a few hundred of this model like in the
fifties, and then they recalled them because they were like
exploding in people's kitchens at breakfast and burning
down their homes. (*He laughs, sobers.*) So only a few hundred
actually exist. I got one from this dealer I know in Colorado
and he had *no* idea what he was selling me.

JESSICA: Huh.

WARREN: I have made toast with it, but nothing bad happened to
me. But I don't really use it too much because it really
depreciates in value. But it's great to know I have one of the
only ones in existence.

JESSICA: What's your favorite thing in this collection?

WARREN: Definitely my Wrigley Field Opening Day baseball cap
my grandfather gave me. No contest.

JESSICA: What's that?

(WARREN *takes out an ancient blue and white baseball cap.*)

WARREN: This is a real collectors' item, like an *amazing* collectors'
item, actually. My mom's dad got it the first day at Wrigley
Field when he was totally like a little kid, in nineteen
fourteen.

(JESSICA *reads what's embroidered on the cap.*)

JESSICA: "Wrigley Field, Home of the Chicago Cubs, Opening
Day." (*Reads off the other side.*) "True Value."

WARREN: True Value Hardware, all *right.*

(*She puts the hat on.*)

WARREN: Looks good, Jessica . . .

(*She smiles. A moment.*)

JESSICA: I didn't know your family was from Chicago.

WARREN: They're not. Just my grandfather. He was actually really cool. When he was a young man, he was like a fairly well-known aviator. You know, with like the fur-lined leather cap with the earflaps, and the whole bit. He actually set a couple of early endurance records in the nineteen twenties . . .

JESSICA: Wow . . . I didn't know that . . .

WARREN: Yeah . . . he was pretty interesting. (*He laughs.*) Like whenever he would meet one of my friends, I'd be like, "Grampa, this is my friend Neil." And my grampa'd be like, "Nice to meet you, Neil. Are you Jewish?" And my friend Neil would be like, "Um . . . Yeah?" And my grampa'd be like, "Neil, in the year nineteen twenty-three I was the greatest Jewish aviator in this country. That's because I was the *only* Jewish aviator in this country. You wanna see a picture?" And then he would break out his clippings, which had these photos of himself in his fuckin' Sopwith Camel that he carried with him *all the time.* He was pretty amusing.

JESSICA: Is he still alive?

WARREN: Nah, nah . . .

JESSICA: Where does your mom live?

WARREN: Santa Barbara.

JESSICA: God, so why don't you go stay with her? That's supposed to be pretty nice.

WARREN: I don't particularly want to live in California, for one thing.

JESSICA: Why not?

WARREN: Because of the *people* in it. Plus my mom lives with her boyfriend . . . And anyway, she's kind of freaked out generally, so it's kind of tough to be around her for very long at one stretch.

JESSICA: Did you . . . didn't you have a sister that died? Or something?

WARREN: Um . . .

(*He hesitates for a long moment.*)

WARREN: . . . Yeah. I did.

JESSICA: So—I mean—is that why you say your mom, your mom is freaked out?

WARREN: I would say it was definitely a prominent factor.

JESSICA: What did your sister die of?

WARREN: Um, she was murdered.

JESSICA: Oh my God, is that true?

WARREN: No, that's just a little joke we have about it in the family.

JESSICA: What?

WARREN: Yeah it's *true.*

JESSICA: I'm sorry: I didn't mean, "Is that true?" I just meant . . . You know, "Oh my God."

WARREN: Yeah . . .

JESSICA: How did it happen? Do you mind talking about it . . . ?

WARREN: Not really. Do you want any pot?

(*He picks up the roach.*)

JESSICA: No, no thanks. But you go ahead.

WARREN: Um— That's all right.

(*He puts down the roach.*)

JESSICA: So what happened? That is so horrible.

WARREN: Um, nothing. She was living with this guy named Julian. And my parents were kind of freaked out that she was living with this guy because she was only eighteen, and he was much older. (*Very long pause.*) Nineteen. It's not my favorite topic.

JESSICA: (*Blushing.*) I'm sorry! . . .

WARREN: That's OK . . .

JESSICA: . . . I'm sorry . . .

WARREN: It's OK . . .

(*Long silence. She is very embarrassed. He holds out the roach to her.*)

WARREN: Do you want any of this?

JESSICA: OK.

(*He lights the roach and gives it to her. She takes a hit, doesn't get much, or coughs, but doesn't relight it or try again. Silence.*)

JESSICA: The Wild City.

(*She turns and looks at him thoughtfully for a moment.*)

JESSICA: Are those your records?

WARREN: Um, yeah. These are my authentic first-release sixties albums, all in perfect condition. Got the whole thing here: Early Mothers, Captain Beefheart, Herman's Hermits, everything. You wanna hear one?

JESSICA: Sure.

(*He puts on a high-velocity Frank Zappa song, e.g., "Mystery Roach," from* 200 Motels.)

JESSICA: All *right!*

(*She nods and starts dancing.*)

JESSICA: Wake this dump up!

WARREN: All right!

(WARREN *starts dancing in his own separate space. He takes a few tentative steps toward her, then she moves unambiguously to him, and they start dancing more or less together.*)

JESSICA: Uh–*huh,* uh–*huh,* uh–*huh* uh–*huh* uh–*huh.*

(*She opens her arms, and* WARREN *steps into them. The music abruptly segues into a Zappa-esque confusion of sound that is impossible to dance to.*)

WARREN: Um—I don't know. I guess you can't really dance to this next song too well.

JESSICA: Well . . .

WARREN: Hold on.

(*He hurries to the stereo and puts on a slow, romantic song, e.g., "Lucille," from* Joe's Garage Part II.)

JESSICA: Oh. OK. Goes for the slow song. I get it.

WARREN: Of course.

JESSICA: OK. I'm game.

(*She starts to take his hands.*)

JESSICA: Wait. (*She lets go.*) I've got a hair in my mouth.

(*She extracts the hair from her mouth, shakes it off her finger, and puts her hands back up. They dance, not entirely gracelessly.*)

WARREN: I'm definitely into actual dancing.

JESSICA: Yeah, I think our generation definitely missed out in the dancing department.

WARREN: Yeah . . . I guess like, whoever the genius was who decided you didn't need *steps* should have come up with something else instead.

JESSICA: Yeah, right?

(*He dips her.*)

JESSICA: Check him *out*. Mr. *Dip*.

(*He brings her back up again*.)

JESSICA: You could be a really good dancer.

WARREN: Thanks: So could you. (*A joke*.) If only society would give us a chance.

JESSICA: Yeah, man!

(*They dance*.)

WARREN: Listen—

JESSICA: Yeah?

WARREN: I just gotta say, I find you incredibly attractive.

JESSICA: OK— Relax, will you?

WARREN: But listen—would you be mortally offended if I kissed you for just a second?

JESSICA: Well, I mean, what's the rush?

WARREN: No rush. I'd just like to get rid of this knot in my stomach.

JESSICA: Oh— Sure, I mean—whatever's expedient.

WARREN: (*Moving closer*.) No— It's just . . .

JESSICA: (*Letting him*.) Yeah . . . ?

(WARREN *kisses her. She kisses back. It quickly turns into heavy teenage-style making out.* JESSICA *breaks away*.)

JESSICA: They're gonna walk in, and I'm gonna be really embarrassed.

WARREN: (*A blatant lie*.) Yeah—me too.

(*She takes a few steps away and looks back at him sharply*.)

JESSICA: They *are* coming back, right?

WARREN: Yeah . . . !

JESSICA: OK. Just checking. (*Pause.*) But I mean . . . do you like me, Warren, or what?

WARREN: Of course I do. Can't you tell?

JESSICA: I don't know. Not really. Maybe you just want to mess around or something.

WARREN: Um, I do. *And* I like you. I completely enjoy talking to you . . .

JESSICA: Well, OK, which would you prefer if you had to choose?

(*Pause.*)

WARREN: That would depend on which one we'd already been doing *more* of.

JESSICA: All right. Never mind. Stupid question. I'm sorry. It's just, I'm always getting drawn into these situations and then getting hurt really badly. So . . .

WARREN: Noted.

JESSICA: You wanna close your eyes for a second?

WARREN: Yes.

(*He closes his eyes.* JESSICA *crosses to him and kisses him, until they are both sprawled inelegantly on* DENNIS*'s horrible mattress, feeling each other up and getting so worked up that* JESSICA *pulls away again, not out of coquetry but just to put on the brakes.*)

JESSICA: OK, gotta take a break.

WARREN: Well . . . I mean—if you want to, we could go some-place else.

JESSICA: What do you mean? Like, to your house or something?

WARREN: Um—no, my house wouldn't work out too well right now . . .

JESSICA: Well, we can't go to *my* house.

WARREN: Well, look, why don't we— Why don't we just go rent the penthouse suite at the *Plaza* or something, and like hang out and order room service and like watch the sun come up over the park.

JESSICA: How could we do that?

WARREN: Because I happen to be extremely liquid at the moment.

JESSICA: Are you serious?

WARREN: Yeah . . . !

JESSICA: Well . . . what about Dennis and Valerie?

WARREN: I'll leave them a note. Or, we can just tell them where we are, and have them meet us there, or we can just hang out by ourselves . . . Whatever we feel like doing.

JESSICA: Um—all right.

WARREN: Really?

JESSICA: Sure. I mean . . . yeah.

WARREN: All right. Let me just get some funding.

(*He goes to the shoe bag and takes out a couple of bricks of cash.*)

JESSICA: Oh my *God*. Is that *money* in there?

WARREN: I'm afraid so.

JESSICA: Where did you get that?

WARREN: These are the proceeds from my unhappy childhood.

JESSICA: The what . . . ?

WARREN: I'll tell you about it later. Are you ready?

JESSICA: I'm ready.

(*She slings her purse over her shoulder. Stops.*)

JESSICA: Shit! I should've called my mother.

WARREN: What for?

JESSICA: I'm just supposed to call her if I'm gonna be out after twelve-thirty.

WARREN: Doesn't that wake her?

JESSICA: She doesn't care, she goes right back to sleep.

WARREN: Do you want to call her now?

JESSICA: No. She's just gonna freak out 'cause I didn't call earlier. I don't know. I'll just deal with it later . . . I don't know why the fuck she's always so *worried* about me.

(*They go out.*)

ACT 2

(*The next day, a little after noon. On the little table is a small laboratory scale, a brown paper bag, an unopened jar of Mannitol, a tablespoon, an upside-down porcelain dinner plate, a nearly unfurled ten dollar bill, and a straight-edged razor.*)

(DENNIS *is sprawled out asleep on his mattress in a crazy tangle of sheets, wearing only a T-shirt and a pair of boxer shorts. The buzzer buzzes.* DENNIS *stirs but does not wake. The buzzer buzzes again. He sits up, then staggers to the intercom and presses the Talk button.*)

DENNIS: What?

WARREN: (*On the intercom.*) It's Warren.

(DENNIS *buzzes him in, unlocks the door and leaves it ajar, then collapses back onto the bed.* WARREN *comes in looking chipper. He carries a small deli bag with a coffee in it.*)

WARREN: Hey.

DENNIS: Where've you been? What happened to you?

WARREN: Nothing. I was with Jessica.

DENNIS: You were with her this whole time?

WARREN: Pretty much.

DENNIS: What time is it?

WARREN: Around noon.

(DENNIS *goes into the bathroom, leaving the door open. Over the following, we hear him pee and flush the toilet.*)

WARREN: So . . . Did you get that Z from Stuey?

DENNIS: (*Off.*) Yeah. It's *great*. Me and Valerie were doing lines with him and *Bergita* for like two and a half hours. Plus he says the heroin he has is like really amazing too.

WARREN: Who's Bergita? The Dutch girl?

(DENNIS *comes back out.*)

DENNIS: Yeah. She was pretty cute. I don't understand how that guy gets girls, man. He is like a classically ugly man.

(*He collapses on the bed again.*)

WARREN: Where's Valerie?

DENNIS: Oh, *Valerie.* Valerie walked in here and took one look at the shards of her sculpture lying in the garbage and went completely insane. She was screaming at me so loud it literally hurt my *ears.* She was like, "You're totally selfish, you do whatever you want, you never apologize to anyone, you have no idea how to deal with people, and you're gonna die alone." Then she burst into tears and fled to her aunt's house in Connecticut. I totally blame you.

WARREN: Sorry about that, man.

DENNIS: I don't give a shit. She's out of her mind.

WARREN: So—is this it?

DENNIS: Yeah.

(WARREN *picks up a brown paper bag off the table and very carefully takes out of it a double-wrapped ziplock baggy containing an ounce of cocaine.*)

WARREN: That's a lot of blow.

DENNIS: Yeah. Now put it down before you break it.

(WARREN *puts down the bag of cocaine.*)

DENNIS: So what happened with you and that girl?

WARREN: Nothing. I had a nice time.

DENNIS: Did you fuck her?

WARREN: Um . . . Yeah. I did.

DENNIS: You did? As in actual penetration?

WARREN: Basically.

DENNIS: No—what do you mean "basically"? Did you or didn't you?

WARREN: No—I did.

DENNIS: So that's amazing.

WARREN: I'm pretty pleased.

DENNIS: *Warren.* Breaks the losing streak.

WARREN: Yeah. I kind of like her. She really likes to argue. But I'm into that.

DENNIS: So where did you go? Her house?

WARREN: No, man, I took her to the fuckin' Vanderbilt Suite at the Plaza Hotel.

DENNIS: No you didn't.

WARREN: Yes I did.

DENNIS: You took her to the *Plaza*?

WARREN: Yeah. I got this really beautiful suite, and we just drank champagne and looked out over the park and made love on the *balcony*. It was pretty intense.

(*Pause.*)

DENNIS: You should have gone to the Pierre.

WARREN: Why do you say that?

DENNIS: Because the Plaza is a dump. My old man says it used to be amazing, but now it's totally run-down and rancid and the Pierre is just a much, much better hotel. You gotta stay at the Pierre or the Carlton or like the Carlyle.

WARREN: Well—I never stayed at any of them, but I definitely thought the Plaza was pretty cool.

DENNIS: So were you actually able to do anything with her? Or did you just like come immediately?

WARREN: I came pretty fast.

DENNIS: Naturally. You only did it once?

WARREN: Well . . . I think she kind of freaked out a little bit afterwards.

DENNIS: What do you mean? What'd she do?

WARREN: Well, she didn't really freak out, but she definitely got pretty quiet. And I was like, "What's the matter? We just had an amazing time together, and I really like you." And she was like, "But I don't even *know* you." So I was like, "Well you know me now." But I don't really know if she agreed with that interpretation.

(DENNIS *crosses to the table and starts opening up the bag of cocaine to show* WARREN.)

DENNIS: Yeah. Don't worry about that. A lot of times your average girl teen will bug out immediately following a swift and
manly conquest. It's no big deal. You didn't do anything to
her that she didn't do to you. Just call her up and, you know,
take her to the *zoo* or something. Only don't sit here and
start getting depressed after you finally got laid with a completely good-looking girl after a *drought* like the fucking
Irish *potato* famine of *eighteen forty-eight*, because you're bringing me down. You should be totally proud of yourself and
not get into your usual self-flagellating stew just because you
came too fast and she freaked out afterwards. (*He laughs.*) Now
come here and look at the crystal formation on this rock. It's
unbelievable.

(WARREN *looks.*)

WARREN: That's a big rock.

DENNIS: It's a big rock. This baby alone would probably pay for
your whole *night* at the Plaza. You know?

WARREN: I doubt it.

DENNIS: Why? How much did you spend?

WARREN: I guess it was around a thousand bills all told, but I
didn't really tally it up yet.

DENNIS: You spent a *thousand dollars* on that girl when she was
totally ready to fuck you for free?

WARREN: I wasn't so sure, man. She seemed kinda skittish.

DENNIS: So, what, now you're in the hole for twenty-five hundred bucks?

WARREN: Twenty-seven.

DENNIS: What is the *matter* with you? How did you spend that
much *money*?

WARREN: I'm not really sure.

DENNIS: OK: You're outta control. You are like hell-bent for destruction and I want nothing more to fuckin' *do* with it! I can't sell twenty-seven hundred dollars worth of blow before tomorrow *morning*.

WARREN: Why not?

DENNIS: Because it's totally *impossible*! I'll make the *calls*, but I can't speed the natural pace of the market. It's just not gonna happen. Besides, your share of the profits only comes to thirteen hundred minus my fuckin' service fee! And even if it *didn't*, I'm not letting you stay here all week with that money, Warren, because when your father finds out you spent that money on drugs, he's gonna think I'm in *cahoots* with you, and then he's gonna forgive *you* and kill *me*.

WARREN: No he's not.

DENNIS: Yes he is! How could you spend another thousand dollars?!

WARREN: It was surprisingly easy.

DENNIS: All right: That's it. Get on the phone, call Christian, tell him we need distribution help. Tell him you'll give him whatever he wants out of your half and if he can't help us move all twenty grams by tonight you're comin' over there to stay with *him*. Because I am officially closing the Dennis Ziegler Home For Runaway Boys. You understand me?

WARREN: Who am I calling? Christian?

DENNIS: Yeah, Christian!

WARREN: All right . . . !

(*As* WARREN *picks up the phone,* DENNIS *roams around the room.*)

DENNIS: Oh you are so stupid, man. You are so stupid. If your father finds you here, man, he's gonna sic that fuckin' *driver* on me and I am totally gonna have to leave town. And this is such a bad time for me.

WARREN: (*Holding the phone.*) Did you have breakfast yet?

DENNIS: No I didn't have breakfast. I just got up.

WARREN: Let's take a run over to Zabar's and pick up a smoked salmon.

DENNIS: DIAL THE PHONE!

(WARREN *dials the phone.*)

WARREN: (*Into the phone.*) Hello Mr. Berkman, is Christian there? . . . Oh, OK. Could you please tell him that Warren Straub called? . . . I'm fine, how are you? . . . Not too much. How's *Mrs.* Berkman?

DENNIS: GET OFF THE PHONE!

WARREN: (*Into the phone.*) Anyway—could you just tell him I called, and he can call me at Dennis Ziegler's house?

(DENNIS *makes a wild, negative, cut-off gesture.*)

WARREN: Actually, just tell him I'll try him later . . . Thanks a lot.

(*He hangs up.*)

DENNIS: What's the *matter* with you?

WARREN: Nothing. Why don't you calm down?

DENNIS: Oh you are really asking for it. Maybe I can get ahold of Philip.

(*The phone rings. They look at it fearfully. It keeps ringing.* DENNIS *picks it up tentatively.*)

DENNIS: (*Into the phone.*) Yeah? . . . BECAUSE *I* DIDN'T *BREAK* YOUR FUCKIN' SCULPTURE, *WARREN* BROKE IT!

(*He slams the phone down as hard as he possibly can. Runs his raging fingers through his hair.*)

WARREN: (*Starts to speak.*)

(DENNIS *grabs the phone and dials furiously. Waits.*)

DENNIS: (*Into the phone.*) I just want you to think about what a sick, unhappy person you are that after all the serious problems we've been having for the last three months over your relentless *identity* crisis—*which has nothing to fuckin' do with me!*—we're finally getting along together like we fuckin' love each other, and you freak out at me *this* much and get me *this* angry at you, because one of my *friends* accidentally broke your semi-Lesbian progressive-school clay *sculpture!* . . . It was on the *shelf* so I could *look* at it! Will you *listen* to yourself? Will you listen to what you're *saying?* . . . YOU TORTURE ME ABOUT A *SCULPTURE*, YOU PSYCHOTIC MONSTER!? I'D LIKE TO RIP YOUR FUCKIN' HEAD OFF!

(*He slams the phone down and kicks it as hard as he can across the room.*)

WARREN: You have a nice touch, man.

DENNIS: Shut up! (*He starts laughing.*) I'm sick, *sick!* All right: Christian's not home and I ain't callin' Philip. What about this shit? Could you sell any of this?

(*He rattles* WARREN'*s open suitcase full of toys.*)

WARREN: Um—yeah. I can sell *all* of it.

DENNIS: Really? For how much? Could you get two thousand dollars for what's in here?

WARREN: I don't know. I never really tallied it up, but I'm fairly sure I could get considerably *more* than that.

DENNIS: Oh, we are selling this *today.* I'm calling Adam Saulk's brother right now.

(*He picks up the phone. Stops.*)

DENNIS: Is that OK?

WARREN: Go ahead.

(DENNIS *dials the phone.*)

DENNIS: All right. Maybe this'll solve everything. (*Into the phone.*) Is that Donald? . . . Dennis Ziegler, man, what's goin' on? . . . I'm all right. Listen, do you know Warren *Straub*? . . . Yeah. So he's got like a lot of really high quality toys and shit from like the fifties and sixties, and about thirty really rare first-release albums— (*Covers the phone. To* WARREN, *who is signaling him.*) *What?*

WARREN: I think you should mention the toaster.

DENNIS: No, he doesn't care about your *toaster*, Warren. (*Into the phone.*) One second, man.

WARREN: Yes he does. It's really rare.

DENNIS: (*Covers the phone.*) It's worth money?

WARREN: *Yeah.*

DENNIS: (*Into the phone.*) Sorry, man—he's also got this incredibly rare toaster from like . . . *eighteen forty-seven.*

WARREN: Nineteen fifty-five.

DENNIS:	WARREN:
(*Into the phone.*) From *nineteen fifty-five.* Like a completely rare edition of toaster. I'm not sure what the actual model is, but— I said I'm not sure what the actual model is, but I definitely know it is one fine toaster. (*Covers the phone.*) Would you shut up!	Tell him they recalled it.
	Tell him they recalled it.
	D. Tell him they recalled it.

(WARREN *shuts up.*)

DENNIS: (*Into the phone.*) Yeah, man—anyway—he was gonna sell some of this shit to his regular boy, but I told him I had a friend who could probably come up with a much better price, and I wanted to try to give you the business if you were interested. But the thing is, Donald? Donald? This stuff is like really good, so I don't wanna waste my time if you're not totally prepared to step up to the plate. You know what I mean there, Donald? . . . Yeah? . . . All right . . . No, this afternoon's not so good for me, man: I'm going to a ball game with my brother . . . No, man, Warren's like ready to *go* . . . Well what are you doing right now? . . . All right, gimme your address. (*Writes down the address.*) All right, man, see you in a few.

(*He hangs up.*)

DENNIS: I am a total business *genius*. I don't even know what this shit is *worth* and I'm already getting you like the best possible price for it. I am just like completely naturally gifted at business.

WARREN: Well . . . There is my usual guy, who's definitely offered me decent money for the whole collection at various times, so—

DENNIS: No, never mind your usual *guy*. You should totally let me handle this transaction for you, Warren, because this guy is like completely intimidated by me, and I'm just gonna get you much more money. All right?

WARREN: Whatever.

DENNIS: All right. Now before I go over there, tell me what would be the best possible money you could *possibly* get for this shit.

WARREN: I don't know. If you include the records, I guess the best price you could hope to get would be like, I don't know, like *maybe* twenty-five at the very outside.

DENNIS: You're seriously telling me this *junk* is worth twenty-five hundred bucks?

WARREN: Yeah. Because it's a really good collection. But you probably won't get that.

DENNIS: All right. Now listen to me, Warren. I am not selling your *baby* toys if you don't tell me it's OK, because I don't want you *guilting* it over my head for the rest of my life. OK? But if you don't want me to, I am totally throwing you out of here right now. Because I have no desire to incur the Wrath of Jason, and you can't just walk in here and dump your *situation* on me and then obstruct every possible solution I come up with just because you're a destructive little *freak* who has to like *wreck* everything so you can get everybody whipped into a *frenzy* over you all the time. But I don't want you telling me later that I forced you into selling your precious belongings, because it's totally up to *you*. All right?

WARREN: No. Go ahead and sell 'em. I don't know what else to do.

(DENNIS *starts getting dressed.*)

DENNIS: All right. If this stuff is worth twenty-five bills then I probably won't have to sell *all* of it, so tell me which of these I should try to hang on to and which I should immediately toss into the gaping maw of Donald Saulk.

WARREN: I guess . . . save the Major Matt Masons for last . . . And if you can, I guess I'd prefer it if you didn't sell the toaster.

(*Pause.*)

DENNIS: I just totally humiliated myself talking up this fuckin' toaster, now you're telling me I can't *sell* it?

WARREN: Not if you don't have to, no. I don't know how much he's gonna offer—

DENNIS: All right. I'll try.

WARREN: And give me the hat.

(DENNIS *picks up the baseball cap.*)

DENNIS: We can't sell this?

WARREN: I don't think so.

DENNIS: Why not? You could get money for this, couldn't you?

WARREN: I know I could, but I'm not selling it.

DENNIS: All right.

(DENNIS *gives* WARREN *the baseball cap and starts packing up the suitcase.*)

(*The buzzer buzzes.*)

DENNIS: It's Jason!

WARREN: It's not Jason!

DENNIS: It's totally Jason! I'm going across the roof!

WARREN: It's not Jason, he doesn't even know I'm here!

DENNIS:	WARREN:
He knows who your *friends* are! You think he didn't figure out where you *went*? You only *have* two friends! All right!	But it's not him, you fuckin' *socio*path: he's throwing a *brunch*!

(*Pause.*)

DENNIS: You answer it.

WARREN: No way.

DENNIS: Why not?

WARREN: Because it's not my house, man.

DENNIS: So what?

WARREN: I don't wanna answer it. What if it's him?

DENNIS: All right. Shut up.

WARREN: I wasn't talking.

DENNIS: Shut *up*!

(DENNIS *goes to the intercom and hits the Talk button.*)

DENNIS: Yeah?

JESSICA: (*On the intercom.*) It's Jessica Goldman. Is Warren there?

DENNIS: (*To* WARREN.) I'm gonna *kill* you, Warren.

WARREN: I didn't know she was coming here.

DENNIS: That scared the shit out of me.

WARREN: Why? Just buzz her in.

(DENNIS *hits the buzzer and goes to the suitcase.*)

DENNIS: All right. Saulk's only on Eighty-first, so I won't be long. I'll do my best, and I'll try to save Major Matt Mason if I can. But he might be called upon to make the ultimate Outer Space sacrifice.

WARREN: I understand, man . . . Farewell, Toaster Amazing.

(WARREN *unhappily watches* DENNIS *pack away the last of the collection and zip up the suitcase.*)

DENNIS: All right. Cheer up, man. Your troubles are almost over.

WARREN: I'm cheerful.

(*There is a knock on the door.* DENNIS *is nearest the door and opens it.* JESSICA *stands in the doorway.*)

JESSICA: Hi, Dennis. How are you?

DENNIS: I'm fine, Jessica. How are *you*?

JESSICA: Fine.

DENNIS: Are you from the Leg Embassy?

(*He is referring to her short skirt.*)

JESSICA: Yeah, I'm the ambassador.

DENNIS: Stay with it.

(JESSICA *comes into the room.*)

JESSICA: (*To* WARREN.) Hey. I was just around the corner so I thought I'd buzz up.

WARREN: (*Bizarrely, to* JESSICA.) Good Morgen to all good Norse-men.

JESSICA: Excuse me?

WARREN: How many Norse Horsemen does it take to Smoke a Herring?

(DENNIS *laughs rudely and loudly at* WARREN's *awkward attempt at eccentric humor and goes into the bathroom, closing the door behind him. We hear the sink running.* WARREN *crosses with awkward confidence toward* JESSICA.)

WARREN: All Norse Horsemen smoke Morgen Cigarettes.

JESSICA: Am I supposed to know what you're talking about?

WARREN: I'm not talking about anything. It's just something to say. Don't you want to kiss me Good Morgen?

(*He comes to her to kiss her. It doesn't go too well. She turns her face or ducks her head so he can't kiss her.*)

JESSICA: (*Low, referring to* DENNIS *in the bathroom.*) Um, can we please not, like . . .

WARREN: Sorry.

JESSICA: That's OK . . .

(*She moves away from him.* DENNIS *comes out of the bathroom. He sits on the floor to put on his sneakers.*)

WARREN: So D. How long you think you're gonna be?

DENNIS: (*Looking at* JESSICA.) I don't know. How much time do you need?

WARREN: (*Confused.*) Um . . . We were gonna get some food . . .

JESSICA: How much *time* do we need?

DENNIS: (*To* WARREN.) So who's stoppin' you?

WARREN: I was actually wondering about the *key*.

JESSICA: (*To* DENNIS.) How much time do we need for *what*?

DENNIS: For whatever dastardly deed you're planning to *indulge* in, Jessica.

JESSICA: I don't think we're gonna be indulging in anything very dastardly, to tell you the truth, Dennis.

WARREN: I thought we were gonna be indulging in some *brunch*.

DENNIS: So *that's* your story, eh? (*A la Snidely Whiplash.*) Yeh heh heh heh . . . !

JESSICA: What is he *talking* about?

WARREN: Denny, man, you're my *best friend*.

DENNIS: (*Getting up.*) All right, kids, I'm outta here. Try to find some way to entertain yourselves.

JESSICA: Don't leave on my account.

DENNIS: Don't worry about it. (*To* WARREN.) Be back in a half.

(DENNIS *exits, with the suitcase.*)

JESSICA: Where's he going?

WARREN: He just has a business transaction to perform.

JESSICA: What is he, like the big drug dealer or something?

WARREN: He's the big everything.

JESSICA: Well . . . Sorry to bust in on you like this—

WARREN: That's OK.

JESSICA: —but I actually just wanted to tell you I can't have brunch.

WARREN: Why not?

JESSICA: Well, when I got home this morning I had this really huge fight with my mom and I think I'd better just be at home today. She kind of freaked out that I never called last night, so now she wants to have some big landmark discussion about how we're gonna handle my living there this year . . .

WARREN: Well . . . Thanks for canceling in person.

JESSICA: Well, I'm sorry, but my mom is really upset and getting along with her is a really big priority for me right now. I tried to call before, but the line was busy.

WARREN: Do you want to make a plan for any time this week?

JESSICA: I think I'd better just chill out a little bit this week, actually.

WARREN: All right.

(*Silence.*)

JESSICA: Well . . . You seem like you're really angry . . .

WARREN: I'm not.

JESSICA: Well that's not the impression you're *conveying*, but . . .

WARREN: No—I guess I just don't understand why you walked ten blocks out of your way so you could be around the corner so you could buzz up and tell me you can't have brunch with me.

JESSICA: Uh, no: I told you I tried to call . . .

WARREN: Yeah—he was on the phone for like two *minutes*.

JESSICA: All right, I'm *sorry.*

WARREN: There's nothing to be sorry about.

JESSICA: All right.

(*She goes slowly to the door and puts her hand on the knob.*)

JESSICA: So . . . can I ask you something?

WARREN: Go ahead.

JESSICA: Did you tell Dennis what happened last night?

(*Pause.*)

WARREN: Um . . . I guess.

JESSICA: Really. What did you say?

WARREN: Nothing. I said we had a nice time.

JESSICA: That's all?

WARREN: Pretty much.

JESSICA: I find that really hard to believe.

WARREN: Why?

JESSICA: I don't know. Don't you guys get into like comparing *notes* and stuff?

WARREN: I'm not really into that.

JESSICA: Well . . . OK . . . It's just— This is getting a little weird now, because when I talked to Valerie, she asked *me* if anything happened with us last night. And for some reason, I guess I didn't really tell her that anything did. So now she's gonna talk to *Dennis*, and I'm gonna look like a total *liar* to someone I'm just starting to be close friends with and who I really care about . . . !

WARREN: Um . . . So . . . I don't really get what's happening now . . . You're mad at me because you lied to Valerie?

JESSICA: *No* . . . I just should have figured that you would like rush off to tell your friends that you *fucked* me—

WARREN: Whoa!

JESSICA: —whereas I might be more inclined to be a little more *discreet* about it till I found out where I stood with you.

WARREN: I didn't fuckin' rush off *any*where!

JESSICA: Yeah, whatever, you know what? It doesn't matter—

WARREN: I came *back* here 'cause I'm *staying* here—

JESSICA: OK, but you know what? It really doesn't matter—

WARREN: And the minute I walked in he like totally *grilled* me—

JESSICA: Oh so you just tell him whatever he wants to know no matter what the consequences are for somebody else?

WARREN: No! Will you let me finish my—

JESSICA: (*On "Let."*) But honestly, Warren? I really don't care who you told, or what you told them, because people are gonna think whatever they think and you know what? There's nothing I can do about it.

WARREN: What people? What are you talking about!

JESSICA: I don't know, but whatever it is I must be wrong because of the way you're *yelling*.

WARREN: You're not anything!

JESSICA: Well, it really—I should just really listen to my instincts, you know? Because your instincts are never wrong. And it was totally against my instinct to come over here last night, and it was definitely against my instinct to *sleep* with you, but I did and it's too late. And now my mom is totally furious at me, I probably ruined my friendship with Valerie, and now like Dennis *Ziegler* thinks I'm like, easy *pickins*, or something—

WARREN: Nobody thinks anything—

JESSICA: And it's not like I even care what he thinks, OK? Because I don't actually *know* him. Or you. Or *Valerie*, for that matter! So it doesn't really matter! I've made new friends before, I can make more new friends now if I have to. So let's just forget the whole thing ever happened, you can chalk one up in your *book*, or whatever—

WARREN: I don't *have* a *book*.

JESSICA: —and I'll just *know* better next time! Hopefully. OK?

(*Pause.*)

WARREN: I don't really get what you're so upset about.

JESSICA: Well: I guess I'm just *insane*.

WARREN: I thought we had a really good time together, and I was actually in a fairly *up* state of mind for once.

JESSICA: I'm sure you were.

WARREN: Well, I didn't mean that in any kind of lascivious way, so I don't know why you want to take it like that. I really like you.

JESSICA: Yeah, whatever.

WARREN: No not whatever! I'm sorry I said anything to Dennis. I definitely caved in to the peer pressure. But I also definitely said as little as possible and was totally respectful of you in the way I talked about you. Even though I was pretty excited about what happened last night, and also about like, maybe like, the prospect of like, I don't know, like, going *out* with you—which I would be very into, if you were. But if you want to think the whole thing meant nothing to me, then go ahead, because that's not the case.

JESSICA: Well . . . You know, I really—

WARREN: It's totally weird, like taking all your clothes off and having sex with someone you barely know, and then being like, "What's up *now*?" You know? Like it's such an intense experience, but then nobody knows what to fuckin' say, even though nothing really bad actually happened. You know?

JESSICA: . . . Well . . . I don't know . . .

WARREN: But I really like you . . . I don't really agree with most of your *opinions* . . .

JESSICA: Oh, thank you.

WARREN: . . . but I don't meet a lot of people who can actually make me *think*, you know? And who can hold their own in an interesting discussion. And who I'm totally hot for at the same time. You know? It's a fairly effective combination.

(*Pause.*)

JESSICA: I don't know, Warren. Things are just really weird in my life right now. And everything you're saying is really sweet, but I have literally no idea whether you mean it or not. It's like my instinct is just *broken* . . . And I guess sometimes actions speak louder than words . . .

WARREN: But what action could I possibly take except to say I'm sorry for whatever it is you think I've done?

JESSICA: (*A joke.*) Presents are always nice. Just kidding.

WARREN: You want a present?

JESSICA: I'm just kidding.

WARREN: Why? I'm sitting on twelve thousand *dollars*. I'll buy you a *sports* car. OK?

JESSICA: That's OK. I don't have a license yet.

WARREN: Well, what do you want?

(*Pause.*)

JESSICA: . . . Are you serious?

WARREN: *Name it.*

JESSICA: OK . . . (*Pause.*) Um . . . Could I have the hat?

(*Pause.*)

WARREN: Definitely.

(*Pause.*)

JESSICA: Really?

WARREN: It's yours.

(*He picks up the baseball cap and holds it out to her.*)

WARREN: Here.

(*Pause.* JESSICA *looks at him uncertainly.*)

JESSICA: . . . Don't if you don't want to.

WARREN: I really want to.

JESSICA: Why?

WARREN: Because I really like you.

(*Pause. She reaches out slowly and takes the hat.*)

JESSICA: Well—I don't know what to say . . .

(WARREN *does not respond.*)

JESSICA: I mean—I can't believe it . . . ! I can't believe that you
    would give me something that means this much to you—I
    don't even know what to say.

WARREN: Good.

(*She puts it on her head and self-consciously "models" it for him.*)

JESSICA: What do you think?

WARREN: . . . Looks great on you . . .

JESSICA: You think?

WARREN: Definitely.

(*She looks at him. He is clearly in distress and can't hide it.*)

JESSICA: Well, you look totally miserable.

WARREN: I'm not.

(*She takes off the hat.*)

JESSICA: Well I'm sorry, but I feel really weird taking your grand-father's hat.

WARREN: Then why'd you fucking ask me for it?

(JESSICA *flushes a deep mortified red.*)

JESSICA:	WARREN:
I was *totally kidding* when I asked you for something—	No you weren't!

JESSICA: —Yes I was! But then you *insisted* I pick something! Only why did you *give* it to me if you don't want me to *have* it?

WARREN: Because I really want you to have it!

JESSICA: But why do you keep *saying* that when you obviously DON'T?

WARREN: NO! God *damn*! What do I have to do, like BEG you to take it from me?

(*A long moment.*)

JESSICA: OK. Sorry.

(*She puts the hat back on her head. Silence.*)

JESSICA: Well . . . I mean . . . Should I just go home?

WARREN: (*Looking at the floor.*) I don't know . . . Do whatever.

JESSICA: Well, then I guess I will.

(*She goes to the door.*)

JESSICA: Should I assume you no longer want to go out this week?

WARREN: I don't think we can. I'm all out of baseball hats.

(JESSICA *takes off the hat*.)

JESSICA: Can I please say something?

WARREN: You try to give me that hat back one more time, I swear to God I'll fuckin' *burn* it . . . !

(*Pause.* JESSICA *puts the baseball cap down on the table*.)

JESSICA: Well . . . That would be up to you.

(*She turns and exits.* WARREN *sits very still for a minute. Then he gets up and carefully puts the hat away with his stuff. He sits at the table and carefully dumps all the cocaine on the dinner plate and looks at it*.)

(*He spoons some Mannitol onto the plate, and starts mixing the two powders together, concentrating intensely*.)

(*The phone rings. He reaches for it and knocks the entire plate of cocaine onto the floor. He doesn't know what to do for a minute. He laughs. The phone keeps ringing. He answers it*.)

WARREN: (*Into the phone*.) Hello?

(*He stands up like he just got an electric shock. He listens for a moment*.)

WARREN: Well, Dad, I guess the jig is up . . . W— Well I— Could I— I was planning on *returning* it . . . Thank you . . . Well, you're actually gonna have to wait like an hour . . . Do whatever you want, but I won't be here . . . Why don't you punch me in the face and throw me out of the apartment? . . . That is definitely my intention . . . Uh-huh . . . I don't know, Dad: What kind of world do *you* think I'm living in? . . .

(*Pause. He sits down. More quietly:*)

WARREN: Yeah. I think about her all the time . . . I don't really know, Dad. I just see her in my imagination, I guess . . . Well,

I feel pretty strongly about the fact that I have a lot better judgment than she did at my age, and it's also not too likely that I'm gonna move in with some thirty-five-year-old guy who beats me up all the time. So I don't really think it's an appropriate comparison. Although I will say that it's a totally obvious one. By which I mean I don't think it's all that clever . . . All right: I know your brunching companions await . . . Well, it is really hard to fully appreciate what your girlfriend has to go through, but it's really fucking fortunate that she has both the good looks and the intelligence to see her through all the rough spots . . . Sounds good . . . Do whatever you want . . . I hate you too.

(*His father hangs up.* WARREN *hangs up too.*)

(*He looks at the cocaine on the floor. He starts to scrape what he can off the floor and onto the plate. But it's an impossible job. He suddenly stomps on the cocaine, smearing it all over the floor with wild kicks. After a moment of this, he stops.*)

(DENNIS *comes in, very freaked out. He puts down the suitcase, now empty.*)

DENNIS: What are you doing? What happened?

WARREN: I knocked the drugs on the floor.

DENNIS: You did *what*?

WARREN: I was trying to mix in the cut.

DENNIS: What? How bad is it?

WARREN: It's pretty bad.

DENNIS: Oh—GOD! OK— All right—I can't even deal with this right now— Listen to me, Warren. Something terrible has happened.

WARREN: What's the matter? Somebody's dead?

DENNIS: Yeah.

WARREN: Who, my mother?

DENNIS: (*Furious.*) No, not your *mother*, you idiot—

WARREN: OK.

DENNIS: It's *Stuey.*

WARREN: Who?

DENNIS: Stuey! Stuey! It's fuckin' Stuey!

WARREN: Stuey who?

DENNIS: Stuart! The Fat Man. Stuart Grossbart. What's the matter with you?

WARREN: Oh shit. *That* Stuey.

DENNIS:	WARREN:
Yeah "that Stuey"! How many fuckin' Stueys do you know?	All right! I couldn't place the name for a second! What happened to him?

DENNIS: I don't know, man. I guess he did too many speedballs. He was with that Dutch chick all night, and they went to sleep and when she woke up this morning she couldn't wake him up, so she turned him over and there was blood coming out of his nose and his *eyes*, and he was dead.

WARREN: Whoa.

DENNIS: I mean I just *saw* the guy last *night.* I am so freaked out. I can't even believe it.

WARREN: How did you find out about it?

DENNIS: 'Cause when I got to Donald Saulk's house he was on the phone with Yoffie. So I got on the phone and Yoffie told me he went over to Stuey's this morning and there were all these cops there, and that girl was sitting there freaked out of her mind crying and screaming and like smoking cigarettes and talking half in English and half in Dutch, and Yoffie told the cops he was Stuey's friend and they told him what happened.

WARREN: *Stuey.*

DENNIS: I guess it's a good thing we didn't do any speedballs. You know?

WARREN: But did we buy bad shit, or what?

DENNIS: I don't think so. I was doing it all night and I didn't wake up with fuckin' blood coming out of *my* nose. Did you?

WARREN: No. But I didn't do any of it yet.

DENNIS: And the *girl* was OK. So I guess he just overdid it. But I am so freaked out. I mean the guy is *dead.* Do you know what that *means*? It's like, he's not gonna be *around* anymore, like at *all.* And it's just got me really fuckin' scared. I mean we are such assholes to be doing all this shit, man. I am totally stopping. I know he was a big fat slob who totally overdid everything and all he ever ate was like sirloin drenched in butter and sour cream, but the guy was like twenty-three years old and now he's just *gone.* You know? Like he is no more.

WARREN: Yeah.

DENNIS: I don't know, man. I guess there's only a certain amount of time you can keep doing this shit before shit starts to happen to you. I mean I am really scared.

WARREN: So did you sell my stuff?

DENNIS: Yeah.

WARREN: Did you have to sell everything?

DENNIS: Oh yeah.

WARREN: How much did you get for it?

DENNIS: I only got nine hundred.

WARREN: What do you mean?!

DENNIS: I mean you had a totally inflated idea of what that shit was worth, so don't make me feel *bad* about it—

WARREN: I know exactly what it was worth and that guy just *rooked* you.

(DENNIS *turns white with rage.*)

DENNIS: I am really gonna fuckin' hit you man! I totally got the best possible deal I could!

WARREN: Then you shouldn't have sold it!

DENNIS: You told me to sell it! At least I didn't knock the fuckin' *coke* on the floor, so don't make me feel *bad* about this, man, all right? I'm freaked out of my mind. So maybe I didn't do so well. I don't know. I'm sorry. It's better than nothing.

WARREN: I guess.

(*Silence.*)

DENNIS: What happened to that girl?

WARREN: She left.

DENNIS: You already had a fight with her?

WARREN: I'm not really sure what happened.

DENNIS: How could you mess that up so fast? What kind of talent for misery do you have, man?

WARREN: I don't know. I guess I'm pretty advanced.

DENNIS: Did my girlfriend call back?

WARREN: No.

DENNIS: I think I went too far with her before. But I can't even deal with it right now. I'm too freaked out.

(DENNIS *lies down on his back.*)

DENNIS: I just can't believe this, man, it's like so completely bizarre. And it's not like I even liked the guy that much, you know? I just *knew* him. You know? But if we had been doing those speedballs last night we could both be *dead* now. Do you understand how *close* that is? I mean . . . It's *death*. *Death*. It's so incredibly heavy, it's like so much heavier than like ninety-five percent of the shit you deal with in the average day that constitutes your supposed life, and it's like so totally off to the *side* it's like completely ridiculous. I mean that was *it*. That was his *life*. Period. The Life of Stuart. A fat Jew from Long Island with a grotesque accent who sold drugs and ate steak and did nothing of note like whatsoever. I don't know, man. I'm like, high on fear. I feel totally high on fear. I'm like—I don't even know what to do with myself. I wanna like go to *cooking* school in *Florence*, or like go into *show* business. I could so totally be a completely great chef it's like ridiculous. Or like an actor or like a director. I should totally direct movies, man, I'd be a genius at it. Like if you take the average person with the average sensibility or sense of humor or the way they look at the world and what thoughts they have or what they think, and you compare it to the way *I* look at shit and the shit I come up with to say, or just the *slant* I put on shit, there's just like no comparison at all. I could totally make movies, man, I would be like one of the greatest moviemakers of all time. Plus I am like so much better at sports than anyone I know except Wally and those big black basketball players, man, but I totally played with those guys and completely earned their respect, and Wally was like, "Denny, man, you are the only white friend I have who I can take uptown and hang out with my friends and not be *embarrassed*." Because I just go up there and hang out with them and like get them so much more stoned than they've ever been in their *life* and like am completely not intimidated by them at all. You know?

WARREN: Yeah.

DENNIS: I'm high on fear, man. I am completely stoned out of my mind on fear. And like you guys think I'm like totally confident and on top of it, but it's not true at all. My fuckin' mother is so fuckin' harsh and wildly extreme that I just got trained to snap back twice as hard the minute anybody starts to fuck with me. That's how I fight with Valerie. Like the minute we get into an argument whatever she says to me I just double it and totally get in her face until she backs down and like has to like, leave the *room*. And it completely works too, because I don't have to take any of the shit I see all my male friends taking from their fuckin' girlfriends, or like the shit my father takes from my mother. I mean all he does is fuckin' lord it over everybody man, over all my brothers and sisters and like all his fuckin' assistants and his dealers and agents and like all these celebrities who buy his art, because he totally knows that he's like a complete living genius and so he's like, "Why should I spend two minutes talking to anybody I don't *want* to?" Except now he's like torturing everyone constantly because he basically never doesn't have to pee, and my mother is freaking out because she's working fourteen hours a day because they cut the money out of all her programs and she's totally predicting major inner-city catastrophe in years to come, and she completely has his balls in a vise. She's like, "Eddie, you're an asshole. Eddie, nobody gives a shit if you have to pee. You always have to pee, so shut up." She just *tramples* him, man. She's like "No matter what you do it doesn't matter, because all you do is sell a bunch of paintings to like, one percent of the population and I'm out there every day like, saving children's *lives* and trying to help real people who are being destroyed by Ronald *Reagan*—so whatever you do and however famous you are it's just a total tissue of conceit, because it's got nothing to do with anybody but rich people." She just makes total emasculated mincemeat out of him and the only thing he can do to fight back is go fuck some twenty-year-old groupie, only now he can't do that anymore because he's so sick, so he's just totally in her power, and all he can do is torture her from like a totally weaker position, and she's like laughing in his face. My family is sick, man, they're *sick*. You think your fuckin' father is crazy? What if like everywhere he went total strangers like worshipped him as a *god*? Wait till his *health* starts to go. Can you imagine what that's like? Like seriously, what does that *feel* like, to be looking ahead like five years and not knowing whether you're still gonna *be* here? You can totally see why people are religious, man. I mean how much better would it be to think you're gonna be *some*where, you know? Instead of absolutely nowhere. Like *gone,* forever. (*Pause.*) That is so fuckin' scary. I am so fuckin' scared right now. (*Pause.*) I gotta call my girlfriend. You have totally fucked me up, by the way! How emblematic of your personality is it that you walk into a room for *ten minutes* and break the *exact item* calculated to wreak the maximum possible amount of havoc, no matter where you are? You're a total troublemaker, Warren. I should totally ban you from my house. I am so keyed up. I can't shut up. I wish Valerie was here. Maybe I should call that girl Natalie and see if she'll come over and give me a blow job. She really likes me, man. She told my sister I had beautiful eyes. (*Pause.*) I do have totally amazing eyes. They're a completely amazing, unique shape. Like most people with my kind of eyes aren't shaped like this at all. My eyes are like totally intense and direct. Like if I look people in the eye, like nine out of ten people can't even hold my *gaze.* Did you do any of that coke?

WARREN: Not yet.

DENNIS: I don't even want to look at it, man. I'm so freaked out. I totally feel like donating it to *charity* or something. (*He laughs.*) That is so not funny . . . I wonder if anybody told his family.

WARREN: I'm sure they did.

DENNIS: I wonder if they'll have a funeral.

WARREN: I'm sure they will.

DENNIS: That's gonna be one big casket. I wonder if anybody'll show up.

WARREN: Why wouldn't they?

DENNIS: Because nobody *liked* the guy! I called like six people, and I was so freaked out, and nobody cared at all. They were all like, "Wow. That's amazing. Is the coke all right?" Now, I don't know if that means they're all like totally callous and unfeeling or whether the guy was just a totally reprehensible human being.

WARREN: Well, he didn't really leave me with any lastingly warm impression. I mean, I'm sorry he's dead, but I read the *newspaper* this morning, too, you know?

DENNIS: Well, all I know is if *I* had a fuckin' funeral, there wouldn't be room to *sit*. Someday I'm gonna make a movie about all of us, man. Like if you made that guy Donald Saulk a character in a movie, with all that shit in his apartment, how heavy would that be? And most people would like find some bad fuckin' actor to like do some caricature sitcom imitation of this guy and totally miss all the intense subtleties and qualities of his personality, and if it was me I would just go in there and use the real *guy*, and it would be so much heavier, and so much funnier. Don't you think?

WARREN: I don't know.

DENNIS: But don't you think I would be like an amazing director?

WARREN: I have no idea, man.

(*Pause.*)

DENNIS: What do you mean you have no idea?

WARREN: I mean I have no idea.

(*Pause.*)

DENNIS: Well I totally would be. I would totally—

WARREN: But you've never *done* it.

DENNIS: What do you mean?

WARREN: I mean you don't know anything *about* it. You just like movies. And have an interest in people's personalities.

DENNIS: No I don't "just like movies." I totally—

WARREN: (*One the second "I."*) I like them too. But I don't necessarily think you'd be a good movie director, because I have no idea if you have the slightest talent for it whatsoever. I'm sorry.

DENNIS: You are really pissing me off.

WARREN: I don't really give a shit, man. Why did you sell my fuckin' toy collection for nine hundred dollars?

DENNIS: Is that what you're mad about? With poor Stuey moldering in the ground?

WARREN: I don't give a fuck about Stuey, and neither do you. I didn't even *know* him.

DENNIS: So call the guy up and get it back and dig your own fuckin' grave, you little asshole! I am totally sick of you and your moronic fuckin' self-imposed *dilemma*! I've been dealing drugs for five years and I never once dropped any of it on the fucking *floor*! Because I am not an *imbecile*! I cannot believe that you do that, and then you have the nerve to give me shit because I undersold your little *toy* box!

(*Pause.*)

WARREN: Why do you have to talk to me that way, man?

DENNIS: Why do I talk to you what way?

WARREN: Why do you have to call me an asshole every five seconds? I don't like it.

DENNIS: What do you mean? We call each other shit all the time. Don't start with me, Warren, because all I've been doing for the last two days is like totally try to help you!

WARREN: I know you're doing *something*, man. But I can barely tell if you're even on my side.

DENNIS: What are you *talking* about? I'm on your side, I'm totally on your side.

WARREN: Then why are you always like, reminding me that I haven't done well with girls for a really long time, man?

DENNIS: Because—

WARREN: And like constantly insulting me and like *teasing* me and telling me how incompetent I am and what a fuckup I am, like this running motif like *every time* we hang out?

DENNIS: Because you *are* a fuckup. So am I! So is everyone we *know.* What is the big deal?

WARREN: And how come every time I said I liked a girl you immediately say she's got a fat ass or like has no tits or she's got a horse face or whatever. You know? Jessica Goldman is the first girl I ever had a chance with who was like clearly good-looking enough that you weren't able to make me feel like a second-rate asshole for wanting to go out with her.

DENNIS: You are really making me mad. That's what you're mad about? Because of that time I said that girl Susan had a horse face? That's just the way I talk, man. We all talk that way, it doesn't mean anything. You can't like suddenly turn around and act all fuckin' hurt and sensitive about that shit, that's the way we *are* with each other. Besides, that girl Susan *did* have a horse face, and everybody else could *see* it. I'm just the only one who *says* it. And when you're with a really good-looking girl I fuckin' say *that.* So don't give me this

shit from the back *benches* of the fuckin' *peanut* gallery
because it's total bullshit, and I am already so *sick* of you
after hanging out with you for less than twenty-four hours
in a row that I'm like two seconds away from beating the
fucking shit out of you, you little fuckin' asshole! (*Pause.*)
What do you *mean* I'm not on your *side*?

WARREN: I'm sure you love me, man, and you're totally like my
personal hero, but I really don't get the feeling that you are.

(*A moment.* DENNIS *steps back. His face twists into a strange shape and
then he breaks out with a surprising choking sob. He starts crying. This
goes on for a moment.* WARREN *watches him coldly.*)

WARREN: What are you crying about?

DENNIS: What do you *think* I'm crying about?!

WARREN: I assume you feel bad about something you think has
happened to you.

DENNIS: *No* . . . It's because you said I was your hero.

WARREN: Oh.

(DENNIS *goes to the kitchenette and blows his nose with a paper towel.
Pause.*)

DENNIS: So what are you saying? You want to like, stop being
friends with me?

WARREN: I don't know, man. I'm not like, breaking *up* with
you . . . I'm not your *girl*friend.

DENNIS: So what are you saying?

WARREN: I don't know.

(*Silence.*)

DENNIS: Well . . . I can't really . . .

(*Silence.*)

WARREN: Let's just drop it.

DENNIS: All right.

(*Silence.*)

WARREN: Can I have that money?

(DENNIS *gives* WARREN *the nine hundred dollars.*)

WARREN: Well . . . I'm only eighteen hundred short.

DENNIS: Well—I'll start moving what's left of this shit today and see how much we can scrape up.

WARREN: It doesn't matter.

(*Silence.*)

DENNIS: You wanna smoke pot?

WARREN: All right.

(DENNIS *goes to his bedside table and takes out a small plastic bag of pot.*)

WARREN: Where did you get that?

DENNIS: I got it from Stuey last night. Christian sold him some. I'd still like to find out where Christian got it. It fuckin' pisses me off that these ragamuffins are like running around copping drugs that I don't know about. I was gonna get some of that heroin from Stuey till it killed him. I hope it's understood in the community that this coke is really good and that Stuey just overdid it.

WARREN: I'm sure it is.

(DENNIS *starts rolling a joint.*)

WARREN: It is sort of amazing that one of us actually died. You know? (*Pause.*) Like my dad is always saying, "Do you know how *bad* you guys would have to fuck up before anything really serious ever happened to you? (*Pause.*) You and all your friends from the Upper West Side who went to that fuckin' school where they think it's gonna cripple you for *life* if they teach you how to *spell*? (*Pause.*) Do you know what happens to other kids who do the kind of shit you guys do? They *die*, man. And the only difference between you and them is my money . . . It's like a big fuckin' safety net, but you can't stretch it too far, man, because your sister fell right through it." (*Pause.*) But the fact is, he's just so freaked out of his mind that he did so well, and it all blew up in his face anyway . . . Like he did this great enterprising thing for himself and his family, and made a fortune in this incredibly tough racket, and got a house on the park without any help from anyone, and he never felt bad for anyone who couldn't do the same thing. But when he was at the height of his powers, he totally lost control of his own daughter, and she ended up getting beaten to death by some guy from the world next door to us. And there was nothing he could do about it. (*Pause.*) So . . . for the last nine years he's been try-ing to literally *pound* his life back into shape. But it's not really going too well, because he's totally by himself. (*Pause.*) You know?

DENNIS: I guess. (*Pause.*) I can't *believe* you don't think I'm on your *side.*

(*Pause.* WARREN *looks at him as if from a very great distance.*)

WARREN: All right, all right. You're on my side.

(DENNIS *lights up.*)

DENNIS: So? What are you gonna do?

WARREN: I don't know, man. I guess I'll just go home.

(DENNIS *smokes pot.* WARREN *sits there.*)

(*The lights fade out.*)

ONE-ACT & SHORT PLAYS

COWTOWN

Allison Moore

Cow Town was commissioned by the Guthrie Theater (Joe Dowling, Artistic Director), in association with The Children's Theatre Company (Peter Brosius, Artistic Director).

CHARACTERS

TRINA: Eighteen, wears dark clothes, boots, and a nose ring. A city kid.
ABBY: Fourteen, Trina's sister. Wears cute, trendy clothes. A city kid.
BETH: Seventeen, wears cute, trendy clothes that look slightly worn, and a little risqué. A farm girl.
BILLY: Fifteen, Beth's brother. Wears Wranglers, Ropers, and a cowboy hat. A farm boy.
JAKE: Seventeen, a good-looking boy. A suburbanite.
DOUG: Seventeen, Jake's buddy. A jock. A suburbanite.
STEPH: Seventeen, one of the cool kids. A suburbanite.
AMANDA: Seventeen, wishes she was one of the cool kids. A suburbanite.
KARA: Sixteen, see above. A suburbanite.
STUDENTS: Additional various students as needed to create hallway scenes.

TIME

The present.

PLACE

Cambridge, Minnesota, where farmland meets strip mall.

(*Sound of birds. Sound of chickens, sound of a cow mooing. Warm light fades up on* ABBY *and* TRINA, *standing on a porch, facing out. A sense of wide open space. Morning.*)

ABBY: It's not so bad.

TRINA: It sucks.

ABBY: It's kinda pretty.

TRINA: I cannot believe we live in the suburbs.

ABBY: There are cows in our yard, Trina.

TRINA: There's an Olive Garden around the corner.

ABBY: It's like three miles away.

TRINA: I'm sorry, Abby, you're right. We only go to school in the suburbs. We live with the rednecks.

ABBY: Would you lighten up?

TRINA: Easy for you to say. You'll be on your little pep squad, and make your little friends. You won't even remember what it was like before.

ABBY: Last year you begged Mom to move—

TRINA: "As Miss Cambridge, Minnesota, I will work to end hunger by donating my butter sculpture from the state fair to all the poor underprivileged children who live in the Ghe-toes in Minneapolis and St. Paul."

ABBY: At least I had friends to leave behind.

TRINA: Dad would never have let this happen.

ABBY: Dad's not here.

(*Pause.*)

She did this for you.

TRINA: It's only one year, right.

ABBY: Unless you're me. Then it's four.

TRINA: Don't worry, Pep Squad. You are going to be fine.

(*Sound of a school bell, lights shift. A flood of high school students, all try-ing to get somewhere, cross from different directions.* ABBY *and* TRINA *step into the fray. Among the other students are* BETH, AMANDA, KARA, JAKE, DOUG, BILLY, *and* STEPH. *Snatches of conversation collide as the students pass each other.*)

EVERYONE: (*Lines overlapping.*)

Hey, wait up!
He's such a jerk.
No, I gotta work today.
Are you coming with?
She's like a fascist, I told her my computer died!
You got the trig worksheet?
Stick it.
I soooo don't want to go to practice.
Did you see what he did to me?

(BETH, AMANDA, *and* KARA*'s lines come between the noise. All motion and sound.* TRINA *and* ABBY *stand near each other, but not with each other, not talking to anyone. They are waiting for the bus.* BILLY *waits alone. In the movement, someone drops a piece of paper.* BILLY *sees it, as he bends down to pick it up,* DOUG *enters with* JAKE *and as he passes behind* BILLY, *he makes obnoxious cow noises, others laugh.*)

KARA: He's right over there.

BETH: Where?

KARA: Behind nose-ring girl?

AMANDA: So gross.

DOUG: (*Shouting.*) Hey Johnson!

KARA: It's Doug.

DOUG: Beth!

BETH: I know who it is.

(*As* BETH *snaps around, she runs into* JAKE.)

JAKE: Whoa—

BETH: I am so sorry.

JAKE: Hey, no problem. We were all just trying to figure out a time to work on the group thing for history?

BETH: Right.

JAKE: We were talking about meeting at Steph's.

BETH: Fine by me.

JAKE: It's not too far?

BETH: We do have a car, Jake.

JAKE: You mean, a car and a tractor?

BETH: Ha ha.

JAKE: I'm kidding. So we'll see you at seven?

BETH: Yeah.

(*A flurry of activity. Buses are arriving.* BETH *watches as* JAKE *moves back toward* DOUG *and* STEPH, *looking at* TRINA *as he passes, smiling.*)

JAKE: Hey.

TRINA: Hey.

DOUG: (*To* JAKE.) Who's that chick?

(*Others retreat. Sound of buses.* BETH, TRINA, ABBY, *and* BILLY *are the only ones left. They board the last bus and sit silently.* TRINA *and* ABBY *sit near one another, but not next to each other.* BILLY *sits alone. He tries to keep from staring at* TRINA, *but cannot help himself.*)

TRINA: Can I help you?

BILLY: Uh, no.

TRINA: Then please stop staring. It's very rude.

(TRINA *unwraps a piece of gum, chews.*)

ABBY: Can I have one?

(TRINA *wordlessly hands* ABBY *a piece.*)

(*To* BETH, *offering her own stick of gum.*) Oh. Hey, do you want some gum?

BETH: Uh, no. Thanks.

ABBY: Sure.

BILLY: (*As* ABBY *puts her piece in her mouth.*) I'll take it.

ABBY: Sorry.

BILLY: Forget it.

BETH: (*Not looking at* BILLY.) Chicken.

BILLY: Am not.

BETH: Then ask her. She has the gum.

(BILLY *looks at* TRINA, *starts to turn away back to his seat.*)

Yeah, that's what I thought.

BILLY: Hey, can I have some gum?

(TRINA *does not respond.*)

Hello?

(*No response.*)

    Excuse me?

BETH: Hey, where you from?

TRINA: Minneapolis.

BETH: Huh.

(*Pause.*)

ABBY: We just moved, like two weeks ago. It's a lot bigger than I thought it would be. School, I mean. I don't know what I was thinking, but when my mom first said we were moving to Cambridge, I thought it would be like—

BETH: Little House, and you'd get to play Laura?

(TRINA *snorts.*)

ABBY: No, just, you know, I thought it would be smaller. But it's not, it's about the same size as my junior high. Do you live on one of the farms out here? Or—

BETH: (*To* TRINA.) I didn't see you on the bus this morning.

TRINA: My mom dropped us.

BETH: Lucky.

TRINA: Lucky would be having a car.

BETH: I changed my mind. Can I have a piece of gum?

(TRINA *hands* BETH *a stick.* BETH *gestures with the piece of gum, but does not chew it.* TRINA *and* BETH *ignore* BILLY *throughout.* ABBY *observes.*)

BILLY: Can I have one, too?

BETH: So where'd you get it done? Your nose ring.

TRINA: In the city?

BETH: I tried to get my belly button pierced at this place in Blaine. They wouldn't let me because I'm not eighteen.

TRINA: Bummer.

BILLY: Wah, wah, come on, give me some gum.

BETH: This girl in my class, Steph? She drove in one night and went to some place like, down by the U. And she gave them this forged permission slip from her mom. It was so fake. It was like, "I, Jan Franklin, being of sound mind and body, give my daughter, Steph, permission to pierce her navel." They totally bought it.

TRINA: They probably just didn't care.

BETH: The Piercing Pagoda definitely cared. The manager was like, "All minors must be accompanied by a parent or legal guardian." Like my mom's gonna come with me to get my belly button pierced.

TRINA: My dad went with me.

BETH: No way.

TRINA: Let me squeeze his hand while they did it. He was pretty cool.

BETH: Did it hurt?

TRINA: They numb it with ice.

BETH: Are your parents divorced or something?

TRINA: My dad's dead.

BETH: Oh. I'm sorry. God.

TRINA: Yeah, my dad caks and suddenly my mom is nostalgic for her farm-girl upbringing. The grief counselor said we should wait two years before any major changes, but apparently that doesn't apply to moving to the middle of nowhere, because farm life will be good for us—never mind that we're not actually farming.

BETH: Oh my God, you bought the Swenson place.

(BILLY *begins repeating the phrase "May I have some gum, please"
under the following.*)

TRINA: I don't know. It's a big white house in the middle of a
    pasture.

BETH: We're totally neighbors. My dad leases the parcel around
    your house.

TRINA: You're the cow people?

BETH: Please don't ever say that again.

TRINA: I just meant, you own the cows we keep seeing.

BETH: It's so embarrassing.

TRINA: No. What's embarrassing? Is pretending to live this "sim-
    ple life" while my mom spends an hour and a half on her
    cell phone during her commute. We might as well have
    moved into one of those fake split-level Victorians behind
    the school. At least you're not posing.

BETH: Yeah, dairy farming is supercool.

TRINA: Family farmers are the only chance the rest of us have to
    stop the corporate bloodsuckers trying to pump us full of
    mad cow disease and growth hormone and frankenfood.

BETH: Okay, how do you even know what frankenfood is?

TRINA: My mom works for Cargill.

BILLY: PLEASE MAY I PLEASE HAVE A PIECE OF GUM,
    PLEASE.

(TRINA *finally looks at* BILLY.)

TRINA: I'm fresh out.

BILLY: You have a whole pack.

TRINA: Sorry.

BILLY: You have a pack right there.

BETH: I almost forgot to chew mine.

(BETH *unwraps her gum, drops the wrapper on the floor, and pops the piece in her mouth.*)

BILLY: Come on! One stinkin' piece!

TRINA: I'll sell it to you.

BILLY: How much?

TRINA: A dollar.

BILLY: No way.

TRINA: Op—price just went up. Now it's five.

BILLY: That one piece probably cost about five cents!

TRINA: Captive market.

BILLY: What?

BETH: She said no, loser, now go away.

BILLY: I don't know what you're saving it for. It's not like any-body's gonna kiss your pus face.

BETH: Ohmigod, what is that smell?

TRINA: I don't—I don't know.

BETH: It's shit! Oh my God, I'm gonna suffocate. Do you smell the shit? I think you've got shit stuck to the bottoms of your shit-kickers, shit brain.

BILLY: Forget it.

(BILLY *retreats, and takes this next in total silence, looking out the window.*)

BETH: Billy have you been standing out in the cow pens pretend-ing you're in the rodeo again? Straddling the milk cows, waving your hat. Billy wants to be a cowboy. Why don't you tell these nice city folk you're going to join Pro Bull-Riding

Tour. Ride bulls with Cody Custer. "Cody Custer is the BEST." "Cody Custer is my HERO." "Cody Custer, I love to watch you ride those bulls! See that bull just bucking and bucking."

(*The bus stops.* BILLY *gets off the bus.*)

This is our stop. Yours is next.

TRINA: Hey—what's your name?

BETH: Beth.

TRINA: My mom drives us in the morning. If you want a ride.

BETH: What time?

TRINA: 7:10, 7:15.

BETH: Okay.

TRINA: We'll pick you up.

(BETH *exits.* ABBY *looks at* TRINA.)

What?

ABBY: Dad did NOT go with you to get your nose pierced.

TRINA: I was having a private conversation?

ABBY: I thought you hated people who litter.

TRINA: What?

ABBY: Forget it.

(*As* TRINA *exits, she drops the pack of gum.* ABBY *picks up the pack of gum, and the wrapper* BETH *dropped earlier, and gets off the bus. Lights shift, isolating* ABBY *as she walks. It is night. Sound of cicadas, wind.* ABBY *unwraps a piece of gum, puts it in her mouth, chews. She unwraps another piece of gum, does the same. She continues this process as she walks, until she comes to the shell of a barn. She circles the outside of it, tentatively, chewing her huge wad of gum, holding all the wrappers. She steps into the structure.* BILLY, *until now unseen by* ABBY, *shines a flashlight on* ABBY.)

BILLY: What are you doing?

ABBY: (*Mouth full of gum.*) Nothing. Who's there?

BILLY: You shouldn't be out here.

ABBY: Billy, right?

BILLY: Place is haunted.

ABBY: So.

BILLY: What's in your mouth?

ABBY: Do you have some paper?

BILLY: Here.

(BILLY *hands her a piece of paper from his back pocket.* ABBY *unfolds it; there is a drawing on it.*)

ABBY: But—

BILLY: It's all right. I got about a thousand of them.

(ABBY *puts her gum wrappers carefully in her pocket, then spits her gum into a corner of* BILLY'S *paper.*)

　　Coulda used one of those wrappers.

ABBY: I'm saving them.

BILLY: For what?

(ABBY *looks at* BILLY'S *drawing.*)

ABBY: It's really good.

BILLY: It's just a sketch.

ABBY: You got the shading for the muscles and everything. It really looks like he's running.

(ABBY *offers the paper back to* BILLY, *who does not take it.*)

You guys live back over there?

BILLY: Yeah.

ABBY: So what's this?

BILLY: Old Shoewalter barn.

ABBY: How do you know it's haunted.

BILLY: 'Cause, I've seen it.

ABBY: What, like ghosts? Oooooooooooo—

BILLY: You shouldn't be walking around out here. My dad leases this land.

ABBY: I'm not hurting anything.

BILLY: Just because you bought the farmhouse doesn't mean you can go anywhere you want. Mr. Swenson still owns the land, and he leases it to my dad.

ABBY: What, is this like your secret hideout? You do your secret things here?

BILLY: Forget it.

(BILLY *starts to leave.*)

ABBY: I'm sorry. Look, hey. Why's it haunted?

BILLY: Why do you care?

ABBY: I don't. I'm just curious. You're probably making it up anyway.

BILLY: You sure you want to know?

ABBY: Yeah.

BILLY: Mr. Shoewalter shot his head off with his hunting rifle. Right here in the barn. Mr. Swenson knocked the house down a couple years back.

ABBY: Why'd he kill himself?

BILLY: My dad says they were gonna foreclose on the farm. This quarter used to be his. It was a pretty small operation, and there wasn't a co-op then. He left a note for Mrs. Shoewalter, telling her he was in the barn and to call Mr. Swenson, because he didn't want her to see him with his brains blown out. And he didn't want to mess her carpet or whatever.

ABBY: Did she go out and look?

BILLY: I don't know. She called Mr. Swenson, though, and Mr. Swenson called my dad.

ABBY: When was this?

BILLY: Probably like ten years. I was little.

ABBY: What happened to his wife?

BILLY: She flipped. She opened all the windows and then just left. Didn't take hardly anything with her, my dad said. Went to some home or something in St. Cloud, near her son. Whole place rotted.

ABBY: I don't think I could not look. I'd want to see.

BILLY: My dad said it was pretty terrible.

ABBY: My dad died, in a car accident. Last August. By the time Trina and I got to the hospital, they were already operating on him. He died in the operating room. So when we saw him, he was already, like, cleaned up, you know? And he looked pretty much normal, cause he didn't have any injuries to his head or anything, his face was just kinda, slack. I think it might make more sense if I had seen the blood.

BILLY: So why'd you all move out here?

ABBY: I guess my mom flipped, too. You got a pencil?

(BILLY *hands her a pencil.* ABBY *has smoothed the drawing on the ground. She takes one of the gum wrappers and places it over part of his drawing, shiny side down. She begins rubbing the wrapper with the pencil.*)

BILLY: What are you doing?

ABBY: Making a belt buckle. For the bull rider. See?

BILLY: You got the silver off.

ABBY: Gum wrappers work the best—only the sticks, though, I can sometimes get gold off of like, the Rolo wrappers? But you have to rub pretty hard.

BILLY: Sometimes they tip the horns, too, with silver? Not on the Tour, but other places—Mexico or Spain. The horns suck on this one. I was mostly working on the back legs. I'll show you.

(BILLY *pulls a book out of his backpack, flips through, showing* ABBY.)

ABBY: Where did you get this?

BILLY: Farm auction. It's got cows, bulls, horses—

ABBY: Oh my god, those are naked people.

BILLY: It's for drawing. You gotta know which muscles to draw, otherwise it just looks posed. See how he's using the back legs to take his weight here? And here in this one, it's these other muscles.

ABBY: Yours is just as good as this one.

BILLY: No way. I won't be able to draw them until I ride. Know what it's like up close.

ABBY: Wouldn't you be scared?

BILLY: There's no time to be scared. That's what Cody Custer said. He's a rider? He said you get scared after, when you remember how close the bull was to goring you, or stepping on your chest. But the second you understand how bad it really was, you remember you're out of the ring. You survived. So you always win.

(*Sound of a school bell.*)

ABBY: Can I keep this?

BILLY: Sure.

(BILLY *and* ABBY *turn out, step out into the hallway, are enveloped and separated by the movement of students and hallway noise. A boy knocks* BILLY *while passing him,* BILLY *disappears.* ABBY *looks for him, he is gone. Students and noise recede, leaving* BETH *and* TRINA *on the porch.*)

BETH: I just thought you'd want to know.

TRINA: Um, thanks?

BETH: It seriously was like you were a celebrity. "What's she like?" "Where's she from?" "What do you guys talk about every morning?" Doug is convinced you're like some kind of pagan priestess.

TRINA: I'm impressed Doug knows the words "pagan priestess."

BETH: I think he actually said "devil worshipper." "Pagan priestess" was Steph's interpretation.

TRINA: I thought you were supposed to be finishing some history thing.

BETH: Jake and I were the only ones who did anything since the last time we met.

TRINA: That's the problem with group projects.

BETH: Jake said he "likes your style."

TRINA: I think you like Jake.

BETH: I just said he was cute.

TRINA: If you don't? Then there's no excuse for the amount of time you spend with his obnoxious friends.

BETH: What do you mean?

TRINA: I mean, Jake seems nice, but come on. Doug and those guys are a little—

BETH: What?

TRINA: I don't know.

BETH: No, what were you going to say?

TRINA: I, I can't say anything. I don't know them.

BETH: Look, Doug can be an asshole sometimes, but he's not really like that. Steph says the guys all expect him to be like that, you know? To be the one to start something, or whatever. And if he doesn't, they're like "What's the matter, Blinkhorn?" "You turning fag on us?"

TRINA: Amanda told me he pinned Billy down in the hall and shoved cow shit in his mouth last year.

BETH: Billy brought a lasso to school and did a roping demonstration for a class project the first week.

TRINA: So he deserves to have someone try to suffocate him with—

BETH: He brought it on himself.

(*Pause.*)

TRINA: I've got an English paper due first period.

BETH: Steph's really cool. She's knows everything there is to know about music. She goes down to the cities all the time, to see bands and everything? She loaned me a bunch of CDs.

TRINA: What kind of music.

BETH: Seriously everything. I haven't even heard of most of it. I can ask her if I can loan them to you?

TRINA: That's okay.

BETH: I know she'd say yes.

TRINA: I don't even know her.

BETH: So come to her party Friday.

TRINA: I'm not gonna crash.

BETH: It's not crashing, you're coming with me.

TRINA: I'll feel weird.

BETH: She told me to bring you.

TRINA: What?

BETH: I see her watching you in the hallway. Like she's trying to
figure you out. She even started wearing a choker like yours.

(BETH *examines* TRINA.)

I bet at your old school you sat at a table way off in the corner of the cafeteria. I bet you've never even been to a party.

(*Pause.*)

You'd like Steph. She's smart, and kinda quiet, actually.

(ABBY *enters, hiding a book under her shirt.*)

TRINA: Hey, Pep Squad, out with your boyfriend again?

BETH: Boyfriend?

TRINA: Didn't you know? Billy is Abby's boyfriend.

ABBY: Shut up.

BETH: What?

TRINA: You show him your pom-poms yet?

ABBY: (*Calling toward the house.*) Mom!

TRINA: Hey, what's under your shirt.

ABBY: None of your business!

(ABBY *sidesteps* TRINA, *but* TRINA *manages to grab the book out from
under* ABBY's *shirt as she passes.*)

TRINA: *An Artist's Anatomy?*

ABBY: Give it back.

BETH: Where'd you get this?

ABBY: I found it.

BETH: Where?

ABBY: In the trash, now give it back.

TRINA: The trash?

ABBY: Leave it alone.

TRINA: Look at this!

(TRINA *pulls out the drawing of the bull.*)

ABBY: That's mine!

TRINA: A bull? Ooo—I bet that's supposed to be Billy on top. Is this what you and Billy do out in the barn?

ABBY: Mom!

TRINA: Mom's not here. Maybe we should put this up on your locker at school. That way everyone will know.

ABBY: I don't care what you do, just give me the book.

BETH: Let her go.

TRINA: She said she found it in the trash. Maybe that's where it belongs.

ABBY: Give it back!

(TRINA *tears a page out of the book as* ABBY *grabs back the book.*)

BETH: Trina!

ABBY: Stop!

(TRINA *drops the book.*)

TRINA: Don't be such a spaz, Pep Squad. You'll ruin your book.

ABBY: I wish you had killed yourself. At least then you weren't mean.

(ABBY *picks up the book and exits into the house.*)

BETH: Let me see that.

(TRINA *hands* BETH BILLY's *picture.* BETH *examines the picture.*)

TRINA: Bus ride's going to be fun now. But she should know better. I mean, like you said: she's bringing it on herself. Right?

BETH: Right. Absolutely.

TRINA: We'll pick you up in the morning?

BETH: 7:15.

(BETH *exits.* TRINA *sees one of the torn pages from the book. She picks it up and hurls it across the stage.* TRINA *reaches up to the porch light, looks out. As she clicks it off, sound of the school bell. Once again, students enter from all directions, the sounds of a crowded hallway, snatches of conversation. The page from the book gets trampled in the traffic.* AMANDA *and* KARA *stand together, looking out into the crowd.* TRINA *steps off the porch area and into the fray. All the girls in the hallway except* ABBY *now wear choker necklaces.*)

AMANDA: Look, maybe she forgot.

KARA: We said lunch. There's Trina. Ask her.

AMANDA: Never mind. I found her.

(BETH *enters with* DOUG *and* STEPH. *They all carry fast-food fountain drinks.* KARA *and* AMANDA *walk off past* BETH *without speaking. As* TRINA *walks, torn pages from* BILLY's *art book drop from her bag without her noticing.* ABBY *sees* BILLY, *is about to say something to him when* DOUG *and some other boys start mooing at him.* BETH *and* STEPH *laugh,* BILLY *turns.* JAKE *enters, picks up one of the pages* TRINA *has dropped, tries to hand it back to her.*)

JAKE: Hey!

TRINA: Hey.

JAKE: I never knew you were into drawing.

TRINA: What?

JAKE: These are a little intense, huh?

TRINA: That's not mine.

JAKE: No, it's cool, I just hope you didn't tear these out of a
   library book—

TRINA: I said it's not mine, it was on the floor.

JAKE: I saw you drop it.

(*Sound of the bell ringing.*)

DOUG: (*Shouting from across the hall.*) Borowski! You missed the
grub run!

TRINA: I have to go.

(*As* TRINA *turns, another page drops behind her.* JAKE *stops to pick it up.*)

DOUG: Some of us gotta eat.

JAKE: And some of us gotta get into college.

DOUG: I got you some fries, but Steph ate them all.

STEPH: I did not!

JAKE: Jeez, thanks a lot, Steph.

DOUG: What the hell is that? A cow?

JAKE: Nothing.

(JAKE *slides the pages into his book as the group moves from the empty-
ing hall, lights begin to fade.*)

   Just something for class.

(*Lights have faded; it is night again. Sound of crickets.* ABBY *at the burned-out barn.*)

ABBY: Billy? Billy?

(BETH, *who has been hiding, snaps her flashlight on* ABBY.)

BETH: Billy's not coming.

ABBY: Where is he?

BETH: I heard him on the phone with you. This place is so nasty.

ABBY: What happened to him?

BETH: Cow's missing. I opened one of the pens.

ABBY: Look, I promised I'd bring his book back—

BETH: You shouldn't have let Trina see.

ABBY: So I'm leaving it here. If he doesn't get it it'll be your fault.

(ABBY *sets the book by the door, and sees* BILLY, *who has been hiding in the dark. He silently puts his finger to his lips, asking her to not reveal his presence to* BETH.)

BETH: He's gonna ruin you. He's a freak. Abby. Everyone knows it.

ABBY: He's not a freak.

BETH: If people find out you've been hanging out with him—

ABBY: I don't care if they find out.

BETH: So why don't you talk to him at school? Why don't you give him his book in the hallway where everybody can see?

ABBY: Because, I—he said to meet him here.

BETH: You know I'm right.

ABBY: If everyone would just leave him alone—

BETH: They won't. People are gonna find out, and when they do? They're gonna stop talking to you. They're gonna say things about you behind your back. Leave little drawings and messages on your locker, on your desk, or take your stuff? I know what it's like. I'm trying to help you.

ABBY: I don't want your help.

BETH: When Doug pinned Billy down in the hall, I was there. I was standing right there, with Amanda and Kara and Brad and Jake and everyone. Everyone was just watching. And while he was doing it, Doug looked right up at me. Everyone saw him looking at me. And I had to make a choice.

ABBY: He's your brother.

BETH: You can pretend like you're better than me, like you would have done something different? But no one is gonna help you when you're the one pinned down in the hall, Abby. Trina is graduating. You've got four years.

(ABBY *looks right at* BILLY.)

ABBY: What did you do? When Doug looked at you, and Billy was right there, on the floor.

BETH: I laughed. And then I walked away.

ABBY: Just leave the book.

(ABBY *starts to exit.*)

BETH: He's gonna be big someday. Like our dad? Some summer he's gonna get tall. He's already strong, he's just small. When he comes back to school nobody's even gonna recognize him. I kept praying it would happen this year. But it's gotta happen sometime. And then they'll leave him alone.

(ABBY *exits silently past* BILLY. BETH *hesitates, then picks up the book, pulls* BILLY'*s drawing from her pocket, and lays it in the pages of the book. She replaces the book, walks off the other direction. Silence, for a moment.* BILLY *appears from his hiding place, with a flashlight. He picks up the book, opens it, the picture falls to the ground.* BILLY *snaps his flashlight off. On the other side,* TRINA *again turns on the porch light.*)

ABBY *has been swinging in the dark. She is sipping Dr. Pepper from a can with a straw.*)

TRINA: The next time you try to slip some bullshit drawing in my books I'm gonna kill you. Did you hear me?

(ABBY *keeps sipping.*)

You're lucky I'm nice. You're lucky I'm not Beth.

(ABBY *keeps sipping.*)

I wasn't even going to say anything to anyone about Billy, but now, I don't know. One more thing like that and I will, I swear to God, Abby.

ABBY: I cut him out.

TRINA: What.

ABBY: Like they cut that lump out of Aunt Dawn's chest.

TRINA: What are you talking about.

ABBY: I was looking right at him, I didn't know if I could do it. Maybe if I practice it'll be easier. He'll be like he's dead, and I'll look at him the way I look at a locker, or a door handle. That's what you said it was like, right? That's the way you said people used to look at you.

(*Pause.*)

TRINA: Look, I'm not mad anymore, just. Don't pull anything like that again. Okay?

ABBY: Remember when we used to be able to sit on our porch and actually see people walking by?

TRINA: And cars.

ABBY: Bikes.

TRINA: Big wheels.

ABBY: Ice cream truck.

(TRINA *hums the ice cream truck song.*)

I remember when they finally let me visit you in the ward, after. And Mom left for a minute to go to the bathroom, and you said, "Are they going to make me go back?" And I didn't know what you meant, so I said, "Where?" And you said, "To school. I can't go back there. You have to talk to them, and tell them I can't go back."

TRINA: Everything was always so easy for you.

ABBY: Was.

TRINA: I'm not gonna say anything about Billy. Okay? I won't tell anyone. I promise.

ABBY: There's nothing to tell. He's a freak. That's it.

TRINA: But. He's your friend.

ABBY: No.

TRINA: Oh.

(ABBY *swings.*)

I remember when I came home with my nose ring. I was so scared. I thought for sure Dad was gonna kill me when he saw it. And he just shook his head and said, "All of life is not like high school."

ABBY: I hope he was right.

TRINA: Me too.

(*Lights begin to fade. Sound of school bell, hallway noises. Students pass all in front of* TRINA *and* ABBY *as they swing. Spot fades up briefly on* BILLY *alone at the barn, drawing intently. Papers fall from the students as they move, without their noticing.*)

(*Lights fade.*)

END OF PLAY

FISHING

Jeff Hoffman

Fishing was the winner of the 1999 Tennessee Williams/New Orleans Literary Festival One-Act Play Contest and was first performed at the University of New Orleans and at Le Petit Theatre du Vieux Carre in March 2000. It was directed by Polly Hudgins; the stage manager was Bonnie Hays; the scenic designer was Joshua Palmer; costume design was by Kasey Allee. The cast was as follows:

SARAH	Samantha Hubbs
FATHER	Stephen B. Cefalu

CHARACTERS

SARAH: A woman in her twenties.
FATHER: Sarah's father, forty to fifty.

SETTING

A quiet and peaceful fishing stream.

TIME

The present, in the morning.

(SARAH, *twenties, is fishing with her* FATHER, *late forties. It's a calm, peaceful morning, and they're fishing in a calm and peaceful stream. A tree branch hangs over the stream. The actors should have real fishing poles in their hands, but the rest can be pantomimed.*)

SARAH: How is it?

FATHER: Being dead?

SARAH: Yes.

FATHER: Can't complain.

SARAH: Sure you could, Dad.

FATHER: No, I shouldn't . . .

SARAH: Not burning in hell?

FATHER: Nope.

SARAH: Surprised?

FATHER: A little actually. Yes.

(Pause.)

Do you still like it? The fishing?

SARAH: I haven't been in years.

FATHER: What's the occasion?

SARAH: I think you know.

FATHER: Do I?

SARAH: You knew I'd go fishing when you died.

FATHER: Did I?

SARAH: Don't ruin this, Dad.

FATHER: No, no. Of course not. Yes, I was hoping you'd come here.

SARAH: And here I am.

FATHER: Yes, here you are.

(*Pause.*)

Did you go to my funeral?

SARAH: Dad . . .

FATHER: I'm sorry. I know. It's none of my business.

SARAH: It's not. No.

(SARAH *casts her line. It's a quick, short flip. She knows what she's doing.*)

FATHER: Goddamn you're good, baby. I always forget how good you are.

(*Pause.*)

You haven't been fishing in years. How 'bout that.

SARAH: Shut up, Dad. Shut up and fish.

FATHER: OK, baby, OK.

(*They fish for a few beats in silence.*)

When did I start sleeping with you?

SARAH: I must have been twelve.

FATHER: Thirteen. Weren't you thirteen?

SARAH: Was I?

FATHER: Yes, I think so.

SARAH: I don't remember.

FATHER: I do.

SARAH: (*Indicating his line.*) You got a bite.

(FATHER *pulls, fumbles. He loses the fish.*)

FATHER: Damn! . . . Damn it!

SARAH: Too bad.

FATHER: They'll be others. There's always others.

(*Pause.*)

SARAH: Dad?

FATHER: Yes, honey?

SARAH: Why'd you come here today?

FATHER: Well, where else would I go? I knew you'd be here.

SARAH: Did I invite you?

FATHER: Yes. Of course you did.

SARAH: I didn't, Dad. I didn't invite you.

FATHER: No, of course you did.

SARAH: No, I didn't.

FATHER: Well, sure you did. Here we are, fishing again. You must have—

SARAH: I DIDN'T INVITE YOU!

FATHER: OK, OK. I'm sorry. You're right. You didn't invite me. But nevertheless. Here I am.

SARAH: Here you are.

(*She casts out her line again.*)

FATHER: Right in the shade, baby. Oh man! You got a gift. A true gift.

(SARAH *doesn't respond. She and her* FATHER *fish in silence for a bit.*)

SARAH: Mom's devastated.

FATHER: Is she?

SARAH: Crushed.

FATHER: My God. I had no idea.

SARAH: She didn't get out of bed for a week.

FATHER: Get out of here . . .

SARAH: I'm serious.

FATHER: Boy, people never stop surprising you.

SARAH: I was amazed.

FATHER: I bet you were.

SARAH: After the way you treated her.

FATHER: I know. I remember.

SARAH: She should be celebrating.

FATHER: I'd be celebrating.

SARAH: But all she can do is cry.

FATHER: Well, it's flattering really.

SARAH: Crying is her one talent.

FATHER: Well, no I wouldn't—

SARAH: Mom is a stupid woman.

FATHER: Now Sarah . . .

SARAH: At the funeral, wearing her dutiful black. Weeping. Wailing. Uncle Tim holding her up.

FATHER: She was a good woman.

SARAH: She was pathetic. At a funeral like yours, you don't accept condolences. You give them back.

FATHER: Don't cry for me, Argentina.

SARAH: Exactly. You know what I'm talking about.

FATHER: Still, you don't find that kind of loyalty anymore.

SARAH: You find it in dogs, Dad.

FATHER: My God, you're right. You do find it in dogs.

SARAH: (*Whimpering.*) Don't hit me! Don't hit me! Don't hit me!

FATHER: (*Whimpering like the mother too.*) I love you! I love you! I love you!

SARAH: Don't leave me! Don't leave me!

FATHER: (*Like a dog.*) Ow! Ow! Owww!

SARAH: Ow! Ow! Owww!

(*They howl and laugh for a bit. Then* SARAH *takes a fishing hook, grabs her* FATHER'*s hand, and sinks the hook into his palm.*)

FATHER: AHHH! AHHH! CHRIST!

(SARAH *keeps pressing the hook into his palm and looks her* FATHER *right in the eyes.*)

OK. All right!

(SARAH *takes the hook out of his hand.*)

Thank you.

SARAH: Cast out. I saw 'em jumping over there.

(SARAH *indicates a spot.* FATHER *casts out in the indicated direction, but he misses badly. He snags his line on the overhanging tree.*)

FATHER: Oh great.

SARAH: Snag?

FATHER: You know it.

SARAH: You gotta go to the side.

(SARAH *casts out side arm, lands her line right where her* FATHER *had been trying for.*)

You put too much arc on it.

(FATHER *wades out toward the snag.*)

FATHER: Yes. Thank you. I realize that.

SARAH: Watch my line.

(FATHER *is wading close to* SARAH's *line.*)

FATHER: I see it. I see it.

SARAH: Were you always this bad?

FATHER: What's that, honey?

SARAH: The way you fish. It's pathetic.

FATHER: I taught you, didn't I?

SARAH: I don't see how. You couldn't land a fish at a hatchery.

FATHER: Fishing's different when you're dead.

SARAH: Is it?

FATHER: Oh yes. You take your time.

SARAH: That's because you're always snagging your line.

FATHER: Well, I used to be better.

SARAH: Yeah?

FATHER: When I taught you, I was much better. Got the magazines. Got the fishing maps. I knew all the sweet spots.

(*Pause.* FATHER *is finally able to unsnag his line.*)

There! Watch out now, baby! I'm gonna give you a run for your money.

(*He casts out. He reels his line in with deep concentration, pulling and jerking the line with precision.* SARAH *reels in her line, but doesn't cast out. She watches her* FATHER *for a moment.*)

SARAH: This isn't really you at all, is it?

FATHER: (*Still concentrating on his line.*) What's that, baby?

SARAH: You weren't like this.

FATHER: Like what?

SARAH: You weren't happy. You weren't funny. You said four words to me a day.

FATHER: What did I say? I don't remember, baby.

SARAH: *Can I come in?* That's what you said.

FATHER: Oh yes, that's right. At night. At your door. I remember.

SARAH: Four words and forty grunts.

FATHER: Always forty?

SARAH: I counted.

FATHER: You did? I never knew that.

SARAH: You never listened to me, and you never talked to me.

FATHER: I was a monster.

SARAH: Yes, you were.

FATHER: But I took you fishing.

SARAH: I went fishing *with* you, and you abided my presence.

FATHER: Abided? I don't know what that means.

SARAH: And you weren't stupid. You ran a business.

FATHER: A small business—and I was lucky.

SARAH: You were manipulative. You were calculating.

FATHER: Maybe I wasn't stupid, but I certainly wasn't calculating.

SARAH: You were evil.

FATHER: No, honey, I just lost control.

SARAH: You lost control *every* day.

FATHER: Not on Sundays.

SARAH: Oh yes, I forgot.

FATHER: Well, see, there you go. Evil men do not send their kids to CCD.

SARAH: (*Relents.*) And you didn't have any wit. No wit whatsoever.

FATHER: There was two Jews walk into a bar and there was how do you get the one-armed Polack out of the tree and that was about it.

SARAH: You wave.

FATHER: Yes. You wave. That was all I needed. Dumb Polacks, greedy Jews, and a can of Bud.

SARAH: It's good you're dead.

FATHER: And fishing of course. I needed my fishing.

SARAH: How'd you ever get by?

FATHER: Whata you mean?

SARAH: At your job. In the world. Everywhere. How did people tolerate you?

FATHER: People loved me.

SARAH: No, they didn't, Dad.

FATHER: How many people came to my funeral, baby?

SARAH: You were rich. That's not love.

FATHER: I wasn't rich.

SARAH: You had money.

FATHER: I had money but I wasn't rich.

SARAH: You built homes.

FATHER: I built *small houses*. Here and there. Nothing very major.

SARAH: (*Remembering what her* FATHER *used to say.*) Developments. Big developments. That's where all the money is.

FATHER: That's right. . . . I sure did enjoy it though.

SARAH: Oh here it comes.

FATHER: Building the places where people live. That's something . . . that's something to be proud of, Sarah.

SARAH: You made them feel safe, didn't you?

FATHER: I'm sorry, honey, but it's true. It's a fact and there's nothing I can do about it. People trusted me and they were justified in that trust: I built them good, sensible houses.

SARAH: It's all very noble.

FATHER: They won't remember me.

SARAH: I'll remember you.

FATHER: Well, you don't count. I think I made that clear.

SARAH: So why did you come here today?

FATHER: I can't go fishing? I'm not allowed all of a sudden?

SARAH: I've moved on. I haven't been home in years. I don't need this anymore.

FATHER: But you have a terrible secret, don't you?

SARAH: I can't even keep track of them all anymore. I keep a list on the fridge.

FATHER: Sexual abuse.

SARAH: Check.

FATHER: Hates her mother.

SARAH: Check.

FATHER: Scared of intimacy.

SARAH: Check. Double check.

FATHER: Loves her father in spite of it all.

(*Short pause.*)

   Check.

(*They both cast out. Silence for a while.*)

SARAH: Should I kill you?

FATHER: Kill me?

SARAH: With a knife, with a chain saw. Really kill you.

FATHER: Oh . . . you think you should?

SARAH: It might be a good idea.

FATHER: It's true. Might do you some good. A little closure.

SARAH: My real father would've never said closure.

FATHER: No, that's true. I didn't use that word.

SARAH: That would be . . . what would that be?

FATHER: That would be a fag word.

SARAH: Yes, that's right. A fag word. What're some other fag words?

FATHER: *Communication.*

SARAH: *Communication,* oh yes. *Communication*'s definitely a fag word. All those psychobabble words.

FATHER: Fag words right on down the line. *Counseling. Therapy* . . .

SARAH: . . . *Aggression* . . . *Resistance* . . . *Impasse!*

FATHER: Oh my God, *Impasse!* I couldn't get enough of that word! We're at an *impasse!*

SARAH: From the lack of *communication* . . .

FATHER: Because of your *aggressive resistance* to *therapy*.

SARAH: Motherfuck them all!

FATHER: That's it, baby! That's a good word! What other words you got?

SARAH: I got *belt*.

FATHER: Damn right you got *belt*. How 'bout *shitface*?

SARAH: *Shitface* is a word.

FATHER: You're damn right *shitface* is a word. *Shitface* is a good all-around useful word. You can put that word in your shoe and kick it around the room.

SARAH: Siddown, *shitface*.

FATHER: Clean up your room, *shitface*.

SARAH: Words that hurt!

FATHER: (*Back to the whimpering.*) Don't hit me! Don't hit me! Don't hit me!

SARAH: I love you! I love you! I love you!

(*They laugh together again for a bit.*)

FATHER: So whata you gonna use?

SARAH: What?

FATHER: To kill me. How you gonna do it?

SARAH: How 'bout a hook, a fishing hook?

FATHER: Appropriate, I'll give you that, but wouldn't it take a long time?

SARAH: Yeah, I guess. You got a gun?

FATHER: Never liked guns.

SARAH: You didn't?

FATHER: You ever see a gun in the house?

SARAH: No, I guess I didn't.

FATHER: Hunting, Sarah. Never went for it.

SARAH: Poor defenseless animals.

FATHER: There you go. I'm a complicated man. That's another example.

SARAH: Oh stop it. You weren't complicated.

FATHER: I wasn't?

SARAH: People are simple. From what I've seen. There's only black and white really.

FATHER: The gray is just the stories we make up to help ourselves feel better.

SARAH: That was my line.

FATHER: Well, I'm sorry. But I saw it coming.

SARAH: Maybe we should get back to the fishing.

FATHER: I couldn't agree more.

(*They both cast out. Pause.*)

The fishing trips. That's a complicated thing isn't it?

SARAH: Not really, no.

FATHER: Well, still. I wasn't mean to you when we were fishing.

SARAH: That's the best you can do? Not mean to me when we were fishing?

FATHER: Yes, actually. It is.

SARAH: Not really all that much of a defense you got goin' there, Pop.

FATHER: Well now listen here, Sarah. There are justifications and there is motivation. And there is rationalization somewhere in there too, although I can never remember exactly where . . .

SARAH: And your point is . . .

FATHER: Ah yes. My point is . . . are any of them gonna help us catch more fish today?

SARAH: That's your point?

FATHER: Well, isn't that what we're here for? I'm not being silly or flippant with this fishing thing. Explanation is impossible, Sarah, but fishing is easy. We both liked to fish, didn't we? You gotta go with what you have.

SARAH: It was something we did together that never made me cry.

FATHER: See, there you go. It's all very simple in the end.

SARAH: I was going to kill you.

FATHER: Well there's that too. Have you thought of a way yet?

SARAH: No. Before. When you were alive. I was really going to kill you.

FATHER: How 'bout drowning? In the stream where we used to fish. Lovely scene. The sun at our backs; your boot on my head. Your mother would find that very moving, I think.

SARAH: But you went and had a heart attack, didn't you?

FATHER: I did. Yes. I ate a lot of meat.

SARAH: So if you would've eaten more broccoli and less hamburger . . .

FATHER: I would not have had a heart attack. My God, you're right. I've never thought about that. Very simple, these things. Cause and effect.

SARAH: And then I could have—

FATHER: Killed me?

SARAH: Done *something* to you. Made you realize. Made you see yourself.

FATHER: Oh I don't think it would've worked. I was a very stubborn man.

SARAH: I would've made it work, Dad.

FATHER: I think you're fooling yourself, honey.

SARAH: I had it all planned. I bought rope. One weekend I went out and bought rope.

FATHER: Rope? What were you going to do with rope?

SARAH: I . . . I'm not sure.

FATHER: See, it was all very abstract. Feelings bubbling to the surface. It didn't mean anything.

SARAH: I still have that rope.

FATHER: Sure, you could use the rope. We got a tree here. I wouldn't mind.

SARAH: I'd string you up and then just keep right on fishing.

FATHER: I can see that. Me up in the breeze there. You strugglin' with a nice brook trout. That's a family postcard what you're describing.

SARAH: People would understand it then.

FATHER: Absolutely they'd understand it then. You wouldn't have to say a word.

SARAH: Everything would be right there in front of them. Plain as day.

FATHER: Nothing more to say, really.

SARAH: No more lying about my past.

FATHER: Can't pretend they don't see something like that. A picture that clear. What a relief it would be for you. . . . Let's do it. Let's do it, honey.

(*Pause.* SARAH *casts out her line again.*)

SARAH: I don't wanna kill you, Dad. I just wanna fish.

FATHER: You're an amazing woman, aren't you?

SARAH: No, I'm not.

FATHER: Sure you are. Letting go of the anger the way you have.

SARAH: Just redirected it, that's all.

FATHER: Mom?

SARAH: I'd string her up in a second.

FATHER: Uncle Tim?

SARAH: Yeah, I'd throw him up there too.

FATHER: Friends?

SARAH: Don't have many.

FATHER: Boyfriend?

SARAH: Please.

FATHER: Girlfriend?

SARAH: You don't know me at all, do you?

FATHER: Of course I don't know you at all. What did you expect?

SARAH: So why come here? Why start anything new?

FATHER: I'm your father.

SARAH: That's all you really need to say, isn't it?

FATHER: When you were a little girl I took you fishing and I never touched you and we both had a good time.

SARAH: And I said: Daddy, can you put the worm on my hook?

FATHER: And I said: No, but I'll show you how.

SARAH: And you did. You showed me how.

FATHER: And it was a sweet little lesson.

SARAH: And I wanna thank you for that.

(*She starts crying.*)

> All I wanna do is say thank you and fish. Isn't that stupid? Isn't that stupid, Dad?

FATHER: No, honey, it's not.

SARAH: Thank you.

FATHER: You don't have to say that.

SARAH: Thank you.

FATHER: It's OK, honey. I don't deserve it.

SARAH: Say you're welcome. Say it.

FATHER: You're welcome.

SARAH: Thank you. Thank you for taking me fishing.

FATHER: You're welcome, honey.

(*Pause.* SARAH *collects herself somewhat.*)

SARAH: You ready to cast out again?

FATHER: I got all day.

SARAH: You ain't goin' anywhere.

FATHER: No, ma'am, I'm stayin' right here with you.

(*Pause, and then they both cast out their lines and slowly reel them back in.*)

(*Gradually, the lights reveal a rope tied in a makeshift noose, thrown over the tree branch that overhangs the water.*)

(FATHER *and* SARAH *look up at it.* FATHER *realizes what* SARAH *has done.*)

(*Still looking up at the rope.*) How is it?

SARAH: Being dead?

FATHER: Yes.

SARAH: Can't complain.

FATHER: Sure you could, honey.

SARAH: No, I shouldn't . . .

FATHER: I didn't know.

SARAH: "One weekend I got a rope" and you didn't know?

FATHER: Yeah, I guess you're right. I should've seen it coming.

SARAH: You got off free your whole life.

FATHER: You were very upset.

SARAH: It was pretty obvious, I think.

FATHER: Cause and effect.

SARAH: It's all very simple in the end, isn't it?

(*Pause.*)

FATHER: Right after my funeral. I don't envy your mother, Sarah.

SARAH: More tears no doubt.

FATHER: Who'll find you I wonder.

SARAH: Will she understand?

FATHER: Your mother?

SARAH: Yes.

FATHER: No, I don't think so.

SARAH: It won't make sense to her?

FATHER: Maybe it'll make sense to her but she won't understand.

SARAH: Well at least it'll make sense to her.

(*Pause.*)

You think she'll realize why I picked this spot?

FATHER: You leave a note?

SARAH: No. . . . You think I should've left a note?

FATHER: Probably should've left a note.

SARAH: She didn't know about our fishing trips, did she? What they meant to us.

FATHER: She didn't know about any of it, Sarah.

SARAH: What?

FATHER: She didn't know about any of it.

SARAH: None of it?

FATHER: Not a clue. I was very careful.

SARAH: I don't believe you.

FATHER: Well, nothing I can do about that. Still, I'm telling you. She didn't know.

SARAH: I should've told her.

FATHER: Probably should've told her.

(*Pause. They look up at the rope again.*)

SARAH: It's a pretty picture though, isn't it?

FATHER: It's well-framed, Sarah. You did a nice job.

SARAH: You see all the poignancy, don't you?

FATHER: Oh yeah. Absolutely. It's all there, baby. Can't miss it.

SARAH: If you have all the particulars.

FATHER: Sure, you need the particulars.

SARAH: Otherwise, it's just . . . what is it, Dad?

FATHER: Otherwise it's just a rope around a tree, honey.

(*Pause as they continue staring at the rope.*)

SARAH: I still like to fish though. After everything, I still love to fish.

FATHER: So do I, baby. . . . So do I.

(*They cast out. They fish together in silence as the lights slowly dim and the music rises.*)

END OF PLAY

HARRIET TUBMAN
VISITS A THERAPIST

Carolyn Gage

Harriet Tubman Visits a Therapist was first produced by Love Creek Productions in New York City. Jennifer Spence directed the following cast:

THE THERAPIST	Deana J. Becker
HARRIET TUBMAN	Emmanuela Souffrant

CHARACTERS

HARRIET TUBMAN: An African American woman, mid-twenties.
THE THERAPIST: An African American woman.

TIME

Another dimension of space-time.

PLACE

Interior of a therapist's office.

"She declares that before her escape from slavery, she used to dream of flying over fields and towns, and rivers and mountains, looking down upon them 'like a bird,' and reaching at last a great fence or sometimes a river, over which she would try to fly, 'but it 'peared like I wouldn't hab de strength, and jes as I was sinkin' down, dere would be ladies all drest in white ober dere, and dey would put out dere arms and pull me 'cross.'"
—from an article about Harriet Tubman
in *The Boston Commonwealth*, 1863

(*Setting: A contemporary therapist's office with pictures of peaceful land-scapes and recovery literature in the bookcase. There is a desk, but the* THERAPIST *has done much to create a nonthreatening, informal atmo-sphere.*)

(*At Rise: The* THERAPIST *is reviewing* HARRIET'*s file. She is a light-skinned African American woman who wears the clothing of a contem-porary middle-class therapist. There is a soft knock on the door. The* THERAPIST *closes the file and rises.*)

THERAPIST: Come in. (*There is another knock, and she crosses to the door and opens it.* HARRIET TUBMAN *stands in the doorway.* HAR-RIET *is a dark-skinned African American woman, about twenty-seven, wearing the clothing of an enslaved field worker.* HARRIET'*s speech and movements are deliberately slow and dull at first. She stands waiting for orders, head bowed.*) Come in. Harriet Tub-man? You're right on time. (*She gestures into the room.* HAR-RIET *lifts her eyes briefly. Her face is expressionless.*) Please . . . Either chair. Make yourself comfortable. (HARRIET *shuffles toward one of the chairs and sits. She keeps her head down. The* THERAPIST *sits in her chair. There is a long silence. The* THERAPIST *sighs and smiles at* HARRIET.) I understand that you have spells of narcolepsy . . . (*No response.*) You have brief periodic spells of deep sleep? (HARRIET *nods briefly, eyes down.*) And they can come on anytime—when you're working? (HAR-RIET *nods again.*) Ever since you were a girl, wasn't it? (HAR-RIET *glances at her quickly, then down again.*) I understand that's when these spells came on—when you were a girl . . .

HARRIET: Dey come on when de man thow'd de chunk o'lead in mah face.

THERAPIST: And you were a girl then?

HARRIET: Not aftuh dat.

THERAPIST: How do you feel about that? (HARRIET *lowers her eyes again.*) I would feel pretty angry if someone threw a lead weight at me. (HARRIET *remains motionless. The* THERAPIST *changes her tone.*) Harriet, do you know why you're here?

HARRIET: Massuh Edward done sent me.

THERAPIST: Do you know why?

HARRIET: Cain't sell no nigga like me.

THERAPIST: I don't think that's why. (HARRIET *looks down.*) I understand why you feel that way. That's a very natural conclusion for a slave to draw. But in this case, I think Mr. Brodas is genuinely concerned about you, and I have reasons for why I say that. Do you want to hear them? (*No response.*) I think Mr. Brodas likes you. He speaks about you with a great deal of pride. He's allowed you to choose your own husband, and John Tubman is a free man. That's a very unusual thing for a slaveowner to do. And he lets you hire out to a shipbuilder—

HARRIET: He take alluh money.

THERAPIST: Well, that's not exactly true. I understand that you get to keep what you make over what you owe him. (HARRIET *snorts.*) I understand you've been able to buy yourself a pair of oxen. That's pretty impressive. (*No response.*) You could even buy your freedom someday.

HARRIET: Time I'ze daid.

THERAPIST: (*The* THERAPIST *studies* HARRIET *for a moment.*) You know I share your feelings about slavery. All day long I listen to women tell me stories that make me sick. Stories of rape—

raping children, of beating—beating pregnant women, stories of murder, or torture, of live burnings, of babies being sold away from their mothers, of chain gangs . . . (HARRIET *looks away.*) But I'm not going to change it, and neither are you. We can drive ourselves crazy thinking about it. We can kill ourselves fighting it. Or we can make the most of what is possible. Like you did, buying your oxen.

HARRIET: (*Eyes down.*) Nat Turner.

THERAPIST: What?

HARRIET: (*Looking at the* THERAPIST *for the first time as she speaks.* HARRIET *drops the dull-witted act.*) Nat Turner. He killed fifty-seven whitefolks.

THERAPIST: (*Taken aback by* HARRIET'*s intensity.*) They hanged Nat Turner.

HARRIET: (*Looking at her hands, acting again.*) Hanged a man las' week over to Bucktown for stealin' chickens.

THERAPIST: (*Losing her temper.*) Nat Turner is the reason you can't read. Did you know that? After his uprising, they made it illegal to teach slaves to read or write. After Nat Turner, we couldn't even meet to go to church, unless a whiteman was the preacher. After Nat Turner, they wouldn't let us talk to each other in the fields, but they wouldn't let us just work either. Oh, no. After Nat Turner, we all had to sing while we worked—oh, except of course, "Go Down, Moses." Now, thanks to Nat Turner, you can die for singing that song.

HARRIET: (*Singing.*)

O GO DOWN, MOSES,
WAY DOWN IN EGYPT'S LAND . . .

THERAPIST: You think I'm an Uncle Tom, don't you?

HARRIET: (*Continues singing.*)

TELL OLE PHARAOH,
LET MY PEOPLE GO . . .

THERAPIST: You think I sold out.

HARRIET: (*Closing her eyes, she raises her voice.*)

OLE PHARAOH SAID HE WOULD GO CROSS.
O GO DOWN, MOSES.
LET MY PEOPLE GO.
AND DON'T GET LOST IN THE WILDERNESS.
LET MY PEOPLE GO.

(HARRIET *looks at the* THERAPIST, *who is silent now.*) Didn't hab
no gun.

THERAPIST: Who didn't have a gun?

HARRIET: Prophet Turner. A sword. Can you see dat? Had hissef
a sword! (*She laughs.*) What he gonna do wid a sword? Slit
open de sow's belly?

THERAPIST: Are you thinking of killing someone?

HARRIET: (*Looking at her hands.*) Mebbe I buy a mule to go 'long
wid de ox.

THERAPIST: (*Sizing her up.*) I'm going to be frank with you. Mr.
Brodas has sent you to me, because he's afraid you're going
to run away.

HARRIET: (*Bursts out laughing.*) Oh, he skeered!

THERAPIST: (*Pleasantly.*) Well, that's why you're here, and I'm
afraid I have to agree with his observation.

HARRIET: (*Enjoying the idea.*) He tell you dat Harriet bin lookin'
mighty greazy. (*She laughs.*)

THERAPIST: "Greazy?"

HARRIET: Gonna slip herself th'oo de massuh's han's. (*She laughs
again.*)

THERAPIST: (*Smiling along with the joke.*) Your husband seems to think you've been "lookin' mighty greasy," too.

HARRIET: (*She stops laughing.*) John say dat? He tell you dat?

THERAPIST: He told Mr. Brodas. (HARRIET *is stunned.*) Harriet, nobody's against you here. Your husband loves you and Mr. Brodas has a great deal of respect for you. But, if you run away, neither one of them is going to be able to save you from the slave catchers—or their dogs. You've got too much to live for to throw your life away like that.

HARRIET: John bin talkin' to Massuh Edward?

THERAPIST: (*Rising.*) Harriet, I want to help you. You are in a very serious situation. Mr. Brodas has asked me to determine whether or not I think you're going to run. (HARRIET *looks at her.*) I'm going to tell him that I'd like to see you for a few more visits, but after that, unless there's a change in your attitude, I will have to tell him the truth. I doubt he'll let you hire out after that. (HARRIET *says nothing. The* THERAPIST *turns suddenly.*) Look at you! You're young, you're healthy, you're in love, you work for wages, your husband is a free man—That's a lot to be thankful for! You have less reason to run than most. (HARRIET *remains silent.*) And what about your family—your mother? She was the one who saved your life when you got the head injury, wasn't she? She was right there with you, wasn't she? Are you going to abandon her? You know you'll never see her again. (HARRIET *looks down.*) And what about John? He's a good man, Harriet. You're pushing away the people who love you in the name of freedom. You're so busy dreaming about a world you don't have, you're missing out on the one right here. Learn to focus on the things you *can* change, learn to appreciate what you have right now—and you can be a great force for good. Little by little, one day at a time, your life will get better and better. (HARRIET *says nothing. The* THERAPIST *sits at her desk and looks out the window.*) I knew a woman once who decided to run. You could say she'd been "lookin' mighty greasy." One night, she took her two daughters— one was six and the other twelve—and she ran. (HARRIET *is keenly interested. The* THERAPIST *turns back to her.*) They caught her, of course, as they catch most runaways.

HARRIET: How far she git?

THERAPIST: To the Delaware border. (HARRIET *nods. The* THERAPIST *narrates the rest of her story with clinical detachment.*) It was the hounds that got her. By the time they called off the dogs, her daughter—the six-year-old—was already dead. And then they took turns raping the twelve-year-old while they made the mother watch. After that, she wouldn't have anything to do with the child. She wouldn't touch her, wouldn't talk to her. She treated her like she didn't exist. Right up until the girl was sold down South. (HARRIET *says nothing.*) Do you think this woman made a wise decision?

HARRIET: She didn't hab no gun?

THERAPIST: What if she did? She was outnumbered. Or do you think she should have shot her daughters?

HARRIET: (*Shrugging.*) Lib in de no'th or die in de South.

THERAPIST: You would shoot your own children?

HARRIET: I seen mah sistuhs—Linah and Soph—seen 'em sol' off on de chain gang, an' dat day I wisht dey wuz daid, an' I bin prayin' dey was daid ev'y day aftuh dat, too.

THERAPIST: Enough to kill them?

HARRIET: Ain't no livin' when dey kin do yo' body any way dey like.

THERAPIST: (*Vehement.*) Oh, yes, there is! We are so much more than our physical bodies—

HARRIET: (*Cutting her off, she rises.*) Look! Now, you look! (*She pulls her shirt out and pulls up the back.*) Heah—you look at dat. You look at what de whiteman done.

THERAPIST: (*Turning away.*) I've seen plenty of scars.

HARRIET: No, you look, cuz you ain't seen dis 'oman's scars. You therapizin' on me, you look. You stan' up heah, an' you look. (*The* THERAPIST *looks.*) You see dat? Dat is a fiel' o' flesh been ploughed by de debil's own han'.

THERAPIST: But you *don't* have to let it scar your soul.

HARRIET: What you talkin' 'bout? Mah soul? Dis heah is mah soul! Dis black Ashanti skin is mah soul! (*She turns to face the* THERAPIST.)

THERAPIST: (*Becoming very clinical.*) And what does it do for you to keep remembering?

HARRIET: (HARRIET *starts to respond with anger, but she stops herself. A smile spreads slowly over her face.*) You is sleepin' wid de massuh.

THERAPIST: (*Hesitating, she chooses her words carefully.*) Sometimes Mr. Brodas visits with me. (HARRIET *is still smiling.*) That doesn't affect my belief that your running away would be suicidal.

HARRIET: (*Lowering her head.*) Yas'm.

THERAPIST: And it doesn't affect the fact that I want to help you.

HARRIET: (*Mumbling.*) No'm.

THERAPIST: You don't have to put on an act for me. (HARRIET *looks up, puzzled.*) I know what you're doing. (*Silence.*) You don't have to please me.

HARRIET: (*Eager to please.*) If you doan' want me to be pleasin', den I won't. No ma'am. Sartainly I won't. You des see how pleasin', Harriet kin be. I kin be de downright unpleasin'est—

THERAPIST: (*Cutting her off.*) Stop it!

HARRIET: Yas'm. (*The two women sit in silence.*)

THERAPIST: (*Starting over.*) I sleep with Mr. Brodas . . . (*Hesitating.*) He's a kind man.

HARRIET: Oh, yas'm, dat he is. He be de bes' massuh in de world! Dat's des what I allus say, dat Massuh Edward, he—

THERAPIST: (*Cutting her off.*) I hate him. (HARRIET *watches her.*) I hate him, because he's white, because he's a slaveowner, because he's a drunkard, because he's a coward and a liar, I hate him because he uses women, I hate him because he doesn't bother to wash when he comes to me. I hate him so much, believe it or not, he doesn't bother me. I hate him so much, I don't let him have anything.

HARRIET: He got yo' body.

THERAPIST: I'm not in it. (HARRIET *says nothing.*) I haven't been in it since I was twelve and I watched the dogs tear my little sister to pieces. I had already left my body before the first whiteman climbed on top of me. And I wasn't in my body when they raped my mother. I wasn't in my body when they sold me down South. And I wasn't in my body when I had a whiteman's baby at thirteen. I wasn't in my body when they sold her five years later. And I wasn't in my body when Mr. Brodas made his proposition. But, you show me your skin, Harriet—let me show you my soul. It's here . . . (*She takes out a locket.*) This is my daughter, Felicity. She lives with me. She has never had to work in the fields, and she never will, because I am buying her freedom. This, this is my soul. I keep myself alive for her . . .

HARRIET: While you is larnin' de other women to be de slaves.

THERAPIST: I teach them how to survive. Look—these are my files. Here are the stories of women who've come to me. Women who didn't go crazy, who didn't kill themselves.

Women I *helped*. And I have helped women, Harriet. Maybe not you. But I have helped women. (*She pauses.* HARRIET *says nothing.*) I give them a safe place to express themselves—to let out their grief and their rage. I help them speak the unspeakable. I listen. I validate their suffering. I teach them strategies for surviving—(*She breaks off.*) You think this is bullshit. (HARRIET *says nothing.*) How many women could live day to day with your level of rage? You don't have children. What do you think that anger would do to a child? And how long do you think you're going to be able to live like this? Oh, you can make a run for it, all right. But Pennsylvania is a long way off. Do you really think you're going to have the stamina to make it? It takes a cool head to go the distance, and I can tell you right now, Harriet Tubman, you don't have it. Your rage will get you over the county line, maybe. But the Delaware border? Unh-unh. Never.

HARRIET: (*The* THERAPIST *has hit a nerve, and* HARRIET *reconsiders.*) So when you work wid de women . . .

THERAPIST: I teach stress management . . . relaxation techniques. Visualization. Sometimes I do a guided meditation with women.

HARRIET: An' dat is what?

THERAPIST: That is where I put the client under hypnosis— which is like your sleeping spells—and then I talk them through an experience they're afraid of—like a whipping, or an auction where their children are going to be sold . . . or I prepare them if they have to submit sexually to their owner. (*She pauses.*) I give them images—I teach them to go away . . . so they can bear it.

HARRIET: An' dis keep de women goin'?

THERAPIST: Yes. Yes, it does. They learn that reality is only another state of consciousness, and it gives them some control. Otherwise, of course, they have none.

HARRIET: (*Making up her mind.*) You bin up no'th.

THERAPIST: I was captured.

HARRIET: You bin to Delaware.

THERAPIST: To the border.

HARRIET: Draw me dat map.

THERAPIST: I can't do that. (HARRIET *looks at her.*) I don't encourage my clients to take reckless chances with their lives.

HARRIET: (*Angry, she rises.*) I got two rights—de right to freedom and de right to die.

THERAPIST: (*The* THERAPIST *rises.*) I have the right to live.

HARRIET: Libbin'! What you talkin', 'oman? You ain't eben inside yo' own skin! (HARRIET, *enraged, turns to go. She opens the door, but is seized by a fit of narcolepsy. The* THERAPIST *helps her to a chair. She watches* HARRIET *for a moment, and then closes the door.*)

THERAPIST: You want the map? All right, Harriet Tubman, I'll give you the map . . . Oh, I'll give you the map. (*She pulls a chair close to the "sleeping"* HARRIET.) Harriet, listen to me. We don't have very much time, and I want you to listen and remember. You are standing in the middle of a field. It's the field behind the Brodas plantation. It's nighttime, Harriet, and you are alone. You are standing in the field, and you are looking back toward the cabins. Can you see them? (HARRIET *doesn't move.*) It's dark, and everyone is asleep, Harriet, everyone except you. You are wide awake, standing in the field. You turn back toward the cabins—and there's your cabin—can you see it? Nod your head if you can see it. (HARRIET *still doesn't move, and the* THERAPIST *discovers the cause of her resistance.*) Harriet, listen to me. You are having to go alone. You are leaving tonight. John is asleep in the cabin. You are leaving without him. Can you see the cabin where

John Tubman is sleeping? (*Slowly,* HARRIET *nods.*) It's a clear night and the stars are out. Look up, and see if you can see one star that's brighter than the others, the one in the "drinking gourd." It should be right over the cabins. Do you see it? (HARRIET *nods.*) Good. That's the North Star. You're going to keep that in front of this shoulder. (*She taps* HARRIET's *left shoulder.*) This shoulder. Now remember that. It's a warm night, Harriet, and you're not afraid. Lift up your arms. Lift them up. (HARRIET *lifts her arms slightly.*) Are you ready? (HARRIET *nods.*) Take a deep breath, and as you breathe in, feel yourself becoming lighter. Breathe in again. You are becoming lighter and lighter, lighter than a feather. Lighter than the smoke of a candle flame. Keep breathing in. You are rising in the warm air. Feel yourself rising. Your toes are just barely touching the ground . . . just barely, and now they're not touching at all. You are rising like smoke, up over the field. Higher and higher. Look down, Harriet, and see the cabins. They're just little boxes under you, as you rise higher and higher, keeping that North Star over this shoulder. (*She touches her again.*) And now you're over the big house . . . You're flying over the edge of the fields now, over Greenbrier Swamp. You can see the black water shining through the trees with the reflection of the moon. And you stay on the edge of the swamp, Harriet. Can you see it? (*She nods.*) And now the swamp is opening up, widening. And you're over the Choptank River. The Choptank River is right under you. And you're flying faster now, because you need to keep going, over the Choptank, and it's getting smaller and smaller. Follow the Choptank, Harriet, about seventy miles on the Choptank River. And see where you are now? See the river, how small it is? It's just a stream now, isn't it? (HARRIET *nods.*) You're very close to the Delaware border now. Very close. There's a farm on the other side of the border, the Cowgill farm in Willow Grove, and that's all you need to know, because once you get to the Cowgill farm, they'll take care of you the rest of the way into Pennsylvania. All you have to do is get to the farm. You understand? (HARRIET *nods.*) So you're going to go down now. Down through the trees, down into Delaware. You're almost on the ground now, almost touching the ground . . . Listen! Listen, Harriet! Hear that? What is it? Listen! (HARRIET *stiffens.*) It's dogs barking, isn't it? Hear them? It's the dogs, Harriet! The dogs! They're after you. You can hear them coming. And you start to run, Harriet. (HARRIET's *breathing accelerates.*) Run! Run! And you're running, but it's night, and you can't see very well. You're tripping over the tree roots and the branches, and the dogs are getting louder and louder. (HARRIET *begins to breathe heavily.*) And now you can hear the men shouting! Listen! They've fired a shot! They hear the dogs, Harriet, and they're after you, and there's nowhere to hide. They're coming. And you're running so fast you can't breathe, and your heart is pounding so hard in your chest it hurts. And now you turn around and you can see them, Harriet. You can see the dogs coming for you. And you know what they're going to do. You've seen them catching possums and squirrels. And you know what they're going to do to you. And you're trying to run, but you trip. You're on the ground, Harriet, and you can't get up. And now, I'm going to count backwards from five—

HARRIET: (*Breaking through with great effort, but still in a trance.*) I see dem! I see dem!

THERAPIST: You see the dogs?

HARRIET: I see de women.

THERAPIST: What women?

HARRIET: De women wid de lights. I see dem in de trees aroun' me. I see dem stretchin' out they han's to me. Dey is callin' my name, an' I am reachin' out my han's to dem.

THERAPIST: There aren't any women with you. You are alone.

HARRIET: No, dat I ain't. I has got de company of so many

women, dat I cain't see dem stars no mo' for de brightness
of de women dat is 'roun me in dem trees. And dey is callin'
out my name, say "Araminta"—dat what dey callin' me—
"Araminta"—like my mamma. Dey is shinin' wid glory,
dese black women, an' dey is reachin' out dey han's to me,
gonna pull me up offa dat groun', gonna snatch me right
'way fum de mouf dem dogs and de han's of de whiteman.
Gonna pull me on ober dat line. Doan matter I cain't walk,
doan' matter I cain't run, doan matter I forget de way—
doan matter, 'cuz dese women, dey been heah befo' and dey
gonna bring me on acrost. Dey is shinin' an' laughin' an'
dey is takin' me by de han' to freedom.

THERAPIST: Are you dying, Harriet?

HARRIET: (*Laughing in her trance.*) No, ma'am! Not befo' I live to
see de lights of Phil'delphia!

THERAPIST: Harriet, these women don't exist.

HARRIET: Oh, yes, dey do. Dese is de women dat lib so good dey
cain't die. Dese is de women fum Africa, de women who
pitch deysefs off de ship, rather die dan lib in de chains ob
slavery. Dese is de women who kilt dey own chilrun 'fo' dey
see dem sol' on de auction block . . . de women who kilt
dey massuhs wid de ax, wid de hoe, wid dey bare han's, de
women dey cain't skeer no mo' cause dey already done do
de wors' an' dey still alibe. Dese is de women larnin' each
other de ways to keep out de whiteman's babies befo' dey
start growin' in de womb ob de black woman's body . . . de
women wid de spells make de whitefolks sick. Dese is de
African women, de Ashanti women.

THERAPIST: (*Quietly.*) I can't see those women.

(*Smiling in her trance,* HARRIET *begins to sing, and the* THERAPIST *talks
over her singing.*)

HARRIET:	THERAPIST:
O GO DOWN, MOSES WAY DOWN IN EGYPT'S LAND TELL OLE PHARAOH LET MY PEOPLE GO.	Harriet, I'm going to count backwards from five. And when I say "one," you will open your eyes. You will be relaxed and fully alert. You will not remember any of this experience. Five . . . four . . . three . . . two . . . ONE.

(HARRIET *opens her eyes, and the two women look at each other. The* THERAPIST *smiles.*)

THERAPIST: How do you feel?

HARRIET: (*After a long pause.*) You sic de dogs on me.

THERAPIST: (*Pretending not to understand.*) I'm sorry?

HARRIET: You sic de dogs on me. De whiteman's dogs.

THERAPIST: I don't know what you're talking about.

HARRIET: De dogs in yo' haid. You ain't buyin' no freedom fo' nobody wid dem dogs in yo' haid.

THERAPIST: (*Opening* HARRIET'*s file.*) Harriet, I am going to have to recommend to Mr. Brodas that you be removed from your present position and put in the fields to work where there is closer supervision.

HARRIET: Put me in de prison—I'ze gone. All de chains in de worl' cain't keep me now. My freedom ain't in the han's of you or Massuh Edward or eben in mah own han's. (*The* THERAPIST *is busy writing.* HARRIET *crosses to the door, and looks back.*) Mebbe I come back. When I do, mebbe I take your daughter.

(*She exits, leaving the* THERAPIST *standing. Blackout.*)

THE END

ICARUS'S MOTHER

Sam Shepard

Icarus's Mother was first produced at the Caffe Cino. It was directed by Michael Smith and played by James Barbosa, John Kramer, Cynthia Harris, Lee Worley, and John Coe. It was subsequently produced by David Wheeler at the Threatre Company at Boston.

CHARACTERS

BILL
JILL
PAT
HOWARD
FRANK

(*The stage is covered with grass. A low hedge upstage runs the width of the stage. Behind the hedge is a pale blue scrim. Center stage is a portable barbecue with smoke rising out of it. The lighting is bright yellow. On the grass down left is a tablecloth with the remnants of a huge meal scattered around it.* BILL *lies on his back down left staring at the sky.* HOWARD *lies up left,* JILL *up right,* PAT *down right, and* FRANK *center stage—all in the same position as* BILL *and staring at the sky. Before the lights come up the sound of birds chirping is heard. The sound lasts for a while. The lights come up very slowly as the sound fades out. The lights come up full. A long pause, then all the people start belching at random. They stop.*)

BILL: (*Still staring at the sky.*) Does he know there's people down here watching him do that?

JILL: Sure.

PAT: It's skywriting.

HOWARD: No, it's not skywriting. It's just a trail. A gas trail.

PAT: I thought it was.

FRANK: It's gas.

BILL: I don't like it. I don't like the looks of it from here. It's distracting.

FRANK: It's a vapor trail. All jets do it.

BILL: I don't like the way he's making it. I mean a semicircle thing like that. In a moon shape.

JILL: I like it.

BILL: If he knows what he's doing, that means he could be signaling or something.

FRANK: Jets don't signal.

PAT: It's gas, Bill.

BILL: You mean that whole long stream of cloud is just excess
gas?

HOWARD: Right.

BILL: He has no other way of getting rid of it?

HOWARD: Nope. (BILL *stands, looking up at the sky.*)

BILL: And he's spreading it all over the sky like that?

HOWARD: That's right.

BILL: He's staying in the same general area, though. How come
he's not moving to some other areas? He's been right above
us for the past hour.

FRANK: He's probably a test pilot or something.

BILL: I think he sees us. I don't like the looks of it.

HOWARD: He's a million miles up. How could he see us?

BILL: He sees our smoke and he's trying to signal. (*Yelling at the
sky.*) Get away from here! Get out of our area! (HOWARD
stands, looking up at the sky.)

HOWARD: He can't hear you, Bill. You'll have to be louder than
that.

BILL: Hey! Get your gas away from here!

FRANK: Sit down.

BILL: We don't know what you want but we don't want you
around here!

JILL: He can't hear you. What's the matter with you?

HOWARD: He can see us, though. He knows we're looking at him.

BILL: If you need help you'll have to come down!

HOWARD: (*Yelling at the sky.*) We ate all the food so we can't give you any!

FRANK: Sit down, you guys.

BILL: Get away from the picnic area! Go somewhere else! Go on! Get away from the park!

JILL: Will you guys cut it out. Leave the poor guy alone. He's just flying. Let him fly.

HOWARD: He's not just flying. If he were just doing that it would be all right. But he's not. He's signaling.

JILL: Who would he be signaling to?

HOWARD: His mother, maybe. Or his wife.

BILL: He could be signaling to anybody.

FRANK: Not likely.

PAT: What if he is? So what?

BILL: So, someone should be told about it. The community should know.

PAT: Let him signal his wife if he wants to. He's probably been away for a while and he just got back. Let him show off a little.

HOWARD: But he's right above us. His wife isn't down here.

JILL: I'm his wife.

BILL: Are you his wife, Jill?

JILL: That's right.

BILL: Then we should tell him, so he doesn't have to waste any
   more time.

HOWARD: Come on down! Your wife's down here!

BILL: Come on down here! (JILL *stands and yells at the sky.*)

JILL: Come here, honey! Here I am! (*She waves.*)

BILL: Come and get her! (FRANK *stands and yells at the sky.*)

FRANK: Come and get your wife, stupid!

(*The following lines should happen on top of each other, with whistling
and ad-lib shouts from all the actors.*)

HOWARD: Come on! Land that thing!

JILL: Here I am, sweetheart! (*Throwing kisses.*)

FRANK: You'd better hurry! (PAT *stands and yells at the sky.*)

PAT: Come on down! Here we are! Yoo hoo!

BILL: Your other wife's here, too!

FRANK: Two wives!

PAT: Come on, sweetie! Where have you been!

JILL: We've been waiting and waiting!

FRANK: Two ripe juicy wives waiting for you!

HOWARD: Come on!

BILL: You've been up there too long, mister!

FRANK: We can see you! Come on down!

BILL: Land that thing!

PAT: Come to me, booby! Boobsy, boobsy, boobsy. (JILL *and* PAT
   start shimmying around the stage.)

HOWARD: We've got your wives, mister pilot! You'd better come
   down or we'll take them away!

BILL: We'll use them ourselves! There's three of us here!

FRANK: He's leaving! Look! Hey!

HOWARD: Hey don't! Come back here!

JILL: He's leaving us! Stop!

PAT: Darling! The children!

BILL: You're running out on your kids! (*They all yell and shake their fists at the sky.*)

JILL: Don't leave us! Come back here!

HOWARD: You're no good, mister pilot!

PAT: Come back! The children!

JILL: Don't leave us, darling! (*They all boo loudly.*)

BILL: What a rotten guy! (*They stop booing and just stare at the sky.*)

FRANK: He's gone.

HOWARD: That makes me sick. (*A pause as they all stare at the sky.*)

PAT: Well, when do they start this thing?

FRANK: Are you in a hurry?

PAT: No. I just want to know so I could take a walk or something in the meantime.

BILL: They don't start till it gets dark.

FRANK: Where are you going to walk to?

PAT: Just down the beach or something. To rest my stomach. That was a big meal, you know.

FRANK: Walking doesn't rest your stomach. When you're full and you walk, that just irritates it.

JILL: He's right.

PAT: All right! I'll walk just to loosen my legs up or something.

I'm not going to lie around here waiting for it to get dark, though.

HOWARD: What happens if they start while you're on your walk?

JILL: That'd be terrible, Pat.

PAT: They shoot them in the sky. I can watch fireworks while I'm walking just as easy. It isn't hard. All I have to do is tilt my head up and watch and continue walking.

BILL: You may trip, though, and there you'd be unconscious on the beach somewhere and we'd have to go looking for you.

JILL: Yeah.

HOWARD: Then we'd miss the fireworks just on account of you, Pat.

FRANK: We'd be looking all over. Through the bushes and up and down the beach for hours. Everyone would miss everything.

JILL: Then maybe someone else would trip while they were looking for you and we'd have two missing people on the beach unconscious instead of just one.

BILL: We might all trip and be there on the beach for weeks unconscious.

PAT: All right! (*She sits; the rest remain standing and close in on her, slowly forming a circle.*)

HOWARD: You can walk if you want to, Pat. While it's still light. We don't mind.

JILL: We don't want to wreck your fun, Patsy.

BILL: But you have to get back before it gets dark. Because that's when the fireworks start. And you don't want to miss them.

FRANK: You don't want to be lost on the beach by yourself and suddenly hear loud booming sounds and suddenly see the sky all lit up with orange and yellow and blue and green and purple and gold and silver lights. (*They gather around* PAT *in a circle, looking down at her as she remains seated.*)

JILL: That'd be scary.

HOWARD: You might run and fall and scream. You might run right into the ocean and drown or run right into the forest.

BILL: They'd have to send helicopters out looking for you.

JILL: Or jets.

BILL: Your husband in the jet would find you. (PAT *stands suddenly.*)

PAT: Shut up! I don't have a husband in a jet and neither does Jill! So stop kidding around! If I want to walk, I will! Just to walk! Just to walk down the beach and not come back till after dark. To loosen my legs up after a big dinner like that.

FRANK: We were just kidding, Pat. (*They all sit slowly around* PAT.)

PAT: Boy! That's something. Trying to scare me into not walking. What a group.

FRANK: We were kidding.

PAT: Shut up, Frank! Jesus. All of a sudden picnics are localized events. We all have to hang around the same area where we eat. We can't even walk. We eat a big steak and we can't walk it off. (HOWARD *stands and grabs* PAT's *hand; he starts pulling her stage left.*)

HOWARD: Let's walk! Come on, Pat. Here we go walking. Where do you want to walk to? (*The rest remain seated.*)

PAT: Cut it out! Let go! Let go of my hand! (*He holds her hand tightly, staring at her.*)

HOWARD: I would like very much to take a walk. You're absolutely right about the steak. We need to walk it off.

PAT: Let go, Howard, or I'll kick you.

BILL: Let her go, Howard.

HOWARD: But she's right. We should all walk after steak dinners. The stomach works best when the whole body's in motion. All the acid gets sloshed around. (PAT *struggles violently to get away,* HOWARD *grabs her other arm and holds her tightly, they face each other.*)

PAT: Let me go! Let go of my arm, Howard! I'll kick you. I really will.

FRANK: Come on. Let her go.

HOWARD: But she's right, Frank.

FRANK: Her husband may come back in his jet plane and see what you're doing. Then you'll be in trouble.

PAT: Very funny.

BILL: He might.

JILL: Then he'll land and do you in with a ray gun or a laser beam.

HOWARD: But we'll be way up the beach. Jets can't land on a little strip of beach. We'll be under some bushes even. He won't even see us. Will he, Pat? (*He shakes her.*) Will he, Pat?

PAT: He might.

JILL: See?

HOWARD: Pat's lying, though. Jets fly at an altitude of approximately five thousand feet and move at a minimum of approximately five hundred miles an hour with an air velocity of approximately—and a wind velocity and the pilot can't even hear or see anything. He's just hung in space and he can't hear or see. Can he, Pat? (*He shakes* PAT *more violently.* PAT *gives no resistance.*) Can he or can't he? No he can't! Oh yes he can! He can see fireworks because fireworks explode at an altitude of approximately five hundred feet and give off powerful light rays and make swell patterns in the blue sky right under his keen old plane! Right? Beautiful. Just think how beautiful, Pat. We'll be down here on the grass and he'll be way, way, way up in the air. And somewhere in between the two of us there'll be a beautiful display of flashing fireworks. I can hardly wait for nighttime. (*He lets go of* PAT. *She moves downstage slowly, then turns and walks slowly upstage; she stands upstage staring at the scrim.* HOWARD *and the others watch her.*)

HOWARD: Of course you have to let yourself go into aeronautics gradually, Pat. You can't expect to grasp the sensation immediately. Especially if you've never been up before. I mean in anything bigger than a Piper Cub or a Beachcraft Bonanza. Single- or double-propeller jobs of that variety usually don't get you beyond say a sore ear or two sore ears from the buzzing they make. The booming of a jet is something quite different.

JILL: She knows that.

HOWARD: Of course the sound isn't all of the problem. Not at all. It's something about being in the cockpit surrounded by glass and knowing that glass is solid, yet it's something you can see through at the same time. That's the feeling. You know what I mean, Pat? Looking through this glass enclosure at miles and miles of geometric cow pastures and lakes and rivers. Looking through and seeing miles and miles of sky that changes color from gray to blue, then back to gray again as you move through it. There's something to look at all around you. Everywhere you turn in the cockpit you have something to see. You have so much to see that you want to be able to stop the plane and just stay in the same position for about half an hour looking all around you. Just turning your seat from one position to the other until you take it all in. Even then you get the feeling that you'd like to spend more than just half an hour. Maybe a whole hour or two hours or maybe a whole day in that very same position. Just gazing from one side to the other. (*He crosses up to* PAT *slowly and stands behind her.*) Then up, then down. Then all the way around until you realize you don't have enough eyes for that. That maybe if you had a few more eyes you could do that but not with just two. Then you get kind of dizzy and sick to the tum tum and your head starts to spin so you clutch the seat with both hands and close your eyes. But even inside your closed eyes you can see the same thing as before. Miles and miles of cow pasture and city and town. Like a movie. Lake after lake with river after river running away from the lake and going to the ocean. House after house turning into city after city and town after town. So you quick open your eyes and try to fix them on the control panel. You concentrate on the controls and the dials and the numbers. You run your hands over the buttons and the circles and squares. You can't look up now or around or from side to side or down. You're straight in front straining not to see with peripheral vision. Out of the sides of your eyes like a bird does but straight ahead. But the sky creeps in out of the corner of each eye and you can't help but see. You can't help but want to look. You can't resist watching it for a second or two or a minute. For just a little bitty while. (JILL *stands.*)

JILL: All right! Leave her alone!

HOWARD: Sorry. (*He crosses back down left and sits;* JILL *crosses up to* PAT *and stands beside her, patting her on the back.*)

JILL: We're all going to see the fireworks together. So there's no point in getting everyone all excited. Pat's going to see them with us and nobody's going to walk anywhere.

FRANK: Oh, thanks a lot. (*He stands;* BILL *and* HOWARD *remain sitting.*) Thanks for the consideration, Jill. My stomach happens to be killing me. I could use a walk. And besides I'd like to see the beach.

BILL: We can walk later. After the fireworks.

FRANK: I can't wait and besides I have to pee too. I really do.

JILL: Well go ahead.

HOWARD: Pee here.

FRANK: No!

HOWARD: Pee in your pants.

FRANK: Look, Howard—

BILL: You can pee in front of us, Frank. It's all right. Pee your heart out.

HOWARD: We don't mind. Really. We're all friends.

JILL: We'll close our eyes, Frank.

FRANK: I would like very much to take a nice little walk and pee by myself, alone. Just for the enjoyment of peeing alone.

BILL: Well go ahead.

FRANK: Thank you. (FRANK *goes off right*.)

HOWARD: How's the girl?

JILL: She's all right. All she needs is some rest.

BILL: Listen, Pat, why don't you and Jill go up the beach with Frank and pee together under the bushes?

HOWARD: And we'll stay and wait for it to get dark.

(*At this point the lights start to fade, almost imperceptibly, to the end of the play.*)

BILL: Pat?

HOWARD: We'll wait here, Pat, and save you a place. We'll save all of you a place to sit.

BILL: How does that sound, Patricia?

HOWARD: It would give you time to rest and settle your stomach and empty your bladder and loosen your legs. What do you think?

BILL: You could take as much time as you wanted.

HOWARD: You could even miss the display altogether if you want to do that. I mean it's not mandatory that you watch it. It's sort of a hoax, if you really want to know the truth. I mean if it's anything at all like the one they had last year.

BILL: Last year's was a joke.

HOWARD: That's right, Pat. Most of them didn't even work. The city spent thirty thousand dollars for twenty-five hundred fireworks last year and fifteen hundred of them exploded before they even got off the launching pad. They just made a little pop, and a stream of smoke came out, and that was it. A joke.

JILL: Some of them were beautiful.

BILL: Some of them *were* beautiful. The big gold and silver ones with sparklers on the ends. Then they had rocket ones that went way up and disappeared and then exploded way out over the ocean. They'd change into different colors. First orange, then blue, then bright yellow. Then this little parachute came floating down very softly with a tiny silver light on it. We just watched it slowly falling through the air hanging from the parachute. It went way out and finally sank into the water and the light went out. Then they'd shoot another one.

PAT: (*Still facing upstage.*) I'm not going to miss the display. I've seen every one of them for the past ten years and I'm not going to miss this one.

JILL: Of course not, Pat. (*She strokes her hair.*)

PAT: They get better and better as the years go by. It's true that some of them didn't work last year and that the city got gypped by the firecracker company. But that doesn't mean it will happen again this year. Besides, as Bill said, some of them were beautiful. It's worth it just to see one beautiful one out of all the duds. If none of them work except just one, it will be worth it to see just that one beautiful flashing thing across the whole sky. I'll wait all night on my back, even if they have to go through the whole stack without one of them working. Even if it's the very, very last one in the whole pile and everybody who came to see them left and went home. Even if I'm the only one left in the whole park and even if all the men who launch the fire-crackers go home in despair and anguish and humiliation. I'll go down there myself and hook up the thing by myself and fire the thing without any help and run back up here and lie on my back and wait and listen and watch the goddam thing explode all over the sky and watch it change colors and make all its sounds and do all the things that a fire-cracker's supposed to do. Then I'll watch it fizzle out and I'll get up slowly and brush the grass off my legs and walk back home and all the people will say what a lucky girl. What a lucky, lucky girl.

JILL: We'll see them, Patty. Don't worry.

BILL: Jill, why don't you take Pat up the beach for a little walk? We'll wait for you. It would do you both good.

JILL: Do you want to walk, Patty?

PAT: Will we be back in time?

JILL: Sure. We'll just take a short walk and come right back. (PAT *turns downstage.*)

PAT: All right. But just a short one.

BILL: That's a girl. (JILL *leads* PAT *by the arm; they go off right.*)

HOWARD: Take your time and we'll save your places.

(BILL *and* HOWARD *look at each other for a second, then they both get up and cross to the barbecue.* HOWARD *picks up the tablecloth and drapes it over the barbecue,* BILL *holds one side of the tablecloth while* HOWARD *holds the other, they look up at the sky, then they lift the tablecloth off the barbecue and allow some smoke to rise; they replace the tablecloth over the barbecue and follow the same procedure, glancing up at the sky; they do this three or four times, then* FRANK *enters from left in bare feet and carrying his shoes.*)

FRANK: What a beach! (HOWARD *and* BILL *turn suddenly to* FRANK *and drop the tablecloth on the ground.*) It's fantastic! The beach is fantastic, you guys. (*They just stare at* FRANK.) You ought to go down there. No beer cans, no seaweed, no nothing. Just beach and water and a few rocks. It's out of the question. We ought to go down there and sit. That'd be the place to watch fireworks from. Right on the sand. We could move our stuff down there. What about it?

HOWARD: There's flak and little particles that fly off in those explosions. It gets in your eyes.

FRANK: Well it would get in our eyes up here just as easy.

HOWARD: Not likely. We're above sea level here.

FRANK: So what?

HOWARD: So the air is denser above sea level and the flak and shrapnel and—well it's just safer up here. Besides there's waves to contend with at sea level. And there's sand and we're away from the smell up here. There's a nice little breeze up here.

FRANK: I'd like to be down there myself. (*He crosses upstage and stares over the hedge as though looking down at a beach.*)

BILL: Why don't you go.

FRANK: I'd like to. It'd be nice lying there with the waves right next to me and explosions in the air.

HOWARD: Go ahead, Frank. We'll stay here.

FRANK: Well we could all go. Like an expedition or an exploration. We could all find out what there is to know about the beach before it gets dark.

BILL: There's nothing to know. The beach is composed of sand which is a product of the decomposition of rock through the process of erosion. Sand is the residue of this decomposition which, through the action and movement of tides controlled by the location of the moon in relation to the position of the other planets in the hemisphere, finds itself accumulating in areas which are known to us as beaches.

FRANK: But it stretches so far out. It'd be nice to walk to the end of it and then walk back.

HOWARD: Go, then! Nobody's stopping you! Have fun! Go roll around in it. (FRANK *turns downstage.*)

FRANK: Boy! You guys are really something. It interests me to know that I've been living in this community for ten years and never knew about this beach. I mean I never knew it was so clean. I expected trash all over and a huge stench from dead fish. But instead I find a long old beach that seems to go out to some kind of a peninsula or something. That's nice to see. I'd like to try hiking out there some day. That's an interesting thing to know. That you could spend a day hiking with a nice group of friendly neighborly neighbors and pack a lunch and make a weekend of it even. Or maybe two weekends' worth, depending on the weather and the friendliness of the neighbors and the cost of the babysitters involved.

BILL: That sounds very nice, Frank.

FRANK: I think so.

BILL: We'll have to try that.

FRANK: Where are the girls?

HOWARD: They left. They said they were going to go look for you.

BILL: They wanted to tell you something.

FRANK: What?

BILL: They wouldn't say. Something important.

FRANK: They're just kidding. (*He crosses down left.*)

HOWARD: No. It was something big, though, because they wouldn't tell us even. We asked them what it was and they said they could only tell you.

FRANK: Something big?

HOWARD: Some kind of secret.

FRANK: Did they giggle about it?

BILL: Yeah but they wouldn't tell. We even threatened them. We told them we'd take them home before the fireworks started if they didn't tell. (FRANK *crosses down right.*)

FRANK: And they still didn't tell?

BILL: Nope. Something exciting, they said.

FRANK: But they giggled a lot?

BILL: Yep.

FRANK: I bet I know what it is.

HOWARD: You do?

FRANK: If it's what I think it is I'll kill both of them. Do you want to know what I think it is?

HOWARD: No. They said it was top secret. We don't want to know until you find out first.

FRANK: Well I already know.

HOWARD: Not for sure. Go find out for sure, then come back and tell us.

FRANK: Okay, but it's really a joke if it's what I think it is. And if it is what I think it is they're going to be in real trouble.

HOWARD: Go find out.

FRANK: Which way did they go? (HOWARD *and* BILL *both point off right.*)

FRANK: Thanks a lot. I'll see you later. (*He goes off right.*)

BILL: Good luck.

(BILL *and* HOWARD *pick up the tablecloth and drape it over the barbecue again; they look up at the sky, then lift the tablecloth. They do this a couple of times, then* JILL *and* PAT *enter from left, laughing hysterically and slapping each other on the back; they are in bare feet and carry their shoes.* BILL *and* HOWARD *drop the tablecloth and turn to the girls.*)

JILL: Too much! What a nut! (*They both double over with laughter as* BILL *and* HOWARD *watch them.* PAT *falls on the ground and rolls around, laughing and holding her sides;* JILL *stands over her.*)

PAT: Oh my side!

JILL: Do you know—do you know what this idiot did? Do you know what she did! She—we're walking up the beach, see—we're walking along like this. (*She walks very slowly with her head down.*) Very slowly and dejected and sad. So suddenly she stops. We both stop and she says, guess what? And I said what? She says I really do—I really do have to pee after all. (*They both break up.*) So I said all right. I'm very serious with her, see. I say all right, Patsy dear, if you have to you have to. So then she said I have to pee so bad I can't even wait. I have to go right now. Right this very minute. So we're in the middle of the beach with nothing around but sand. No bushes or nothing. So she whips down her pants and crouches right there in the middle of the beach very seriously. And I'm standing there looking around. Sort of standing guard. And do you know what happens? (*They crack up.*) All of a sudden I have to pee too. I mean really bad like she has to. So I whip my pants down and crouch down right beside her. There we are sitting side by side on the beach together. (*She crouches down in the position.*) Like a couple of desert nomads or something. So. You know how it is when you have to pee so bad that you can't pee at all? (BILL *and* HOWARD *nod their heads.*) Well that's what happened. Neither one of us could get anything out and we were straining and groaning and along comes our friend in the jet plane. Except this time he's very low. Right above our heads.

Zoom! So there we were. We couldn't stand up because then he'd really see us. And we couldn't run because there was nowhere to run to. So we just sat and pretended we were playing with shells or something. But he kept it up. He kept flying back and forth right above our heads. So do you know what this nut does? (HOWARD *and* BILL *shake their heads.*) She starts waving to him and throwing kisses. Then he really went nuts. He started doing flips and slides with that jet like you've never seen before. (*She stands with her arms outstretched like a plane.*) He went way up and then dropped like a seagull or something. We thought he was going to crash even. Then I started waving and the guy went insane. He flew that thing upside down and backwards and every way you could imagine. And we were cracking up all over the place. We started rolling in the sand and showing him our legs. Then we did some of those nasty dances like they do in the bars. Then we both went nuts or something and we took off our pants and ran right into the water yelling and screaming and waving at his plane.

PAT: (*Lying on her back and staring at the sky.*) Then he did a beautiful thing. He started to climb. And he went way, way up about twenty thousand feet or forty thousand feet. And he wrote this big sentence across the sky with his vapor trail. He wrote "E equals MC squared" in huge letters. It was really nice.

BILL: Are you sure he saw you?

JILL: Well he wasn't doing all those tricks for nothing.

BILL: But are you sure it was the same guy?

JILL: Of course.

HOWARD: It couldn't have been anyone else?

JILL: Not a chance.

HOWARD: Because Frank told us that guy crashed. (PAT *stands suddenly.*)

PAT: What?

HOWARD: He said that he saw that very same jet go down in the middle of the ocean.

PAT: When?

HOWARD: Just before you came back.

JILL: So where did Frank go?

BILL: To get some help. They're trying to fish him out right now.

PAT: You mean he crashed into the water?

BILL: That's what he told us. It could be a different guy, though.

JILL: I doubt it.

HOWARD: The plane exploded just before it hit the water.

PAT: No!

BILL: That's what Frank said.

JILL: Well let's try to find him, Pat.

BILL: He went that way. (*He points off right.*)

PAT: Aren't you guys coming?

HOWARD: We'll wait here.

JILL: Come on, Pat.

(*She pulls* PAT *by the arm, they go off right.* HOWARD *and* BILL *pause to look at the sky, then grab the tablecloth quickly; they are about to drape it over the barbecue when* FRANK *enters slowly from left. He seems to wander around the stage undeliberately and staring blankly in front of him.* HOWARD *and* BILL *drop the tablecloth and watch* FRANK.)

HOWARD: Frank? (FRANK *continues to walk as he speaks; he moves all over the stage in a daze as* HOWARD *and* BILL *watch.*)

FRANK: Boy, oh boy, oh boy, oh boy. You guys. You guys have missed the fireworks altogether. You should have seen—this

is something to behold, this is. This is the nineteenth wonder of the western, international world brought to you by
Nabisco Cracker Corporation for the preservation of historians to come and for historians to go by. This is. If only the
weather and the atmospheric conditions had been better
than they were it would have beaten the Hindenburg by far
more than it did. (*The lights by this time have become very dim,
so that the scrim takes on a translucent quality.*) By that I mean to
say a recognized world tragedy of the greatest proportion
and exhilaration to make the backs of the very bravest shudder with cold sensations and the hands moisten with the
thickest sweat ever before known, ever. And the eyes to
blink in disbelief and the temples swell with pounds and the
nose run with thick sticky pus. Oh you guys should have
come, you guys should have. What a light! (*There is a tremendous boom offstage, followed in a few seconds by flashes of light
onstage changing from orange to blue to yellow and then returning
to the dim lighting of before; the flashes should come from directly
above them. This all occurs while* FRANK *continues, oblivious to
everything but what he's saying;* HOWARD *and* BILL *remain in their
positions.*) And to happen while walking head down looking
at your toes and counting your steps. To happen under private conditions on sand. To be thinking about killing your
baby boy or your baby girl or your wife or your wife's sister
or your pet dog. And to come to a standstill. (*Another boom
followed by the same lighting and returning to the dim; the sound of
a vast crowd of people starts faintly and builds in volume to the end
of the play.*) To stop still in your tracks, thinking about the
night to come and how long it takes to build a beach given
the right amount of sand and the right amount of time and
the right amount of water to push everything up. Bigger
bodies of water with more rain and less sun. More water
than land ever. In volume, in density, in the stratospheric
conditions. And to hear a sound so shrieking that it ain't
even a sound at all but goes beyond that into the inside of
the center of each ear and rattles you up so you don't know
exactly or for sure if you'll ever hear again or if it actually

exactly matters. And it pulls your head straight up off your shoulders in a straight line with the parallel lines of each leg and so each tendon leading to your jawbone strains to its utmost. (*Another boom followed by the lighting; the crowd increases.*) So your eyes bob back and roll around in their sockets and you see the silver-sleek jet, streamlined for speed, turn itself upside down and lie on its back and swoop up, then give itself in so it looks like it's floating. Then another boom and it falls head down just gliding under its own weight. Passing cloud after cloud and picking up its own speed under its own momentum, out of control. Under its own force, falling straight down and passing through flocks of geese on their way back from where they came from. Going beyond itself with the pilot screaming and the clouds breaking up. (*Another boom and light.*) And the windows cracking and the wings tearing off. Going through seagulls now, it's so close. Heading straight for the top of the flat blue water. Almost touching in slow motion and blowing itself up six inches above sea level to the dismay of ducks bobbing along. And lighting up the air with a gold tint and a yellow tint and smacking the water so that waves go up to five hundred feet in silver white and blue. Exploding the water for a hundred miles in diameter around itself. Sending a wake to Japan. An eruption of froth and smoke and flame blowing itself up over and over again. Going on and on till the community comes out to see for itself. (*Another boom and light.*) Till the houses open because of the light, they can't sleep. And the booming goes on. And the porches are filled with kids in pajamas on top of their fathers shielding their eyes. And their mothers hold their fathers with their mouths open and the light pouring in and their cats running for cover. (*The booming sounds come closer together now and the lighting keeps up a perpetual change from color to color in bright flashes; the crowd noise gets very loud.* FRANK *moves faster around the stage, almost shouting the lines;* HOWARD *and* BILL *hold hands and stand very close together.*) And the sound keeps up and the doors open farther and farther back into the city. And the whole sky is

lit. The sirens come and the screaming starts. The kids climb
down and run to the beach with their mothers chasing and
their fathers chasing them. Oh what a sight to see with your
very own eyes. How lucky to be the first one there! And the
tide breaks open and the waves go up!

BILL: Stop it, Frank!

FRANK: The water goes up to fifteen hundred feet and smashes
the trees, and the firemen come. The beach sinks below the
surface. The seagulls drown in flocks of ten thousand. There's
a line of people two hundred deep. Standing in line to watch
the display. And the pilot bobbing in the very center of a
ring of fire that's closing in. His white helmet bobbing up
and bobbing down. His hand reaching for his other hand
and the fire moves in and covers him up and the line of two
hundred bow their heads and moan together with the light
in their faces. Oh you guys should have come! You guys
should have been there! You guys— (*He staggers off left.*
HOWARD *and* BILL *stand very still, facing out to the audience and
holding hands.* JILL *rushes on from right.*)

JILL: Come on, you guys! The plane went down. Come and
look! Come on!

HOWARD: Get away from here!

JILL: Everybody's down there! It's fantastic. The plane crashed,
Bill! It really did!

BILL: Get away from the picnic area!

JILL: All right. But you guys are missing out. (*She runs off right,*
HOWARD *and* BILL *stand very still, the crowd noise becomes deafen-
ing, the lights dim slowly out, the sound stops.*)

THE END

ON THE EDGE

Craig Pospisil

On the Edge received its New York premiere at the Vital Theatre Company (Stephen Sunderlin, Producing Artistic Director; Julie Hamberg, Associate Artistic Director) as part of the 8th Vital Signs New Works Festival on October 30, 2003. It was directed by Tom Rowan, and the cast was as follows:

GENE   Rob O'Hare
SAMMY   Anastasia Barnes

The play was also produced as part of the Turnip Theatre Company's 7th Annual Fifteen Minute Play Festival (Joseph Massa, Artistic Director; Gloria Falzer, Managing Director). It was directed by Anthony P. Pennino, and the cast included:

GENE   Clayton Hodges
SAMMY   Rachel Jackson

(*It is night, and* GENE, *a young man of seventeen, stands on a ledge on the outside of a New York City building, ten stories up in the air. He is plastered to the wall and is very careful with any movement. He forces himself to look down at the street and scans it for a few seconds before looking up again.*)

(*Several feet away from him there is a dimly lit, open window. From inside the apartment low levels of rock music and snatches of conversation from a party can sometimes be heard.*)

(*After a few moments,* SAMMY, *a young woman of seventeen, appears in the window.* GENE *freezes, hoping not to be seen by her.* SAMMY *sticks an unlit cigarette in her mouth and pulls a match out of a matchbook. She strikes the match against the book a couple of times, but it won't light. She tosses the match out the window . . . and notices* GENE.)

(*Long pause. They look at one another.*)

SAMMY: Hey.

GENE: Hey.

(SAMMY *glances down at the sidewalk below and back at* GENE *as she tears another match from the book. Before she can try lighting it though* GENE *speaks up.*)

GENE: Ah . . . would you mind waiting a couple minutes?

SAMMY: Hm?

GENE: Cigarette smoke really bothers me.

SAMMY: Oh. Sure.

(GENE *looks down and scans the sidewalk again.* SAMMY *watches him.*)

SAMMY: So, what's up? You're missing the party.

GENE: I'm just hanging out.

SAMMY: That's cool. (*Pause.*) How's the view?

GENE: I can see my building from here.

SAMMY: (*Slight pause.*) I know you. You're in my physics class, right?

GENE: Yeah.

SAMMY: What's your name?

GENE: Gene.

SAMMY: Right. Right.

GENE: You're Samantha. Sammy.

SAMMY: Yeah. How'd you know?

GENE: . . . you're in my physics class.

SAMMY: Oh. Yeah. (*Pause.*) So, what're you doing?

GENE: What does it look like I'm doing?

SAMMY: It looks like a major bid for attention.

GENE: With *my* parents? I stopped trying.

SAMMY: (*Pause.*) So, what's the deal?

GENE: (*Shrugs.*) I decided life's just not worth it.

SAMMY: Bummer. (*Pause.*) So, what're you waiting for?

GENE: Amanda.

SAMMY: Amanda Harris?

(GENE *nods.* SAMMY *looks over her shoulder into the apartment and then back at* GENE.)

SAMMY: You want me to get her?

GENE: No, I'm waiting for her to leave.

SAMMY: But then you'll miss her.

GENE: Not by much.

SAMMY: Whoa. That's harsh.

GENE: Yeah, well . . . so's life.

SAMMY: So, what happened? She dump you?

GENE: We weren't dating.

SAMMY: So, she wouldn't go out with you.

GENE: . . . uh, not really.

SAMMY: (*Slight pause.*) Did you ask her out? (*Pause.*) Gene?

GENE: I don't wanna talk about it.

SAMMY: Hey, I just want to be able to tell people why you did it.
I mean, I'm sure to be interviewed by the news and the
tabloids. After they hose you off the sidewalk.

GENE: They'll know.

SAMMY: Did you leave a note?

GENE: (*Slight pause.*) No.

SAMMY: Do you want some paper?

GENE: Would you go away?

SAMMY: If you don't leave a note, how's anyone gonna know
why you did it?

GENE: Because I'm gonna scream her name out as I fall, okay?!

SAMMY: (*Pause.*) What if you can't finish?

GENE: What?

SAMMY: I mean, do you have this timed out? How long will it take? Probably the sort of thing I could figure out if I paid attention during physics. But, I mean, what if you only get to say, "Aman—!" before you hit?

GENE: I'll finish.

SAMMY: There's a breeze. What if the wind takes the sound away?

GENE: I'll make sure they hear me.

SAMMY: I'm just trying to help.

GENE: I think I can handle it. (*Pause.*) You know, this isn't gonna be pretty. I'm gonna split open on the sidewalk when I hit. If I don't jump far enough, I might impale myself on that iron fencing. So, unless you wanna have nightmares about this for the rest of your life, you might wanna go.

SAMMY: No, I'm cool. (*Pause.*) I don't think Amanda knows you like her so much.

GENE: I don't like her. I *love* her.

SAMMY: Whatever. You should tell her.

GENE: (*Pause.*) I can't.

SAMMY: It's gotta be easier than this.

GENE: Yeah, but this makes more of a statement.

SAMMY: A statement about what?

GENE: It's just more dramatic, okay?!

SAMMY: Oh! I know where else I've seen you. You're in all the plays at school, right?

GENE: Yeah.

SAMMY: No wonder.

GENE: "No wonder" what?

SAMMY: You theater people are weird.

GENE: We are not!

SAMMY: Dude, you're on a ledge.

GENE: You don't understand.

SAMMY: Maybe not. (*Slight pause.*) Does your shrink understand?

GENE: I don't go to a shrink!

SAMMY: Something to think about. (*Slight pause.*) But, you know, Amanda's not so great. She's got a hot body, yeah, but she's kinda obvious. I mean, she's the sort of pretty you like to look at, but I can't imagine what I'd talk to her about.

GENE: No, she's really nice. She always smiles at me in the halls at school, and sometimes I run into her when I'm walking my dog, and we say hi, and then she talks to Molly and pets her. She's not like you think. (*Slight pause.*) I love her voice. It's kind of rough, but sweet.

SAMMY: Yeah, she's got a kinda sexy voice. (*Pause.*) So, where do you live?

GENE: What?

SAMMY: I live near Amanda too. East Seventy-eighth between Park and Lex. Where are you?

GENE: Why do you want to know?

SAMMY: Jeez, I'm just curious. I thought maybe we could share a cab across the park.

GENE: After I kill myself?!

SAMMY: Oh, yeah, right. I forgot.

GENE: Stick around. You'll see.

SAMMY: Uh-huh. (*Pause.*) Wait a minute. You said you could see your building. This is the West Side. You don't live near Amanda.

GENE: (*Slight pause.*) I didn't say I did. I said I saw her walking my dog.

SAMMY: Oh, man.

GENE: What?

SAMMY: Tell me you don't drag your dog across town, hoping you'll run into her.

GENE: No. We just go for long walks.

SAMMY: Oh, man! You're like a stalker.

GENE: I am not.

SAMMY: Oh, wow. Now that's an angle for the tabloids. Wait 'til I tell people.

GENE: No! Don't! (*Slight pause.*) Please.

SAMMY: Then come back inside and talk to her.

GENE: No. I can't.

SAMMY: Why not? I'll help you find—*[her.]*

GENE: (*Interrupting.*) Because she's got her tongue halfway down Bobby Chamberlain's throat, okay?!! (*Pause.*) I ran into her when I was walking Molly last weekend, and we talked and she said she was coming to M.J.'s party tonight, and I said I was too, and she said, "Great. I'll see you there. We can hang out." I've been waiting all week for this party. I thought, "Perfect. We'll talk a little and then I'll ask her out." I've wanted to for months, but first she was dating Dean and then Chris, but. . . . Well, I got here right at eight. I was the first one here. And I waited near the door. And I waited. And waited. And I drank a lot while I was waiting . . . and then she came in. And Bobby had his arm around her neck.

(*Pause.*) So, then I had to go throw up for a while. And when I got back she was making out with him on the couch. So then I went to throw up a little more, and as I came out of the bathroom, I saw them duck into M.J.'s mother's bedroom. (*Slight pause.*) All I wanted was to hold her hand and smell her hair . . . and she's down the hall fucking him!

(*Long pause.*)

SAMMY: Bobby's kinda cute, you know.

GENE: What?!

SAMMY: Well, he is.

GENE: He's an idiot. We've been going to school together for six years and he still can't remember my name. He's always . . . I mean, it's like other people just don't. . . , He's an asshole!

SAMMY: Hey, he's not my type, but a lot of girls go for him.

GENE: Oh, go away! Please?!

SAMMY: The thing is you shouldn't have waited to ask her.

GENE: Like I don't know that! Like that's not the reason I'm out here. I'm a loser. I'm weak! No one wants to be around me. I get it! I know, okay?! (*Slight pause.*) I can't take it anymore, all right?! I'm tired. I'm tired of trying to "just keep smiling," like my mother says. Or go, "Well, some people are late bloomers." (*Pause.*) I can't.

(*Long pause.*)

SAMMY: Gene. . . .

GENE: What?

SAMMY: I've got bad news.

GENE: You're fucked up, you know that!

SAMMY: Amanda's gone.

GENE: (*Slight pause.*) Bullshit. I'm not falling for that.

SAMMY: You must've missed her while we were talking. I bummed that cigarette from her as she and Bobby left.

GENE: No! You're lying! I've been watching. I couldn't have missed her.

SAMMY: Okay, fine. Keep waiting then. I'm going back inside.

GENE: No, wait!

SAMMY: What?

GENE: You're just gonna go in there and tell people or call the cops. Or you'll tell Amanda not to leave.

SAMMY: I'm telling you, Gene, she's already gone.

GENE: I was watching.

SAMMY: Fine, she's still here. Me, I need a drink.

GENE: If you go, I'll jump.

SAMMY: Yeah, so? I thought you were gonna jump anyway.

GENE: But I'll jump now. And it'll be your fault.

SAMMY: I can live with that.

(SAMMY *turns and disappears into the apartment.*)

GENE: Hey! Sammy? Sammy?! (*Slight pause.*) Bitch!

(SAMMY *suddenly reappears in the window.*)

SAMMY: Wha'd you call me?!

(GENE *flinches and struggles to keep his balance.*)

GENE: Jesus Christ! Don't do that.

SAMMY: What did you call me?

GENE: Oh, give me a break.

SAMMY: No one calls me that!

GENE: Everyone calls you that!

SAMMY: What?

GENE: Everyone calls you a bitch. (*Slight pause.*) And after tonight I know why!

SAMMY: Knock it off, asshole!

GENE: Or what?

(SAMMY *climbs out onto the ledge and starts inching her way toward* GENE.)

GENE: What the hell are you doing?!

SAMMY: I'm gonna make you shut up.

GENE: You stay away! You . . . oh, I get it. This is like reverse psychology, right? You say you're gonna push me, so I say, "No, no, I want to live."

SAMMY: No, I'm just pushing you.

GENE: I'll take you with me!

SAMMY: Like I care.

GENE: Okay-I'm-sorry-I'm-sorry. I'm sorry.

(SAMMY *stops. She is about a foot or so away from him.*)

SAMMY: Fine, whatever. Forget it. (*She looks around for the first time.*) Hey . . . this is kinda cool out here.

(*There is a pause as* GENE *gets his breath back.*)

GENE: Oh, man, I am so fucked up.

SAMMY: You just need to talk to a shrink or something.

GENE: I don't think I could.

SAMMY: It's not so hard.

GENE: (*Slight pause.*) You go to one?

SAMMY: Yeah.

GENE: How come?

SAMMY: My parents make me go.

GENE: You're kidding. Why?

SAMMY: They're worried I'm a lesbian.

GENE: Oh, that's fucked! Why do they think that?

SAMMY: 'Cause I'm a lesbian.

GENE: (*Pause.*) What?

SAMMY: I like girls.

GENE: Really?

SAMMY: Yeah.

GENE: Whoa. (*Slight pause.*) What's that like?

SAMMY: I don't know. Probably like you liking girls.

GENE: Does anyone else know?

SAMMY: (*Slight pause.*) No.

GENE: What does your shrink say?

SAMMY: Not much.

GENE: What do you say?

SAMMY: That I don't have a problem liking girls.

GENE: Is that true?

SAMMY: Yeah. I mean, it's. . . . No. I don't have a problem with it. My folks are kinda messed up about the idea, though. They said they'd like disown me or not pay for college or something. It's a drag.

GENE: So, what are you going to do?

SAMMY: I don't know. Try to hold out until I get through school and college and then get away or something.

GENE: That sucks.

SAMMY: I guess.

(*They are silent for a moment.*)

GENE: My parents are nuts, but . . . not like that.

SAMMY: Good.

GENE: You wanna go back in?

SAMMY: In a minute. It's kinda fun out here.

GENE: Yeah, it's a rush when the wind blows by.

SAMMY: Yeah?

GENE: Yeah. Wait . . . here it comes.

(*They stand there feeling the breeze. As the wind picks up, they spread their arms flat against the wall for extra support. Their hands touch, and* GENE *and* SAMMY *look at each other. Smiling, they take each other's hand and feel the wind blowing by.*)

(*The lights fade to black.*)

END OF PLAY

PHOTOGRAPHS FROM S-21

Catherine Filloux

To Davin K. Hun

Photographs from S-21 premiered at the HB Playwrights Foundation Theatre in June 1998. It was originally directed by Eva Saks and William Carden, with the following cast:

YOUNG WOMAN   Dawn Akemi Saito
YOUNG MAN   Andrew Pang
(ALTERNATE) YOUNG MAN   David Jung

CHARACTERS

YOUNG WOMAN: A young Cambodian woman who wears black pajamas and an ID tag.
YOUNG MAN: A young Cambodian man with the same pajamas and tag.

TIME

August 1997.

PLACE

A modern museum.

PROGRAM NOTE

A show entitled "Photographs from S-21: 1975–1979" was exhibited at the Museum of Modern Art in New York in the summer of 1997.

(*A* YOUNG WOMAN *and a* YOUNG MAN *pose, frozen, in the huge life-size frames of their black-and-white photos, facing each other. They both wear black pajamas and ID tags. The* YOUNG WOMAN's *ID is a long number, with some Cambodian handwriting and a date. The* YOUNG MAN's *is simply a tag with the number 3. They both stare at the camera the moment after blindfolds were taken from their eyes. There is a light shining at the bottom of the* WOMAN's *frame.*)

(*The* WOMAN *lets out a soft wail.*)

YOUNG WOMAN: I can't go on.

YOUNG MAN: . . . What did you say?

YOUNG WOMAN: I don't know where I am.

YOUNG MAN: Me neither . . .

YOUNG WOMAN: Who are you? All day long I listen to voices. I understand nothing, but I understand you.

YOUNG MAN: I am across from you. On the wall. Look, can you see me?

YOUNG WOMAN: No, my eyes are weak. They blindfolded me for a long time. Then suddenly they took off the blindfold and took my photo.

YOUNG MAN: Yes, the same with me. But I can see you.

YOUNG WOMAN: Who are you?

YOUNG MAN: A photograph, on the wall, like you.

YOUNG WOMAN: It is unbearable. During the day the people pass. They stare into my eyes. At night, there is no air. Like the inside of a cushion.

(*A beat.*)

YOUNG MAN: Would you like to move from where you are and meet me at the center of the room? There is a bench. Then you could see *me*.

YOUNG WOMAN: I can't move.

YOUNG MAN: Try and I will try.

YOUNG WOMAN: I don't know who you are.

YOUNG MAN: I speak your language.

YOUNG WOMAN: They spoke my language.

YOUNG MAN: Who?

YOUNG WOMAN: The Khmer Rouge.

YOUNG MAN: I'm not Khmer Rouge.

(*He breaks out of the photo to show her.*)

Look, no red scarf. That's why I'm here. I ran away.

(*A beat.*)

Would you like me to describe you? So that you know I can see you.

YOUNG WOMAN: No . . . I am ashamed.

YOUNG MAN: Why?

YOUNG WOMAN: My black pajamas.

YOUNG MAN: I wear the same.

YOUNG WOMAN: The number they pinned on me.

YOUNG MAN: I am Number Three.

YOUNG WOMAN: My number is much longer.

YOUNG MAN: Yes. There is also a date on your identification . . . It says, "Seventeen, Five, Seventy-eight."

YOUNG WOMAN: You must have very good eyesight.

YOUNG MAN: Thank you. I have been staring at you for a long time. You are always there, except when the crowds become big and block you, or the guard turns off the light . . . I see so many things in you, now . . . Fear, determination, beauty, surprise . . . your eyes are like water in a lake that reflects the passing seasons . . . I have begun to see you like that . . .

YOUNG WOMAN: The date on my identification is May 17, 1978.

(*He moves toward her.*)

YOUNG MAN: There is something strange at the bottom of your picture. It is blurred . . . I cannot make it out . . .

YOUNG WOMAN: *No.*

YOUNG MAN: . . . I see it. Something just inside the frame, moving skyward . . .

YOUNG WOMAN: No, there is nothing. (*A beat.*) My husband *cried* when they killed his mother.

YOUNG MAN: They killed you if you cried.

YOUNG WOMAN: I know. In the labor camp. They cracked her skull with a shovel because she was too slow working. We could not even bury her. So now she is *kmauit*—a restless ghost . . .

(*The* YOUNG MAN *moves to the bench.*)

YOUNG MAN: I always envy the visitors who sit here. Sometimes they sit in groups. Families. They read the books that are here. They write in a book too.

YOUNG WOMAN: Sometimes the people come like a parade. They walk in and out. Like a stream, staring into my eyes. Their eyes are all different colors. Blue. Green. Yellow. Like lights.

YOUNG MAN: It's nice to find someone who speaks the same language.

(*He stretches out on the bench.*)

Are you sure you don't want to stretch your legs? . . . You know we aren't the only ones on the wall. There are twenty-two of us. Cambodians. Or at least that's what I think I see. All being posed for photos at "S-21."

YOUNG WOMAN: S-21 used to have another name . . . "Tuol Sleng."

(*He looks through the guest book on the table and reads.*)

YOUNG MAN: Someone's written something here in our language! Listen. "*Do not forget.* Signed, Sovindara Hun. New York City." (*A beat.*) We're in America . . .

(*The* WOMAN *moves from her photograph very stiffly.*)

Hey, you did it! . . . Please, come sit down. This is comfortable.

YOUNG WOMAN: No, let me stand for a moment. I'm dizzy.

YOUNG MAN: You want me to coin you?

YOUNG WOMAN: No, no, no.

YOUNG MAN: I have a coin!

(*He rolls up the cuff of his pajama pants and feels in the lining.*)

I sewed this little pocket, when I returned from the labor camp to my grandmother's. I'd heard she was dying and they gave me permission to go see her. I asked her for a needle and thread and I made a secret pocket. I hid some gold she gave me and some coins. My lighter. A lot of good it did me.

(*He takes out the coin.*)

Come on, sit down. Here, give me your arm. I'm sorry, I don't have any oil . . .

(*She sits and he starts to rub her arm forcefully with the coin.*)

How does it feel?

YOUNG WOMAN: (*In awe.*) I do not believe it.

YOUNG MAN: What do you mean?

YOUNG WOMAN: I am in a dream.

YOUNG MAN: No, you're in America . . .

YOUNG WOMAN: America?

YOUNG MAN: You know, rich people, lots of cars. Willie Nelson.

YOUNG WOMAN: Oh, yes . . . Is that why they sent you to S-21? Because they found the gold?

YOUNG MAN: No, they never got the gold!

(*He quickly takes a piece of gold out of the secret pocket and shows her, delighted.*)

Look, it's right here. I tricked them!

(*He puts it back in his pocket.*)

Here give me your other arm.

(*He touches one of her hands, which is always clenched in a fist. She pulls away.*)

You're shaking.

YOUNG WOMAN: I'm always cold. Shaking with fright.

YOUNG MAN: They're not here.

(*She looks at her uniform and ID tag.*)

YOUNG WOMAN: They can't be far away . . .

(*He puts his arm around her.*)

YOUNG MAN: Here, let me warm you, darling.

YOUNG WOMAN: Why do you call me that?

YOUNG MAN: I called my sister that . . . We're dead, so you don't have to be scared . . . I mean, that is the truth . . . I wish we had something to eat . . . What kind of food do you wish for, if you could have anything?

YOUNG WOMAN: But we are *here*, Number Three.

YOUNG MAN: Don't call me that. I have a name.

YOUNG WOMAN: Who knows it now?

YOUNG MAN: You.

(*He puts his palms together and bows.*)

"Vuthy."

(*She puts her palm and fist together, bowing back.*)

YOUNG WOMAN: Tuol Sleng was a school, Vuthy. As a girl I went there to learn to read and write. That's where they took me on May 17, 1978. I walked in and remembered forming my letters so carefully, reading the words . . . *They* killed you if you could read and write . . .

YOUNG MAN: I know. (*He points to the frame.*) It's strange to be here now.

YOUNG WOMAN: America.

YOUNG MAN: I don't know if we're really here.

YOUNG WOMAN: We feel real.

(*He resumes his position in the frame.*)

YOUNG MAN: Maybe it's because we're in the photographs. And people pass by. And every time their eyes touch ours, we're back there again.

YOUNG WOMAN: They look at me so strange. Like they are asking me a question.

YOUNG MAN: Yes.

YOUNG WOMAN: I can never turn away.

YOUNG MAN: Caught.

YOUNG WOMAN: Who are they, who look?

YOUNG MAN: Ghosts, maybe . . . Ghosts of the Khmer Rouge.

YOUNG WOMAN: But they do not look the same.

YOUNG MAN: Why else would they come back again and again to see us? To check on us?

YOUNG WOMAN: Perhaps, you are right, Vuthy. Perhaps they are the enemy, disguised . . .

(*The* YOUNG MAN *moves away.*)

(*Urgently.*) Where are you going? Please don't leave me here. You don't know what can happen.

YOUNG MAN: I just want to see what is nearby. The people always seem to be passing through on their way to something called "Picasso."

(*He exits and she follows, but stops.*)

YOUNG WOMAN: Vuthy, come back! . . .

(*She stands alone. She reenters her frame and starts to take her position.*)

No, no, no, no. (*She leans down.*) No, no, no . . .

(*The* YOUNG MAN *hurries back in.*)

YOUNG MAN: Darling, what's happened? What's wrong?

(*The* YOUNG WOMAN *stares into space, totally lost.*)

Darling, tell me what happened. Please tell me what happened to you.

(*She says nothing at all.*)

There, there. (*He takes out the gold.*) Why don't you take this piece of gold?

(*She takes it, absently.*)

Isn't it beautiful? Hold it to the light.

(*She doesn't.*)

Well, I'll tell you what I saw, next door. More photographs. Of horses, of flowers, of bananas, just bananas. A boy swimming, a girl dancing, cars—we're in America—dirt, there were photos of dirt, yes. Hills. Houses, square houses with windows, airplanes, old people with lots of wrinkles, a little girl with a short dress, a bicycle, a woman with a hat—smoking a cigarette, a city with many lights. Walls and walls of this, I stopped when I heard your screaming, but it went on and on . . . I want to show you. It's easy. Just follow me. We'll go past the photographs, find a door . . . Or perhaps we don't need doors, since we're ghosts . . .

YOUNG WOMAN: How can I be dead and feel like this?

(*The* YOUNG MAN *has no answer.*)

What happened to you?

YOUNG MAN: Shocked me with an electric current, starved me, shackled me to the other men, made me sleep in my own . . .

YOUNG WOMAN: Why did they send you to S-21?

YOUNG MAN: I ran away from the camp. I ate insects and rats, slept underwater . . . You want to know my real crime? I stayed alive.

YOUNG WOMAN: And after they took off the blindfold?

YOUNG MAN: . . . My blood joined the blood of others on the floor . . .

(*A beat.*)

YOUNG WOMAN: . . . Vuthy?

YOUNG MAN: Yes?

YOUNG WOMAN: You saw right.

(*He looks at her, waiting.*)

There was something at the bottom of my photo . . . A child's hand . . .

YOUNG MAN: (*Softly.*) Oh, yes, I looked at it for so long . . .

YOUNG WOMAN: (*Reliving it.*) They took off the blindfold. My daughter reached up to me. *I did not move.* (*Softly.*) Did not move . . . They shot her first . . . I did not protect her.

(*She reaches down to take the hand of the imaginary child.*)

She reached up her hand . . .

(*He takes her hand.*)

YOUNG MAN: Come, we don't want to be ghosts, haunting people at night, making them afraid to fall asleep . . .

YOUNG WOMAN: I have no one left to haunt. All my family is gone.

YOUNG MAN: We must have some peace, darling. A proper funeral for us.

YOUNG WOMAN: . . . I don't deserve peace . . .

(*He takes her hand and they begin to leave. They are captured in a shaft of light during their odyssey outside.*)

Are we outside?

YOUNG MAN: Yes. The cement feels strange on my feet.

YOUNG WOMAN: Rough. Is it raining?

YOUNG MAN: No, it is a fountain. A proper funeral or we will remain ghosts. Come, stand in the water. (*He leads her into the fountain.*) Close your eyes. (*He caresses her.*)

Shhshhh . . .

(*He takes incense from his pocket and lights it with his lighter. He bows before her. She holds out her clenched fist to him.*)

YOUNG WOMAN: When I am newly born in my next life, I will still remember the Khmer Rouge.

(*She opens her hand and he takes a child's hair ribbon from her palm. Blackout.*)

(*The* YOUNG WOMAN *and* MAN *reappear in their frames. A flash and the click of a shutter.*)

END OF PLAY

SHARI SAYS

Craig Fols

CHARACTERS

ARIANNE: Twenty-six, stunningly beautiful movie-star looks, blonde, from the Midwest.
DOUG: Twenty-six, dark-haired, great body, studly actor.
GREG: Twenty-six, pretty-looking good looks.
AMY: Twenty-six, dark-haired, beautiful.

TIME

The present.

PLACE

New York City.

The action of the play takes place in and around Arianne's apartment on the Upper West Side of Manhattan. The apartment is suggested by a few pieces of newish furniture: a sofa, a rug, a telephone. The furniture in the apartment should look as if it was purchased at Ikea or Crate and Barrel yesterday. Other settings (the cafe, the park, the analyst's office) should be extremely simple to allow as fluid a staging as possible. A small table in Arianne's apartment might double as a cafe table, and so on.

Scene 1

(*A one-bedroom apartment on the Upper West Side, New York City. The living area, simply suggested.*)

(ARIANNE, *an extremely attractive blonde in her middle twenties, wearing exercise clothes, is discovered at rise talking to* DOUG, *an extremely attractive, dark-haired, rugged-looking guy, also early twenties.* DOUG *wears jeans, a T-shirt, and cowboy boots.*)

ARIANNE: Shari says no. Shari says I shouldn't. Shari says what's the point, really, after everything is said and done? Shari . . .

DOUG: Fuck Shari. I'm tired of hearing what she has to say.

(DOUG *turns on his heels and exits.*)

(*Sound of door slamming.*)

(ARIANNE *looks after him.*)

(*Lights out.*)

Scene 2

(ARIANNE *on the phone.*)

ARIANNE: We broke up. (*Pause.*) Shari. (*Pause.*) He couldn't handle it.

(*Pause. Lights out.*)

Scene 3

(*Party in progress.* ARIANNE, AMY [*a very attractive brunette*], *and* GREG *drinking martinis from big glasses.*)

GREG: This is wonderful.

ARIANNE: Do you really think so?

GREG: I love a good martini.

AMY: Who doesn't?

(*Pause.*)

GREG: Where's Doug?

ARIANNE: He moved out.

AMY: Oh, no.

GREG: I didn't . . .

ARIANNE: Last week. We broke up and he moved out.

GREG: I didn't . . .

AMY: Were you having problems?

ARIANNE: I guess so.

(*Lights out.*)

Scene 4

(DOUG *seated alone, talking.*)

DOUG: Fuckin' Shari, man. What a bitch. Tells her what to do, and she does it. Tells her what to eat, which gym to join. Everything. Three times a day, at least, they're on the phone. I'm lying there in bed with a hard-on, she's calling Shari. You figure.

(*Lights out.*)

Scene 5

(*The apartment.* AMY *and* ARIANNE.)

AMY: We need to talk.

ARIANNE: Okay.

AMY: I hear that Doug is seeing someone else.

ARIANNE: Oh, really?

AMY: I hear they're getting serious.

ARIANNE: Who told you that?

AMY: Don't pretend to be so unaffected.

ARIANNE: I'm not pretending. I am unaffected.

AMY: I hear . . .

ARIANNE: Where did you get this information, exactly? (*Pause.* AMY *says nothing.*) No, really. What is the source of this information? That you're passing on.

AMY: Well. To tell you the truth . . .

ARIANNE: To tell the truth, you're the one who's seeing Douglas. Isn't that true?

AMY: How did you find out?

ARIANNE: Isn't it obvious? Shari.

Scene 6

(GREG *seated, talking.*)

GREG: I'm in love with my agent. Isn't that ridiculous? Especially since I'm gay, and she isn't very attractive, anyway. Actually, she's kind of wildly unattractive, if you want to know the truth, she's fat and . . . unappealing in just about every way. But she's all I think about. Actually, that's not true. When I masturbate I think of Doug, another of Shari's clients, but the rest of the time I think about Shari. What is she going to think of me, what kinds of roles will she send me out for? Does she want to fuck me? Which I think she does. To tell you the truth, I think she wants to fuck all her clients. And who could blame her?

Scene 7

(ARIANNE *in her apartment.* AMY *and* DOUG *enter, hand in hand.*)

ARIANNE: I'm so glad you two could make it.

AMY: We wouldn't have missed it for the world.

DOUG: Is Greg here?

ARIANNE: He's in the bathroom.

(*Long awkward pause.*)

DOUG: What time is she expected?

ARIANNE: Six-thirty.

AMY: That's . . .

DOUG: Twenty minutes.

(GREG *enters. He crosses behind* ARIANNE, *puts his arms around her, nuzzles the back of her neck.*)

GREG: Hi.

ARIANNE: Hi.

GREG: Hi Amy. Hi Doug.

AMY: Hi, Greg.

DOUG: Hi.

AMY: Do you think this will really be a surprise?

DOUG: It was to me. (*To* ARIANNE.) Did you get the cake?

ARIANNE: (*While* GREG *nuzzles her ear.*) It's in the icebox.

AMY: I'll get it.

(AMY *exits.*)

DOUG: Icebox?

ARIANNE: I'm from the Midwest.

(*The phone rings.* ARIANNE *disengages from* GREG *and answers it.*)

Hello? No, of course not. No, it's no problem. I understand completely. Of course you can have a rain check. I'll tell you what. I'll put the coconut oil in the freezer, and we can do it another time. Bye.

(AMY *has entered from the kitchen with the birthday cake.*)

(ARIANNE *hangs up the phone.*)

She isn't coming.

(*Lights out.*)

Scene 8

(AMY *and* ARIANNE *at a table in a cafe.*)

AMY: So what's the story with you and Greg?

ARIANNE: What do you mean?

AMY: You seemed awfully affectionate the other night.

ARIANNE: We've always been.

AMY: I know, but . . .

(GREG *enters, a little breathless. He kisses* ARIANNE, *joins the two women at the table.*)

GREG: Hi, Pooky. Sorry I'm late.

ARIANNE: I ordered you a decaf cappuccino.

AMY: I thought that was for you.

ARIANNE: The water's for me. I'm on a diet.

(DOUG *enters, wearing an apron, carrying a tray with coffee and water.*)

(GREG *seems surprised to see* DOUG.)

DOUG: Hey, Greg. See something you like?

(*Lights out.*)

Scene 9

(AMY *alone, talking.*)

AMY: I just think she likes her better than she likes me. Maybe I'm paranoid, or acting out, or maybe it's my low self-esteem talking, but I don't think so. I think she likes her better than she likes me because she's blonde, or maybe because she has bigger tits than I do, or maybe it's because she's basically a nicer person. Anyway, whatever the reason, it's really starting to get me down.

Scene 10

(*The apartment.* DOUG *is lying on the couch, one leg slung over the back.*)

(*Sound of door opening, keys.*)

GREG'S VOICE: Honey, I'm home.

(GREG *enters carrying groceries.*)

DOUG: She's not here. She won't be home for a little while.

(*Lights out.*)

Scene 11

(ARIANNE *alone, talking.*)

ARIANNE: Well of course I always knew my boyfriend was gay, but it came as a surprise, nonetheless. To walk in like that and find them . . . on my new sofa. It was . . . disquieting. And I know why he did it. My last one, I mean, not this one. This one really is gay. But the last one . . . the last one just did it to get back at me.

(*Lights out.*)

Scene 12

(ARIANNE *and* GREG *at the cafe table.*)

GREG: (*Handing her keys.*) Here are your keys.

ARIANNE: Thank you.

GREG: Don't worry. I didn't copy them. I won't walk in on you in the middle of the night or something. I'm not a stalker.

ARIANNE: Whatever.

GREG: Where's Doug? Doesn't he work at this cafe anymore?

ARIANNE: Shari got him a series.

GREG: Oh.

ARIANNE: (*Calling the waiter.*) Check.

(*Lights out.*)

Scene 13

(*The park.* ARIANNE *and* DOUG *on a bench.*)

DOUG: Thanks for meeting me.

ARIANNE: Uh-huh.

DOUG: I thought the park because, I don't know. I just have too many associations with the rest of New York.

ARIANNE: I know what you mean.

DOUG: Your apartment, my apartment, that cafe . . .

ARIANNE: Our analyst's office . . . I know exactly how you feel.

DOUG: Do you? That's why I'm so happy to be leaving.

ARIANNE: Are you? That's good. I'm glad.

DOUG: L.A. Wow. I don't know what to expect.

ARIANNE: That's for sure.

DOUG: New associations. New friends. New people.

ARIANNE: If you're sure that's what you want.

DOUG: I am. Mostly. Except that there are times when I . . . there are some things I know I'll miss.

ARIANNE: Really?

DOUG: People, mostly, and particular people in particular.

ARIANNE: I see.

DOUG: As a matter of fact, that's why I wanted to see you. That's why I wanted us to see each other. There are . . . there's something I wanted to run by you.

ARIANNE: Okay.

DOUG: I mean, I know this might be the wrong time to talk about it, with me heading to the airport in twenty minutes, but I was thinking, I was thinking about L.A., and the future, and this series, and if it does well, if I do well, if the series gets picked up and everything, and I'm out there, with a job, and an income, and a kind of steady life and everything . . .

ARIANNE: Uh–huh . . .

DOUG: Well, then. I think it might be time to make a change, to make an alteration, in my style of living and everything.

ARIANNE: I'm not sure I know what you're talking about.

DOUG: I'm thinking of leaving Shari.

ARIANNE: Oh. (*Pause.*) I think that would be a good idea.

(ARIANNE *reaches across and takes* DOUG's *hand. They sit on the bench, staring out into the night. Sounds of New York traffic.*)

END OF PLAY

SMALL WORLD

Tracey Scott Wilson

CHARACTERS

MAN 1
MAN 2
MAN 3
WOMAN 1
WOMAN 2
WOMAN 3

(Lights up on 3 couples meeting at separate benches. They have never met before. It is a first date for all. Until specified, MAN 1 only speaks to WOMAN 1, MAN 2 only speaks to WOMAN 2, and MAN 3 only speaks to WOMAN 3. When it reads, MAN 1, 2, and so on, the characters are speaking simultaneously. Also (. . .) indicates that the characters are finishing the previous sentence.)

MAN 1: Stacy?

WOMAN 1: Bob?

MAN 2: Lucy?

WOMAN 2: Bill?

MAN 3: Alice?

WOMAN 3: Tim?

ALL: Hi!

MAN 1: I've never been on one of these blind . . .

MAN 2: . . . computer . . .

MAN 3: . . . newspaper ad . . .

MAN 1, 2, 3: dates before.

WOMAN 1, 2, 3: Neither have I.

(They sit.)

MAN 1, 2: It's beautiful here in the park.

MAN 3: Maybe we should have gone to the park.

WOMAN 1, 2: Yes.

WOMAN 3: No.

MAN 3: Oh.

WOMAN 3: I have allergies. (*Pause.*) But still you . . .

WOMAN 1, 2, 3: . . . couldn't ask for a more . . .

WOMAN 1: Beautiful . . .

WOMAN 2: Wonderful . . .

WOMAN 3: Pretty . . .

WOMAN 1, 2, 3: day today.

MAN 1, 2: Would you like to go for a walk around the . . .

MAN 1: Lake.

MAN 2: Flower garden.

MAN 3: Wanna go to a movie?

WOMAN 1: Maybe in a minute.

WOMAN 2: I'd like to sit here for a few minutes.

WOMAN 3: Can we talk first?

MAN 1, 2, 3: OK.

ALL: So . . .

WOMAN 1, 2: I understand you work in . . .

WOMAN 1: . . . the health care . . .

WOMAN 2: . . . the music . . .

WOMAN 1, 2: industry.

WOMAN 3: I am so lonely.

MAN 1: Yes, I am a home health aid for the elderly.

MAN 2: Yes, I'm writing a book on jazz.

MAN 3: I . . . uh . . .

WOMAN 1, 2: That's . . .

WOMAN 1: Wonderful.

WOMAN 2: Exciting.

WOMAN 3: Please help me.

MAN 1, 2: So . . .

MAN 3: Uh . . .

MAN 1, 2: What do you do?

MAN 3: How can I help you?

WOMAN 1: Oh, I'm just an office manager for a small office.

WOMAN 2: I'm a computer consultant.

WOMAN 3: Just be real with me.

WOMAN 1, 2: But I really want to . . .

WOMAN 3: Be really, really, really, really, really real with me.

WOMAN 1: . . . work in TV.

WOMAN 2: . . . own a farm someday.

WOMAN 3: Unorchestrate your emotions to my song.

MAN 1: Interesting.

MAN 2: Great.

MAN 3: Wait a minute.

MAN 1: I have a friend . . .

MAN 2: I know someone . . .

MAN 3: Have you read that book . . . ?

MAN 1: Works in TV.

MAN 2: Who owns a farm.

MAN 3: (*Recalling title of book.*) Think It . . .

WOMAN 3: Say It . . .

MAN 3: Speak It . . .

MAN 3, WOMAN 3: Now! *The Interactive Guide to Kicking Your Inner Child's Ass.*

MAN 1: She says TV is . . .

MAN 2: He says farming is . . .

MAN 3: I love that book.

MAN 1, 2: a lot of work.

MAN 3: It changed my life.

MAN 1, 2: . . . but rewarding.

WOMAN 1: Yeah.

WOMAN 2: Yup.

WOMAN 3: It changed my life too. (*Pause.*) Before I read that book I was so polite all the time. I was into . . .

WOMAN 3, MAN 3: Pseudo-Ultra-Judo-Fake Bonding.

WOMAN 3: Like it says in the book! I would have met you here today and just had a . . .

WOMAN 1, 2: So . . .

WOMAN 3: shallow conversation . . .

WOMAN 1, 2: It must be really rewarding to . . .

WOMAN 3: . . . about nothing.

WOMAN 1: . . . help the elderly . . .

WOMAN 2: . . . write about jazz.

WOMAN 3: But because of that book I feel strong enough to say to you: HELP ME!

MAN 1, 2: It's so rewarding.

MAN 1: I couldn't even begin to tell you.

MAN 2: Jazz is my life.

MAN 3: I will help you. What's wrong?

WOMAN 3: You see I'm not really over my . . .

(*Lights up on* MAN 1.)

WOMAN 3: . . . last boyfriend.

MAN 1: (*To* WOMAN 1.) Some people get depressed when they look at the elderly.

WOMAN 3: He told me he was a home health aide for the elderly.

MAN 1: (*To* WOMAN 1.) But I don't. I feel hopeful . . .

WOMAN 3: But he only had one patient.

MAN 1: . . . to have lived so long and experienced so much.

WOMAN 3: . . . his mother.

MAN 1: (*To* WOMAN 1.) It's a beautiful thing.

WOMAN 1: (*To* MAN 1.) Wow . . .

MAN 3: Ewwwww.

WOMAN 3: Every time I would go over to his house, he would excuse himself every few minutes and go into another room. I just thought he had a bladder problem, but then one day I heard someone talking. I asked him (*To* MAN 1.) who was that? . . .

MAN 1: (*To* WOMAN 3.) No one. You're hearing things. I live
  alone.

WOMAN 3: (*To* MAN 3.) But one day, I tiptoed behind him and
  peeked in the room. There was an old woman in a chair. He
  was calling her . . .

MAN 1: Momma.

WOMAN 3: (*To* MAN 3.) I was very understanding. (*To* MAN 1.)
Oh, honey. Is this your mother? You take care of her too? That's
nothing to be ashamed of. It's sweet. Your mother and all those
others too. (*To* MAN 3.) Then this woman, who is like so wrin-
kled a prune would stare in awe, says . . .

WOMAN 2: (*As mother.*) Who are you! Who are you! I'm his one
  and only patient! His one and only! Get out! I'm the only
  one who gets her feet shaved around here. You're stepping
  on my toenail clippings! GET OUT! GET OUT!

WOMAN 3: Two days later he was like:

MAN 1: (*To* WOMAN 3.) I tried to be a home health worker, but
  Momma takes up all of my time. I love Momma, I love
  Momma, I love Momma. I do. Before that she and Grandma
  took up all of my time. I love Grandma, I love Grandma, I
  love Grandma. I do. But Grandma is dead now, and
  soon . . . Momma will be dead too. Then you can move
  into my house, and we'll have kids. Two boys and two girls.
  We'll teach them to be good little home health workers,
  too, cause, like Momma says, by the time we grow old our
  Social Security check won't buy us a cup of milk.

WOMAN 1: (*To* MAN 1.) You are so noble.

MAN 3: Ew.

WOMAN 3: But still I think of him.

MAN 3: I know what you mean. I'm still hung up on my girlfriend too.

(*Lights up on* WOMAN 2.)

MAN 3: She said she wanted to be a farmer.

WOMAN 2: (*To* MAN 2.) I know it's a lot of work, but to be out in the fresh country air . . .

MAN 3: . . . a chicken farmer.

WOMAN 2: (*To* MAN 2.) Communing with nature every day. Feeding the land. Feeding the chickens.

MAN 3: But that is not all she wanted to do with those chickens.

(MAN 3 *squirms in his chair.*)

WOMAN 2: (*To* MAN 3.) What's wrong with you?

MAN 3: I've got hay in my butt. God, that is the last time we go to a farm.

WOMAN 2: What? No!

MAN 3: Yes, it is.

WOMAN 2: But farming is my life.

MAN 3: But you don't own a farm, I don't understand why we have to sneak in other people's barns to make love all the time. At first, it was exciting, but now it's just weird.

WOMAN 2: You're so conventional.

MAN 3: I am not . . . I . . .

(*There is the sound of a chicken.*)

MAN 3: What was that?

(*Sound of a chicken.*)

WOMAN 2: Nothing.

MAN 3: Yes, it was.

(*Sound of a chicken.*)

MAN 3: It sounded like . . . (*To* WOMAN 3.) I opened the door and there were all these chickens. Chickens everywhere.

MAN 3: (*To* WOMAN 2.) What the . . .

WOMAN 2: Don't touch them. I love them. See how soft and gentle.

MAN 3: You can't . . . We can't keep chickens in the apartment.

WOMAN 2: Quiet. Don't yell in front of them. (*Pause.*) See, they are sweet and gentle. Like kittens with feathers. But sexy. Very sexy. That clucking drives me wild. Please just touch the chickens, baby! Touch the chickens!

MAN 2: (*To* WOMAN 2.) I love nature too.

WOMAN 3: (*To* MAN 3.) Yuuccch.

MAN 3: What is wrong with us?

WOMAN 3: For me it has been a pattern. A pattern of unhealthy relationships. The other guy I dated.

(*Light up on* MAN 2.)

WOMAN 3: A die-hard jazz lover.

MAN 2: (*To* WOMAN 2.) Jazz is truly the only great American art form.

WOMAN 3: So I thought.

MAN 2: In its rhythms we hear America. In its tunes we see ourselves.

WOMAN 3: I studied everything I could about jazz just so I could get close to him. I bought thousands of recordings. One day I bought him this rare Miles Davis recording. It took me six months to find it. I was going to surprise him and slip it in his record collection. I must have hit some secret door because . . . (*To* MAN 2.) Honey . . .

MAN 2: Yeah, baby.

WOMAN 3: Uh . . . I wanted to give you this. (*Hands him CD.*)

MAN 2: Oh wow. Miles Davis session number 73. Oh wow baby, thank you, thank you.

WOMAN 3: Uh-huh. Um . . . I was going to put it in with your other records . . . and surprise you.

MAN 2: Uh-huh. This is perfect.

WOMAN 3: And I found this.

(WOMAN 3 *shows him CD.*)

MAN 2: Oh . . . Uh . . . Yeah, you know. I was holding that for my . . . mother. My mother . . .

WOMAN 3: (*To* MAN 3.) A Yanni CD.

WOMAN 3: (*To* MAN 2.) No, you weren't.

(*She dumps a whole batch of CDs at his feet.*)

WOMAN 3: Yanni, John Tesh, Enya, Celine Dion, Phil Collins . . . What is this about? I thought you were cool.

MAN 2: Hey! Be careful. You're going to scratch them. (*Pause.*) One night I couldn't sleep, all right. So, I turned on the radio. They were playing "Desert Siren" by Yanni. (*He hums tune.*) It was so relaxing. (*He hums tune.*) So calming. (*He hums tune.*) Yanni is beautiful. (*He hums tune.*) Someday he'll be appreciated. (*He hums tune.*) Someday . . . (*He hums.*) Someday.

WOMAN 2: (*To* MAN 2.) I want you to teach me everything you know about music.

MAN 3: (*Shudders.*) John Tesh. Ewww.

WOMAN 3: So, you see. It must be me.

MAN 3: No, no, no. Don't assume that. I dated this woman.

WOMAN 1: (*To* MAN 1.) I know TV is supposed to be this vast wasteland.

MAN 3: Who wanted to work in TV.

WOMAN 1: (*To* MAN 1.) But I think it is a powerful and effective medium . . .

MAN 3: So, she watched a lot of TV.

WOMAN 1: (*To* MAN 1.) . . . to communicate and express ideas.

MAN 3: But then I noticed she began to watch only one program.

(*Theme from* The Jeffersons *plays.*)

MAN 3: (*To* WOMAN 1.) Honey, do we have to watch . . .

WOMAN 1: Shhhhh.

MAN 3: But you've seen this episode a hundred times already.

WOMAN 1: Shhhhh.

MAN 3: All day and night, *The Jeffersons.* She would tape the show and watch it in fast forward and reverse.

WOMAN 1: (*Pointing to TV.*) See! Right there! Right there!

MAN 3: What?

WOMAN 1: Lionel just said . . . Pop Taht Tuoba Erus Ton Mi.

MAN 3: What?

WOMAN 1: He said: Pop Taht Tuoba Erus Ton Mi.

MAN 3: What? What are you saying?

WOMAN 1: Oh, I have a little language for Lionel. You see, I believe he's giving me a message, so I speak his lines backwards so I can understand.

MAN 3: Giving you a message?

WOMAN 1: Yes. Us. Us a message. To the world.

MAN 3: Uh . . .

WOMAN 1: Did you know Lionel created the show *Good Times* . . .

MAN 3: Uh . . . Honey . . .

WOMAN 1: And the man that replaced him on the show was his brother. His very own brother.

MAN 3: Honey, I . . .

WOMAN 1: But he's gone now. No word of him since 1979. I can't find him. But I will. I know I will. Pop Taht Tuoba Erus Ton Mi Pop. Taht Tuoba Erus Ton Mi Pop. Taht Tuoba Erus Ton Mi.

MAN 1: (*To* WOMAN 1.) I've never thought of TV that way before.

WOMAN 3: (*To* MAN 3.) I'll never watch *The Jeffersons* again. (*Pause.*) In honor of you.

MAN 3: Listen, I have to tell you . . .

MAN 1, 2, 3: I really like you.

MAN 1: You're wonderful . . .

MAN 2: . . . Terrific . . .

MAN 3: You've touched my inner song and let me tell you baby, it ain't playing Yanni.

(*Girls smile and laugh in unison.*)

WOMAN 1, 2, 3: Well . . .

WOMAN 1: I think you're great . . .

WOMAN 2: Fantastic . . .

WOMAN 3: You've touched my inner song . . .

WOMAN 1, 2, 3: . . . too.

MAN 1, 2, 3: I would love to . . .

MAN 1: Get to know you.

MAN 2: Spend some more time with you.

MAN 3: Coordinate your soul with mine.

WOMAN 1, 2, 3: (*They all sigh.*) Great!

MAN 1, 2: But first I have to . . .

MAN 1: Stop at home for a minute.

MAN 2: Stop by the record store.

MAN 3: My afternoon is completely free.

WOMAN 1: Oh, I suppose you have to check on your patients?

WOMAN 2: Are you buying the latest jazz CD?

MAN 1, 2: Uh . . . Yeah . . . Yeah . . .

WOMAN 1, 2: Oh, that works out because I have to . . .

WOMAN 1: Set my VCR to record a program.

WOMAN 2: Stop by this new chicken farm.

WOMAN 3: My afternoon is free too.

WOMAN 1, 2, MAN 1, 2: So, I'll meet you later then.

ALL: Great!

WOMAN 1, 2, 3: But I tell you, I just can't believe someone like you . . .

WOMAN 1: . . . isn't taken . . .

WOMAN 2: . . . hasn't been snatched up yet . . .

WOMAN 3: . . . is free . . .

MAN 1, 2, 3: Well, I can't believe you are . . .

MAN 1: . . . available . . .

MAN 2: . . . not married . . .

MAN 3: . . . unattached.

ALL: There are just so many crazy people out there.

(*They all laugh.*)

WOMAN 1: I'm telling you . . .

MAN 1: You got that right.

WOMAN 2: Tell me about it . . .

MAN 2: I could tell you stories.

WOMAN 3: Hell, between the two of us . . .

MAN 3: I guess we dated every crazy person out there.

WOMAN 1, 2: My last boyfriend . . .

MAN 1, 2: . . . girlfriend . . .

(*Lights up on* MAN 3 *and* WOMAN 3.)

MAN 1, 2, WOMAN 1, 2: . . . was a pathological liar!

(*They gasp in disbelief.*)

WOMAN 1: Really?

MAN 1: No kidding.

WOMAN 2: What are the chances of that?

MAN 2: It really is a small world. (*Pause.*) A small world.

SWEET HUNK O' TRASH

Eric Lane

Sweet Hunk O' Trash premiered in the first annual All Day Sucker produced by Circle East (Michael Warren Powell, Artistic Director) at Circle-in-the-Square Downtown in New York City, June 1996. Thomas Morissey directed the following cast:

ROB   Andrew Stein
EARL   Jimmy Georgiades

Sweet Hunk O' Trash was produced by Orange Thoughts Productions as part of the full-length play *Cater-Waiter* at HERE in New York City, January 1997. The play was directed by Martha Banta; the set design was by Kate Kennedy; the lighting design was by Matthew Frey; the costume design was by Susan J. Slack; the sound design was by Paul Aston; the production stage manager was Gerry Cosgrove. The cast of *Sweet Hunk O' Trash* was as follows:

ROB   Tim Deak
EARL   Jimmy Georgiades

CHARACTERS

ROB: Cute, sweet, vulnerable, somewhat guarded.
EARL: Butch, gentle, direct, with a sense of humor. A protector.

PLACE

A volunteer dance.

(*The song "Tribal Dance" plays.*
ROB *stands.* EARL *walks up, stands next to him.*
EARL *looks out. Starts to bop to music.*
ROB *sneaks a look. Looks out.*
EARL *looks at him. Looks away.*
ROB *looks over. Looks away. Smiles.*
ROB *looks again, catches* EARL*'s eye, quickly looks away.*
ROB *looks.* EARL *is still looking at him.*)

ROB: Hi.

EARL: Hi.

ROB: I'm Rob.

EARL: Earl.

ROB: Hi, Earl.

EARL: Hi.

ROB: Hi.

(*Music fades to low underneath.* ROB *looks down at floor.*)

EARL: You wanna dance or something?

ROB: No thanks.

EARL: Me either. I hate this shit.

ROB: What?

EARL: This music. Bum-budda-bum-budda-bum . . . Drive you fuckin' nutz. The monotony, you know.

ROB: Right. It is kinda monotonous.

EARL: Monotonous, yeah. What kinda music you like?

ROB: Show tunes.

EARL: (*Hates show tunes.*) Oh.

ROB: Other stuff, too. But I volunteer. We sing in the hospital. A bunch of us. Show tunes. Whatever. In hospitals. So.

EARL: Me, too.

ROB: You sing?

EARL: (*Shakes head "no."*) Volunteer.

ROB: Doing what?

EARL: I hold people.

ROB: Oh.

EARL: Just like, you know, hold them. People gotta be touched, don't you think?

ROB: Sure.

EARL: Sure. Just look at a baby, you see it. You take two piles of babies, one touched, the other not touched. The touched ones is bigger, guaranteed.

ROB: So you hold them.

EARL: Yeah. Maybe just a few minutes each time. But I hold them. I guess you do it with your voice.

ROB: What?

EARL: Your singing. Show tunes. Kinda like the same. (ROB *smiles.*) People sick, ones like married, do a lot better. There are studies. You read that?

ROB: No, but it makes sense.

EARL: Makes sense . . . Science.

ROB: Right.

EARL: Or just couples. Not married, just together. You wanna dance?

ROB: Maybe later.

EARL: Yeah, wait for a good song. I hate this house stuff. Bum-budda. Bum-budda . . .

ROB: Bum. (EARL *smiles*.) How'd you get started? Volunteering.

EARL: I found a baby.

ROB: You found a baby?

(*Music fades out*.)

EARL: Yeah, in the garbage. My friend, Randy, you ask him what he does, he says he works for the city. You ask him, doing what? Sanitation. Me, I'm a garbage man. What I got to be ashamed. I'm not the one throwing out this junk. You wanna learn about a culture, look at their garbage. You'd be amazed at the shit people throw out.

ROB: What happened to the baby?

EARL: Took her to the hospital. Nobody wanted to touch her. She had AIDS. Two months old. Nobody wanted to touch her. So I started going. I don't know. I guess it got me thinking. I thought about going to massage school. You know, study. But it wasn't really about that. So I just go. To the hospital.

ROB: Is she okay?

EARL: Yeah, she's okay. Maybe sometime you come with me.

ROB: I'd like that.

EARL: You could sing to her. Emma. That's what I call her. You could sing her a song.

ROB: I'd like that. (*A beat.*) Earl, I— (*He stops.*)

EARL: What?

ROB: I've been on one date the past year.

EARL: You should get out more. (ROB *laughs.*)

ROB: No, um. Look. Well, like last date I went on, everything was going fine, 'til I mention my lover died. Suddenly the guy I'm with. Well, the arms cross. The legs cross. He turns away. We finish dinner, but suddenly everything like . . . I don't think he knew he was doing it but—Anyway.

EARL: What a shithead.

ROB: Scared, I guess.

EARL: I guess.

ROB: Just scared. (EARL *and he look at each other.*) Earl, do you want to dance?

(EARL *takes* ROB*'s hands. Music fades up.* ROB *moves into* EARL*'s arms. They slow dance, in contrast to the music. At first,* ROB *is surprised, then decides to go with it. They dance.*)

(*Lights fade.*)

TIME FLIES

David Ives

*this play is for
John Rando,
Anne O'Sullivan,
Arnie Burton,
and Willis Sparks,
who made it fly*

CHARACTERS

MAY: A mayfly.
HORACE: A mayfly.
A FROG
DAVID ATTENBOROUGH

PLACE

A pond. Evening.

(*Evening. A pond. The chirr of tree toads, and the buzz of a huge swarm of insects. Upstage, a thicket of tall cattails. Downstage, a deep green love seat. Overhead, an enormous full moon.*)

(*A loud cuckoo sounds, like the mechanical "cuckoo" of a clock.*)

(*Lights come up on two mayflies:* HORACE *and* MAY, *buzzing as they "fly" in. They are dressed like singles on an evening out, he in a jacket and tie, she in a party dress—but they have insectlike antennae, long tubelike tails, and on their backs, translucent wings. Outsize horn-rim glasses give the impression of very large eyes. May has distinctly hairy legs.*)

HORACE and MAY: Bzzzzzzzzzzzzzzzzz . . .

(*Their wings stop fluttering, as they "settle."*)

MAY: Well here we are. This is my place.

HORACE: Already? That was fast.

MAY: Swell party, huh.

HORACE: Yeah. Quite a swarm.

MAY: Thank you for flying me home.

HORACE: No. Sure. I'm happy to. Absolutely. My pleasure. I mean—you're very, very, very welcome.

(*Their eyes lock and they near each other as if for a kiss, their wings fluttering a little.*)

Bzzzzzzzz . . .

MAY: Bzzzzzzzz . . .

(*Before their jaws can meet: "CUCKOO!"—and* HORACE *breaks away.*)

HORACE: It's that late, is it. Anyway, it was very nice meeting you—I'm sorry, is it April?

MAY: May.

HORACE: May. Yes. Later than I thought, huh.

(*They laugh politely.*)

MAY: That's very funny, Virgil.

HORACE: It's Horace, actually.

MAY: I'm sorry. The buzz at that party was so loud.

HORACE: So you're "May the mayfly."

MAY: Yeah. Guess my parents didn't have much imagination. May, mayfly.

HORACE: You don't, ah, live with your parents, do you, May?

MAY: No, my parents died around dawn this morning.

HORACE: Isn't that funny. Mine died around dawn too.

MAY: Maybe it's fate.

HORACE: Is that what it izzzzzzzz . . . ?

MAY: Bzzzzzzzz . . .

HORACE: Bzzzzzzzzzzzzz . . .

(*They near for a kiss, but* HORACE *breaks away.*)

Well, I'd better be going now. Good night.

MAY: Do you want a drink?

HORACE: I'd love a drink, actually . . .

MAY: Let me just turn on a couple of fireflies. (MAY *tickles the underside of a couple of two-foot-long fireflies hanging like a chandelier, and the fireflies light up.*)

HORACE: Wow. Great pond! (*Indicating the love seat.*) I love the lily pad.

MAY: The lily pad was here. It kinda grew on me. (*Polite laugh.*) Care to take the load off your wings?

HORACE: That's all right. I'll just—you know—hover. But will you look at that . . . ! (*Turning,* HORACE *bats* MAY *with his wings.*)

MAY: Oof!

HORACE: I'm sorry. Did we collide?

MAY: No. No. It's fine.

HORACE: I've only had my wings about six hours.

MAY: Really! So have I . . . ! Wasn't molting disgusting?

HORACE: Eugh. I'm glad that's over.

MAY: Care for some music? I've got The Beatles, The Byrds, The Crickets . . .

HORACE: I love the Crickets.

MAY: Well so do I . . . (*She kicks a large, insect-shaped coffee table, and we hear the buzz of crickets.*)

HORACE: (*As they boogie to that.*) So are you going out with any— I mean, are there any other mayflies in the neighborhood?

MAY: No, it's mostly wasps.

HORACE: So, you live here by your, um, all by yourself? Alone?

MAY: All by my lonesome.

HORACE: And will you look at that moon.

MAY: You know that's the first moon I've ever seen?

HORACE: That's the first moon *I've* ever seen . . . !

MAY: Isn't that funny.

HORACE: When were you born?

MAY: About seven-thirty this morning.

HORACE: So was I! Seven thirty-three!

MAY: Isn't that funny.

HORACE: Or maybe it's fate.

(*They near each other again, as if for a kiss.*)

    Bzzzzzzz . . .

MAY: Bzzzzzzzzz . . . I think that moon is having a very emotional effect on me.

HORACE: Me too.

MAY: It must be nature.

HORACE: Me too.

MAY: Or maybe it's fate.

HORACE: Me too . . .

MAY: Bzzzzzzzzzz . . .

HORACE: Bzzzzzzzzzzzzzzz . . .

(*They draw their tails very close. Suddenly:*)

A FROG: (*Amplified, over loudspeaker.*) Ribbit, ribbit!

HORACE: A frog!

MAY: A frog!

HORACE and MAY: The frogs are coming, the frogs are coming! (*They "fly" around the stage in a panic. Ad lib.*) A frog, a frog! The frogs are coming, the frogs are coming! (*They finally stop, breathless.*)

MAY: It's okay. It's okay.

HORACE: Oh my goodness.

MAY: I think he's gone now.

HORACE: Oh my goodness, that scared me.

MAY: That is the only drawback to living here. The frogs.

HORACE: You know, I like frog films and frog literature. I just don't like frogs.

MAY: And they're so rude if you're not a frog yourself.

HORACE: Look at me. I'm shaking.

MAY: Why don't I fix you something. Would you like a grasshopper? Or a stinger?

HORACE: Just some stagnant water would be fine.

MAY: A little duckweed in that? Some algae?

HORACE: Straight up is fine.

MAY: (*As she pours his drink.*) Sure I couldn't tempt you to try the lily pad?

HORACE: Well, maybe for just a second. (HORACE *flutters down onto the love seat.*) Zzzzzzz . . .

MAY: (*Handing him a glass.*) Here you go. Cheers, Horace.

HORACE: Long life, May.

(*They clink glasses.*)

MAY: Do you want to watch some tube?

HORACE: Sure. What's on?

MAY: Let's see. (*She checks a green* TV Guide.) There is . . . *The Love Bug, M. Butterfly, The Spider's Stratagem, Travels with My Ant, Angels and Insects, The Fly* . . .

HORACE: The original, or Jeff Goldblum?

MAY: Jeff Goldblum.

HORACE: Eugh. Too gruesome.

MAY: *Born Yesterday*. And *Life on Earth*.

HORACE: What's on that?

MAY: "Swamp Life," with Sir David Attenborough.

HORACE: That sounds good.

MAY: Shall we try it?

HORACE: Carpe diem.

MAY: Carpe diem? What's that?

HORACE: I don't know. It's Latin.

MAY: What's Latin?

HORACE: I don't know. I'm just a mayfly.

(*"Cuckoo!"*)

And we're right on time for it.

(MAY *presses a remote control and* DAVID ATTENBOROUGH *appears, wearing a safari jacket.*)

DAVID ATTENBOROUGH: Hello, I'm David Attenborough. Welcome to "Swamp Life."

MAY: Isn't this comfy.

HORACE: Is my wing in your way?

MAY: No. It's fine.

DAVID ATTENBOROUGH: You may not believe it, but within this seemingly lifeless puddle, there thrives a teeming world of vibrant life.

HORACE: May, look—isn't that your pond?

MAY: I think that is my pond!

HORACE: He said "puddle."

DAVID ATTENBOROUGH: This puddle is only several inches across, but its stagnant water plays host to over fourteen gazillion different species.

MAY: It is my pond!

DAVID ATTENBOROUGH: Every species here is engaged in a constant, desperate battle for survival. Feeding—meeting—mating—breeding—dying. And mating. And meeting. And mating. And feeding. And dying. Mating. Mating. Meeting. Breeding. Brooding. Braiding—those that can braid. Feeding. Mating . . .

MAY: All right, Sir Dave!

DAVID ATTENBOROUGH: Mating, mating, mating, and mating.

HORACE: Only one thing on his mind.

MAY: The filth on television these days.

DAVID ATTENBOROUGH: Tonight we start off with one of the saddest creatures of this environment.

HORACE: The dung beetle.

MAY: The toad.

DAVID ATTENBOROUGH: The lowly mayfly.

HORACE: Did he say "the mayfly"?

MAY: I think he said "the *lowly* mayfly."

DAVID ATTENBOROUGH: Yes. The lowly mayfly. Like these two mayflies, for instance.

HORACE: May—I think that's us!

MAY: Oh my God . . .

HORACE and MAY: (*Together.*) We're on television!

HORACE: I don't believe it!

MAY: I wish my mother was here to see this!

HORACE: This is amazing!

MAY: Oh God, I look terrible!

HORACE: You look very good.

MAY: I can't look at this.

DAVID ATTENBOROUGH: As you can see, the lowly mayfly is not one of nature's most attractive creatures.

MAY: At least we don't wear safari jackets.

HORACE: I wish he'd stop saying "lowly mayfly."

DAVID ATTENBOROUGH: The lowly mayfly has a very distinctive khkhkhkhkhkhkhkhkhkkh . . . (*He makes the sound of TV "static."*)

MAY: I think there's something wrong with my antenna . . . (*She adjusts the antenna on her head.*)

HORACE: You don't have cable?

MAY: Not on this pond.

DAVID ATTENBOROUGH: (*Stops the static sound.*) . . . and sixty tons of droppings.

HORACE: That fixed it.

MAY: Can I offer you some food? I've got some plankton in the pond. And some very nice gnat.

HORACE: I do love good gnat.

MAY: I'll set it out, you can pick. (*She rises and gets some food, as:*)

DAVID ATTENBOROUGH: The lowly mayfly first appeared some 350 million years ago . . .

MAY: That's impressive.

DAVID ATTENBOROUGH: . . . and is of the order Ephemeroptera, meaning, "living for a single day."

MAY: I did not know that!

HORACE: "Living for a single day." Huh . . .

MAY: (*Setting out a tray on the coffee table.*) There you go.

HORACE: Gosh, May. That's beautiful.

MAY: There's curried gnat, salted gnat, Scottish smoked gnat . . .

HORACE: I love that.

MAY: . . . gnat with pesto, gnat au naturelle, and Gnat King Cole.

HORACE: I don't think I could finish a whole one.

MAY: "Gnat" to worry.

(*They laugh politely.*)

That's larva dip there in the center. Just dig in.

DAVID ATTENBOROUGH: As for the life of the common mayfly . . .

HORACE: Oh. We're "common" now.

DAVID ATTENBOROUGH: . . . it is a simple round of meeting, mating, meeting, mating—

MAY: Here we go again.

DAVID ATTENBOROUGH: —breeding, feeding, feeding . . .

HORACE: This dip is fabulous.

DAVID ATTENBOROUGH: . . . and dying.

MAY: Leaf?

HORACE: Thank you.

(MAY *breaks a leaf off a plant and hands it to* HORACE.)

DAVID ATTENBOROUGH: Mayflies are a major food source for trout and salmon.

MAY: Will you look at that savagery?

HORACE: That poor, poor mayfly.

DAVID ATTENBOROUGH: Fishermen like to bait hooks with mayfly look-alikes.

MAY: Bastards!—Excuse me.

DAVID ATTENBOROUGH: And then there is the giant bullfrog.

FROG: (*Amplified, over loudspeaker.*) Ribbit, ribbit!

HORACE and MAY: The frogs are coming, the frogs are coming!

(*They "fly" around the stage in a panic—and end up "flying" right into each other's arms.*)

HORACE: Well there.

MAY: Hello.

DAVID ATTENBOROUGH: Welcome to "Swamp Life." (DAVID ATTEN-BOROUGH *exits.*)

MAY: (*Hypnotized by* HORACE.) Funny how we flew right into each other's wings.

HORACE: It is funny.

MAY: Or fate.

HORACE: Do you think he's gone?

MAY: David Attenborough?

HORACE: The frog.

MAY: What frog. Bzzzz . . .

HORACE: Bzzzzz . . .

DAVID ATTENBOROUGH'S VOICE: As you see, mayflies can be quite affectionate . . .

HORACE and MAY: Bzzzzzzzzzzzz . . .

DAVID ATTENBOROUGH'S VOICE: . . . mutually palpating their proboscises.

HORACE: You know, I've been wanting to palpate your proboscis all evening.

MAY: I think it was larva at first sight.

HORACE and MAY: (*Rubbing proboscises together.*) Zzzzzzzzzzzzz-zzzzzzzzzzzzzzzzzz . . .

MAY: (*Very British, "Brief Encounter."*) Oh darling, darling.

HORACE: Oh do darling do let's always be good to each other, shall we?

MAY: Let's do do that, darling, always, always.

HORACE: Always?

MAY: Always.

HORACE and MAY: Zzzzzzzzzzzzzzzzzzzzzzzzzzzzzzzzzzzz!

MAY: Rub my antennae. Rub my antennae. (HORACE *rubs* MAY's *antennae with his hands.*)

DAVID ATTENBOROUGH'S VOICE: Sometimes mayflies rub antennae together.

MAY: Oh yes. Yes. Just like that. Yes. Keep going. Harder. Rub harder.

HORACE: Rub mine now. Rub my antennae. Oh yes. Yes. Yes. Yes. There's the rub. There's the rub. Go. Go. Go!

DAVID ATTENBOROUGH'S VOICE: Isn't that a picture. Now get a load of mating.

(HORACE *gets into mounting position, behind* MAY. *He rubs her antennae while she wolfs down the gnat-food in front of her.*)

HORACE and MAY: Bzzzzzzzzzzzzzzzzzzzzzzzzzzzzzzzzzzzzzzzzzz!

DAVID ATTENBOROUGH'S VOICE: Unfortunately for this insect, the mayfly has a life span of only one day.

(HORACE *and* MAY *stop buzzing, abruptly.*)

HORACE: What was that . . . ?

DAVID ATTENBOROUGH'S VOICE: The mayfly has a life span of only one day—living just long enough to meet, mate, have offspring, and die.

MAY: Did he say "meet, mate, have offspring, and DIE"—?

DAVID ATTENBOROUGH'S VOICE: I did. In fact, mayflies born at seven-thirty in the morning will die by the next dawn.

HORACE: (*Whimpers softly at the thought.*)

DAVID ATTENBOROUGH'S VOICE: But so much for the lowly mayfly. Let's move on to the newt.

(*"Cuckoo!"*)

HORACE *and* MAY: We're going to die . . . We're going to die! Mayday, mayday! We're going to die!

(*Weeping and wailing, they kneel, beat their breasts, cross themselves, daven, and tear their hair.*)

(*"Cuckoo!"*)

HORACE: What time is it? What time is it?

MAY: I don't wear a watch. I'm a lowly mayfly!

HORACE: (*Weeping.*) Wah-ha-ha-ha!

MAY: (*Suddenly sober.*) Well isn't this beautiful.

HORACE: (*Gasping for breath.*) Oh my goodness. I think I'm having an asthma attack. Can mayflies have asthma?

MAY: I don't know. Ask Mr. Safari Jacket.

HORACE: Maybe if I put a paper bag over my head . . .

MAY: So this is my sex life?

HORACE: Do you have a paper bag?

MAY: One bang, a bambino, and boom—that's it?

HORACE: Do you have a paper bag?

MAY: For the common mayfly, foreplay segues right into funeral.

HORACE: Do you have a paper bag?

MAY: I don't have time to look for a paper bag, I'm going to be *dead* very shortly, all right?

(*"Cuckoo!"*)

HORACE: Oh come on! That wasn't a whole hour!

(*"Cuckoo!"*)

Time is moving so fast now.

(*"Cuckoo!"*)

HORACE and MAY: Shut up!

(*"Cuckoo!"*)

HORACE: (*Suddenly sober.*) This explains everything. We were born this morning, we hit puberty in midafternoon, our biological clocks went BONG, and here we are. Hot to copulate.

MAY: For the one brief miserable time we get to do it.

HORACE: Yeah.

MAY: Talk about a quickie.

HORACE: Wait a minute, wait a minute.

MAY: Talk fast.

HORACE: What makes you think it would be so brief?

MAY: Oh, I'm sorry. Did I insult your vast sexual experience?

HORACE: Are you more experienced than I am, Dr. Ruth? Luring me here to your pad?

MAY: I see. I see. Blame me!

HORACE: Can I remind you we only get one shot at this?

MAY: So I can rule out multiple orgasms, is that it?

HORACE: I'm just saying there's not a lot of time to hone one's erotic technique, okay?

MAY: Hmp!

HORACE: And I'm trying to sort out some very big entomontological questions here rather quickly, do you mind?

MAY: And I'm just the babe here, is that it? I'm just a piece of tail.

HORACE: I'm not the one who suggested TV.

MAY: I'm not the one who wanted to watch *Life on Earth*. "Oh— 'Swamp Life.' That sounds *interesting*."

FROG: Ribbit, ribbit.

HORACE: (*Calmly.*) There's a frog up there.

MAY: Oh, I'm really scared. I'm terrified.

FROG: Ribbit, ribbit!

HORACE: (*Calling to the* FROG.) We're right down here! Come and get us!

MAY: Breeding. Dying. Breeding. Dying. So this is the whole purpose of mayflies? To make more mayflies?

HORACE: Does this world *need* more mayflies?

MAY: We're a major food source for trout and salmon.

HORACE: How nice for the salmon.

MAY: Do you want more food?

HORACE: I've lost a bit of my appetite, all right?

MAY: Oh. Excuse me.

HORACE: I'm sorry. Really, May.

MAY: (*Starts to cry.*) Males!

HORACE: Leaf?

(*He plucks another leaf and hands it to her.*)

MAY: Thank you.

HORACE: Really. I didn't mean to snap at you.

MAY: Oh, you've been very nice.

(*"CUCKOO!" They jump.*)

Under the circumstances.

HORACE: I'm sorry.

MAY: No, I'm sorry.

HORACE: No, I'm sorry.

MAY: No, I'm sorry.

HORACE: No, I'm sorry.

MAY: We'd better stop apologizing, we're going to be dead soon.

HORACE: I'm sorry.

MAY: Oh Horace, I had such plans. I had such wonderful plans. I wanted to see Paris.

HORACE: What's Paris?

MAY: I have no fucking idea.

HORACE: Maybe we'll come back as caviar and find out.

(*They laugh a little at that.*)

I was just hoping to live till Tuesday.

MAY: (*Making a small joke.*) What's a Tuesday?

(*They laugh a little more at that.*)

The sun's going to be up soon. I'm scared, Horace. I'm so scared.

HORACE: You know, May, we don't have much time, and really, we hardly know each other—but I'm going to say it. I think you're swell. I think you're divine. From your buggy eyes to the thick raspy hair on your legs to the intoxicating scent of your secretions.

MAY: Eeeuw.

HORACE: Eeeuw? No. I say *woof.* And I say who cares if life is a swamp and we're just a couple of small bugs in a very small pond. I say live, May! I say . . . darn it . . . live!

MAY: But how?

HORACE: Well, I don't honestly know that . . .

(ATTENBOROUGH *appears.*)

DAVID ATTENBOROUGH: You could fly to Paris.

MAY: We could fly to Paris!

HORACE: Do we have time to fly to Paris?

MAY: Carpe diem!

HORACE: What is carpe diem?

DAVID ATTENBOROUGH: It means "bon voyage."

HORACE and MAY: And we're outta here!

(*They fly off to Paris as . . .*)

(*Blackout.*)

WAR AT HOME

STUDENTS RESPOND TO SEPTEMBER 11TH

Nicole Quinn & Nina Shengold

And Joe Augustine, Jason Backenroth, Katie Brooks, Anna Burstein, Deana Dor, Al Favata, Phoenix Greco, Allison LaPlatney, Jesse Leavitt, Melissa Leo, Robin Markle-Kellar, Genni Minnisali, Dyami Nason-Regan, Justine Nye, Sam Packard, Amish Patel, Snehal Patel, Halley Petersen-Jobsis, Abby Pilmenstein, Elias Primoff, Shayla Raleigh, Joseph Reeder, Callie Rockwell, Josh Rubenstein, Sierra Rudy, Kate Sarrantonio, Ilyana Sawka, Jessie Schain, Michelle Shirak, Alison Sickler, Mica Stanmyer, Raquel Steres, Tullah Sutcliffe, Jamie Wilber, Emily Wolford, Ilana Workman, Thomas Workman, Shelley Wyant, Sandy Zerbe, Mike Zimmerman

---

War at Home premiered at Rondout Valley High School in Accord, New York, on December 7, 2001.

CHARACTERS

STUDENTS:
ARTIST
BULLY
CHEERLEADER
FIREBRAND
FRESHMAN
GADFLY
INTROVERT
JOCK
MUSICIAN
MUSLIM
PATRIOT
SLACKER DUDE
WORRIER
ENSEMBLE MEMBERS

OTHERS:
ANNOUNCER
ARAB MAN
ARAB WOMAN
HOLLYWOOD EXECUTIVE
HOLLYWOOD SCREENWRITER
MOTHER
NEIGHBOR
TEACHER

HOW THIS PLAY WAS WRITTEN

Shortly after September 11, two writers attended a peace ceremony on the soccer field of Rondout Valley High School, 100 miles north of Ground Zero. We were moved by the students' passion and eloquence as they spoke at an open mike, and decided to create a theater piece from their words and experiences.

We met with the Drama and Diversity Clubs and invited the students to participate in a series of workshops. Over thirty writers showed up. At each session, we asked several questions, ranging from "How did you first hear the news?" to "How do you feel when you see the American flag?" The students wrote their responses on the spot and turned in their writings anonymously, so that they could feel free to express controversial opinions and private fears. We also gave each student a folder and urged them to bring in anything they read in the paper or on the Internet that spoke to them. We edited these together into a kind of theatrical quilt, organizing the material into characters with different voices and points of view. Then we cast these roles and rehearsed the script. Many of the student writers also performed in the cast, but the words they spoke (and viewpoints expressed) were not necessarily their own.

This play can be performed simply, on a bare stage with scripts in hand, or in a more polished production. Music plays an essential role, and live music, no matter how simple the instrumentation, will help to establish a rhythm and tone for each scene. Any number of students can participate in the ensemble, and speaking roles may be combined or redivided to suit your needs. You can use teachers, community members, or other adults as the nonstudent characters, or cast students in these roles as well. Most of the roles can be played by actors of any race or gender; the more diverse, the better.

Special thanks to Juilliard violinist William Harvey for permission to use his letter, and to everyone who worked on the play's first production. It was a joy and a privilege to work with these honest, impassioned, and fearless young people. We hope that their words may be useful to others.

NINA SHENGOLD AND NICOLE QUINN

December 7, 2001

(A makeshift shrine on the empty stage: an assortment of candles, flowers, and flags on a central platform, in front of two huge canvas flats that echo the shape of the Twin Towers, with a newsprint and photo collage of the Lower Manhattan skyline along the base.)

(STUDENTS are scattered throughout the theater ["at home"]. Flute music plays as the audience enters.)

P.A. ANNOUNCER: Good morning, it's Tuesday, September 11th, 2001. Homeroom.

(A school bell rings. STUDENTS respond as if it's their alarm clock, with sleepy groans, stretches, etc. They begin to speak from wherever they are, slowly making their way to the stage ["school"] as the houselights dim.)

PATRIOT: 6:00 a.m.

JOCK: Late.

ARTIST: Too early.

JOCK/FRESHMAN/WORRIER: Late!

FIREBRAND: *(Groggy.)* 6:15.

MOTHER: Wake up, second day of school.

FIREBRAND: *(Still groggy.)* 6:25.

MOTHER: Wake up, time to get up.

FIREBRAND: *(Yes, still groggy.)* 6:35.

MOTHER: You're going to be late.

FIREBRAND: (*Rousing herself with effort.*) 6:45.

MOTHER: It's about time. What do you want for lunch?

SLACKER DUDE: So tired. Don't want to go to school.

GADFLY: Falling asleep in the shower.

CHEERLEADER: Blue jeans, a white tank top, and a long-sleeved pink shirt with embroidered flowers along the V-neckline. I blow-dry my hair and put on my makeup.

ARTIST: Exhausted. Wear yesterday's clothes.

CHEERLEADER: I look cute and can't wait to see my friends.

GADFLY: I'm mad there's a dress code, so I wear a T-shirt with grapes on the bust and the words, "gently squeezed by loving hands."

BULLY: Shredded wheat sucks.

CHEERLEADER: Blueberry yogurt.

MUSLIM: Whole wheat toast with strawberry jam.

GADFLY: Doritos or Cheese Nips?

MOTHER: You'll catch a chill if you take a shower and then stand at the bus stop.

FIREBRAND: How will I catch a chill? I have no hair!

TEACHER: I stayed up late, so I wake up late. Don't have time to bathe. Gulp coffee on the way to school. I don't spend enough time with the kids. Hear about them secondhand. Note to self: play with kids.

NEIGHBOR: My neighbor's son peels out of the driveway with rap music blaring. *Teenagers!* (*Yelling.*) It's 7:00 a.m.!

BULLY: (*Yelling right back.*) Eat my dust!

INTROVERT: I ride my bike to school, thinking it's cold and how dumb it is riding my bike.

ARTIST: I ride the bus as usual, listening to the middle schoolers scream as usual.

FRESHMAN: Getting sneered at because I'm a freshman.

ARTIST: Thinking insignificant little thoughts about my insignificant little life.

PATRIOT: Are these jeans too tight?

WORRIER: Do I have my lunch money?

ARTIST: Who's gonna be in my study hall?

WORRIER: Can I REALLY find my classes?

MOTHER: Hey-ya! Lift that leg, Billy Blanks, the Tae-Bo king, flashing a toothy grin from the TV screen. Do I have to?

NEIGHBOR: (*Shooing a squirrel.*) Get out of my garden! Shoo!

INTROVERT: A regular day. Everyone saying hey and people, as usual, having their sarcastic comments to me.

ARTIST: This is going to be a really hard year. Some of my teachers really suck. There's no one in my lunch.

SLACKER DUDE: Just want to go to sleep.

ARTIST: Don't want winter to come. It feels so empty.

(*School bell rings.* STUDENTS *disperse into "hallway" positions.*)

JOCK: My first gym class. Gonna kick ass.

FRESHMAN: English.

INTROVERT: Chemistry.

ARTIST: Health, not study hall. Yuck.

WORRIER: Ceramics?

FIREBRAND: I'm sitting in the auditorium, thinking, how lame.

TEACHER: Third period prep. I walk off into the woods for a smoke, commune with nature, solitude from the swarm. On my way back into my room I pass a study hall. The sound of the radio catches my attention, and I think, that's a pretty laid-back study hall, teacher lets 'em listen to the radio.

WORRIER: Two teachers are talking. They sound scared.

PATRIOT: Spanish class. Hear something about New York City, some kind of plane crash.

WORRIER: A plane crash? That's not *too* bad.

FIREBRAND: My friend mutters something about . . .

INTROVERT: (*Freaked, to herself.*) . . . People flying 747s into buildings.

FIREBRAND: She's on Mars.

ARTIST: Hey, is there a fire drill today?

GADFLY: Uh, I don't know since we're like getting bombed.

ARTIST: What are you talking about?

GADFLY: Uh yeah, dumbwit, didn't you hear?

ARTIST: Shut up, what are you talking about? (*To audience.*) I'm thinking, what a stupid joke, 'cause I knew it was a joke.

GADFLY: Yeah, two planes bombed New York.

ARTIST: Hey, what's she talking about? She just said we got bombed or something.

CHEERLEADER: No, it's true.

ARTIST: It's *true*?

WORRIER/PATRIOT/MUSLIM/FRESHMAN/BULLY: WHAT??

(*Lines start to overlap, building in hysteria.* BULLY *turns to* JOCK.)

BULLY: Hey man, did you hear what happened?

JOCK: No, man, what?

BULLY: The World Trade Center was bombed!

JOCK: What the f——?

BULLY: Yeah!

INTROVERT: All of my teachers are acting weird. I'm weirded out.

PATRIOT: One of the towers *collapsed*!

TEACHER: Radios on. Rumors flying. Did you hear—

PATRIOT: I heard—

WORRIER: What did *you* hear?

SLACKER DUDE: (*To* JOCK.) Dude, our country just got like totally annihilated, man!

CHEERLEADER: (*Overhearing, turns.*) What??

SLACKER DUDE: Yes! Dude, the Pentagon's like the shit of our whole country. We're going *down*!

JOCK: Whoa!

CHEERLEADER: Oh my God, are you serious?

PATRIOT: Is this really happening?

MUSLIM: What's going on?

CHEERLEADER: It's completely crazy!

(*Her boyfriend,* JOCK, *hugs her.*)

BULLY: Who did this?

INTROVERT: We're gonna die.

ARTIST: My dad's in New York!!!

TEACHER: I was seven when President Kennedy was shot. Duck and cover drills. Panic.

WORRIER: Why don't they *tell* us what's going on??

P.A. ANNOUNCEMENT: ". . . So if you are in need of assistance for mental health, we want you to know that we're here for you."

(SLACKER *and* GADFLY *crack up.* ARTIST *starts quietly sobbing.*)

FIREBRAND: The world outside Rondout could blow up and we'd never know.

(*School bell rings.*)

P.A. ANNOUNCER: First Period. Social Studies.

(*The* STUDENTS *scatter across the stage. Some in small "family" groups, with nonspeaking characters acting as parents and siblings, others alone.*)

SLACKER DUDE: When I got home my mom was waiting outside, I was like, damn it.

REBEL: Turned on CNN.

SLACKER DUDE: NPR.

JOCK: CBS.

ARTIST: The plane crashing into the building, over and over again in endless reruns.

MUSLIM: People running, chased by a huge cloud of smoke and debris.

GADFLY: A somber five-year-old boy, clutching a fireman's hat half his size.

CHEERLEADER: This woman still covered with dust, talking about how she saw a woman running with her baby, just being trampled. At that point all my emotions came flowing out like a river. I just cried and cried, and then I was angry and confused and just about every other emotion I could possibly feel.

REBEL: We all sat down the rest of the night and watched TV.

When we ate dinner we left it on to see if anything else would happen.

BULLY: Forget homework.

FIREBRAND: Homework: Notes for English. Today is Tuesday, "named for the Norse God of War."

INTROVERT: When I got home, my parents were screaming at me, so I walked out.

JOCK: My dad said that we as a country had brought this on ourselves, and I agreed.

CHEERLEADER: My mom and I cried when we saw people sing "Land of Liberty."

PATRIOT: (*Singing.*) "God Bless America . . ."

FRESHMAN: Yeah, well of course I cried!

ARTIST: Angry at myself for crying. Feeling unjustified because I'd heard from my dad and that was my main concern. An e-mail: "Hi, I'm okay. Love, Dad." Well, that is simply far too real. I can't accept the simplicity of it.

FRESHMAN: I cried till it hurt.

BULLY: I felt nothing.

INTROVERT: Everything.

MUSLIM: I'm terrified every time someone overtly notices my brown skin. Afraid of their anger.

WORRIER: Afraid.

CHEERLEADER: I felt very sad, and I can't explain, there aren't enough words in the world to explain what my heart felt at that moment.

ARTIST: That night the house was quiet, everyone thinking and very sad.

GADFLY: . . . thinking Aaliyah had just died, and that woman got hit on the bus to work.

WORRIER: I can't decide if I'm more nervous with my door open or shut.

PATRIOT: I'm one of those people that believe in the saying, "Don't think of it as a loss, think of this person as one more angel in heaven."

WORRIER: Bad people. War. Bombs. War.

JOCK: My mom wouldn't stop complaining about how she didn't believe my brother and I understood the magnitude of what happened. Ever since, the TV has been on, it's like she's obsessed.

ARTIST: My life is still unimportant compared to those who don't have one anymore.

WORRIER: I puked.

ARTIST: I was scared. I took the dog outside and saw two planes in the sky. The guy next door told me it was okay, that they were supposed to be there.

MUSLIM: Am I safe? I heard that someone at school was talking about beating me up.

FRESHMAN: My mom didn't want me to go back to school. I said, "Mom, I'm not going to hide in fear of these people! I'm going to school tomorrow."

GADFLY: Food. Always comforting. Carbos and fat. Macaroni and cheese.

FIREBRAND: I didn't need comfort. I didn't want comfort. There was a candlelight vigil at the rec center. I went to the movies instead.

WORRIER: I am certain that Pakistan's center will not hold and it will destabilize and be overrun by Islamic fanatics, who will wield the nuclear bomb, as a catalyst for World War III, thus fulfilling Nostradamus's prediction of the third Antichrist coming out of the Middle East. This frightens me.

SLACKER DUDE: I am unaffected. I am sadly comfortable.

INTROVERT: I went to my room and put on my favorite song to cheer me up. The song is "The Immigrant" by the Prodigals. I only sing one part of the song 'cuz it means something to me. It goes . . .

"You can drink when you're dry
You can laugh till you cry
But the tears in your eyes keep on falling . . ."

I love that part. Then I went to bed hoping everything would be the same tomorrow. It wasn't.

(*The school bell rings.*)

P.A. ANNOUNCER: Second Period. Accounting.

(*The full* GROUP *sits on the floor in rows, as if in a classroom, hands raised. They lower their hands in turn as* TEACHER *calls on them to speak.*)

CHEERLEADER: I have friends I babysit for who live in the city and I couldn't get ahold of them for what seemed like forever.

MOTHER: I kept dialing over and over. The circuits are busy, the circuits are busy, all circuits are busy.

ARTIST:
My mom called my grandmother and I found out that she watched the second plane crash from her apartment's balcony.

GADFLY:
I talked to some friends in New York. They told me about being evacuated and National Guardsmen on every corner.

FIREBRAND: My friends live twelve blocks from Ground Zero. They're Internet shopping for gas masks.

NEIGHBOR: Whenever the phone rang, I grabbed it.

FRESHMAN/WORRIER/ARTIST: Hello?

NEIGHBOR: My mother.

MUSLIM/SLACKER/PATRIOT/GADFLY/JOCK: Hello?

NEIGHBOR: On East Ninety-third Street, five miles away, they couldn't even see the smoke.

ALL STUDENTS: *Hello?*

NEIGHBOR: "It's so *quiet*," she said, and her voice sounded lost.

WORRIER: My friend . . .

FIREBRAND: My cousin . . .

ARTIST: My dad . . .

GADFLY: My sister-in-law's brother's girlfriend . . .

WORRIER:	FIREBRAND:	ARTIST:
. . . Was crying . . .	. . . Was near there.	. . . Was supposed to be in the city.

MUSLIM/SLACKER DUDE/JOCK: I didn't know anyone.

JOCK: So many people. Who were they?

WORRIER/INTROVERT/ENSEMBLE MEMBERS: I didn't know anyone.

BULLY: I know someone who died in the attacks. I don't remember him all that well, but his name is Gerry Nevins and he has two sons that are seven and five.

PATRIOT: My aunt who lives in California works for American Airlines, and a regular flight that she takes all the time is the one from Boston to LAX. But for some reason she wasn't on that particular flight. All her coworkers who she is close with were killed. My uncle wants her to quit her job. He told her he'd sell the house, the cars, whatever it takes so she'd be there to raise their kids.

FIREBRAND: I lost a friend in New York that day, but not in the way most would think. He was talking to me over the Net during the evening, and he said all Arabs were stupid, so I told him what a total moron he was and told him to fuck off. We haven't spoken since.

SLACKER DUDE: I called my friend at 8:30 and I was like, "Are you okay?"

ENSEMBLE MEMBER: Yeah, ha, I'm fine.

SLACKER DUDE: Man, I'm sick to death of all this death and destruction.

ENSEMBLE MEMBER: Oh yeah! Me too.

TEACHER: We were down in the city a week ago. Ate in an Indian restaurant on Sixth Street and took the subway to Battery Park for a sunset ride on the Staten Island Ferry. On the way back, the Twin Towers were lit and the harbor looked gorgeous. The kids begged me to take the elevator up to the observation deck . . .

FRESHMAN/MUSICIAN: Please, Daddy. Pleeeeeeease . . . ?

TEACHER: Some other time.

WORRIER: So many people.

JOCK: Who *were* they??

MOTHER: Hiya! Lift that leg again! Billy Blanks urging me to hurt myself more. Make me sweat. I try to remember the order of my day. What comes after this torture is through? Football? Dance class? Who needs to be where when? What's for dinner? Feed the dog. Laundry. Christ! When do I write? Avocado. Mmm . . . that's what I'll eat when this is over. No. Ice cream, cookies . . . shut up. Just lift that friggin' leg one more time. Phone's ringing. Now what? Do I screen? Do I pause?

    "Hello?" It's my husband's brother, Jake. He's in D.C.

He asks if Paul's in the city. "Yeah. He had a meeting this morning." He wants to know where. "I don't know. Am I supposed to be your brother's keeper?" His voice sounds strange. "Is the meeting at the Trade Center?" I don't know, maybe. Turn on my TV? I do. I see Billy midsquat and reluctantly watch him dissolve into a smoking tower. Voices are saying things. Words. But I don't hear them. My stomach goes hollow. My legs give out. "I'll call you back."

Call his cell phone. I punch in the numbers. Mess it up. Punch again. Shit!! And again. Recorded message about busy circuits. Paul's office. I don't know the number by heart. Find it, his friggin' business card. I keep glancing at the screen. Disbelief. Horror. Another plane plows into tower two. Fear. My life. My family. Too much death already. Mama. My brother. My sister's cancer. Not my husband too! Please God, not that! Oh . . . the phone, someone's talking. It's Eric in the office, "I don't think he's there. But, shit, Nico, we've got a crew on the hundred and third floor in tower one. I've got them on walkie. They're stuck in the stairwell. No way down. One guy made it to the roof. Nothing there. Am I saying the right things? I don't know what to do." I'm thinkin', Jesus, Eric, I'm having my own fucking crisis here. But instead I say, "You're doing great, Eric. Just stay calm, they need you to stay calm."

It's 9:30 a.m. I hang up. I call the cell. I call the cell. I call the cell. I'm now intimate with the series of tones. The annoying sameness of the message. I call the office. "Eric . . ?" Before I can say anything he's launched into it, "I lost them. They were crying. It was too hot. The line went dead. I think they jumped."

It's 9:45 and my panic level is at an all-time high. I have reached target heart rate without even one Billy kick. "Eric? Are you okay?" ". . . No," he says. "I'm not." "Go home," I tell him. "Go home and kiss your son." I hang up.

The towers have collapsed! How many people were still in there? And on the planes? Where is my frickin' husband?!

If he's not dead, I'm going to kill him for not calling. Where is he?! It's 10:00 a.m. I'm punching the air in pure frustration. The phone rings. "Hello?!" I try to rein in the hysteria which has risen in my throat. "Hi, Neeks, just thought I'd check in to let you know I'm okay. I'm with this guy who's called everyone he knows to let them know he's alive. Can you believe that?" I smile. I nod. I cry.

(*The bell rings.*)

P.A. ANNOUNCER: Third Period. Creative Writing. "Somewhere in Hollywood . . ."

(*Snot-nosed* STUDIO EXECUTIVE *sails on in a rolling office chair, followed by opportunistic* SCREENWRITER. *Very L.A.*)

EXECUTIVE: We love sequels! Action movie sequels. Horror sequels. This sure feels like a movie, doesn't it? I kept expecting to see Bruce Willis jump out of the Twin Towers, machine guns blazing, carrying stranded victims to safety. Die-Hard Nine, or Ten, or whatever it is now, I lost track. So what have you got for me?

SCREENWRITER: "Gulf War II: Operation Infinite Justice . . ."

(EXECUTIVE *grimaces/groans.*)

. . . OK, er, "Enduring Freedom."

EXECUTIVE: Better.

SCREENWRITER: It'll be great! Just like "Gulf War: Operation Desert Storm." Same plot points, same themes, same characters, same ending . . . we hope.

EXECUTIVE: Tell me more.

SCREENWRITER: The hero. Literally, George Bush II. Same advisors, same politics, same name, same charming accent, but *new* catchphrases! Like "This is a war between freedom and fear."

EXECUTIVE: Love it.

SCREENWRITER: The villain, Osama bin Laden, is Saddam Hussein II, Hitler III. "He's worse than Hitler!"

EXECUTIVE: Isn't that the tagline we used last time?

SCREENWRITER: Osama's just like Saddam: powerful, cruel, intelligent, sneaky, he doesn't like us but people like him. We armed Saddam. And we made Osama: the CIA trained him to fight the USSR.

EXECUTIVE: Massive plot holes. One of the biggest being, why do they hate us?

SCREENWRITER: . . . They hate freedom?

EXECUTIVE: Please, no complex answers that cause us to look into ourselves or our foreign policy, not in an action movie.

SCREENWRITER: Oil.

EXECUTIVE: Oil . . .

SCREENWRITER: . . . Oil! We'd be building a pipeline through Afghanistan if they didn't hate us.

(EXECUTIVE *nods, interest piqued.*)

EXECUTIVE: Collateral damage?

SCREENWRITER: Plenty. Civilians get killed while the bad guys hide in bunkers, caves, and palaces. Oops. We all make mistakes. Our intentions are good.

EXECUTIVE: The Gulf War was cool, wasn't it? Like a video game. Think of the licensing ops. Lots of great visuals: violent, though sanitized.

SCREENWRITER: Right. We don't see the villagers getting killed, the desperate people stepping on land mines in an attempt to reach the food we drop, or the rations landing on people, since we don't attach parachutes to them.

EXECUTIVE: Every movie needs comic relief.

SCREENWRITER: What we do see are big, cool explosions. We win! We go in, blow a bunch of stuff up, we get out with just a few smudges.

EXECUTIVE: So did Saddam.

SCREENWRITER: And so will bin Laden.

EXECUTIVE: We'll bring them both back for "Gulf War III: Operation God Is on Our Side!"

(*They shake on the deal and drag-race offstage in their rolling chairs.*)

(*School bell rings.*)

P.A. ANNOUNCER: Fourth Period. U.S. History.

(MUSICIAN *carries on an American flag and all* STUDENTS *line up in rows for the Pledge of Allegiance.* GADFLY *and* ARTIST *stand in semi-respectful silence with their arms at their sides.* FIREBRAND *folds her arms and glowers aggressively.*)

GROUP: I pledge allegiance to the flag
　　　　Of the United States of America—

(GROUP *freezes as each steps forward to speak to the audience in turn.*)

PATRIOT: A patriotic tingle surrounding my skin.

GROUP: And to the Republic for which it stands—

JOCK: Softball fields. Cheeseburgers. I feel, American.

GROUP: One nation, under God—

ARTIST: My allegiance doesn't lie in a piece of colored cloth.

GROUP: Indivisible—

CHEERLEADER: Seeing all those flags on the cars makes me think, "Wow, we're all in this together."

BULLY: United we stand!

GROUP: With liberty and justice for all.

GADFLY: But only if you fly the flag, toe the line, keep your mouth shut.

GROUP: (*Faster.*) I pledge allegiance to the flag
Of the United States of America

(*Lower volume and continue under the following speeches, repeating as needed.*)

NEIGHBOR: You know what, though? I'm worried because I *don't* have a flag on my car. I'm afraid somebody will shoot me. I went into three stores to buy one and they were sold out.

FIREBRAND: What I want to know is who's *selling* these things? They are *everywhere.* And where are they made? Sweatshop labor in where, Indonesia, Hong Kong, Detroit?

FRESHMAN: I want to be a proud American.

ARTIST: I'm not proud of muscles flexed with megaton warheads.

PATRIOT: The flag represents our country. Even through the worst tragedies we can survive . . . make a comeback and show everyone that we're strong.

WORRIER: I heard that a man burned a flag in the street, yelling, "Allah! Allah!" while people got out of their cars and beat him to the ground.

BULLY: He deserved it!

(*Group pledge comes to an end, getting louder on the last phrase.*)

GROUP: . . . with liberty and justice for all.

(MUSICIAN *carries the flag back out as* STUDENTS *remove hands from hearts, relaxing, addressing each other as well as the audience as they move into their next position.*)

CHEERLEADER: When we started bombing Afghanistan, I was glad we were doing something.

FRESHMAN: Some people, my dad for example, say war is the best and only solution sometimes. I don't want to believe that.

SLACKER DUDE: Dude, America is so fucked up, man. I can't believe we're bombing!

BULLY: Bomb them all.

ARTIST: Now we're terrorists too.

BULLY: Blow them off the face of the earth.

ARTIST: We're just asking for more.

MUSLIM: I've never had so many nightmares in my life as I've had this past month. Worried about my family.

BULLY: Nuke 'em.

ARTIST: It isn't worth killing civilians to make us look strong.

INTROVERT: I have no opinion.

FIREBRAND: Have you noticed how much less news coverage there is of us bombing *them*?

GADFLY: The crater formerly known as Afghanistan.

FIREBRAND: Ash-ghanistan.

SLACKER DUDE: I mostly don't talk about it. It's just in my head.

FRESHMAN: I'm glad that we're bombing. I think.

JOCK: I don't want to be drafted.

(*School bell rings.*)

P.A. ANNOUNCER: Fifth Period. Foreign Language.

(*A Middle Eastern instrument plays a muezzinlike call. A* MAN *in traditional Arab robes, a head wrap covering most of his face, walks slowly down the aisle of the auditorium.* STUDENTS *cluster to look.* MUSLIM *hangs back from the rest of the group.*)

CHEERLEADER/ARTIST/WORRIER/BULLY: Who is he?

MUSLIM: What is he thinking?

CHEERLEADER: What does he believe?

WORRIER: Whose side is he on?

BULLY: *Them.*

ARTIST: I look away, then feel guilty and give him a smile.

INTROVERT: Who *are* they??

ARTIST: (*Smile still pasted.*) I hope he won't think I'm a racist. He looks like Muhith's father. Muhith Mussabir, my best friend in fifth grade. What happened to him?

MOTHER: I jump to conclusions based on appearance. My whole life, it's been people doing that to me. And yet . . .

NEIGHBOR: I don't exactly want to accuse anybody who looks Middle Eastern, but who can you trust now?

JOCK: Celebration in the streets of Nebula.

CHEERLEADER: Little children throwing candy.

JOCK: People chanting:

MUSLIM/JOCK/PATRIOT/CHEERLEADER: "God is good."

BULLY: They're Muslims.

MUSLIM: Why do they hate us so much?

(*A heavily veiled* WOMAN *joins the* MAN.)

GADFLY: The women of Afghanistan.

FIREBRAND: Buried alive in mass graves.

GADFLY: Raped teenagers.

FIREBRAND: Flies inside diseased homes.

GADFLY: It's illegal to smile in public.

FIREBRAND: Women killed for exposing a wrist.

BULLY: We should just bomb them all.

ARTIST: Maybe I shouldn't smile.

JOCK: I heard that the gas station guy was arrested.

BULLY: Hey man, you're making money on the American dream! We deserve it!

PATRIOT: I'm buying American gas!

MUSLIM: I'm scared for my family.

INTROVERT: I'm scared.

WORRIER: Biological warfare. Anthrax.

PATRIOT: I mean, I have plans and stuff for my life. I really don't want to get some stupid disease and die before I have a chance to do anything.

ARTIST: I hate not knowing.

PATRIOT: I heard there was a bomb on the Mid-Hudson Bridge.

FIREBRAND: A bomb *threat*.

PATRIOT: Whatever.

ARTIST: Scary shit. Everybody's so paranoid, and I guess they have some right to be.

FIREBRAND: Timothy McVeigh was a typical American boy and look what *he* did!

GADFLY: Anyone can be a terrorist.

FIREBRAND: Timothy McVeigh. So now do we beat up all skinny white guys?

GADFLY: Like *you*?

MOTHER: The reservoir . . . the orange plastic cones look so flimsy.

NEIGHBOR: Our water.

MOTHER: Right where our kids ride their bicycles.

NEIGHBOR: It's 11:00 a.m. and I'm still in my PJs, okay? I've got work I'm supposed to be doing. I don't sleep anymore. I'm in the vanguard of the freaked-out.

So on Sunday I'm down at Emmanuel's, buying some shrimp for my dinner, and this man at the fish counter is saying the Citgo in town is shut down, and five other Pakistani-run gas and convenience stores, in Shokan, Rosendale, Ellenville. Why? So the FBI can investigate links to the Taliban. The fish guy goes off on a racist rant and I walk away with my jaw dropped. Then I drive by the Citgo, and it *is* closed. And I think, the world as I know it is over. I live in this safe little haven, I don't lock my house, I leave keys in the car overnight. And now that's all over. It's here in my yard.

I mean, let's say Osama bin Laden is buying up gas and convenience stores all around the New York City water supply. They're drivable bombs. You get a gas truck into your station, you hit the driver over the head, and drive away with a movable bomb. You can blow it up, ram it right into the reservoir, poison the water. And the guys in those stations, they're *not* friendly, they're not even neutral, they're actively hostile. It's not like the Greek deli owners or Korean grocery stands in New York—these guys don't *want* to fit in, they give you an attitude. And they're all *men*. Where are the women??

Okay, now is this racist caca? If so, how awful of me to buy into it. My mother was in Auschwitz; how dare I? I don't want to be blaming, the way that the Jews have been blamed. I don't want to spread fear. On the other hand, if it *is* true . . . And this is why I can't get out of bed in the morning.

(*She looks directly at Arab-dressed* MAN *and* WOMAN.)

If this is terrorism, it works. I'm terrified.

(*School bell rings.*)

(*Arab-dressed* MAN *and* WOMAN *exit with graceful dignity.* STUDENTS *move back into "classroom" formation as* SLACKER DUDE *and* WORRIER *rise to give a report.*)

P.A. ANNOUNCER: Sixth Period. Modified Math.

SLACKER DUDE: OK, so the date of the attack is, like, 9-1-1? The emergency number, how weird is that??

WORRIER: And it's all elevens:

9+1+1= 11
September 11 is the 254th day of the year: 2+5+4= 11
The first plane to hit the towers was Flight 11
Flight 11: 92 on board. 9+2=11
New York was the 11th state in the Union
New York City, 11 letters
The Pentagon, 11 letters
Afghanistan, 11 letters

SLACKER DUDE: Whoa, man, my NAME has eleven letters. How scared should I be? I'm going into hiding, like NOW. The terrorists are after me! There must be someplace on Planet Earth I can hide . . . but no, "PLANET EARTH" has eleven letters! Maybe Nostradamus can help me—no WAY, he's got eleven letters too! The Red Cross? T-H-E R-E-D C . . . eleven letters! Somebody help me. Send me e-mail! No, don't—"SEND ME E-MAIL" has eleven letters too!!! Will this never end? I'm going insane! "GOING INSANE" . . . eleven letters! Nooooooooooooooooooo!!!!!!

(*He sinks to his knees.* WORRIER *leans in close.*)

WORRIER: How many letters in "RONDOUT HIGH"?

SLACKER DUDE: ELEVEN!!!

(*The bell rings.* STUDENTS *exit, except for* FRESHMAN.)

P.A. ANNOUNCER: Seventh Period. Music in Our Lives.

(*A* STUDENT MUSICIAN *enters, tuning and warming up as the* FRESH-MAN *steps up to the microphone.*)

FRESHMAN: I read this last night on the Internet. A letter from a Juilliard student, Monday, September 17. (*Reading.*) Yesterday I had the most moving experience of my life. Juilliard organized a quartet to go play at the Armory. The Armory is a huge military building where families of people missing from Tuesday's disaster go to wait for their loved ones. The entire building, the size of a city block, was covered with missing posters. Thousands of posters, spread out to eight feet above the ground, each featuring a different smiling face. I made my way into the huge central room, and found my Juilliard buddies.

(MUSICIAN *plays a brief classical excerpt.*)

For two hours we sight-read quartets (with only three people!). I'll never forget the grief counselor from the Connecticut State Police who listened the whole time, or the woman who listened only to "Memory" from *Cats*, crying the whole time. At seven, the other two players had to leave; they'd been playing since one and couldn't go on.

I volunteered to stay and play solo. A man in fatigues who introduced himself as Sergeant Major asked me if I'd mind playing for his soldiers as they came back from digging in the rubble at Ground Zero. Masseuses had volunteered to give his men massages, he said, and he didn't think anything would be more soothing than getting a massage and listening to violin music. So for the new four hours, I played everything I could from memory: *Eine Kleine Nachtmusik,* "Silent Night," "My Country 'Tis of Thee," "Eel in the Sink."

(MUSICIAN *will pick out stray phrases of various pieces as listed [titles may be changed to accommodate his/her repertoire].*)

Never have I played for a more grateful audience. By the end, my intonation was shot and I had no bow control. I would have lost any competition I was playing in, but it didn't matter. The men would come up the stairs in full gear, remove their helmets, look at me, and smile.

At 11:20 I was introduced to Colonel Slack, head of the Division. After thanking me, he said, "Boy, today was the toughest day yet. I made the mistake of going back into the pit. I'll never do that again." Eager to hear a firsthand account, I asked, "What did you see?" He stopped, swallowed hard and said, "What you'd expect to see."

(MUSICIAN *starts playing "Amazing Grace."*)

(*After a few bars.*) The colonel stood still as I played a lengthy rendition of "Amazing Grace," which he claimed was the best he'd ever heard. I didn't think I could play anymore. I asked the Sergeant Major if it would be appropriate if I played the National Anthem. He shouted above the chaos of the milling soldiers to call them to attention, and I played the National Anthem as the three hundred men of the Sixty-ninth Division saluted an invisible flag.

As I rode the taxi back to Juilliard—free, of course, since taxi service in New York is free right now—I was numb. Not only was this evening the proudest I've ever felt to be an American, it was my most meaningful as a musician and a person as well. At school, kids are hypercritical of each other and very competitive. Teachers expect technical perfection. But this wasn't about that. The soldiers didn't care that I had so many memory slips I lost count. I've never understood so fully what it means to communicate music to other people.

And I'll never forget that when I asked the colonel to describe the pit, he couldn't. Words only go so far, and even music can only go a little bit further from there.

(READER *turns to listen in silence as* MUSICIAN *continues to play "Amazing Grace." The final bell rings.*)

P.A. ANNOUNCER: Eighth Period. Global Studies.

(*The* CAST *appears at the back of the auditorium, moving slowly down both aisles with lit votive candles. Two at a time they step up onstage, placing their candles in front of the Towers, observing a moment of silence as they leave this makeshift shrine. They cluster in small groups, each grieving in his or her own way: some comfort or hug each other, some pray, some stand withdrawn and silent. When all are in place, one student starts to sing. First one voice, then another, then a groundswell.*)

STUDENTS: (*Singing a cappella.*)

> We shall overcome
> We shall overcome
> We shall overcome some day.
> Way down deep in my heart,
> I do believe that we shall overcome some day.

(*A world music beat as* STUDENTS *and other* CHARACTERS *come together, moving from their separate groups into a unified whole. They join hands and move to the front of the stage to lead the audience in song.*)

(*Curtain call and audience exit music: Medley of kick-ass rock songs recently banned from the radio as "too political."*)

END OF PLAY

EXCERPTS

AVEN'U BOYS

Frank Pugliese

Aven'U Boys was originally produced by Naked Angels, opening on September 23, 1989. It was directed by Pippin Parker; the set design was by David Hohmann; the lighting design was by Chris Kondek; the costume design was by Carmel Dundon; the assistant director was Christie Wagner; the fight choreography was by B. H. Barry. The cast was as follows:

WENDY	Marisa Tomei
ANN	Nancy Travis
LINDA	Kasi Lemmons
ED	Patrick Breen
CHARLIE	Fisher Stevens
ROCKY	Rob Morrow

CHARACTERS
(for the Act 2, Scene 3 excerpt)

WENDY

CHARLIE

(*Lights up on* WENDY *lying on the couch of her and* CHARLIE's *place.* CHARLIE's *in the next room quietly trying to dress the baby. The sound of a TV is heard.*)

WENDY: Hey what ya doin'?

CHARLIE: (*Off.*) Nothin'!

WENDY: You gotta be doin' somethin'.

CHARLIE: (*Off.*) Nothin'. Just dressin'!

WENDY: You goin' out again?

CHARLIE: (*Off; pause.*) Bowlin' night.

WENDY: Bowlin' night? Ya ain't bowled on a Friday night since ya was a kid.

CHARLIE: (*Off.*) The bar's havin' a bowlin' night.

WENDY: Bunch a drunks bowlin'. Maybe I should come?

CHARLIE: (*Off.*) No, no it's just for the guys.

WENDY: Rocky goin'?

CHARLIE: (*Off.*) Nah, he don't come around much no more.

WENDY: Charlie, you're missin' the best part, they're gonna burn him now. You eva notice how crazy these Indians are in these movies? Somethin' like you guys at a bowlin' alley.

CHARLIE: (*Off.*) Sounds more like a party at your mother's!

WENDY: Only half-naked shit-hole is my husband. Who jumps into the shower with a bottle of vodka and my eighteen-year-old niece.

CHARLIE: (*Off.*) She's on the high school swimming team.

WENDY: She's also head cheerleader. Don't mean you gotta cheer some head.

CHARLIE: (*Off.*) She ain't blood.

WENDY: And they were almost likin' you. Is Charlie sleepin'?

CHARLIE: (*Off.*) He's always sleepin'.

WENDY: It's all the noise.

(*We hear a burp.*)

WENDY: What was that? Was that the kid?

CHARLIE: (*Off.*) That was me.

WENDY: IS HE UP?

CHARLIE: (*Off.*) Sleepin' like a baby.

(*Another burp.*)

WENDY: Why don't I come in there?

CHARLIE: (*Off.*) Nah, I'm coming out, just buttoning my coat.

WENDY: God, you should see his flesh melt!

(CHARLIE *walks into the living room, carefully carrying a bowling bag.*)

CHARLIE: Well, gotta go.

WENDY: You sure you wanna go bowlin'? We ain't been home alone for a month now. Stay home. We'll play gin, strip, and fuck like the old days.

CHARLIE: Don't wanna be late.

(*Wanting to leave, he turns and the bowling bag burps. They both look at the bag.*)

WENDY: Your bowling bag burped.

CHARLIE: That was me.

WENDY: What's in there?

CHARLIE: Nothin', a bowlin' ball.

WENDY: WHAT THE FUCK IS MY BABY DOIN' IN THAT BOWLING BAG . . . ? I'LL KILL YOU.

CHARLIE: There ain't no baby in there. He's in the crib.

WENDY: Let me see.

(*She goes for the bag. He pulls away.*)

CHARLIE: No.

WENDY: GIVE ME MY BABY.

CHARLIE: Look we're just going out for a walk.

WENDY: In a bowlin' bag? IT'S FREEZING OUT THERE, HE'S GONNA FREEZE TO DEATH.

CHARLIE: He ain't cold, he's in the bowlin' bag.

WENDY: HE'LL SUFFOCATE.

CHARLIE: Nah, there's some little holes to air out my shoes.

(*He goes to open the bag. She grabs one of the handles.*)

WENDY: THE KID'S STAYIN' HOME.

CHARLIE: What you doin'?

WENDY: He ain't goin'.

(*They start to tug.*)

CHARLIE: Let go of the fuckin' kid. We're going to my mother. You happy now? That's all, just to my mother.

WENDY: Your mother. The one who feeds him macaroni like he's dying or somethin'.

CHARLIE: He can use it.

WENDY: The kid's stayin'. I don't want her makin' him a fat little pig.

CHARLIE: LET GO, OR I'LL CRACK YOU.

WENDY: Let go and stop it. YOU CRAZY OR SOMETHIN'? YOU'RE GONNA KILL HIM.

CHARLIE: YOU LET GO.

WENDY: NO.

CHARLIE: LET GO OR I'M GONNA BREAK YOUR FACE.

(*They pull with such force that they both let go. The bag falls to the ground. The baby starts to cry.*)

WENDY: Oh my God.

CHARLIE: See what you done, you stupid bitch? You almost broke my bowlin' bag.

(*She goes for the baby. He lunges forward and grabs the bag.*)

WENDY: I HATE YOU. You're trying to kill him.

CHARLIE: Calm down. I'll be right back. He's my kid too.

WENDY: GIVE ME MY BABY. I HATE YOU, I HATE YOU.

CHARLIE: Yeah, yeah. Everybody hates everybody. So don't be cryin' so much. Look, you got what you want. I married you. And you got your office girl career you made such a big stink about. So stop givin' me shit.

WENDY: Where you goin'? Is it some girl?

CHARLIE: Yeah, I got fifteen blow jobs lined up for tonight.

WENDY: Yeah, well I'm going out too.

CHARLIE: (*Puts bag down on couch as he puts on his coat.*) Go ahead, go out with one of them office boys you always talk about.

WENDY: You liked it all right. Men still find me attractive.

CHARLIE: Yeah, you make me sick.

WENDY: Give me my baby. GIVE ME MY BABY. (*She jumps for the baby on the couch.*)

CHARLIE: GET OUTTA HERE.

WENDY: Give me my baby!

CHARLIE: You're really pissin' me off.

(*He punches her. She staggers and falls as he exits with the bag.*)

WENDY: Leave him. He's Rocky's kid. He's my kid.

(CHARLIE *returns.*)

CHARLIE: He's whose kid?

WENDY: Rocky's.

CHARLIE: What, I can't hear you?

WENDY: Rocky.

CHARLIE: I can't hear you. Are you saying something?

WENDY: IT'S ROCKY'S KID!

CHARLIE: What?

WENDY: Rocky. I fuck him all the time. Before work. At lunch. After work. Just you're the only jerk dumb enough to marry me.

(*She's crying.* CHARLIE *gives her a hug. Pause.*)

CHARLIE: Finders keepers, losers weepers. (*Punches her in the eye and she twists into the fetal position. As he leaves:*) He's mine now.

THE LOOP

Warren Leight

The original showcase production of *The Loop* was at the Harold Clurman Theatre, New York City, on September 8, 1994. Susann Brinkley directed Felicity Huffman as Yvette and Todd Weeks as Jules.

CHARACTERS
(for the Act 1, Scene 5 excerpt)

JULES: Amy's not-too-swift husband. A decent, mild-mannered guy, mid-twenties.
YVETTE: A tough, heartbreaking hooker.

NOTE

Almost every scene in the full-length La Ronde-like play takes place in a bedroom.

Scene 5

(*A cramped New York hotel room that's been ransacked.* JULES [*late-twenties, boyish*] *and* YVETTE [*a local "masseuse," same age, more mileage*] *have just been held up. The assailant tied them together, back to back.*)

JULES: OK—I have a plan.

YVETTE: Jules, isn't it . . . a little late for that?

JULES: Look, I did the best I could.

YVETTE: You're right. I'm sorry. What you did, or tried to do, was very heroic. I'm sure most guys in your position would not have come to my defense. Even as little as you did.

JULES: Well I'm sure I just did what any—What do you mean, my position?

YVETTE: In New York. A hooker in your hotel room. A burglar comes in. A lot of guys would not risk physical harm. Fuck.

JULES: The ropes too tight?

YVETTE: I've been tied up tighter. It's just, I hate to spend the night.

JULES: Don't worry. I'm going to get us out of here. Here's the plan. On the count of three—we're going to scream. OK? Ready. One.

YVETTE: No. Bad plan.

JULES: Two.

YVETTE: Shut up. Shut up.

JULES: Three. HELLL—

YVETTE: (*Elbows him hard.*) SHUT THE FUCK UP!

JULES: Oww. What did you do that for?

YVETTE: Jules—it's a bad plan. If we scream, the cops are going to come, and when they get here, they are going to take one look at you, and then they are going to put my ass in jail.

JULES: Cops?

YVETTE: Jules, we've been robbed. We're tied up. Who do you think is going to come . . . the prize patrol?

JULES: They won't put you in jail.

YVETTE: If they find out that I came over to give you a massage, they're going to book me as an accessory. I swear to God that is—

(*The phone rings.*)

JULES: Shit.

YVETTE: I'll get it. Ha. Ha.

JULES: That's my wife.

YVETTE: Again?

JULES: She's going to worry about me.

YVETTE: The hotel will take a message. Although these places— two hundred ninety a night—and they let it ring and ring and ring.

Lady give it a rest. He's tied up. (*To* JULES.) What is her problem?

(*Phone stops ringing.*)

JULES: I always call, when we're apart. Before I go to bed. You know. It's not like me . . . to stay out.

YVETTE: So tell her what happened.

(JULES *does not think this is a good idea.*)

　　You went out, your last night in town, you and the guys got a little blotto. You came in and passed out.

(*Phone rings again.*)

　　What do you guys have, like phone sex every night? "Oh Jules . . . I'm wet . . . please. Give it to me."

JULES: Is that really necessary?

YVETTE: Then, like you come and she fakes coming and—

JULES: My wife does not fake . . . orgasm.

YVETTE: Ha.

JULES: She doesn't.

YVETTE: Every man tells me this.

JULES and YVETTE: Believe me . . . I know.

YVETTE: Fine. Suit yourself.

JULES: I wish she faked orgasms. I wish I could meet someone, just once, who faked orgasm. How do you meet these women? Where are they? Everyone I've been with . . . it's like, they're pre-orgasmic. They're taking some classes, but they still have some issues about the whole thing. Or—

YVETTE: Everyone you've been with?

JULES: Except for this actress. Once. Daniella. *She* was unbelievable.

YVETTE: What happened to her?

JULES: She's marrying my father-in-law. It's a long story. But all the others, and there haven't been that many, they've got like a road map. Touch me here. Soft. Now fast. There. Left. Right. Did you ever try to drive and read a map at the same time?

YVETTE: I don't understand these women.

JULES: What?

YVETTE: I mean—how hard is it to come?

JULES: Well, I mean . . . obviously it's a mutual . . . you know the mood, the setting . . .

YVETTE: I can come on the subway . . . looking at a Salem ad.

JULES: You're just saying that.

YVETTE: The one with the hose, and the water. I mean . . . what is the big deal. The first time I had sex, it was like, he put it in me . . . ten seconds later. Kaboom. I thought, where have penises been all my life? What is the big deal?

JULES: People are different.

YVETTE: I can come here. Kiss my ear. My ears are sensitive.

(*He tries to kiss her. Can't quite turn around enough.*)

Or my neck sometimes. Just blow on it.

(*He starts to. Stops, then starts again as she moans.*)

Oh Goooooooddd. Jules that was so hot.

JULES: Did you just—

YVETTE: A little one.

JULES: You don't have to do that. I appreciate it, but—

YVETTE: I wasn't faking.

JULES: That's very sweet of you.

YVETTE: I wasn't trying to be sweet. I'm a medical miracle. That's why this is such a good line of work for me.

JULES: What kind of childhood did you have?

YVETTE: Magical.

JULES: Was your father mean to you?

YVETTE: I didn't see him much.

JULES: He abandoned you.

YVETTE: No. He was a truck driver. On the road. But when he was home, sometimes, he was . . . moody. He'd just go nuts. Knock over the furniture, throw things. Little Evie was the only one who could reach him when he was like that.

JULES: Where was your mother?

YVETTE: Dead.

JULES: I'm sorry.

YVETTE: She died when I was seven. After that . . . (*She stops here.*)

JULES: Did he molest you?

YVETTE: (*As if he's crazy.*) What?

JULES: He did, didn't he?

YVETTE: What are you talking about?

JULES: The bastard.

YVETTE: Are you getting off on this?

JULES: No. I'm very sorry . . . for you. What he . . .

YVETTE: He didn't molest me.

JULES: I'm sure it's hard to talk about.

YVETTE: He didn't molest me. He wasn't even a Teamster. I just said it because I thought you . . . guys like to hear that stuff.

JULES: You said it because it was real. You don't have to lie anymore. Sometimes, after the wife dies . . . things happen. It's
not your fault.

YVETTE: I made that up too.

JULES: What?

YVETTE: She didn't die. She just, you know . . . kind of watched
TV and ate frozen food.

JULES: But you said . . .

YVETTE: Look—I . . . guys seem to like these stories. I tell them
what they want to hear. It's exhausting but it's what you
have to do. It's a client business.

JULES: You don't have to lie to me.

YVETTE: Suit yourself.

JULES: (*After a pause.*) My dad drank.

YVETTE: Did I ask you?

JULES: I just thought, you know . . . sometimes it's good to
talk . . .

(*She refuses to say anything. The phone rings.*)

Oh God. (*He tries to get up to answer it. No go.*)

YVETTE: What is this woman's problem? She's calling like a fucking cuckoo clock.

JULES: She loves me.

YVETTE: Are you rich?

JULES: No. She is.

YVETTE: Oh—you're fucked.

JULES: Oh God.

YVETTE: You see what I'm getting at.

JULES: I just remembered. I have a breakfast in the morning. Before my flight. With my wife's father.

YVETTE: Eight different ways.

JULES: We have to get help. OK?

YVETTE: No.

JULES: One. Two.

YVETTE: JULES.

JULES: Three. (*He tries to scream—it comes out wrong. He's crying instead.*) HEL-ah-uu-huh-huh.

YVETTE: Jules, you're pulling the rope.

(*The phone starts to ring again.*)

JULES: (*Cries uncontrollably.*) Why? What did I . . . why me? I— I—

YVETTE: Jesus Christ, do you have to cry?

JULES: I'm . . . I'm so-sor—sob sob sob.

YVETTE: I hate when men cry. Jules—snuff it. I mean, you know, you're not the only one having a tough night here. First I come over on a fucking mission of mercy, and you like freak out—did anyone in the hotel see you? Are you sure? What did they say at the desk? Thanks, like I'm what, bad for your image?

JULES: I'm . . . I was—

YVETTE: *Then* we're about to get down to business, when, boom, psycho dick bursts in and you give the most pathetic rescue attempt I have ever seen, which gets him so mad he not only takes your money, he takes *my* money. Your clothes. My clothes . . .

JULES: My wife left a suitcase in the closet. I can loan you some.

YVETTE: He took that too, Mr. See No Evil.

JULES: What?

YVETTE: And now, the only thing you can think of is to scream until the cops come. And when they come, you'll lose your job—

JULES: Are you sure?

YVETTE: And I'll go to jail.

JULES: No. No. Are you sure he took her suitcase?

YVETTE: Are you listening to me?

JULES: Why would he take her dresses?

YVETTE: Why did she leave them?

JULES: Do you have a boyfriend?

YVETTE: Do you have an attention span?

JULES: I'm sure the police will be fair. They don't put people in jail for no reason.

YVETTE: Where did you grow up?

JULES: Canada.

YVETTE: Figures.

JULES: I think you should be a little more trusting of people.

YVETTE: Jules—they're going to put my ass in jail. The only way to avoid that is for you to tell them I'm an old friend of yours.

JULES: To lie.

YVETTE: Yes, to lie.

JULES: You're wrong. It's just not how things work. I'm going to have to file an insurance claim on all of this, and you can't lie on those forms. You have to sign your name. I'll tell the truth, but because I'm telling the truth—everything will be okay.

YVETTE: What are you going to tell your wife?

JULES: The truth.

YVETTE: Her father?

JULES: The truth again.

YVETTE: And everything will work out all right?

JULES: I think so.

YVETTE: Then why were you crying?

JULES: I don't know. (*Losing it.*) Everything is going to be all right. None of this is going to change anything. My wife loves me. I'm a good worker. You didn't rob me. No one is going to be punished for something that none of us are to blame for. Because . . . because . . . just because.

YVETTE: Suddenly, I am so relieved.

JULES: You see. Things aren't so bad.

YVETTE: For a while, I thought I would have to listen to you cry all night. But now, you've gone completely insane. But with your insanity has come a certain . . . sweetness.

JULES: And I am not going to let them put you in jail. You didn't do anything at all, and you won't have to get in trouble for it.

YVETTE: It might be easier to tell a little white lie.

JULES: Trust me, Yvette. I'm going to take care of everything.

YVETTE: Really.

JULES: Absolutely.

YVETTE: Jules . . .

JULES: One.

YVETTE: You're very sweet . . .

JULES: Two.

YVETTE: Three.

JULES and YVETTE: HELLLP!

MISADVENTURE

Donald Margulies

Misadventure is excerpted from the full-length play *Back Story,* based on characters created by Joan Ackermann. Eighteen playwrights wrote scenes and/or monologues based on Ackermann's story of a brother and sister from Pittsfield, Massachusetts.

Back Story was commissioned by Actors Theatre of Louisville and premiered at the Humana Festival of New American Plays in March 2000. It was directed by Pascaline Bellegarde, Aimée Hayes, Dano Madden, Meredith McDonough, and Sullivan Canaday White; the set design was by Paul Owen; the lighting design was by Greg Sullivan; the costume design was by Kevin McLeod; the sound design was by Darron L. West and Martin R. Desjardins; the properties design was by Mark Walston; the production stage manager was Amber D. Martin; the dramaturgs were Michael Bigelow Dixon and Amy Wegener; the assistant dramaturg was Kerry Mulvaney. The cast was as follows:

ETHAN   Phil Bolin, Cary Calebs, Patrick Dall'Occhio, Jeff Jenkins, Tom Johnson, Cabe McCarty, Tom Moglia, Stephen Sislen, Mark Watson, Zach Welsheimer, Travis York

AINSLEY   Shawna Joy Anderson, Molly M. Binder, Rachel Burttram, Christy Collier, Samantha Desz, Melody G. Fenster, Aimée Kleisner, Kimberly Megna, Holly W. Sims, Heather Springsteen, Jessica Wortham

(*The parking lot of the Danville, New Hampshire, police station.* AINS-
LEY*'s fuming.* ETHAN*'s sheepish. It's cold.*)

AINSLEY: (*To policeman offstage; laced with sarcasm.*) Thank you, Offi-
cer. Thanks a lot. (*To* ETHAN.) Get in the car.

ETHAN: (*Refusing.*) Un-uh.

AINSLEY: Get. In. The. Car.

ETHAN: No way.

AINSLEY: Ethan! Get in the car!

ETHAN: I refuse to get in the car when you're like this.

AINSLEY: Like what?

ETHAN: You're mad at me.

AINSLEY: I am not mad at you.

ETHAN: Yes you are; I can tell: Your nostrils are doing that thing.

AINSLEY: What thing?

ETHAN: *You* know, they kinda . . . (*He demonstrates by flaring his
nostrils.*)

AINSLEY: GETINTHECAR!

ETHAN: What if you lose control and crash into a tree or something?

AINSLEY: I'm not gonna lose control.

ETHAN: How do *you* know? You might get this uncontrollable urge to smack me repeatedly, and *then* what?

AINSLEY: I am not gonna smack you! Get in the car!

ETHAN: I've had enough trauma for one evening, thank you.

AINSLEY: *You've* had enough trauma?!

ETHAN: Yes! The stigma of incarceration will haunt me for years.

AINSLEY: (*Softly.*) Get in the car. (*He shakes his head.*) Ethan, I am too tired and too pissed off—

ETHAN: Ah ha! (*She let her anger slip.*)

AINSLEY: (*Continuous.*) —to be having this argument with you in a police station parking lot in Nowhere, New Hampshire. I'm cold and I want to go home.

ETHAN: I like the cold; the cold feels good. It's sobering me up. I feel more awake than I've ever felt in my life.

AINSLEY: What were you *thinking*?! What in the world were you *thinking*?!

ETHAN: I don't know.

AINSLEY: You don't *know*? Were you trying to *kill* yourself? Huh? Were you? (*He shrugs.*)

ETHAN: No. I don't know. Maybe.

AINSLEY: Maybe?! MAYBE?!

ETHAN: I don't *know*, I said.

AINSLEY: You selfish boy! You stupid selfish boy!

ETHAN: Good. Let it out. I'm glad we're talking now; it's much better than that nostril thing.

AINSLEY: How DARE you be reckless with your life! How DARE you!

ETHAN: Shhh! You're disturbing the peace. You want them to throw *both* of us in jail?

AINSLEY: What's *my* life worth if you trash yours? Huh? Have you thought about that?!! I'll have to live the next seventy-five years haunted every goddamn day by your pimply, ghostly self! We're not just sibs, you stupid moron, we're soul mates! Don't you know that by now?!

ETHAN: (*Childlike, surprised by the depth of her rage, he nods; a beat, softly.*) I'm sorry.

AINSLEY: You drink yourself sick and go hitching on the Interstate?! Are you crazy?! Have I taught you nothing?!

ETHAN: Hey. A. I said I was sorry.

AINSLEY: Never mind being drunk and weaving on the shoulder with cars and trucks whizzing by at eighty miles an hour! Never mind that! What if a crazy person stopped to pick you up—a Jeffrey Dahmer-type or something—

ETHAN: (*Amused.*) What?!

AINSLEY: —and took you away so you were never heard from again! Some Boy Scouts would come across your jawbone one day in the woods! It's a good thing the cops picked you up and threw you in jail. You could've been roadkill!

ETHAN: You're nuts, you know that? You've been watching too much television.

AINSLEY: Don't mock me! There ARE crazy people out there, you know, they're not just CREATED by the media, they exist! There are truly bad and sick people out there in the world who want nothing more than to destroy other people's happiness! (*He cracks up.*) Stop laughing! STOP IT!! It isn't funny! You scared me, Ethan! You scared me to death!! (*She throws punches at him; he protects his head with his hands, laughing until she really hurts him.*)

ETHAN: Ow! (*She stops. Silence.*) That hurt.

AINSLEY: Good.

ETHAN: I can explain.

AINSLEY: Nothing you could possibly say . . .

ETHAN: Aren't you even gonna give me my due process? Aren't you?

AINSLEY: I don't see why I should.

ETHAN: I'm just a kid, you know.

AINSLEY: Oh, God. Is that your excuse? Is that your piss-ant excuse?!

ETHAN: Kids are *supposed* to act out and do reckless things. Right? If not while I'm young, when? When I'm old? When I'm forty?

AINSLEY: The key is surviving long enough to attain wisdom.

ETHAN: Okay, so let's chalk it up to the folly of youth. Okay? I've learned my lesson: I drank a whole lot of really shitty bourbon with some asshole I don't even like whose approval I inexplicably crave and blew Pizza Hut pizza all down my front and onto my brand-new running shoes. Don't you think I'm humiliated enough? I just *bought* these shoes. Like a week ago.

AINSLEY: If you'd *killed* yourself . . . ! If you'd gotten yourself killed for some stupid, peer-pressure, macho, adolescent, alcoholic misadventure. . . . If I'd *lost* you 'cause of it. . . . If I'd *lost* you . . . (*She finally lets herself weep; she turns away from him. He's impressed. Silence.*) Pizza Hut, huh. No wonder you smell like a dairy farmer.

ETHAN: I can't even smell it anymore.

AINSLEY: Trust me.

ETHAN: Oh, yeah, why should I trust *you*?

AINSLEY: Because you'd better. Because if you don't trust *me,* brother, you are a goner. You are toast. (*A beat.*) Now get in the car.

ETHAN: Still mad at me?

AINSLEY: (*Smiling.*) Get in the fucking car?

ETHAN: (*Smiles; a beat, as he gets into the car.*) Can we stop somewhere to get something to eat? I'm starving.

AINSLEY: We'll see. Phew. You stink. (*She starts the car.*)

NIGHT OUT

Sunil Kuruvilla

Night Out is part of a collection of scenes and monologues called *Snapshot,* which was written by seventeen playwrights, all inspired by a single photograph by Lee Friedlander titled *Mount Rushmore, South Dakota, 1969. Snapshot* was commissioned by Actors Theatre of Louisville and premiered at the Humana Festival of New American Plays in March 2002. It was directed by Russell Vanderbroucke; the set design was by Paul Owen; the lighting design was by Tony Penna; the costume design was by John White; the sound design was by Colbert Davis; the properties design was by Doc Manning; the production stage manager was Sarah Hodges; the dramaturgs were Amy Wegener and Tanya Palmer. The cast of *Night Out* was as follows:

MAN   Donovan Sherman
WOMAN   Ellie Clark

(*Two a.m. A small town in upstate New York. A* MAN, *twenty-four, and a* WOMAN, *twenty-eight, search in the snow beside her house, looking for his keys. She uses a flashlight while he struggles in the dark, bending low so he can see the ground.*)

WOMAN: They're gone.

MAN: Don't say that.

WOMAN: There's too much snow.

(*They continue searching.*)

WOMAN: How many did you lose?

MAN: Thirty. I told you.

WOMAN: Why so many?

MAN: My school keys are on that ring.

WOMAN: It would leave a big mark.

MAN: I need your light.

WOMAN: Be nice.

(*The* WOMAN *comes close to share her flashlight.*)

MAN: Stay there.

(*The* WOMAN *goes back to her area and continues looking.*)

WOMAN: Stop moving around. We're not going to find your keys
    if you mess up the snow.

MAN: What time is it?

WOMAN: We still have a few hours.

MAN: More than that!

WOMAN: It's getting light out.

MAN: No it's not.

WOMAN: You want me to check the time?

MAN: What if he leaves work early?

WOMAN: He won't.

MAN: He could get sick and come home.

WOMAN: Don't say that.

MAN: Where are they?

WOMAN: My fingers are cold.

MAN: You didn't put them somewhere?

WOMAN: Why did you come outside?

MAN: To put Kleenex in the garbage.

WOMAN: You couldn't do it when you left?

MAN: I'm always afraid you'll forget and leave it under your bed. I hate having that smell in the room. You have Triple A?

WOMAN: No.

MAN: You're sure?

WOMAN: We don't.

MAN: Why not? Everyone does.

WOMAN: Do you?

MAN: You're sure you didn't hide them?

WOMAN: No I said.

(MAN *drops to his knees feeling the snow with his hands.*)

MAN: I have to get my car out of your driveway.

WOMAN: We can call a tow truck.

MAN: You know how expensive that is?

WOMAN: Don't worry about the money.

MAN: Where do I tow it? Three hours back to the Catskills? You have no idea.

WOMAN: I can pay.

(*The* MAN *stands and walks around, searching.*)

WOMAN: Stop moving around.

MAN: Look inside.

WOMAN: We did.

MAN: If they're inside and your husband finds them later on. Didn't think of that did you? What if my keys are inside?

WOMAN: You dropped by to see him. You wanted to say sorry.

MAN: A year later?

WOMAN: You could.

MAN: I drive all this way to apologize for kissing you last Christmas? I've avoided him all this time—suddenly I'm right here, middle of the night? You think he's an idiot?

(MAN *falls to his knees and runs his fingers in the snow.*)

MAN: Give me your flashlight.

(*The* WOMAN *keeps her flashlight, watching the* MAN *search in the snow.*)

MAN: You must have put them somewhere.

(WOMAN *starts to go inside.*)

MAN: Where are you going?

WOMAN: Inside.

MAN: No. Just stand there.

WOMAN: Why?

(*Silence.*)

MAN: Where'd you put my keys?

(*They stare at each other.*)

(*Silence.*)

(*The* MAN *goes back to searching in the snow.*)

WOMAN: Stop moving around.

MAN: Go inside.

WOMAN: Look at the snow.

MAN: I don't care.

WOMAN: Look at the snow.

(*The* MAN *looks at the snow, then at the* WOMAN.)

WOMAN: Even if we find your keys—it's a mess. He'll see all the footprints.

(*Silence.*)

MAN: Someone tried to break in.

WOMAN: In this town?

MAN: It could happen.

WOMAN: No it couldn't.

MAN: Maybe.

WOMAN: You don't live here.

MAN: Just say it.

WOMAN: He'll ask if I phoned the sheriff.

MAN: Say yes.

WOMAN: What if he checks?

MAN: You turned the light on then. You turned on the light and the person ran away. Say that. Sound upset. You don't know who it was but you scared him off.

(*The two stare at each other.*)

MAN: You're pretty sure he won't come back ever again.

CONTRIBUTORS

JENNY LYN BADER won the Edith Oliver Award for comedy at the O'Neill Playwrights Conference. Her full-length plays include *Manhattan Casanova* (John Drew Theatre at Guild Hall) and *The Omega Traveller* (Cherry Lane Alternative). One-acts include *Worldness* (Humana Festival of New American Plays) and *Miss America* (NY Int'l Fringe Festival, "Best of the Fringe"). She has been a frequent contributor to *The New York Times* and a Lark Playwriting Fellow.

DOUGLAS CARTER BEANE is the author of *Mondo Drama, Music from a Sparkling Planet, The Country Club, As Bees in Honey Drown* (Outer Critic's Circle John Gassner Award), and *Advice from a Caterpillar.* His first original screenplay, *To Wong Foo, Thanks for Everything, Julie Newmar,* was produced by Steven Spielberg. Mr. Beane's career as a producer and artistic director began with his creation of the popular New York theater company, The Drama Dept.

CATHERINE FILLOUX's plays include *The Beauty Inside, Silence of God, Eyes of the Heart, Mary and Myra,* and *Three Continents.* Her plays have been produced around the United States. *Photographs from S-21* has toured the world. Filloux has received awards from the Kennedy Center, O'Neill, Rockefeller MAP Fund, Asian Cultural Council, and a Fulbright. She is a member of New Dramatists and lives in New York with her husband John Daggett.

CRAIG FOLS is an actor and playwright living in New York City. His first play *Buck Simple* was published in *The Best American Short Plays, 1994–95*. He has also been published in Heinemann's *Elvis Monologues* and *Take Ten II* by Vintage Books.

CAROLYN GAGE is a lesbian-feminist playwright, performer, director, and activist. The author of four books on lesbian theater and forty-five plays, musicals, and one-woman shows, she specializes in nontraditional roles for women, especially those reclaiming famous lesbians whose stories have been distorted or erased from history. Gage's collection of plays *The Second Coming of Joan of Arc and Other Plays* was named national finalist for the Lambda Literary Award in drama.

JESSICA GOLDBERG's plays include *Get What You Need, Sex Parasite, Affair Play, Good Thing, Hologram Theory*, and *Stuck*. *Refuge* was the recipient of the 1999 Susan Smith Blackburn Prize; it has been translated and produced in German, Swedish, Norwegian, Spanish, and Catalan.

JEFF HOFFMAN received an MFA in playwrighting and poetry from the University of Texas where he was a Michener Fellow at the James A. Michener Center for Writers. In 2002 he was a Chesterfield Screenwriting Fellow with Paramount Pictures. In 2004–2005 he will be a Wallace E. Stegner Fellow in poetry at Stanford University.

DAVID IVES is probably best known for his evenings of one-act comedies: *All in the Timing* (available from Vintage Books) and *Time Flies* (available from Grove). His full-length comic fantasia, *Polish Joke,* was produced by Manhattan Theatre Club. Mr. Ives's young-adult novel, *Monsieur Eek,* is published by HarperCollins.

SUNIL KURUVILLA has developed his plays at various places including New York Theatre Workshop, Williamstown Theatre Festival, and the Sundance Institute. He has written screenplays for Showtime and CTV. Mr. Kuruvilla has a master's degree in creative writing from the University of Windsor and a master's degree in playwriting from the Yale School of Drama. His favorite food is corn-on-the-cob, generously buttered, lightly salted.

ERIC LANE's plays include *Heart of the City, Times of War, Cater-Waiter,* and *Dancing on Checkers' Grave.* Honors include the Berrilla Kerr Playwriting Award, La Mama Playwright Development Award, and a Writers Guild Award. Mr. Lane has written and produced two short films: *First Breath* and *Cater-Waiter,* which he also directed. He has received numerous Yaddo fellowships and the St. James Cavalier Centre for Creativity fellowship in Malta.

WARREN LEIGHT's *Side Man* won the 1999 Tony Award for Best Play. His other theater includes *Glimmer, Glimmer and Shine, No Foreigners Beyond This Point,* and *James and Annie.* He is currently a coexecutive producer on *Law & Order: Criminal Intent.* Mr. Leight is vice president of the Writers Guild of America, East Council, and a member of the Dramatists Guild Council.

KENNETH LONERGAN's plays include *This Is Our Youth* and *Lobby Hero.* His work has been performed by Naked Angels, Atlantic Theatre Company, London's Royal Court Theatre, and the first annual Young Playwrights' Festival at Circle Rep. He wrote the film *Analyze This* and has twice been nominated for the Academy Award for his screenplays, *Gangs of New York* and *You Can Count on Me,* which he also directed.

DONALD MARGULIES received the 2000 Pulitzer Prize for his play *Dinner with Friends.* His plays include *Collected Stories, The Model Apartment, What's Wrong with This Picture?, The Loman Family Picnic,* and *Found a Peanut.* Honors include an Obie Award, grants from the Guggenheim Foundation, NYFA, and the NEA. Mr. Margulies is an instructor at Yale University and a council member of the Dramatists Guild.

ALLISON MOORE is a displaced Texan currently living in Minneapolis, where she has won the Jerome Fellowship and the McKnight Advancement Grant at the Playwrights' Center. Her plays include *Eighteen* and *Urgent Fury.* Her work has been produced at the Cherry Lane Alternative, Kitchen Dog Theatre, Actors Theatre of Louisville, and the Playwrights' Center. Ms. Moore is a graduate of Southern Methodist University and received her MFA from the Iowa Playwrights Workshop.

CRAIG POSPISIL is the author of *Months on End* and *Somewhere in Between,* published by Dramatists Play Service, and *It's Not You,* which is included in *Take Ten II: More Ten-Minute Plays.* His work has been produced in New York, Los Angeles, across the United States, and internationally. Other plays include *The Dunes* and *Catch as Catch Can.* He edited the collections *Outstanding Men's Monologues, 2001–2002* and *Outstanding Women's Monologues, 2001–2002.*

FRANK PUGLIESE wrote the Obie Award–winning play *Aven'U Boys.* His plays include *Hope is the Thing with Feathers* (The Drama Dept.), *The Summer Winds* (NY Stage & Film), *The King of Connecticut, The Talk,* and *The Alarm* (all with Naked Angels). Films include *Shot in the Heart, Infamous, Born to Run,* and the upcoming *Italian,* which he will direct. Mr. Pugliese was artistic director of Naked Angels. He teaches playwriting and screenwriting at Columbia University.

NICOLE QUINN has written screenplays for HBO, Showtime, and network television, and adapted Edward Abbey's *Desert Solitaire* for Jodie Foster's Egg Pictures. Her screenplay *Racing Daylight* was a winner of the "First Fifteen" at the Tanglewood Film Festival. Her plays have been performed at Actors & Writers, Makor, and other theaters.

NINA SHENGOLD won the ABC Playwright Award for *Homesteaders* and the Writers Guild Award for her teleplay *Labor of*

Love. Her short plays, including *Emotional Baggage, No Shoulder, Finger Food, Lives of the Great Waitresses,* and others, have been produced throughout the country. *Romeo/Juliet,* her five-actor, seventy-five-minute edit of Shakespeare's play, is published by Broadway Play Publishing.

SAM SHEPARD has written over forty plays, including the Pulitzer Prize–winning *Buried Child, A Lie of the Mind, Fool for Love, Curse of the Starving Class, True West, Suicide in B Flat,* and *The Tooth of Crime.* He was playwright-in-residence at San Francisco's Magic Theatre and won eleven Obie Awards for his many off-Broadway productions. He is an Oscar-nominated actor (*The Right Stuff*) and Golden Palm–winning screenwriter (*Paris, Texas*).

ANNIE WEISMAN's plays include: *A Totally Meaningful Ritual* (ASK Theatre Projects commission, developed at Sundance Theatre Lab); *Be Aggressive* (La Jolla Playhouse premiere); and *Hold Please* (South Coast Rep commission and premiere). Weisman has an NEA/TCG residency at South Coast Rep and commissions from Trinity Rep, Mark Taper Forum, and La Jolla Playhouse. She writes for the Showtime series *Dead Like Me* and graduated from Williams College.

TRACEY SCOTT WILSON's works include *Order My Steps* (Cornerstone Theater's Black Faith/AIDS project), *I Don't Know Why That Caged Bird Won't Shut Up, Exhibit #9* (New Perspectives Theatre and Theatre Outrageous coproduction), *Leader of the People* (New Georges Theatre), and *The Story* (The Public Theater/NYSF). She earned a Van Lier Fellowship from NY Theatre Workshop, a residency at Sundance Ucross, and is the winner of the 2001 Helen Merrill Emerging Playwright Award.

ABOUT THE EDITORS

ERIC LANE and NINA SHENGOLD are editors of eleven contemporary play collections. Their other titles for Vintage Books include *Plays for Actresses, Leading Women: Plays for Actresses II, Take Ten: New Ten-Minute Plays, Take Ten II: More Ten-Minute Plays,* and the upcoming *Talk to Me: Monologue Plays.* For Viking Penguin, they edited *The Actor's Book of Contemporary Stage Monologues, The Actor's Book of Scenes from New Plays, Moving Parts: Monologues from Contemporary Plays, The Actor's Book of Gay and Lesbian Plays* (Lambda Literary Award nominee), and *Telling Tales: New One-Act Plays.*

NINA SHENGOLD received the ABC Playwright Award and the L.A. Weekly Award for *Homesteaders,* published by Samuel French. Her *Romeo/Juliet,* a five-actor adaptation of Shakespeare's play, is published by Broadway Play Publishing. Her ten-minute plays have been performed at the Actors Theatre of Louisville and dozens of other theaters. Ms. Shengold won the Writers Guild Award and a GLAAD Award nomination for her teleplay *Labor of Love,* starring Marcia Gay Harden; other screenplays include *Blind Spot,* with Joanne Woodward and Laura Linney, *Unwed Father, Double Platinum,* and a film adaptation of Jane Smiley's *Good Will.* She is artistic director of the upstate New York theater company Actors & Writers. Her first novel, *Clearcut,* is forthcoming from Anchor Books.

ERIC LANE is an award-winning playwright and filmmaker. Plays include *Heart of the City, Times of War, Shellac, Cater-Waiter,* and *Dancing on Checkers' Grave,* which starred Jennifer Aniston. Mr. Lane has written and produced two short films: *First Breath* stars Victor Williams, Kelly Karbacz, and Melissa Leo, and was directed by Jimmy Georgiades. *Cater-Waiter,* which Mr. Lane also directed, stars David Drake, Tim Deak, Lisa Kron, and John Kelly. For his work on TV's *Ryan's Hope,* he received a Writers Guild Award. Honors include the Berrilla Kerr Playwriting Award, La Mama Playwright Development Award, numerous Yaddo fellowships, and a St. James Cavalier Centre for Creativity fellowship in Malta. Mr. Lane is an honors graduate of Brown University, and is artistic director of Orange Thoughts Productions, a not-for-profit theater and film company in New York City.

INDEX

★F = Female, M = Male

EIGHT OR MORE CHARACTERS

PERMISSIONS
ACKNOWLEDGMENTS

LEADING WOMEN
Plays for Actresses II

Eric Lane and Nina Shengold again gathered an abundance of strong
female roles in an anthology of works by award-winning authors and
cutting-edge newer voices. The characters who populate these full-
length plays, ten-minute plays, and monologues include a vivid
cross-section of female experience: girl gang members, Southern
debutantes, pilots, teachers, and rebel teenagers. Each play in
Leading Women is a boon for talented actresses everywhere.

Drama/0-375-72666-7

TALK TO ME
Monologue Plays

This unique collection of monologue plays includes a breathtaking
array of human voices and stories by master playwrights and emerging new writers. Each of the plays, ranging from one-act to ten-
minute plays to full-length works, creates a rich and specific world.
Because each monologue is complete, rather than an excerpt, *Talk to
Me* is an unprecedented source for actors in search of material for
auditions, classes, and performances, as well as a literary gold mine
for anyone who loves drama.

Drama/1-4000-7615-3

VINTAGE BOOKS
Available at your local bookstore, or call toll-free to order:
1-800-793-2665 (credit cards only).